GROWTH IN A TIME OF CHANGE

GROWTH IN A TIME OF CHANGE

Global and Country Perspectives on a New Agenda

HYEON-WOOK KIM
AND
ZIA QURESHI

EDITORS

BROOKINGS INSTITUTION PRESS
Washington, D.C.

Library of Congress Cataloging-in-Publication Data

Names: Kim, Hyeon-Wook, editor. | Qureshi, Zia, 1953– editor.
Title: Growth in a time of change : global and country perspectives on a new agenda / edited by Hyeon-Wook Kim, Zia Qureshi.
Description: Washington, D.C. : Brookings Institution Press, [2020] | Includes bibliographical references and index.
Identifiers: LCCN 2019026911 (print) | LCCN 2019026912 (ebook) | ISBN 9780815737759 (paperback) | ISBN 9780815737766 (epub)
Subjects: LCSH: Economic development. | Economic development— Korea (South) | Technological innovations—Economic aspects. | Technological innovations—Economic aspects—Korea (South) | Economic history. | Korea (South)—Economic conditions.
Classification: LCC HD82 .G765 2020 (print) | LCC HD82 (ebook) | DDC 338.95195—dc23
LC record available at https://lccn.loc.gov/2019026911
LC ebook record available at https://lccn.loc.gov/2019026912

9 8 7 6 5 4 3 2 1

Typeset in Janson Text

Composition by Westchester Publishing Services

Contents

PART II

Country Perspectives on a Changing
Growth Agenda: Korea

Preface

Technology and other forces are reshaping the global growth agenda in significant ways. Growth paradigms are shifting as continuing major advances in digital technologies transform markets and the nature of work and business. New dynamics unleashed by change have profound implications for future trajectories of economic growth as well as for the inclusiveness of growth and income distribution.

Change creates both new opportunities and new challenges. Much will depend on how policies and institutions respond. Fresh thinking and policy innovations will be needed to address new issues. Economies with more flexibility in markets and greater responsiveness in policies will be better positioned to harness change to produce more robust and inclusive growth outcomes.

This book is the first of a two-book research project that examines how the growth agenda is evolving, focusing especially on the impacts of technological change. The project examines the transformation of the growth agenda from both global and country perspectives. Entitled *A New Growth Agenda*, the project is a collaboration between the Global Economy and Development Program at the Brookings Institution and the Korea Development Institute.

Addressing a subset of issues in the changing growth agenda, and re-flecting the project's mix of global and country perspectives, this book is structured in two parts. Part I analyzes some key dimensions of change in the global context for growth. Part II addresses some new issues in the growth agenda from the perspective of an individual major economy—Korea. Korea's case provides a reflection of some of the trends observed at the global level as well as some interesting contrasts.

In Part I the authors analyze how technological change, shifts in invest-ment, and demographic transition are affecting potential economic growth globally and across major groups of economies. They explore possible sce-narios for the global economy as the digital revolution and advances in ar-tificial intelligence drive rapid technological change, including impacts on growth, jobs, income distribution, international trade balances, and global capital flows. Technology is causing shifts in countries' international com-parative advantage and ushering in a new phase of globalization marked by a rapid increase in cross-border digital flows. The authors assess the implica-tions of these developments for the future of sectors such as manufacturing and for international trade.

Rising income and wealth inequalities are a major concern globally. Against this backdrop, in Part II the authors analyze trends in wage in-equality and labor's share of income in Korea in terms of the role played by technology, industrial concentration, shifts in the demand for skills rela-tive to supply, and other factors. They also examine how macroeconomic developments and technological change are influencing the behavior of households and firms in the Korean economy in terms of their decisions to consume, save, and invest.

Throughout the book, the authors, in their analysis of the changing growth and distributional dynamics and the digital transformation of glo-balization, place emphasis on drawing implications for policy—at national and international levels. In addition to policymakers, we hope that this book, and its successor volume, will appeal more widely to those with an interest in the unfolding significant economic change that defines our time.

Hyeon-Wook Kim and Zia Qureshi

Acknowledgments

This book is the outcome of a collaborative project between the Brookings Institution and the Korea Development Institute (KDI). Hyeon-Wook Kim (KDI) and Zia Qureshi (Brookings) coedited the book. The editors would like to thank Jeong Pyo Choi, president of KDI, and Homi Kharas, interim vice president of the Global Economy and Development Program at Brookings, for the support from the two institutions.

The book consists of chapters contributed by a team of authors. The team included—in addition to the editors, who contributed chapter 1 and chapter 6, which provide overviews of Part I and Part II of the book, respectively—the following: Sinem Kilic Celik, M. Ayhan Kose, and Franziska Ohnsorge (chapter 2); Warwick J. McKibbin and Adam Triggs (chapter 3); Brahima Coulibaly and Karim Foda (chapter 4); Joshua P. Meltzer (chapter 5); Youngsun Koh (chapter 7); Jiyoon Oh (chapter 8); Duksang Cho (chapter 9); and Young-il Kim (chapter 10). The editors would like to thank their coauthors for their valuable contributions.

The chapters were initially presented as papers at a conference held at Brookings on January 8, 2019, and were subsequently finalized in light of the comments received. Discussants of the papers included Martin Baily, Barry Bosworth, Chad Bown, Oya Celasun, Mitali Das, Mary Hallward-Driemeier, Ana Revenga, and Luis Servén. Their comments and suggestions are gratefully acknowledged. Helpful comments were also received from session chairs and other participants in the conference, including Alistair Dieppe, Simeon Djankov, David Dollar, Tarhan Feyzioglu, Daehee Jeong, Dong Soo Kang, Seongtae Kim, William Maloney, and Changyong Rhee.

Sebastian Strauss ably provided research support. For assistance with administrative, budgetary, and coordination matters, thanks are due to Caroline Conroy, Kristina Server, Jacqueline Sharkey, Molly Sugrue, and Valeriya Ten.

The Brookings Institution Press provided excellent editorial and production support. The editors would like to thank Bill Finan, Elliott Beard, and Cecilia González at the Brookings Institution Press and Angela Piliouras and the team at Westchester Publishing Services.

PART I

The Changing Global Context for Growth

ONE

Technology, Change, and a
New Growth Agenda

ZIA QURESHI

Global economic growth has been lackluster for more than a decade
now. Growth slowed sharply after the global financial crisis of 2007–08,
but the underlying growth trajectory had started to weaken in most
major economies well before the crisis. Recovery from the shock of the
crisis has been uneven and, in general, slow and weak. Growth appeared
to pick up steam in a synchronized way across economies in 2017 and
early 2018, but the acceleration proved short-lived and faded by late
2018.[1]

The persistent sluggish growth is happening at a time when the global
economy has been exposed to important forces of change. Foremost
among these has been technology. There has been a boom in new technologies, spearheaded by digital technologies. Technology-enabled innovation is a major spur to productivity growth, the key driver of long-term
economic growth. Yet, paradoxically, productivity growth has slowed
rather than accelerated in most economies. Among advanced economies

since approximately 2005, growth in productivity has averaged barely half of the pace of the previous fifteen years.[2]

There is much ongoing debate on this "productivity paradox"—why has productivity slowed amid a wave of technological advances?[3] Firms at the technological frontier have reaped major productivity gains from these advances, but the impact on productivity more widely across firms and the economy at large has been weak. The new technologies have tended to produce "winner-takes-most" outcomes. Market structures appear to have become less competitive, and performance gaps between dominant firms and other firms have become wider and persistent, dragging aggregate productivity growth lower. Looking ahead, restoring greater vigor to economic growth will depend crucially on harnessing the potential of the new technologies to produce stronger and more broad-based increases in productivity.

Investment, especially fixed capital formation, also has shown a persistent weakness. In most major economies, investment rates fell sharply after the global financial crisis but were already trending downward. A decade later, long after the crisis-related disruptions to investment waned, investment rates in most major economies remain below trend rates before the slowdown. Within this picture of subdued overall investment, the composition of investment has been changing, with "intangible capital," such as software and digital platforms, growing in importance.[4] The persistent weakness of investment despite historically low interest rates after the crisis and recovery in corporate profitability presents another puzzle—an "investment paradox"—and has prompted increased concerns about risks of "secular stagnation."[5]

The productivity and investment paradoxes have been interconnected and mutually reinforcing. Low investment contributed to subdued productivity growth by limiting capital deepening and by slowing the adoption of new technologies that typically are embodied in new capital when deployed into actual production. Weaker prospects for productivity growth, in turn, contributed to depressed investment. A weakening of competition in markets, mentioned above in relation to subdued productivity growth, appears to have been a factor behind subdued investment as well.[6]

Technology is having profound effects on labor markets. Automation and digital advances are shifting labor demand away from routine low- to middle-level skills to higher-level and more sophisticated technical and managerial skills. They are altering the nature and future of work. As the demand for skills shifts, supply has been slow to respond. The education, training, and retraining of workers in skills that complement the new technologies have lagged. Mismatches between required and available skills have increased. On the one hand, growing ranks of workers face diminishing demand for their current skills. On the other hand, the supply of workers equipped with the new skills required by the digital economy has not been growing fast enough. The resulting skill shortages have constrained the broader diffusion of the new technologies within economies, limiting their impact on productivity and growth. How the technology-driven shifts in labor markets are managed will greatly affect the dynamics of jobs, productivity, and growth.[7]

Many major economies also face the challenge of aging populations, which means slower growth of labor input into production (this may be partly offset by longer working lives as more and more people opt to work longer). In advanced economies, this effect is reinforced by the leveling off of labor force participation and educational attainment. These trends put an even greater focus on productivity—and the technological innovations that drive it—to deliver economic growth as the impulse for growth from factor accumulation weakens.

Three basic ingredients drive economic growth—labor, capital, and productivity. As outlined above, all three are facing new issues that have been affecting growth dynamics and help explain the persistence of slower growth. Many of these issues revolve around the unfolding effects of rapid technological change and how it has interacted with markets and policies.

The growth picture is further complicated by other important trends. The growth challenge is not only to restore stronger growth but also to make it more inclusive. Income inequality has been rising over the past two to three decades within most major economies, and the increase has been particularly pronounced in some countries, such as the United States. Since the early 1980s, income inequality in the United States, as measured by the broadest indicator of inequality (the Gini index), has increased by more than 15 percent. The income share of the richest 1 percent has more than doubled, to around 22 percent, and their share of overall wealth has risen to around 40 percent.[8] Technological change has been a key factor influencing these income distribution dynamics.

The new technologies favoring capital and higher-level skills have contributed to a decline in labor's share of income and to greater wage inequality. These distributional effects have been reinforced by the rise of dominant "superstar" firms characterized by a combination of supernormal profits and low labor income shares. Competition policy failures have added to the winner-takes-most dynamics of the new technologies in giving rise to more concentrated market structures with more market power and high economic rents.[9] The shift toward more monopolistic industry structures and greater market power of dominant firms worked to make the distribution of capital income also more unequal. The rise in overall income inequality thus has consisted of a shift of income from labor to capital and a more unequal distribution of both labor and capital income.

The political setting for policymaking has become more challenging. Rising inequality and growing anxiety about the future of work and jobs have contributed to increased social tensions and political divisiveness. Populism has surged in many countries. Nationalist and protectionist sentiment has been on the rise as well, with a backlash against globalization that, alongside technological change, is seen to have contributed to rising inequality through job losses and wage stagnation for lower-skilled workers.

While income inequality has been rising in many countries in recent decades, inequality between countries has been falling, thanks to the rise of faster-growing emerging economies that are narrowing the income gap with advanced economies. Technological change poses new challenges for this process of economic convergence. Manufacturing-led growth in emerging economies has been the dominant driver of convergence, propelled by the comparative advantage enjoyed by these economies in labor-intensive manufacturing based on their large pools of low-skilled, low-wage workers. This source of comparative advantage will matter less as automation of low-skilled work progresses, disrupting traditional pathways to development.[10]

In sum, the growth agenda is being reshaped by significant change in the world economy from technology and other forces. And transformative change continues as digital technologies push further with advances in artificial intelligence, robotics, the Internet of Things, and cyber-physical systems—advances that could unleash a "Fourth Industrial Revolution" (4IR). Globalization is going increasingly digital, a transformation that, analogous to 4IR, has been termed "Globalization 4.0."[11] As technology drives change, it creates both new opportunities and challenges. How policies and institutions respond is key to determining how this change translates into outcomes for growth, jobs, and income distribution.

Technological change recently has not delivered its full potential in boosting productivity and economic growth. It has pushed income inequality higher and generated fears about a "robocalypse"—massive job losses from automation.[12] Globalization also has contributed to rising inequality within economies, although technological change has been a bigger, more pervasive factor. The correct response to these challenges is not a Luddite retreat from technology or a slip back into protectionism. Ongoing advances in digital technologies hold considerable potential to lift the trajectory of productivity and economic growth and enhance human welfare. As much as two-thirds of potential productivity growth in major economies over the next decade could be related to the new digital technologies.[13] But technological change is inherently disruptive and entails difficult transitions. It also inevitably creates winners and losers, as does globalization. Policies have a crucial role to play in ensuring that the potential economic gains from these forces are captured effectively and inclusively. Unfortunately, policies and institutions have been slow to adapt to the challenges of change. With better and more responsive policies, better outcomes are possible.

The core of the forward policy agenda is to better harness the potential of the new technologies to produce more robust and inclusive economic growth. Reforms must seek to improve the enabling environment for firms and workers—to broaden access to opportunities that come from technological change and to enhance capabilities to adjust to the new challenges. Competition policies should be revamped for the digital age to ensure that markets continue to provide an open and level playing field for firms, keep competition strong, and check the growth of monopolistic structures. With the intangible asset of knowledge becoming an increasingly important driver of economic success, the innovation ecosystem (research and development policies, patent regimes) should be improved to promote wider diffusion of advances in knowledge embodied in the new technologies.[14] Infrastructure that supports digitization should be strengthened. Investment in skills must be boosted, with stronger and smarter programs for worker upskilling and reskilling and lifelong learning to respond to shifts in the demand for skills resulting from technological change—and from globalization. Labor market policies and social protection systems must be adapted to the realities of a more dynamic job market—as part of an overhaul of social contracts. Tax systems should be reviewed in light of the new tax challenges of the digital economy and the income distribution dynamics.

The politics of reform is inevitably complex. Reform may seem even more daunting in the current political climate. But one thing reform action should not be paralyzed by is continued trite debates about conflicts between growth and equity. Research shows that this is a false dichotomy. The slowdown in productivity and economic growth and the rise in income inequality over the past couple of decades are linked by broadly common causes, chief among which is the interplay between technological change and policy and market failures. The agenda to reverse these trends, as outlined above, also is broadly common.[15] Policies to promote equity are often seen narrowly in terms of redistribution of the gains from economic growth through government taxes and transfers. But the interlinked dynamics of productivity, growth, and equity suggest that there is a much broader policy agenda of "predistribution" that can make the process of economic growth itself more inclusive—and more robust at the same time.[16]

Much of the attention of policymakers in major economies over the past decade has been focused on addressing the aftermath of the global financial crisis and the ensuing recession—issues relating to deficient aggregate demand, credit market disruptions, and financial sector repair. Major financial crises cast a long shadow.[17] Some legacies of the last crisis remain—notably high debt levels, public and private. Looking ahead, more attention needs to be devoted to deeper reforms in markets, policies, and institutions on which longer-term prospects for growth and shared prosperity will depend, and especially to how this agenda is being reshaped by technology.

Reforms are needed at the international level as well so that rules of engagement between countries in trade and other areas are fair. But the dominant part of the agenda to make globalization work better and for all rests with policies at the national level, such as those related to competition, upskilling/reskilling workers, and social protection mentioned above. With globalization going increasingly digital—cross-border digital flows are now the most dynamic element of global flows—an important area for international cooperation will be the development of necessary new disciplines for digital flows that support open access, fair competition, and well-balanced intellectual property rights that reward innovation but prevent intellectual monopolies.

The Changing Global Context for Growth

This book is the first in a series under a joint project of the Brookings Institution and the Korea Development Institute that aims to address how the growth agenda is evolving with change in the world economy, in particular from technological transformation. The project's title—*A New Growth Agenda*—reflects its motivation and focus. As the foregoing discussion indicates, this is a large topic, well beyond the scope of a single work to address exhaustively. Each book under the project will focus on a select set of issues in the changing growth agenda, with the aim cumulatively to develop a fuller exploration of the agenda.[18]

The project examines how the growth agenda is being reshaped both from global and from country perspectives. This book first analyzes, in Part I, how the global context for growth is changing. In Part II it addresses some new issues in the growth agenda from the perspective of an individual economy, Korea. Korea's case provides both a reflection of some of the trends observed at the global level and some interesting contrasts. This chapter includes an overview of Part I. Chapter 6 provides an overview of Part II.

The Challenge of Reviving Slowing Potential Growth

How are the forces of change affecting potential growth—maximum sustainable growth in the medium to long term as determined by the underlying productive capacity—in the world economy? In chapter 2, Celik, Kose, and Ohnsorge find that potential growth has declined across most economies and that it could fall further in coming years in the absence of policy reforms to counter the forces driving the slowdown. Their analysis presents a picture of a growth environment where a business-as-usual approach to policy risks a persistent slowing of growth but where policies that are responsive to the new challenges can reap sizable rewards in lifting growth.

Global potential growth in the five-year period 2013–17 is estimated at 2.5 percent a year, which is 0.5 percentage point below its long-term average over the past two decades (1998–2017). This includes a fall of 0.5 percentage point in advanced economies, to a potential growth rate of 1.4 percent, and a fall of 0.6 percentage point in emerging and developing economies (EMDEs), to a potential growth rate of 4.8 percent. The fall in potential growth is still larger when measured against the higher potential growth of a decade ago (2003–07): 0.9 percentage point globally, 0.8 percentage point in advanced economies, and 1.1 percentage points in EMDEs. The slowdown in potential growth is broad-based across advanced economies and EMDEs. Among the latter, it has been more pervasive in middle-income economies.

The analysis finds that the slowdown in global potential growth reflects persistent weaknesses in all three major drivers of growth: physical capital, workforce and human capital, and productivity. Roughly half of the slow-down is estimated to be on account of weaker investment and capital accumulation. Just under a quarter is estimated to result from slower growth of labor input related to demographic trends such as aging and changes in labor force participation rates. More than a quarter reflects slower growth in total factor productivity.[19] Weaker capital accumulation and productivity growth, to varying degrees, are common factors in most economies. The picture with respect to growth in workforce varies, with aging an increasingly important factor in advanced economies and some mature emerging economies, in contrast to many developing economies, such as those in South Asia and sub-Saharan Africa, which have more favorable demographics.

Global potential growth could slow further if these trends in the fundamental drivers of growth continue. The business-as-usual scenario developed in chapter 2 indicates that global potential growth could decline further by 0.2 percenage point over the ten-year period 2018–27, including a 0.1 percentage point fall in advanced economies and 0.5 percentage point fall in EMDEs.

Fortunately, these outcomes are not inevitable. Chapter 2 concludes on a positive note that responsive policies can help reverse the current negative growth dynamics. It sets out a range of options that policymakers could consider. Investment could be boosted by improving the policy and institutional environment for private investment and creating room in public finances to increase complementary public investments, such as addressing shortfalls in key infrastructure. Productivity growth could be stimulated by policies to spur innovation, enhance competition, and promote broad diffusion of technological advances. Advancing an open international trade system would help as well. Education and training could be strengthened to raise the quantity and quality of human capital and build skills demanded by the new technologies. Labor force participation rates could be boosted by labor market reforms, encouragement of participation by women, and mitigation of the effects of aging through retirement policy reform, lifelong learning, and migration. Scenarios developed in chapter 2 indicate that a combination of such reforms could lift potential growth over the period 2018–27 by 0.7–0.8 percentage point in advanced economies and EMDEs.

How Technology May Alter Future Growth Paths

One major source of uncertainty about future growth is technology. There is an active debate about how the digital revolution may affect the future path of productivity. "Techno-pessimists" believe that today's digital technologies are much less consequential than past major technological breakthroughs, such as the internal combustion engine and electrification, in their ability to drive rapid and sustained increases in productivity. They expect the weakness in productivity growth to persist. "Techno-optimists," on the other hand, believe that the digital revolution is truly transformative but that the realization of its full potential to spur productivity growth has been held back by the inevitable adoption and diffusion lags facing new technologies. They are of the view that productivity growth will accelerate and will be greatly boosted by the next wave of innovations—notably, advances in artificial intelligence and cyber-physical systems—that can take the digital revolution to a new level. These alternative futures for technology and its impact on productivity have very different implications for global growth and the global economy.[20]

In chapter 3, McKibbin and Triggs explore alternative technology-enabled productivity growth scenarios and analyze their implications for growth, jobs, and flows of trade and capital, and what they mean for policymakers. One scenario is that the weak productivity growth of recent years persists into the future, as predicted by the techno-pessimists. The other scenarios explore a future takeoff in productivity growth, as envisaged by the techno-optimists, ranging from a global surge in productivity to surges in productivity favoring advanced economies and sectors that have invested more in digital technologies.

The exploration of these scenarios provides important analytic and policy insights. In a scenario where the technological frontier and productivity in advanced economies grow slowly and depress economic growth there, the potential for technology catch-up in EMDEs remains large, which could underpin continued strong growth in these economies. Indeed, these economies could gain from increased capital inflows as the relative return on investment there rises. Capturing this potential for stronger growth would depend on supportive policies within these economies and openness in international markets to flows of trade, capital, and technology. A scenario where rapid technological advances produce a surge in productivity globally would lift growth in all economies, advanced and emerging. A variety of constraints could keep economies from reaping the full benefits of a technology-driven productivity boom in the form of stronger and inclusive growth. Flexibility in markets will be key to facilitating adjustments in the face of disruptions from technological transformation. It will be important to maintain strong competition in product markets, promote depth and flexibility in financial markets to manage the reallocation of capital that goes with structural shifts, and ensure that labor markets support labor mobility and enable workers to share in the gains of the productivity boom. The insights from the scenarios reinforce many of the policy messages of chapter 2 on boosting potential growth.

Scenario simulations show that rapid technological change may not be inimical to workers, contrary to prevalent fears about large job losses. Higher productivity and growth resulting from technological advances support higher employment and wages, with new jobs replacing those no longer needed. While this transition may be challenging, it can be eased by policies that re-equip workers and support their mobility.

A scenario in which productivity surges only in advanced economies that invest more in digital innovation, such as the United States and other major economies, highlights the potentially crucial importance of such investment in tomorrow's economy. These economies reap most of the growth dividends in this scenario. Other economies with strong export links to these economies can benefit from spillover effects, but the rest, including many among EMDEs, risk losing out on the productivity boom.

The eurozone presents an interesting case in the context of such an asymmetric productivity growth scenario. A productivity boom in the eurozone's core economies (Germany and France) while productivity lags in economies in the periphery could put a particularly strong strain on the latter, given the group's common monetary policy and exchange rate, and threaten the eurozone's stability. This implies the need for productivity-enhancing reforms in the periphery plus building more flexibility into the eurozone's macroeconomic frameworks and considering deeper integration.

Shifting Dynamics in Global Manufacturing

Technology is transforming the growth dynamics in manufacturing, a sector that historically has played a key role in economic advancement of countries. Since the Industrial Revolution, manufacturing has powered the economic rise of economies—first the rise of today's advanced economies and, more recently, that of China and other successful emerging economies of East Asia. In a development paradigm that came to be known as the "flying geese" model, as economies moved up the manufacturing ladder and wages there rose, lower-skill manufacturing tasks shifted to economies with lower wage costs.[21] This process over time helped economic convergence between the early industrializers and those that followed. But as Coulibaly and Foda discuss in chapter 4, the digital revolution is disrupting this development paradigm.

The new technologies are shifting production toward higher capital and skill intensity, with routine lower-skill production tasks increasingly being automated. As a result, comparative advantage based on low-cost, low-skilled labor is eroding. Manufacturing tasks in global value chains (GVCs) that were previously offshored to low-wage-cost developing economies could be reshored to advanced economies. The expected shedding of low-skill tasks by China (the world's largest manufacturer, accounting for about a quarter of global manufacturing output) to other economies as its own labor costs rise may not happen as these tasks become automated and remain in China (the country has already emerged as a leader in investment in robots). China and other successful manufacturing economies in East Asia are also increasing the domestic value-added component of their manufacturing output by building domestic supply chains that provide intermediate inputs that previously were imported. The growth of GVCs in manufacturing may slow, and the bar for entering them may rise. These trends are already in evidence and will likely intensify as the 4IR technologies advance. Contrary to the paradigm of convergence, these trends could strengthen and consolidate the position of existing major manufacturing hubs in North America, Europe, and East Asia.

Technology is also leading to an increasing servicification of manufacturing. Along the manufacturing value chain, the contribution of services is growing as the value added by upstream and downstream activities rises relative to that of production and assembly. These upstream and downstream activities—such as research and development, design, branding and marketing, and user services embedded in products—are intensive in higher-level and specialized skills and digital infrastructure and technologies. Services trade has been expanding much faster than goods trade, and GVCs are becoming more service-intensive.[22]

For developing economies, given these trends, the traditional route to development through manufacturing based on low to moderately skilled labor will become much tougher. Industrialization as a development path for these economies, however, is certainly not foreclosed. Economies that proactively adapt to the new challenges can continue to carve out comparative advantage and build viable manufacturing industries to help drive their growth and create higher-productivity jobs for their growing labor force. Success will depend increasingly on upgrading the workforce and developing skills complementary to new technologies, building stronger infrastructure in support of digitization and trade logistics, and improving the business environment for innovation and investment, including regulatory frameworks suitable for the digital age. As discussed in chapter 3, there is large potential in these economies for productivity growth and improved competitiveness through technology catch-up. Improved capabilities through such efforts would enable these economies to take advantage of increasing domestic demand fueled by growing populations and rising middle classes. By 2030, EMDEs could account for more than half of all global consumption, with EMDEs excluding China accounting for 35 percent.[23] The faster growth of demand within these economies could also attract more investment from outside that aims to locate production closer to points of growing consumption. For example, increasingly, Chinese manufacturing firms relocating to Africa primarily serve local markets.

The same technologies that limit opportunities in traditional manufacturing can open new avenues for growth. Digital platforms and logistics technologies are lowering transaction costs to connect to global markets. They are increasing opportunities for countries to tap into the burgeoning trade in services facilitated by digitization. Countries rich in natural endowments can move up the value chain from simple commodity exporting to agricultural and food processing and horticulture and can better exploit tourism possibilities. African economies, for example, may have sizable potential for growth in industries that depart from the traditional smokestack manufacturing model of industrialization.[24] The new technologies offer leapfrogging possibilities in development, such as in finance and communications; African economies have seen rapid growth in mobile telephony and pioneered innovations in digital finance to link large populations to financial markets and the formal economy. Technology does disrupt job markets, but such disruptions may not inevitably lead to large numbers of technologically unemployed workers. As some jobs disappear or are reshaped in traditional manufacturing or other sectors, demand for new and modified jobs rises: witness the rise of 4 million app developers in India.[25]

Technology is reshaping the global manufacturing landscape, and indeed disrupting many other sectors. It will alter traditional pathways to growth and development. But it also offers multiple new pathways for countries that demonstrate responsiveness and skill in managing the transition.

Globalization Going Digital

The digital revolution is ushering in a new phase of globalization. While growth in traditional trade flows has slowed in the past decade, globalization overall has not. With soaring cross-border flows of data and information, globalization is going increasingly digital. In chapter 5, Meltzer examines this transformation. Between 2005 and 2015, cross-border data flows rose 45-fold, and they are expected to grow another ninefold by 2020. In addition to transmitting valuable streams of data, information, and ideas, digital flows facilitate the movement of goods, services, finance, and people. Virtually every type of cross-border transaction now has a digital component. All considered, digital flows might already be exerting a larger impact on global economic growth than traditional flows of traded goods.[26]

The digital transformation of globalization creates new opportunities for boosting trade, productivity, and economic growth from which all economies can benefit. Advanced economies and successful emerging economies, such as China, at the leading edge of the new technologies have had a head start. Boosted by first-mover advantages and scale and network economies associated with digital technologies, their companies, such as Facebook and Google, have rapidly acquired dominant positions in the global digital space. Services trade has been in the vanguard of digital globalization. Digitally deliverable services, including those embodied in goods, now exceed one-half of total U.S. exports. But digitization of international flows is creating opportunities more widely across economies. Digital platforms such as Alibaba, Amazon, and eBay are making it easier for enterprises in developing economies, including small and midsize enterprises, to connect to the global marketplace. They are facilitating entry into GVCs for trading goods and services. Cloud computing is broadening access to digital software and storage. Two-sided digital platforms, such as Uber and Airbnb, are creating new microentrepreneurs in an expanding "crowd-based capitalism."[27] Digital platforms for professional services are beginning to create a more global labor market. Individuals around the world are using the internet and global digital platforms to learn, research, and build networks.

Not all countries are making the most of this potential. Digital globalization increases the premium on enhancement of national capabilities in terms of building worker skills for the digital economy and strengthening infrastructure to enhance digital access and international connectedness. Also important is a policy environment that supports openness, competition, and business dynamism. This is not an agenda exclusively for developing economies. Advanced economies are better connected to international digital networks, but they too must exert greater effort to help workers reskill and transition to tomorrow's jobs and adapt regulatory frameworks to the digital age to address new issues relating to competition policies, patent regimes, and management of data that drive the digital economy (data ownership, access, privacy, security). The gains from digital globalization and how inclusively they are shared, between and within economies, will depend greatly on policymakers' responsiveness to these challenges.

Making globalization work better and for all will also require greater cooperation at the international level. Not only must past gains in establishing a rules-based international system be protected from the recent rise of nationalist and protectionist sentiment but new rules and cooperative arrangements must be devised to underpin the new phase of globalization driven by digital transformation. This includes adequate disciplines for digital trade, including cross-border data flows and the fast-growing digitally deliverable services. Digital protectionism, such as data localization measures with a protectionist intent and other restrictions on cross-border data flows and market access for digitally deliverable services, has been on the rise. Data protection and cybersecurity require stronger international cooperation in regulation and enforcement. Competition policy needs to become more global to address cross-border business practices that restrict competition. The superstars of the digital economy—the tech giants—typically are multinationals that affect market concentration and competition in many countries. In a more knowledge-intensive globalization, appropriate frameworks governing intellectual property take on added significance. Digital globalization, involving an increasingly intangible nature of cross-border business, will also require enhanced international cooperation in tax matters.

Global policymaking and institutional frameworks have not kept pace with the advance of globalization, and this gap could widen as digital technologies transform international flows of goods, services, finance, skills, knowledge, and innovation. Up-to-date global rules that support an open and fair framework for these flows as they evolve will be an important complement to reforms at the national level to ensure that advances in globalization and technology produce better outcomes for productivity, growth, and inclusiveness. Greater international cooperation may appear daunting in today's political environment of ascendant nationalist populism. Eventually, however, there will be a need to adapt international frameworks to the demands of the twenty-first century.

Conclusion

Technology and other forces are reshaping the global growth agenda in major ways. Growth paradigms are shifting with markets and the future of work and business. The only constant in the economic landscape, it seems, is change. And change may only accelerate as artificial intelligence and other innovations drive the digital revolution further. Today's technological advances hold much promise for boosting productivity, growth, and human welfare. But the realization of these gains is not automatic. Policies have a crucial role to play in determining what outcomes are achieved. Change is creating both opportunities and challenges. Economies with more flexibility in markets and greater responsiveness in policies will be better positioned to capture the opportunities and meet the challenges.

The era of smart machines demands smarter policies. Technological innovation is creating the need for policy innovation as it transforms markets. New thinking and policy adaptations will be needed in areas such as competition policies, innovation systems and knowledge diffusion, infrastructure underpinning the digital economy, upskilling and reskilling of workers, social protection regimes, and tax policies. At the international level, new rules will need to be established as globalization goes increasingly digital. There is currently active research and debate in many of these areas, which should help guide policymakers.

Both technological change and globalization have contributed to the recent rise in income inequality in many economies—and the associated rise in social discontent and political tumult. But such distributional consequences of change are not preordained. Much depends on policy responses. Notwithstanding the fact that change is inevitably disruptive and creates winners and losers, more inclusive outcomes are possible. Effective responses will require policies that help people adapt to the change and take advantage of the future opportunities it brings.

NOTES

1. The IMF's World Economic Outlook, April 2018 (International Monetary Fund 2018) presented an outlook of "synchronized acceleration" of global growth. In the World Economic Outlook, April 2019 (International Monetary Fund 2019), the assessment of the outlook for global growth shifted to one of "synchronized deceleration."

2. See Organization for Economic Cooperation and Development (2015, 2018) for data on, and analysis of, productivity trends in major economies.

3. Some argue that the "productivity paradox" may simply reflect mismeasurement since current statistical methods do not fully capture improvements in the quality of goods and services and the value created by new goods and services, especially those in the digital space. Research finds that these factors do lead to an underestimation of productivity growth but that this can explain only a relatively small part of the measured slowdown in productivity growth (Byrne, Fernald, and Reinsdorf 2016; Syverson 2016). For the most part, the productivity slowdown and the related paradox are real, not illusory.

4. For more on the rise of "intangible capital" and its economic implications, including for investment, see, for example, Haskel and Westlake (2017), and Crouzet and Eberly (2018).

5. See, for example, Summers (2016).

6. A growing body of research in OECD economies documents a trend toward a decline in competition in markets and finds that it may be hurting both growth (innovation, productivity, investment) and income distribution. See, for example, De Loecker and Eeckhout (2017, 2018); Gutiérrez and Philippon (2017); Eggertsson, Robbins, and Wold (2018); Furman and Orszag (2018); Rajan (2019); Stiglitz (2019); and Tepper (2019).

7. Several recent studies examine the labor market implications of the digital economy (changing demand for skills, future of jobs) and what they mean for policy. See, for example, Acemoglu and Restrepo (2018); World Bank (2018); and Organization for Economic Cooperation and Development (2019).

8. For trends in income and wealth distribution in major economies, see, for example, Alvaredo and others (2018).

9. For an analysis of the rise of "superstars" and its implications, see, for example, Autor and others (2017) and McKinsey Global Institute (2018a).

10. Rodrik (2015) develops the changing dynamics of manufacturing's role in growth under the theme of "premature deindustrialization." See also Hallward-Driemeier and Nayyar (2018).

11. See Schwab (2016); Baldwin (2018); and World Economic Forum (2019) for more discussion on the nature and scope of the change captured in the terms "4IR" and "Globalization 4.0."

12. "Robocalypse" is a term used by Autor and Salomons (2017) to capture the threat to jobs from automation.

13. See McKinsey Global Institute (2018b).

14. Several recent studies have focused on the role of overly broad and stringent patent systems as a factor limiting innovation and its wide diffusion and weakening competition. "The copyright and patent laws we have today look more like intellectual monopoly than intellectual property" (Lindsey and Teles 2017). See also Baker, Jayadev, and Stiglitz (2017).

15. For more discussion on the nexus between technology, productivity, and income distribution, the shared dynamics between the slowdown in productivity growth and the rise in income inequality, and the interconnected agenda to revive productivity growth and reduce inequality, see Brookings Institution and Chumir Foundation (2019). See also Tyson and Spence (2017).

16. The term "predistribution," coined by Jacob Hacker (2011), embodies the idea that the state should try to prevent high income inequality from occurring in the first place rather than reducing it through the tax and transfer system once it has occurred, as happens under redistribution. Ricardo Hausmann (2015) draws a similar distinction between policies for redistribution and inclusion (in the growth process).

17. See, for example, Reinhart and Rogoff (2014) on the depth and persistence of the macrofinancial impacts of major financial crises and the long process of recovery.

18. To keep the scope of the work manageable, the project does not specifically address climate change and its implications for the growth agenda. Though beyond the scope of this work, harmonizing climate action and economic growth is clearly a key part of change in the future growth agenda. For a detailed discussion of the links between climate and growth, see Global Commission on the Economy and Climate (2018), especially the chapter entitled "The New Growth Agenda."

19. Growth in total factor productivity (also referred to as multifactor productivity) represents output growth not accounted for by increases in factor inputs—capital and labor. It therefore captures growth in output resulting from improvements in how these inputs are allocated and used in production, as a result of technological innovation, higher-quality managerial and worker skills, and more efficient business organization and processes.

20. For a techno-pessimistic view, see, for example, Gordon (2016). For a techno-optimistic view, see Brynjolfsson and McAfee (2014) and Nordhaus (2015). For a synthesis of the debate, see Qureshi (2016).

21. See Akamatsu (1962).

22. See, for example, McKinsey Global Institute (2019).

23. McKinsey Global Institute (2019).

24. See Newfarmer, Page, and Tarp (2019).

25. See, for example, Acemoglu and Restrepo (2018) and World Bank (2018) for how this dynamic adjustment process of old jobs and tasks giving way to new ones as technology shifts has played out during previous major episodes of technological change and how it may evolve in this era of the digital revolution.

26. See McKinsey Global Institute (2016) and Lund and Tyson (2018).

27. Sundarajan (2016). See also Brynjolfsson and McAfee (2017).

REFERENCES

Acemoglu, Daron, and Pascual Restrepo. 2018. "The Race between Man and Machine: Implications of Technology for Growth, Factor Shares, and Employment." *American Economic Review* 108, no. 6, pp. 1488–1542.

Akamatsu, Kaname. 1962. "A Historical Pattern of Economic Growth in Developing Countries." *The Developing Economies* 1, no. S1, pp. 3–25.

Alvaredo, Facundo, Lucas Chancel, Thomas Piketty, Emmanuel Saez, and Gabriel Zucman. 2018. *World Inequality Report 2018*. World Inequality Lab.

Autor, David, and Anna Salomons. 2017. "Robocalypse Now: Does Productivity Growth Threaten Employment?" in *Proceedings of the ECB Forum on Central Banking: Investment and Growth in Advanced Economies* (Sintra, Portugal: European Central Bank).

Autor, David, David Dorn, Lawrence Katz, Christina Patterson, and John Van Reenen. 2017. "The Fall of the Labor Share and the Rise of Superstar Firms," NBER Working Paper 23396 (Cambridge, Mass.: National Bureau of Economic Research).

Baker, Dean, Arjun Jayadev, and Joseph Stiglitz. 2017. *Innovation, Intellectual Property, and Development: A Better Set of Approaches for the 21st Century* (Washington, D.C.: Center for Economic and Policy Research).

Baldwin, Richard. 2018. "If This Is Globalization 4.0, What Were the Other Three?" *Vox, CEPR Policy Portal*, December 2018.

Brookings Institution and Chumir Foundation. 2019. *Productive Equity: The Twin Challenges of Reviving Productivity and Reducing Inequality*. Report. Washington, D.C.

Brynjolfsson, Erik, and Andrew McAfee. 2014. *The Second Machine Age: Work, Progress, and Prosperity in a Time of Brilliant Technologies* (New York: W. W. Norton).

———. 2017. *Machine, Platform, Crowd: Harnessing Our Digital Future* (New York: W. W. Norton).

Byrne, David, John Fernald, and Marshall Reinsdorf. 2016. "Does the United States Have a Productivity Slowdown or a Measurement Problem?" *Brookings Papers on Economic Activity* (Spring 2016), pp. 109–82.

Crouzet, Nicolas, and Janice Eberly. 2018. "Understanding Weak Capital Investment: The Role of Market Concentration and Intangibles." Paper prepared for the Jackson Hole Economic Policy Symposium, Federal Reserve Bank of Kansas City, August 2018.

De Loecker, Jan, and Jan Eeckhout. 2017. "The Rise of Market Power and the Macroeconomic Implications," NBER Working Paper 23687 (Cambridge, Mass.: National Bureau of Economic Research).

———. 2018. "Global Market Power," NBER Working Paper 24768 (Cambridge, Mass.: National Bureau of Economic Research).

Eggertsson, Gauti, Jacob Robbins, and Ella Getz Wold. 2018. "Kaldor and Piketty's Facts: The Rise of Monopoly Power in the United States," NBER Working Paper 24287 (Cambridge, Mass.: National Bureau of Economic Research).

Furman, Jason, and Peter Orszag. 2018. "A Firm-Level Perspective on the Role of Rents in the Rise in Inequality." In *Toward a Just Society: Joseph Stiglitz and Twenty-First Century Economics*, edited by Martin Guzman (Columbia University Press).

Global Commission on the Economy and Climate. 2018. *Unlocking the Inclusive Growth Story of the 21ˢᵗ Century: Accelerating Climate Action in Urgent Times* (Washington, D.C.: The New Climate Economy).

Gordon, Robert. 2016. *The Rise and Fall of American Growth: The U.S. Standard of Living since the Civil War* (Princeton University Press).

Gutiérrez, Germán, and Thomas Philippon. 2017. "Declining Competition and Investment in the U.S.," NBER Working Paper 23583 (Cambridge, Mass.: National Bureau of Economic Research).

Hacker, Jacob. 2011. "The Institutional Foundations of Middle Class Democracy." *Policy Network* (May 6).

Hallward-Driemeier, Mary, and Gaurav Nayyar. 2018. *Trouble in the Making? The Future of Manufacturing-Led Development* (Washington, D.C.: World Bank).

Haskel, Jonathan, and Stian Westlake. 2017. *Capitalism without Capital: The Rise of the Intangible Economy* (Princeton University Press).

Hausmann, Ricardo. 2015. "Redistribution or Inclusion." *Project Syndicate*, January 30 (www.project-syndicate.org/commentary/income-inequality -opportunity-costs-by-ricardo-hausmann-2015-01).

International Monetary Fund. 2018. *World Economic Outlook, April 2018: Cyclical Upswing, Structural Change* (Washington, D.C.).

———. 2019. *World Economic Outlook, April 2019: Growth Slowdown, Precarious Recovery* (Washington, D.C.).

Lindsey, Brink, and Steven Teles. 2017. *The Captured Economy: How the Powerful Enrich Themselves, Slow Down Growth, and Increase Inequality* (Oxford University Press).

Lund, Susan, and Laura Tyson. 2018. "Globalization Is Not in Retreat: Digital Technology and the Future of Trade." *Foreign Affairs* (May/June).

McKinsey Global Institute. 2016. *Digital Globalization: The New Era of Global Flows*. McKinsey & Company.

———. 2018a. *Superstars: The Dynamics of Firms, Sectors, and Cities Leading the Global Economy*. McKinsey & Company.

———. 2018b. *Solving the Productivity Puzzle: The Role of Demand and the Promise of Digitization*. McKinsey & Company.

———. 2019. *Globalization in Transition: The Future of Trade and Value Chains*. McKinsey & Company.

Newfarmer, Richard, John Page, and Finn Tarp. 2019. *Industries without Smokestacks: Industrialization in Africa Reconsidered* (Oxford University Press).

Nordhaus, William. 2015. "Are We Approaching an Economic Singularity? Information Technology and the Future of Economic Growth," NBER Working Paper 21547 (Cambridge, Mass.: National Bureau of Economic Research).

Organization for Economic Cooperation and Development. 2015. *The Future of Productivity*. Paris.

———. 2018. *OECD Compendium of Productivity Indicators, 2018*. Paris.

———. 2019. *The Future of Work: OECD Employment Outlook 2019*. Paris.

Qureshi, Zia. 2016. "The Productivity Outlook: Pessimists versus Optimists," Research Brief (Brookings Institution).

Rajan, Raghuram. 2019. "Disruption, Concentration, and the New Economy." PS OnPoint. *Project Syndicate*, January 15 (www.project-syndicate.org/onpoint/disruption-concentration-and-the-new-economy-by-raghuram-rajan-2019-01).

Reinhart, Carmen, and Kenneth Rogoff. 2014. "Recovering from Financial Crises: Evidence from 100 Episodes." *American Economic Review* 104, no. 5, pp. 50–55.

Rodrik, Dani. 2015. "Premature Deindustrialization," NBER Working Paper 20935 (Cambridge, Mass.: National Bureau of Economic Research).

Schwab, Klaus. 2016. *The Fourth Industrial Revolution* (Geneva: World Economic Forum).

Stiglitz, Joseph. 2019. *People, Power, and Profits: Progressive Capitalism for an Age of Discontent* (New York: W. W. Norton).

Summers, Lawrence. 2016. "The Age of Secular Stagnation: What It Is and What to Do about It." *Foreign Affairs* (March/April).

Sundarajan, Arun. 2016. *The Sharing Economy: The End of Employment and the Rise of Crowd-Based Capitalism* (MIT Press).

Syverson, Chad. 2016. "Challenges to Mismeasurement Explanations for the U.S. Productivity Slowdown," NBER Working Paper 21974 (Cambridge, Mass.: National Bureau of Economic Research).

Tepper, Jonathan. 2019. *The Myth of Capitalism: Monopolies and the Death of Competition* (Hoboken, N.J.: Wiley).

Tyson, Laura, and Michael Spence. 2017. "Exploring the Effects of Technology on Income and Wealth Inequality," in *After Piketty: The Agenda for Economics and Inequality*, edited by J. Bradford DeLong, Heather Boushey, and Marshall Steinbaum (Harvard University Press).

World Bank. 2018. *The Changing Nature of Work: World Development Report 2019*. Washington, D.C.

World Economic Forum. 2019. "Globalization 4.0: Shaping a New Global Architecture in the Age of the Fourth Industrial Revolution." White Paper. Geneva.

TWO

Subdued Potential Growth

Sources and Remedies

SINEM KILIC CELIK, M. AYHAN KOSE, AND FRANZISKA OHNSORGE

The global economy regained some strength over the period between mid-2016 and 2018, but potential output growth—the rate at which an economy would grow when labor and capital are fully employed—has continued to remain weak (see figure 2-1). In the years 2013–17, after the global financial crisis of 2007–08, global potential growth fell short of its long-term average and was well below its pre-crisis average. This weakness was broad-based, affecting both advanced economies, where it was evident even before the financial crisis, and emerging and developing economies (EMDEs), where there was a short-lived pre-crisis uptick. The decline raises concerns about the durability of the cyclical recovery as well.

Since the growth rate of per capita potential output is the overriding long-run force for sustained reductions in poverty, this trend is also cause for concern about the international community's ability to meet broader

FIGURE 2-1. **Global Growth**

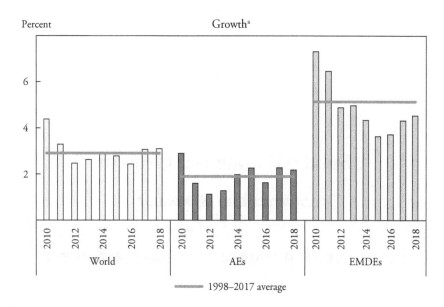

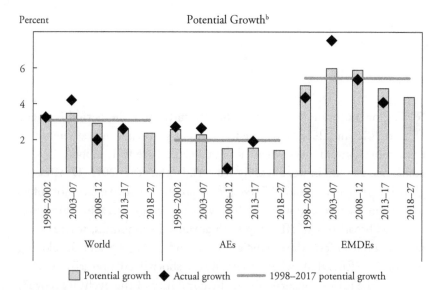

Source: Penn World Tables and World Bank.

a. Sample of 181 countries.

b. Based on production function approach and GDP-weighted averages for a sample of thirty advanced economies (AEs) and fifty emerging and developing economies (EMDEs).

development goals.[1] In some regions, especially commodity-exporting ones such as Eastern Europe and Central Asia and the Middle East and North Africa, the post-crisis slowdown in potential growth could set back per capita income convergence by more than a decade.

Against this backdrop, this chapter addresses the following questions:

- How has potential growth evolved since the turn of the century?
- What have been the drivers of potential growth?
- What are the prospects for potential growth?
- What policy options are available to lift potential growth?

To help answer these questions, we examine the evolution of potential growth in a large sample of countries, with a strong regional focus (table 2-1). Since potential output is not directly observable, economists estimate it from long time series of actual output, employment, capital stocks, and productivity. We use a comprehensive database of potential output growth.[2] For clarity, and in keeping with a longer-term focus, this study uses the production function approach.[3]

This chapter makes several contributions to the large literature on potential growth. First, the focus in this study is on the broader EMDE universe, whereas other studies have documented a potential growth slowdown in advanced economies and Asian economies.[4] Second, the chapter examines global trends in the structural drivers of potential growth, including total factor productivity (TFP) growth, labor supply growth, and investment in human and physical capital. Third, it explores policy options to lift potential growth. These include measures to improve education and reforms to health care and labor markets. In contrast to earlier studies, the discussion of policy options to lift potential growth is directly derived from this empirical exercise.[5]

Our principal conclusions are as follows:

- The global financial crisis has ushered in a period of persistently weak potential growth. During 2013–17, global potential growth (2.5 percent a year) fell 0.5 percentage point below its longer-term (1998–2017) average and even further below its average a decade earlier (2003–07). Potential output decelerated in advanced economies to 1.4 percent a year during 2013–17, which is 0.5 percentage

Table 2-1. *Sample and Region Coverage*

Advanced Economies		Emerging Market and Developing Economies		
Austria	**EAP**	China	**LAC**	Argentina
Belgium		Indonesia		Barbados
Canada		Philippines		Brazil
Cyprus		Thailand		Chile
Czech Republic				Colombia
Denmark	**ECA**	Bulgaria		Costa Rica
Estonia		Croatia		Ecuador
Finland		Hungary		Guatemala
France		Kazakhstan		Honduras
Germany		Moldova		Jamaica
Greece		Poland		Mexico
Hong Kong SAR, China		Russia		Panama
Iceland		Turkey		Paraguay
Ireland		Ukraine		Peru
Israel				Uruguay
Italy	**MNA**	Bahrain		
Japan		Egypt	**SSA**	Benin
Korea		Islamic Republic of Iran		Botswana
Latvia		Jordan		Cameroon
Luxembourg		Kuwait		Côte d'Ivoire
Netherlands		Saudi Arabia		Kenya
Norway		Tunisia		Lesotho
Portugal				Mauritius
Slovak Republic	**SAR**	India		Mozambique
Slovenia		Sri Lanka		Niger
Spain				Rwanda
Sweden				Senegal
Switzerland				South Africa
United Kingdom				Swaziland
United States				

point below its long-term average. Similarly, EMDE potential growth slowed to 4.8 percent a year, 0.6 percentage point below its longer-term average. This weakness in potential growth has been broad-based, affecting almost half of EMDEs and 87 percent of advanced economies in the sample, together representing 69 percent of global gross domestic product (GDP).

• A host of factors have contributed to this post-crisis shortfall in potential growth below longer-term averages. Half of the deceleration reflects weaker-than-average rates of capital accumulation. Just over one-quarter of the slowdown is due to weaker TFP growth, and just under one-quarter of the moderation is attributable to demographic trends.

- The slowdown in potential growth may extend into the next decade. Trends in its fundamental drivers suggest that global potential growth may slow further by 0.2 percentage point on average over the period 2018–27. While the decline in potential growth is expected to be 0.1 percentage point a year in advanced economies, EMDE potential growth could ease much more, by 0.5 percentage point. The projected slowdown from 2013 to 2017 would affect EMDEs and advanced economies that account for 73 percent of global GDP.
- Policies could help reverse these trends and boost global growth. For advanced economies, labor market reforms (especially targeting pension systems) may have the highest potential to stem the decline in potential growth. Among EMDEs, in particular, education, health, and labor market reforms could significantly increase potential growth. A combination of these policies could lift potential growth in EMDEs over the next decade by 0.8 percentage point and more in East Asia and the Pacific (EAP) and Europe and Central Asia (ECA).

To sustain higher potential growth, countries need to reform labor and product markets, strengthen human and physical capital, and build environments conducive to business and household investment. The onus is particularly on the largest emerging markets and advanced economies, whose growth momentum generates spillovers for other EMDEs.

This chapter draws on a comprehensive database that estimates potential growth using all standard approaches for up to 181 countries for 1980–2017 (extending to 2027 for eighty countries) based on work by Kilic Celik and coauthors. The remainder of the chapter presents only results using a production function approach for thirty advanced economies and fifty emerging market and developing economies for the period 1998–2027, which together account for 91 percent of global GDP.[6]

Evolution of Potential Growth: What Happened?

Slowdown in Global Potential Growth

Global potential growth fell to 2.5 percent a year during 2013–17. This is below its longer-term (1998–2017) average of 3 percent a year and even further below its average a decade earlier (2003–07; figure 2-2). The potential growth weakness was broad-based and robust to the specific choice of potential growth measures. During 2013–17 potential growth was below its longer-term average in 87 percent of advanced economies and in almost half of EMDEs. Economies with potential growth below its longer-term average accounted for roughly 70 percent of global GDP.

Per capita estimates also show a trend deceleration. These estimates suggest that there was a persistent slowdown in global potential growth beneath the temporary cyclical shocks that appear to have been the main reasons for the post-crisis slowdown in actual growth from elevated pre-crisis levels. In advanced economies, the potential growth slowdown set in before the global financial crisis, whereas EMDEs enjoyed a short-lived pre-crisis surge in potential growth that subsequently faded.

ADVANCED ECONOMIES. After a sharp decline during 2008–12—the period of the global financial crisis, the eurozone crisis, and pronounced investment weakness—potential growth stabilized in 2013–17 as investment growth recovered.[7] However, at 1.4 percent a year from 2013 through 2017, potential growth in advanced economies remained about 0.5 percentage point below its longer-term average. The decline was particularly pronounced in some countries in Asia. For example, Korea's potential growth slowed more than 1 percentage point in 2013–17 to 3.2 percent from 4.2 percent a decade earlier.[8]

EMDEs. In the initial wake of the global financial crisis, a surge in public investment underpinned EMDE potential growth, offsetting softening productivity and labor supply growth. As EMDE policy stimulus was unwound, and as investment growth plummeted in commodity-exporting EMDEs following the oil price slide in mid-2014, EMDE potential growth slowed sharply to 4.8 percent a year in 2013–17, 0.6 percentage point below its longer-term average.[9]

FIGURE 2-2. **Evolution of Potential Growth**[a]

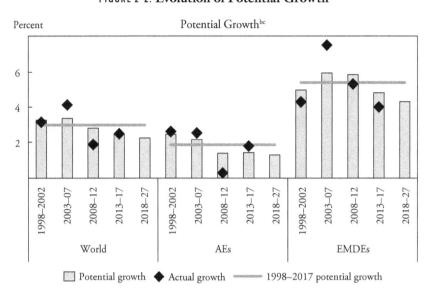

Percent   Potential Growth[bc]

☐ Potential growth   ◆ Actual growth   ▬▬ 1998–2017 potential growth

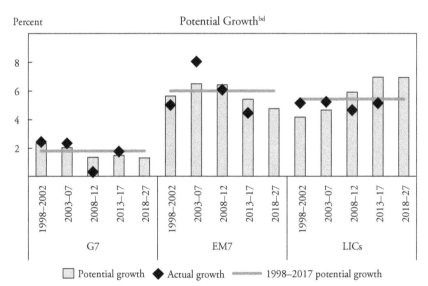

Percent   Potential Growth[bd]

☐ Potential growth   ◆ Actual growth   ▬▬ 1998–2017 potential growth

Source: Penn World Tables and World Bank.

a. Based on potential growth derived using the production function approach.

b. GDP-weighted average.

c. Sample includes thirty advanced economies (AEs), and fifty emerging market and developing economies (EMDEs).

d. G7 includes Canada, France, Germany, Italy, Japan, the United Kingdom, and the United States. EM7 includes Brazil, China, India, Indonesia, Mexico, Russia, and Turkey. Low-income countries (LICs) includes five countries: Benin, Burundi, Mozambique, Niger, and Senegal.

(continued)

FIGURE 2-2. (continued)

Percent   Contribution of Potential Growth and Business Cycle to Actual Growth[bce]

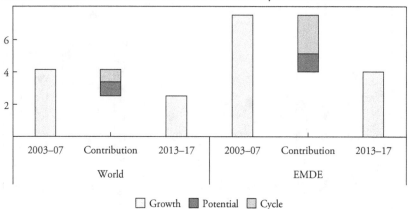

☐ Growth   ■ Potential   ☐ Cycle

Percent   Share of Economies and GDP with Potential Growth below
1998–2017 Average[f]

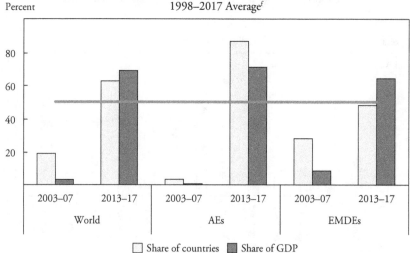

☐ Share of countries   ■ Share of GDP

e. Light bars denote average actual global growth during 2003–07 and 2013–17. Dark bars denote the contribution of global potential growth to the change in actual growth between the two five-year periods; medium bars denote contribution of the cyclical component of global growth to change in actual global growth between the two five-year periods.

f. Number of economies and their share of global GDP among thirty advanced economies and fifty EMDEs with potential growth in each period below its longer-term average (1998–2017). Horizontal line indicates 50 percent.

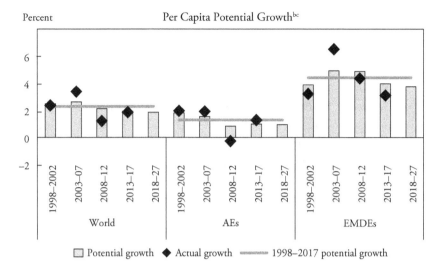

Per Capita Potential Growth[bc]

Percent

Potential growth ◆ Actual growth ▬ 1998–2017 potential growth

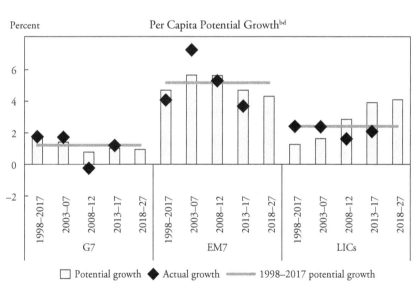

Per Capita Potential Growth[bd]

Percent

☐ Potential growth ◆ Actual growth ▬ 1998–2017 potential growth

REGIONAL PATTERNS. Potential growth has fallen furthest in EMDE regions that had benefited from rapid per capita income convergence or that hosted many commodity-exporting EMDEs (figure 2-3).

- Middle East and North Africa (MNA). The shortfall of potential growth during 2013–17 from its longer-term (1998–2017) average was one of the sharpest in the Middle East and North Africa (1.2 percentage point), where investment growth plunged amid the oil price drop of mid-2014, a period of violent conflict and policy uncertainty in parts of the region.

- Europe and Central Asia (ECA), Latin America and the Caribbean (LAC). During 2013–17, potential growth also fell 0.5 and 0.2 percentage point, respectively, below its longer-term average in Europe and Central Asia and Latin America and the Caribbean. The ECA region's past two decades of rapid integration into European production networks has gradually diminished its potential for further catch-up productivity growth. The region also hosts several energy exporters that suffered deep recession or slowdown following the mid-2014 decline in oil prices. Weak productivity growth and less favorable demographics reduced potential growth in LAC.[10]

- East Asia and the Pacific (EAP). In 2013–17, potential growth in China fell 1.3 percentage point below its longer-term average as policy efforts succeeded in rebalancing growth away from investment toward more sustainable growth engines, combined with slowing productivity and working-age population growth. Elsewhere in EAP, potential growth rose 0.7 percentage point on robust capital accumulation and strengthening TFP growth.

- South Asia Region (SAR) and sub-Saharan Africa (SSA). During 2013–17, favorable demographics helped lift potential growth in SAR and SSA. In SAR, potential growth was negatively affected by investment weakness such that growth in 2013–17 broadly matched its longer-term average. In SSA, potential output accelerated by 0.4 percentage point during 2013–17 over its longer-term average. This demographic dividend was complemented by rapid capital accumulation over the previous two decades as re-

FIGURE 2-3. Regental Potential Growth

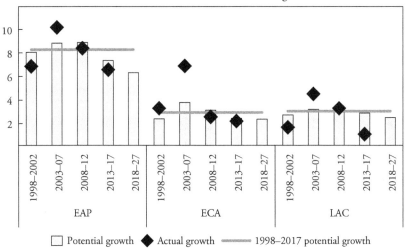

Percent — Potential Growth in Select EMDE Regions[ac]

□ Potential growth ◆ Actual growth ▬▬▬ 1998–2017 potential growth

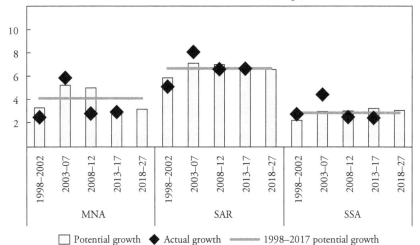

Percent — Potential Growth in Select EMDE Regions[bc]

□ Potential growth ◆ Actual growth ▬▬▬ 1998–2017 potential growth

Source: Penn World Tables and World Bank.

a. EAP = East Asia and the Pacific, ECA = Europe and Central Asia, LAC = Latin America and the Caribbean.
b. MNA = Middle East and North Africa, SAR = South Asia Region, and SSA = Sub-Saharan Africa.
c. GDP-weighted averages using potential growth estimate based on production function approach.

(continued)

FIGURE 2-3. (continued)

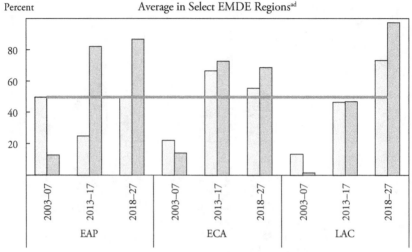

Share of Economies and GDP with Potential Growth below 1998–2017 Average in Select EMDE Regions[ad]

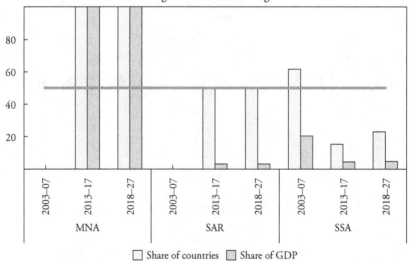

Share of Economies and GDP with Potential Growth below 1998–2017 Average in Select EMDE Regions[bd]

d. Horizontal line indicates 50 percent. Number of economies and their share of GDP in the region among fifty EMDEs with potential growth in each region.

source discoveries were developed into operating mines and oil fields and governments undertook large-scale public infrastructure investments. The commodity price slide after 2011 has raised concerns about the sustainability of such potential growth.

Drivers of the Slowdown in Potential Growth

Of the 0.5 percentage point shortfall in post-crisis (2013–17) global potential growth below its longer-term (1998–2017) average, about half can be attributed to weaker capital accumulation (0.2 percentage point) and the remainder to weaker TFP growth and slower labor supply growth (0.1 percentage point, respectively). Weak global capital accumulation mainly reflected investment weakness in advanced economies, in the wake of financial crises in the United States and Europe, and a policy-driven rebalancing away from investment in China.[11] Unfavorable demographics and slowing TFP growth were features of both advanced economies and EMDEs (figure 2-4).

Total Factor Productivity Growth

CHANNELS OF TRANSMISSION. By allowing output to expand with a given amount of factor inputs, TFP growth has historically been the critical driver of sustained growth in per capita output and prosperity.[12] TFP growth can rise with the adoption of new technologies, adaptation of existing technologies, introduction of more efficient processes, or changes in management practices.[13] Differences in TFP account for about two-thirds of the variation in per capita income across the world.[14] Higher productivity lifts firms' marginal product and reduces their marginal cost, which allows firms to increase their demand for factors of production. Technological advances reduce the price of capital equipment, encouraging further capital accumulation, which in turn embodies further improvements in productivity.[15]

EVOLUTION OF POTENTIAL TFP GROWTH. Global potential TFP growth—the part of TFP growth that is stripped of its wide cyclical swings—slowed from about 1.3 percent a year in 2003–07 to about 1 percent a year during 2013–17 but with wide heterogeneity (figure 2-5).

In advanced economies, productivity growth showed signs of flattening well before the global financial crisis. For some advanced economies, the productivity growth slowdown during the early 2000s has been described

FIGURE 2-4. Drivers of Potential Growth[a]

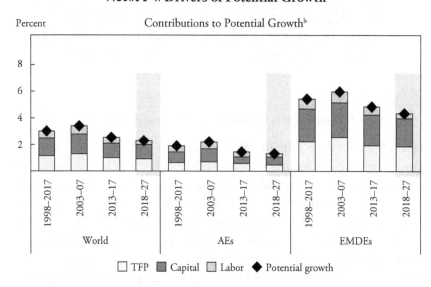

Percent — Contributions to Potential Growth[b]

TFP □ Capital ■ Labor ■ ◆ Potential growth

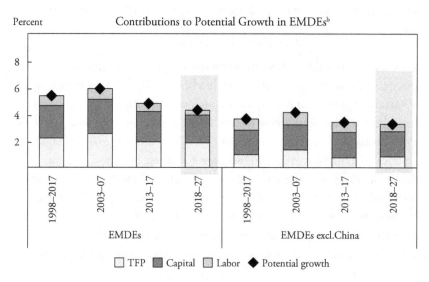

Percent — Contributions to Potential Growth in EMDEs[b]

TFP □ Capital ■ Labor ■ ◆ Potential growth

Source: Penn World Tables and World Bank.

a. GDP-weighted averages of production function-based potential growth estimates. TFP stands for total factor productivity growth.

b. Sample includes thirty advanced economies (AEs) and fifty emerging and developing economies (EMDEs).

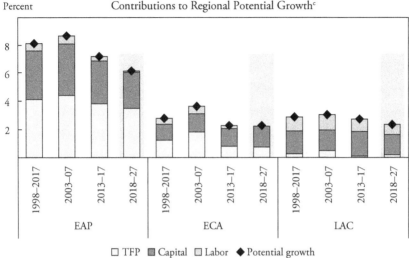

Percent   Contributions to Regional Potential Growth[c]

□ TFP   ■ Capital   □ Labor   ◆ Potential growth

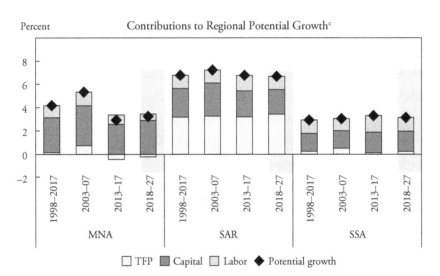

Percent   Contributions to Regional Potential Growth[c]

□ TFP   ■ Capital   □ Labor   ◆ Potential growth

c. Regional samples include largest available sample for each region to ensure broad-based coverage. EAP = East Asia and the Pacific, ECA = Europe and Central Asia, LAC = Latin America and the Caribbean, MNA = Middle East and North Africa, SAR = South Asia Region, and SSA = Sub-Saharan Africa.

FIGURE 2-5. Total Factor Productivity Growth[a]

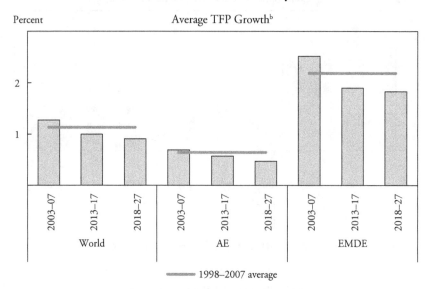

Percent — Average TFP Growth[b]

━━━━ 1998–2007 average

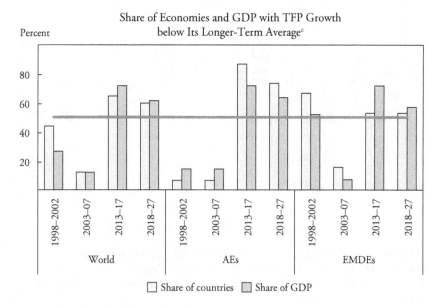

Percent — Share of Economies and GDP with TFP Growth below Its Longer-Term Average[c]

□ Share of countries ▨ Share of GDP

Source: Penn World Tables and World Bank.

a. TFP growth stands for total factor productivity growth. This figure refers to potential TFP growth.

b. GDP-weighted average of total factor productivity growth. Includes fifty emerging and developing economies (EMDEs) and thirty advanced economies (AEs).

c. Number of economies among thirty AEs and fifty EMDEs in which potential total factor productivity growth is lower than its longer-term average (1998–2017).

as a return to productivity growth before the surge of information and communications technologies in the mid-1990s.[16]

By contrast, TFP growth in EMDEs surged to 2.5 percent a year in
2003–07, reflecting productivity-enhancing investment, partly financed by
capital inflows.[17] Reforms of policy frameworks after the EMDE financial
crises in the late 1990s and early 2000s and greater integration into global
value chains provided an environment conducive to rapid productivity
growth. However, since the global financial crisis, TFP growth in EMDEs
slowed to 1.9 percent a year in 2013–17.

SOURCES OF THE TFP GROWTH SLOWDOWN. Some drivers of the TFP growth
slowdown are likely to be structural and persistent. TFP growth may have
slowed as a wave of information and communications technologies matured.
The pace of cross-country diffusion of technology may have diminished as
global value chains stopped growing. Aging workforces may have impeded
the adoption of new ideas. In commodity exporters, a downgrading of expectations for long-term profitability of resource projects would have reduced investment and, with it, embodied productivity gains. Finally, the
large-scale factor reallocation, especially from agriculture to manufacturing, that has supported robust EMDE productivity growth over the past
two decades appears to be slowing.

THE ROLE OF HUMAN CAPITAL. Over the past three decades, TFP growth in
EMDEs has been supported by growing human capital. In countries with
better-educated and healthier working-age populations, both TFP growth
and labor force participation rates tend to be higher. EMDEs have made
rapid strides toward improving education and health outcomes over the past
two decades.

- On average in EMDEs, secondary school completion rates increased by 7 percentage points between 1998–2002 and 2013–17.
  The average completion rate of 27 percent is about two-thirds of
  the advanced-economy average.
- Tertiary completion rates rose by about one-half, to 10 percent
  in 2013–17, but this figure is still about half of the advanced-
  economy average.

- Life expectancy rose by four years, to an average life expectancy of seventy-one years, about ten years less than the advanced-economy average.

These substantial improvements in human capital mitigated adverse developments weighing on EMDE potential growth between 1998–2002 and 2013–17 and helped raise potential growth in regions where progress was particularly large. The largest improvements between 1998–2002 and 2013–17 were made in sub-Saharan Africa, where secondary completion rates almost doubled, to approach the advanced-economy average of 40 percent, and life expectancy rose by seven years to almost sixty years. Life expectancy also rose considerably (by four years) in South Asia to seventy-two years.

Physical Capital Accumulation

CHANNELS OF TRANSMISSION. Investment can lift potential output growth through direct and indirect channels. Directly, investment is the source of capital accumulation, which raises labor productivity and potential output—as long as investment is not channeled into excess capacity and wasted.[18] Indirectly, investment can raise total factor productivity because technological improvements are often embodied in investment.[19]

EVOLUTION OF INVESTMENT GROWTH. Global investment growth slowed by half between 2010 and 2016, as investment weakness shifted from advanced economies to EMDEs over this period. Investment growth in advanced economies declined during the eurozone crisis and, after a brief rebound, again after the oil price decline that disrupted energy sector investment in the United States. In EMDEs, investment growth slowed sharply following the global financial crisis, from double-digit rates in the immediate wake of the crisis to a post-crisis low of 3 percent in 2016. Despite signs of bottoming out in 2017, investment growth has been well below its pre-crisis average as well as its longer-term average in more than half of the EMDEs in the sample (figure 2-6). In EMDEs, both public and private investments were weak. Public investment accounted for about 31 percent of total investment in EMDEs and about 15 percent of advanced-economy investment during 2010–15.[20] After 2011 public investment growth remained anemic following the stimulus-related surge of 2008–09, and private investment growth slowed sharply after 2011.

FIGURE 2-6. Investment Growth

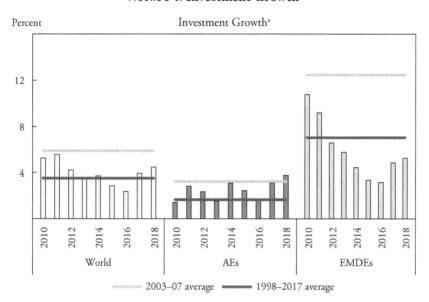

Percent — Investment Growth[a]

World   AEs   EMDEs

.... 2003–07 average   ——— 1998–2017 average

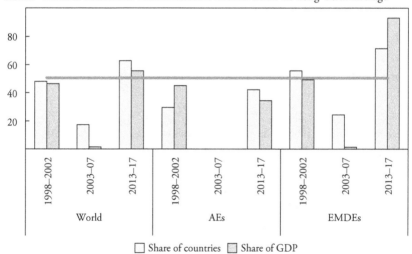

Percent   Share of Economies with Investment Growth below Its Long-Term Average[b]

World   AEs   EMDEs

☐ Share of countries   ▨ Share of GDP

Source: Penn World Tables and World Bank.

a. Investment-weighted averages. For a sample of thirty-seven advanced economies (AEs) and 145 emerging and developing economies (EMDEs).
b. Share of 139 countries in which investment growth is below the longer-term average (1998–2017). Horizontal line indicates 50 percent.

SOURCES OF INVESTMENT WEAKNESS. Whereas investment weakness in advanced economies mainly reflected sluggish demand and output growth, in EMDEs a broader range of factors has been at play. In commodity importers, slowing FDI inflows and spillovers from soft activity in major advanced economies accounted for much of the slowdown in investment growth after 2011. In commodity-exporting countries, a sharp deterioration in their terms of trade (particularly for energy exporters), slowing growth in China, and mounting private debt burdens accounted for much of the slowdown in investment growth. In several EMDEs, political and policy uncertainty was a key factor in investment contractions or slowdowns.[21] Investment weakness may also reflect the declining price of capital goods or a growing role of poorly measured intangible capital, such as design, research and development, marketing, and training.[22]

CONSEQUENCES OF INVESTMENT WEAKNESS. Cyclical factors, although transitory themselves, can have long-lasting effects on potential output growth. More than half of EMDEs in the sample suffered at least one year of investment contraction during 2013–17. In some, investment contractions were triggered by the prolonged slump of commodity prices from their peak in early 2011. In others, it was accompanied by heightened domestic political or geopolitical tensions. Such episodes typically foreshadow weaker potential growth in the three years surrounding the trough of the investment contraction.

Labor Supply

CHANNELS OF TRANSMISSION. Growing working-age populations have been associated with "demographic dividends" to growth. Higher working-age shares of populations have been accompanied by higher capital accumulation and employment (figure 2-7).[23] Shifts toward an older age structure of the population affect potential output in several ways. Population aging may reduce the working-age population, which directly reduces the potential labor supply. There are also less direct effects of population aging. For example, aging increases the share of the population with below-average labor force participation rates. Aging populations have been associated with slower labor productivity growth for various industries and occupations.[24]

Another important driver of increased labor supply can be labor force participation among less well represented groups, including women, young,

FIGURE 2-7. **Demographics**

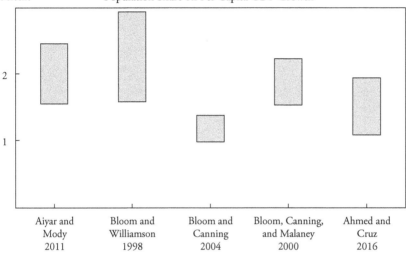

Impact of 1 Percentage Point Higher Growth of Working-Age
Population Share on Per Capita GDP Growth[a]

Percent

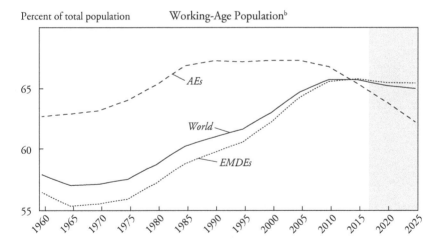

Percent of total population — Working-Age Population[b]

Source: United Nations World Population Prospects: The 2017 Revision.

a. The sample in each study differs. Aiyar and Mody (2011) survey Indian states, 1961–2001;
Bloom and Williamson (1998) survey seventy-eight countries, 1965–90; Bloom and Canning
(2004) survey over seventy countries, 1965–95; Bloom, Canning, and Malaney (2000) survey
seventy countries, 1965–90; Ahmed and Cruz (2016) survey 160 countries, 1960–2010.
b. Population-weighted averages. The working-age population is defined as people aged 15–64 years.

(*continued*)

FIGURE 2-7. (continued)

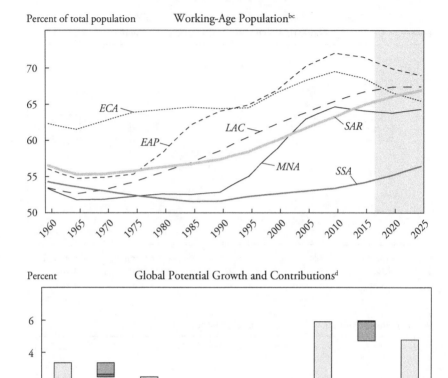

Percent of total population — Working-Age Population[bc]

Percent — Global Potential Growth and Contributions[d]

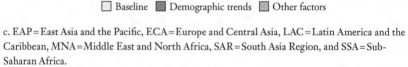

☐ Baseline ■ Demographic trends ▨ Other factors

c. EAP = East Asia and the Pacific, ECA = Europe and Central Asia, LAC = Latin America and the Caribbean, MNA = Middle East and North Africa, SAR = South Asia Region, and SSA = Sub-Saharan Africa.

d. GDP-weighted averages. Other factors include contribution from policy changes, cohort effects, changes in population growth, convergence-driven productivity growth, and investment. "Contribution" reflects percentage point changes between the averages of 2003–07 and 2013–17.

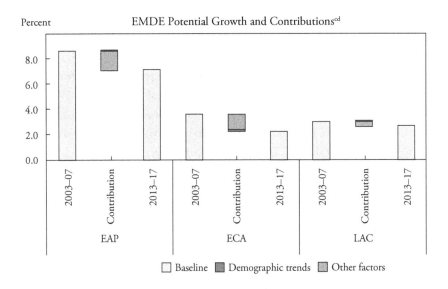

Percent   EMDE Potential Growth and Contributions[cd]

□ Baseline   ■ Demographic trends   ▨ Other factors

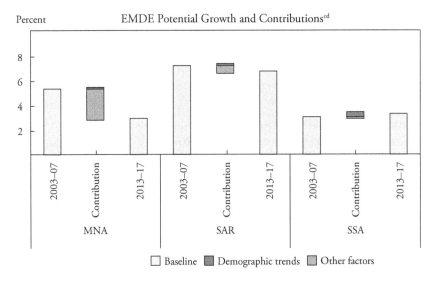

Percent   EMDE Potential Growth and Contributions[cd]

□ Baseline   ■ Demographic trends   ▨ Other factors

and old workers. Rising female labor force participation rates have been attributed to better educational attainment (opening access to higher-earning jobs), lower fertility rates, a technology-driven shift toward non-manual skills, and cheaper home production (lowering the opportunity cost of working).[25] Meanwhile, population aging has contributed to a decline in labor force participation, which tends to be lower among older workers.[26]

EVOLUTION OF DEMOGRAPHICS. In the past five decades, growth was supported by rapidly growing working-age populations—until the mid-1980s in advanced economies and around 2010 in EMDEs (figure 2-7). Since 2000, countries with rising working-age population shares accounted for half of global output growth and three-quarters of global GDP levels. With the retirement of the baby boom generation and lower fertility rates, demographic trends have become less favorable to growth and will continue to be so over the next decade. In advanced economies, the working-age share of the population is set to decline, from 65.4 percent in 2015 to 62.3 percent by 2025. In EMDEs the working-age share of the population peaked at 65.8 percent in 2015 and is expected to stabilize around this level over the next decade. While the largest declines are expected in EAP and ECA, working-age shares of the population are expected to rise in sub-Saharan Africa and South Asia.

In addition to the changing age composition of the population, expanding female labor force participation has increased the labor supply, especially in EMDEs. Female labor force participation was broadly stable over the two decades, from 1998–2002 to 2013–17, though with a wide divergence across EMDE regions. Supported by surging school enrollment and completion rates, female labor force participation rates in LAC rose by almost 6 percentage points between 1998–2002 and 2013–17. In contrast, despite some (more modest) improvements in education, they declined in the SAR by almost as much over the same period. Among EMDEs, female labor force participation remains less than three-quarters of male labor force participation.

THE ROLE OF DEMOGRAPHICS IN POTENTIAL GROWTH. The overall effect of demographics on potential growth—via TFP growth and labor supply growth—can be assessed using the production function approach. The estimates compare baseline potential growth estimates against counterfactual scenarios in which the composition of the population for all age groups and genders remains at their 1998 values.[27]

The contribution of aging to potential growth is calculated as the difference between actual potential growth and a counterfactual derived from an "unchanged demographics" scenario. The counterfactual scenario is one in which population shares are fixed at 1998 levels (for historical contributions) or 2017 levels (for forward-looking scenarios) in the calculation of labor force participation rates and TFP growth. All other variables, including fitted labor force participation rates for each age group and gender, remain the same in both scenarios. Hence, aggregated labor supply differs between the two scenarios only because different age groups (with different inclinations to participate in the labor force) have different population shares.

The contribution of migration to potential growth is calculated as the difference between actual potential growth and a counterfactual derived from a "no-migration" scenario. The counterfactual scenario is one in which population, population shares, fertility, and life expectancy indicators are estimated under zero international migration for each country, as calculated in the UN Population Statistics (UN 2017).

The results suggest that, in 2013–17, population aging lowered global potential growth by 0.2 percentage point from its 2003–07 average. Advanced economies accounted for this entire decline. In EMDEs, except in Europe and Central Asia, growing and younger working-age populations lifted potential growth marginally over the same period. Trends in female labor force participation benefited some EMDE regions' potential growth while weighing on potential growth in others. Over the longer term (1998–2017), higher female labor force participation contributed 0.3 percentage point to potential growth in LAC, while it did not contribute appreciably to longer-term potential growth in the SAR.

Prospects for Potential Growth: What Could Happen?

The factors weighing on potential growth over 2013–17 are likely to persist over the next decade. Demographic trends are expected to become less favorable. This will weigh on potential growth even if trend improvements in human capital and female labor force participation (and, for advanced economies, migration) continue. Although investment growth is expected to recover from its recent weakness, it is unlikely to return to elevated pre-crisis levels. Short of unexpected surges in productivity growth—perhaps as a result of dissipating crisis legacies or unanticipated technological breakthroughs—these trends imply an outlook for mediocre potential growth.

Baseline Scenario Assumptions

The forward-looking scenario presented here applies the production function approach to assumed paths for capital, population statistics, and education and health outcomes. The baseline scenario is one of "follow the same path" in that it assumes that all policy variables follow their long-term average trends. The scenario assumes that all population-related variables (including age and gender structure of the population, fertility, and life expectancy) evolve as in the UN Population Projections under the assumption of median fertility, normal mortality, and "normal" (trend) migration.[28]

- Past trend improvements in each economy's education and health outcomes are expected to continue. Secondary and tertiary *enrollment* rates by gender are assumed to grow through the forecast horizon at their average growth during 1998–2017 but are capped at 100 percent. Economy-wide averages are calculated as the population-weighted average (2000–16) of these gender-specific rates.
- Secondary and tertiary education *completion* rates by gender and age group are assumed to grow at their average rate during 1998–2017. Economy-wide averages are calculated as the population-weighted average (2000–16) of these gender- and group-specific rates.
- In line with historical experience, investment growth is assumed to remain constant at its long-term average.[29]

Evolution of Drivers of Global Potential Growth

Under this baseline scenario, the fundamental drivers of potential growth all point to continued softening.

- A slowing pace of capital accumulation, especially in China, will be offset by growing capital accumulation in advanced economies. In EMDEs other than China, the pace of capital accumulation will remain broadly steady as investment growth keeps pace with recovering output growth after its pronounced weakness of 2015–16.
- Subdued investment and less room for catch-up productivity growth as per capita income differentials narrow for EMDEs will

sap productivity growth. This could reduce potential growth by about 0.1 percentage point.

- Even if education and health outcomes continue to improve in line with their longer-term trends, aging populations combined with withdrawal from the labor market of older cohorts of workers could reduce global potential growth by another 0.2 percentage point on average. That said, in advanced economies, migration could dampen the slowdown in potential growth by about 0.1 percentage point by supporting labor force growth.

Global Potential Growth

Thus, absent significant policy changes or productivity breakthroughs, global potential growth could decline by 0.2 percentage point, to 2.3 percent a year in 2018–27 (figure 2-8). Two-thirds of the sample's economies, accounting for 78 percent of global output, would be left with potential growth below the longer-term average.

Advanced-economy potential growth could slow by 0.1 percentage point to 1.3 percent a year. This deceleration in potential output mostly reflects an expected decline in TFP growth and a further slowdown in labor supply due to population aging. These trends are expected to be only partially offset by a recovery in capital accumulation from post-crisis weakness.[30]

EMDE potential growth could slow by 0.5 percentage point to an average 4.3 percent a year during the next decade, well below its longer-term average. This slowdown would mostly reflect demographic trends (across most EMDEs) and weaker capital accumulation in China, as China's policy-guided investment slowdown continues (elsewhere capital accumulation is expected to recover partially from its post-crisis weakness). While China will account for 0.4 percentage point of the 0.5 percentage point decline in EMDE potential growth, the decline will be broad-based, affecting almost two-thirds of EMDEs in the sample.

The slowdown would also be sizable for the largest EMDEs, which could generate adverse spillovers to other EMDEs that the production function approach does not explicitly account for.[31] Largely owing to weakening demographic trends and China's slowing capital accumulation, potential growth in the seven largest emerging markets (EM7) is expected to slow by 1.1 percentage point on average, of which China accounts for more than three-quarters. Aging (and, in some cases, shrinking) populations are expected to reduce G7 potential growth by 0.2 percentage point on average.

FIGURE 2-8. **Potential Growth Prospects**

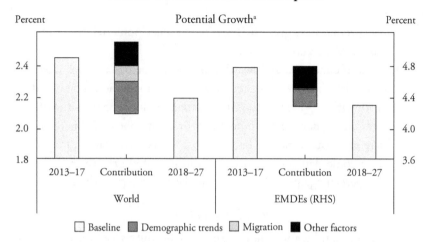

Potential Growth[a]

Legend: □ Baseline ■ Demographic trends □ Migration ■ Other factors

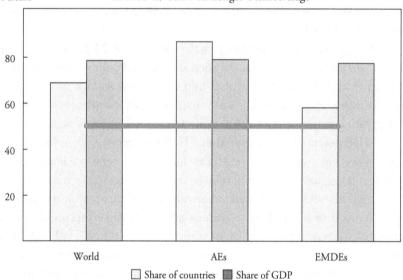

Share of Countries and GDP of Countries with Potential Growth
in 2018–27 below Its Longer-Term Average[b]

Legend: □ Share of countries ■ Share of GDP

Source: World Bank estimates.

a. GDP-weighted averages. Derived using the production function-based potential growth. "Other factors" reflects declining population growth, convergence-related productivity growth, policy changes, cohort effects, and a slowdown in investment growth relative to output growth. "Contribution" reflects the percentage point changes between the averages of 2013–17 and 2018–27. "RHS" stands for right-hand side.

b. Share of countries and share of GDP of eighty countries in which potential growth in 2018–27 is below longer-term average potential growth (1998–2017), in percent of all countries or global GDP among eighty advanced economies (AEs) and emerging and developing economies (EMDEs). Horizontal line indicates 50 percent.

Regional Potential Growth

Potential growth is expected to slow over the next decade in all regions and fall below the longer-term average in all regions except SSA. In most regions, working-age shares of the population are expected to shrink. In the SAR and SSA, working-age shares of the population are expected to rise, but a shift is expected within the working-age population toward older cohorts with weaker labor market attachment.

- **EAP, LAC.** Potential growth is expected to moderate in EAP as policy efforts in China succeed in shifting toward more sustainable growth engines and the region's working-age population ages. China's potential growth is expected to slow to 6.5 percent on average in 2018–27, from 9.1 percent on average during 1998–2017 (see figure 2-4). Elsewhere in EAP, potential growth is expected to remain solid. In LAC, demographic trends and the legacy of weak investment over the past half-decade will weigh on potential growth.
- **ECA, SAR, SSA.** Shrinking labor supplies and weak investment will weigh on potential growth in ECA and the SAR as investment fails to return to the elevated levels seen before the oil price plunge and onset of policy uncertainty in mid-2014. In SSA, an expected slowdown in potential growth largely reflects population aging in South Africa, while elsewhere in SSA potential growth is expected to remain broadly steady at a robust 5 percent.
- **MNA.** Potential growth is expected to strengthen somewhat in the Middle East and North Africa. Investment and productivity growth are expected to be strong, provided conflict and geopolitical risks do not intensify.

Policy Options to Lift Potential Growth

The production function framework can be applied to examine stylized policy scenarios. The impact of better policy outcomes is estimated as the difference between the baseline scenario and potential growth under a counterfactual scenario of higher growth of physical or human capital or labor supply. All counterfactual scenarios model a repeat of a country's best ten-year improvement, up to reasonable ceilings. The potential growth dividend of the scenarios therefore depends on each country's track record as well as its room for improvement. The estimate provided in these stylized scenarios may well be lower bounds because they disregard nonlinearities in reform impacts as well as synergies between different reform measures.

- **Higher physical capital.** The investment growth rate in each country is assumed to rise by its highest increase in any ten-year period during 1998–2017.
- **Better human capital.** Educational outcome indicators— secondary and tertiary enrollment and completion rates—are assumed to rise in each country by as much as the maximum improvement over any ten-year period during 1998–2017. Enrollment rates remain capped at 100 percent. Completion rates are capped at the maximum across advanced economies in 2016. Life expectancy is assumed to rise in each country as much as the largest improvement over any ten-year period during 1998–2017 but not above the median advanced-economy life expectancy in 2016 (capped at 100 years).
- **Labor market reform.** For each age group in each country, female labor force participation rates are assumed to rise by the largest increase over any ten-year period during 1998–2017 but not to exceed male labor force participation rates in the same age group. Separately, a pension reform with labor market implications is modeled. For each gender and each country, labor force participation rates for workers aged 55, 60, and 65 or older are assumed to rise to the rates of workers that are five years younger— that is, those age 50, 55, and 60. The increase is assumed to occur gradually over twenty years for each gender in each country.

Raising Physical Capital

The United Nations Conference on Trade and Development (UNCTAD) estimated that unfilled global investment needs amount to up to 3 percent of global GDP.[32] In particular, all EMDE regions have sizable investment needs.[33] Depending on the availability of financing, these could be filled through either public or private investment or a combination of both in public–private partnerships. Increasing public investment can be an effective policy tool to support short-term demand while also helping to raise future potential growth.[34] Although the rapid increase in public debt over 2008–17 has constrained fiscal space in most countries, there remains scope to shift existing government expenditures toward public investment to make government operations more growth friendly.[35] Moreover, in many countries, government revenue ratios remain low, indicating that in some cases tax revenues could be raised, including by expanding tax bases or improving the quality of tax administration.[36]

In addition, policies can support productivity-enhancing private investment. Innovation-related investment tends to be low in EMDE firms, partly because of the limited availability of complementary inputs such as trained engineers or effective organization techniques.[37] Policy efforts to expand the supply of complementary inputs and capabilities and to raise the returns on investment through intellectual property rights protection may foster private investment.

If, over the next decade, each country raised its investment growth as much as its largest increase over any historical ten-year interval, global investment-to-GDP ratios would rise by 2.3 percentage points of GDP. Investment-to-GDP ratios would rise somewhat more in EMDEs, by 2.9 percentage points of GDP. It is estimated that such an investment boost would raise global potential output by 2 percent by 2027, reversing the slowdown under the baseline scenario. EMDE potential output would rise even more (5 percent cumulatively by 2027; figure 2-9).

Implicit in these scenarios is the premise that the additional investment would be used productively. In the context of EMDEs, there is some evidence that absorptive capacity can limit the success of large scaling up of public investment, although this adverse effect is small in lower-income and capital-scarce countries.[38]

Raising Human Capital

Measures to raise human capital could lift both labor supply and TFP growth: a better-educated workforce is more securely attached to the labor market and more productive. In particular, a better-educated workforce may be better able to adjust to technological disruptions that reduce employment and wages by replacing jobs.[39] In the framework used here, human capital has two dimensions, educational attainment and health outcomes (proxied by life expectancy).

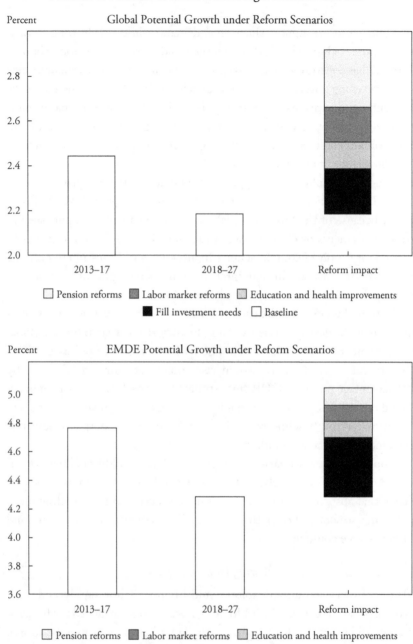

FIGURE 2-9. Policies to Stem Declining Potential Growth[a]

Global Potential Growth under Reform Scenarios

Percent

☐ Pension reforms ■ Labor market reforms ☐ Education and health improvements
■ Fill investment needs ☐ Baseline

EMDE Potential Growth under Reform Scenarios

Percent

☐ Pension reforms ■ Labor market reforms ☐ Education and health improvements
■ Fill investment needs ☐ Baseline

Source: World Bank estimates.

a. GDP-weighted averages.

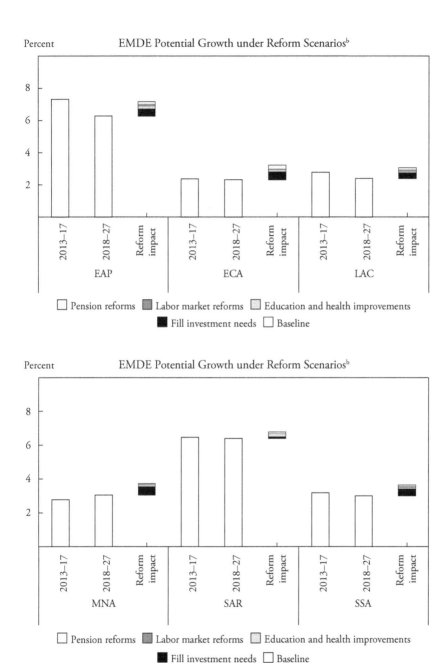

Percent   EMDE Potential Growth under Reform Scenarios[b]

Pension reforms   Labor market reforms   Education and health improvements   Fill investment needs   Baseline

EAP   ECA   LAC

2013–17   2018–27   Reform impact

Percent   EMDE Potential Growth under Reform Scenarios[b]

Pension reforms   Labor market reforms   Education and health improvements   Fill investment needs   Baseline

MNA   SAR   SSA

2013–17   2018–27   Reform impact

b. EAP = East Asia and the Pacific, ECA = Europe and Central Asia, LAC = Latin America and the Caribbean, MNA = Middle East and North Africa, SAR = South Asia Region, and SSA = Sub-Saharan Africa.

EDUCATION. While secondary school enrollment rates are near advanced-economy levels in the average EMDE, tertiary school enrollment rates (40 percent) and secondary and tertiary school completion rates (27 percent and 10 percent, respectively) were less than two-thirds of the advanced-economy average in 2013–17 on average. In addition to expanding access to education, as captured by these measures, improving the quality of education to improve education outcomes is critical.[40] There are a number of policies that can improve education outcomes. At the national level, these include policies targeted at better training for teachers, greater teacher accountability, and performance incentives.[41] The development of metrics to assess and accelerate progress toward learning goals is a prerequisite for policy actions to improve educational outcomes.[42] At the student level, useful policies include efforts to tailor teaching to the requirements of students. Grants may encourage school attendance by disadvantaged students. Better early childhood nutrition and cognitive development improve students' capacity to learn.[43]

In a stylized policy scenario, education-related policy indicators—secondary and tertiary enrollment and completion rates—are assumed to rise over 2018–27 in each EMDE by as much as their largest historical improvement in any ten-year period. This would imply that EMDEs, on average, would raise secondary school completion rates by 5 percentage points and secondary and tertiary enrollment rates by 7 percentage points over the next decade. In EMDE regions that have made particularly large strides in improving education outcomes but still have ample room for further improvements, such as the SAR, secondary school completion rates could rise as much as 16 percentage points over the next decade.

Rapid technological change and a more interdisciplinary perspective may also require new education strategies that allow workers to be flexible and adapt their knowledge and expertise throughout their careers. More than a third of the skills demanded in today's world have been estimated to be no longer desirable for future occupations by 2020.[44] Hence, the ability to mobilize knowledge and rapidly adapt skill sets may be a critical competency for workers to meet the demands of future labor markets.[45]

HEALTH POLICIES. At seventy-one years on average in 2013–17, life expectancy in EMDEs is still below that in advanced economies (eighty-two years). Although regions such as the SAR and SSA have raised life expectancy by four to seven years since the turn of the century, it remains about one-eighth below advanced-economy levels.

Policy interventions to improve public health, and to ensure productive working lives, range widely. Better sanitation and access to clean water would improve public health: 9 percent of the global disease burden may be attributable to unsafe water, inadequate sanitation, and insufficient hygiene.[46] In addition, improvements in health care provision can be spurred by well-defined and regularly monitored performance indicators.[47] Comprehensive coverage of health services has been followed by better health outcomes in countries with higher per capita incomes.[48] At the local level, programs targeted at local health service providers or groups of patients have generated considerable improvements in health care services and outcomes. For example, in Rwanda, performance-based incentive payments helped significantly improve health indicators for children.[49] In India, enhanced training of primary health care providers led to better identification and treatment of patient ailments.[50]

In a stylized scenario of improved health, life expectancy is assumed to rise over 2018–27 in each EMDE by as much as its largest improvement over any historical ten-year period. This would imply an increase in life expectancy in EMDEs by 2.5 years, on average, but as much as 3.8 years in the MNA by 2027.

IMPACT ON POTENTIAL GROWTH. These stylized scenarios suggest that improvements in education and health outcomes—via their effect on labor supply and TFP growth—could lift global and EMDE potential growth by 0.2 percentage point on average. In some EMDE regions with a strong track record of boosting human capital and ample room for improving education and health outcomes, such as in EAP, potential growth could rise by one-and-a-half times as much.

Raising the Labor Supply

At 49 percent, on average, in 2013–17, global female labor force participation remains two-thirds that of men (75 percent), and it is even lower in EMDEs. Similarly, in both EMDEs and advanced economies, the average labor force participation rate among workers aged 55 or older is about half that of 30- to 45-year-old workers, and labor force participation among 19- to 29-year-olds is only four-fifths that of their 30- to 45-year-old peers. Labor supply can be raised by drawing a greater share of the working-age population into the labor force. This can be achieved through policies to "activate" discouraged workers or groups with historically low participation rates, such as women and younger or older workers.

In advanced economies and EMDEs, active labor market policies and reforms to social benefits were followed by higher labor force participation rates.[51] Less-rigid employment protection regulation and lower minimum wages have had mixed effects on employment and labor force participation and, at times, unintended side effects such as lower labor force participation of disadvantaged groups.[52]

In EMDEs, policies aimed at other objectives have sometimes brought important collateral benefits that improve labor force participation. For example, in Nigeria, better access to finance and training programs increased female labor force participation by encouraging new firm startups.[53] In Uruguay, the extension of the school day was associated with higher adult labor force participation.[54] In Eastern Europe and Central Asia, shifting health care systems toward services targeted at the elderly has helped extend productive lifetimes, and providing support services to women with families has helped encourage labor force participation.[55]

RAISING FEMALE LABOR FORCE PARTICIPATION. Female labor force participation rates—along cohort, age-, and country-specific dimensions—are assumed to rise over the next decade by the largest historical ten-year improvement in each EMDE (in a stylized labor market reform scenario), although they will not exceed the rates of same-aged men. On average, this would imply raising female labor force participation rates by 10 percentage points by 2027. The premise underlying this assumption is that, over the decade, sufficient jobs will be created to absorb this additional labor supply.

In such a stylized labor market reform scenario, global and EMDE potential growth could rise by 0.2 percentage point and 0.1 percentage point, respectively, on average, over 2018–27. Again, such a renewed reform push could yield the largest dividends for EMDE regions, such as Latin America and the Caribbean, with both a strong track record and sizable remaining gaps between male and female labor force participation rates.

RAISING LABOR FORCE PARTICIPATION OF OLDER WORKERS. The scenario assumes a pension reform that gradually raises labor force participation in each five-year age group from 55 years onward. Separately in each country and for each gender, labor force participation rates for workers in the age groups of 55–59 years, 60–64 years, and 65 years or older are assumed to rise to the rates of age groups that are five years younger—that is, those who are 50–54, 55–59, and 60–64. The increase is assumed to occur gradually over twenty years for each gender in each country.

In such a stylized pension reform scenario, global and advanced economy potential growth could rise by 0.3 percentage point on average over 2018–27. For EMDEs, the effect is smaller, 0.1 percentage point. The largest boost to growth would materialize in EAP and ECA, the two regions with the most rapidly aging populations.

Raising Productivity

The scenario analysis thus far is restricted to reforms that can be quantified in the production function framework used here. Other reforms could raise total factor productivity. Institutional reforms could help lift productivity growth. Better institutional quality, such as control of corruption, application of the rule of law, and improved political stability, has accompanied higher and more stable growth. At the firm level, more friendly business climates have favored firm productivity and a shift from informal activities to more productive formal activities.

Fiscal structural reforms could also yield important productivity dividends. Several studies have highlighted the long-term growth dividends of fiscal reforms, especially when combined with other structural reforms.[56] In OECD countries, the growth-enhancing effects of a budget-neutral shift in government spending toward health, education, and transport often becomes apparent after five years.[57] More broadly, low- and lower-middle-income countries with a greater share of nonwage government spending tend to have higher long-term growth.[58] On the revenue side, also, a budget-neutral increase in the efficiency of the tax system could raise long-term growth. Sixty percent of fiscal reform episodes in 112 countries—such as switching from labor taxation to consumption taxation and shifting spending toward health, education, and infrastructure—were followed by growth accelerations of more than 1 percentage point.[59] Over the longer term, fiscal reforms such as the establishment of fiscal rules have also proven growth enhancing in countries in the European Union.[60]

OTHER REFORMS/REGULATIONS. Kilic Celik and coauthors find that governance and business climate reforms are associated with increases in both potential TFP growth and investment growth.[61] Reform spurts, which are defined as one-standard-error changes in one of the four Worldwide Governance Indicators, are followed by a statistically significant 0.1 percent increase in potential TFP growth and around a 3 percentage points increase in investment growth two to four years after the reform spurts.

Conclusion: Reforms for Growth

The stylized scenarios above suggest that a combination of additional investment, better educational and health outcomes, and reforms in labor markets, business climate, and governance could stem or even reverse the expected decline in potential growth over the next decade (figure 2-9). The human and physical capital and labor market reform scenarios above are associated with 0.7 percentage point higher global growth.

In advanced economies, reforms associated with human and physical capital and labor markets could enhance potential growth by 0.7 percentage point. Although the impact of policies aiming at readying human capital for future labor market demands is difficult to quantify for advanced economies in general, labor market reforms (especially pension reforms) may have a significant impact on potential growth going forward. In some countries, meeting physical investment needs may still yield sizable increases in potential growth. For example, while Korea may still improve its potential growth by investing in physical capital, it can also benefit from engaging more in labor market reforms with a similar impact on potential growth (0.3 percentage point for each case).

The human and physical capital and labor market reform scenarios above are associated with 0.8 percentage point higher EMDE potential growth. For EMDEs, this would more than offset the 0.5 percentage point slowdown in potential growth expected under the baseline scenario. Any reform package has to take into account several additional considerations.

- **Synergies.** Implementing multiple reforms simultaneously rather than piecemeal can generate mutually reinforcing synergies. For example, in OECD countries, labor and product market reforms, FDI, and trade regulation potentially yield important synergies.[62] In another example, land, fiscal, and social benefit reforms yield larger growth benefits in China when implemented jointly.[63] In addition, cross-country synergies from coordinated reforms may

arise. The potential for growth spillovers puts a premium on reform efforts in advanced economies that have large repercussions
for their EMDE trading partners.

- **Country-specific reform priorities.** In practice, reform priorities differ across countries, calling for tailored policies.[64] For
  example, school enrollment and completion rates in several economies in the MNA region exceed the EMDE average. However,
  education reforms continue to be needed to address poor scores
  on international tests and pervasive skills mismatches in the labor
  market.[65]

- **Timing.** Reform payoffs may take more time to materialize than
  in the stylized scenarios discussed here. There is some evidence
  that reforms have had the largest growth dividends when they
  were well-timed—at least in the context of advanced economies.
  For example, labor market reforms may lift growth more during
  economic upswings, when job entrants can more easily find jobs
  appropriate to their skills, than downturns.[66]

NOTES

We thank Martin Baily and Zia Qureshi for their comments. We appreciate
feedback from Eduardo Borenzstein, Kevin Clinton, Brahima Coulibaly, Antonio Fatas, Thomas Helbling, Homi Kharas, Ugo Panizza, and Jonathan
Temple. Xinghao Gong provided excellent research assistance.

1. Research suggests that two-thirds of cross-country differences in growth
of the poorest households' income are accounted for by differences in average
income growth (Dollar, Kleineberg, and Kraay 2013; Barro 2000). Mechanisms
by which overall growth helps reduce inequality differ but include its impact
on raising the demand for agricultural output, which helps poor land holders,
as well as rising urbanization and higher wages (Yankow 2006; Gould 2007;
Ravallion and Datt 2002).

2. Kilic Celik and others (forthcoming). Most of the existing literature on
potential growth involves estimating the role of output gaps in driving inflation
or domestic monetary policy in the context of individual countries (in about half
of sixty-seven publications for individual EMDEs surveyed by the authors).

3. Other measures of potential growth incorporate short-term supply shocks
that dissipate over time (Kilic Celik and others, forthcoming).

4. International Monetary Fund (2015); Dabla-Norris and others (2015);
Asian Development Bank (2016); and Organisation for Economic Co-operation
and Development (2014).

5. Other studies have investigated the link between actual growth or productivity growth and structural reforms, focusing on the near-term benefits (Prati, Onorato, and Papageorgiou 2013), productivity effects (Dabla-Norris, Ho, and Kyobe 2015; Adler and others 2017), or a sample consisting of mostly advanced economies (Banerji and others 2017; International Monetary Fund 2015, 2016b).

6. The fifty EMDEs include four economies in East Asia and the Pacific, nine economies in Europe and Central Asia, fifteen economies in Latin America and the Caribbean, seven economies in the Middle East and North Africa, two economies in South Asia, and thirteen economies in sub-Saharan Africa (Kilic Celik and others, forthcoming. Please see table 2-1 for the list of countries in each group and region. Data for more than one-third of them (and about half of the sample's EMDEs in Europe and Central Asia and sub-Saharan Africa) are missing before 1997, and no data for EMDEs are available before 1991. Hence, to ensure broad country coverage, the sample period is restricted to 1998–2027.

7. As in the broader set of advanced economies, potential growth in the world's seven largest economies (the G7)—Canada, France, Germany, Italy, Japan, the United Kingdom, and the United States—was, at 1.5 percent on average in 2013–17, 0.3 percentage point below its longer-term average.

8. Our estimates of potential growth for Korea are in line with those of other studies. Potential growth is estimated at around 3 percent during 2013–17 (Organisation for Economic Co-operation and Development 2018b: 3.2 percent for 2015–17; International Monetary Fund 2018: 2.5–3.0 percent; Bank of Korea 2017: 3.0–3.5 percent in the 2010s).

9. The potential growth slowdown from pre-crisis rates was also evident in the seven largest emerging market (EM7) economies—Brazil, China, India, Indonesia, Mexico, Russia, and Turkey. On average during 2013–17, EM7 potential growth slowed to 5.4 percent. Almost three-quarters of this decline in EM7 potential growth between 2003–07 and 2013–17 reflected slowing potential growth in China.

10. In contrast to production function–based potential growth measures, potential growth estimates based on filtering techniques have slowed sharply in Latin American countries and sub-Saharan Africa, the predominantly host commodity exporters, where actual growth decelerated steeply in the commodity price slide from 2011.

11. There are some exceptions in advanced economies. For example, capital accumulation was still one of the driving forces of potential growth in Korea. In fact, the contribution of capital accumulation was stable in the past half-decade and broadly in line with its longer-term average. The slowdown of Korea's potential growth mainly reflected slowing TFP growth and slower labor supply growth.

12. Romer (1986); Lucas (1988); Grossman and Helpman (1991).

13. European Bank for Reconstruction and Development (2014).

14. Jones (2016).

15. Greenwood, Hercowitz, and Krusell (1997); Sakeflaris and Wilson (2004).

16. See Gordon (2013); Cette, Fernald, and Mojon (2016). Baily and Montalbano (2016) attribute (some of the) surge in U.S. productivity growth in the mid-1990s to improvements in productivity measurement, especially in the services sector.

17. The regression results suggest that for many EMDEs, catch-up productivity growth is a key driver of overall TFP growth (for details, see Kilic Celik and others, forthcoming).

18. Devarajan, Swaroop, and Zhou (1996); Presbitero (2016).

19. Solow (1962).

20. See World Bank (2017a).

21. Kose and others (2017).

22. Corrado and Hulten (2010); Ollivaud, Guillemette, and Turner (2016).

23. Bloom and Canning (2004); International Monetary Fund (2004). The benefits from a rising working-age population have been particularly pronounced in Asia (Bloom and others 2010; Bloom and others 2007; Aiyar and Mody 2011). Demographic change over the period 1960–95 for eighty-six countries has been estimated to account for approximately 20 percent of per capita output growth, and more in Asia and Europe (Kelley and Schmidt 2005). Cruz and Ahmed (2016) estimated that a 1 percent increase in the working-age population share was associated with a more-than-proportional increase in GDP per capita growth in 160 countries between 1960–2010. Other studies of the relationship between demographics and growth include Higgins and Williamson (1997); Eastwood and Lipton (2011); and Kelley and Schmidt (1995, 2007).

24. Maestas, Mullen, and Powell (2016).

25. These factors have been explored by Mincer (1962); Goldin (1994); Hill (1983); Killingsworth and Heckman (1986); and Connelly (1992).

26. Maestas, Mullen, and Powell (2016).

27. Such thought experiments are widely used to assess the impact of demographics on growth or growth projections (Bloom, Canning, and Fink 2010; European Commission 2015).

28. Cohort effects are assumed to stay constant at their latest level throughout the forecast horizon, starting in 2018.

29. Considering the policy-driven rebalancing away from investment in China, investment growth rates are assumed to be constant at their last five-year average (2013–17).

30. One of the exceptions is Korea. Under the baseline scenario, the slowdown of potential output growth (0.6 percentage point per year) to 2.6 percent over the next decade results from the population aging and expected slowdown in capital accumulation. These findings are in line with other studies (International

Monetary Fund 2018: 2.5 percent for 2017–19; Bank of Korea 2017: 2.8–2.9 percent for 2016–20).

31. A 1 percentage point decline in growth in the seven largest emerging markets (EM7) could slow growth in other EMDEs by 0.9 percentage point over the following three years. A similarly sized decline in G7 growth could have a one-half to three times larger impact than an EM7 slowdown (Huidrom, Kose, and Ohnsorge 2017). The EM7 countries are China, Russia, India, Brazil, Turkey, Mexico, and Indonesia.

32. United Nations Conference on Trade and Development (2014).

33. Vashakmadze and others (2017).

34. World Bank (2017a); Calderón and Servén (2010a, 2010b, and 2014).

35. World Bank (2017b).

36. World Bank (2015).

37. Cirera and Maloney (2017).

38. Presbitero (2016).

39. Acemoglu and Restrepo (2017a). The impact of such technological disruptions on output may not be clear-cut. For example, in aging societies, technological change to replace jobs may relieve pressures resulting from a shrinking labor supply (Acemoglu and Restrepo 2017b, 2017c). In addition, automation may expand labor demand by creating new tasks for which labor has a comparative advantage (Acemoglu and Restrepo 2016).

40. World Bank (2017c).

41. Evans and Popova (2016).

42. World Bank (2017c). Other measures such as reducing student–teacher ratios and additional years of schooling have effects that differ widely depending on country circumstances (Evans and Popova 2016; Hanushek and Woessmann 2008).

43. On three policies, see, respectively, Kremer, Brannen, and Glennerster (2013); Glewwe and Muralidharan (2015); and Tsimpo Nkengne, Etang Ndip, and Wodon (2017).

44. World Economic Forum (2016).

45. Organisation for Economic Co-operation and Development (2018a).

46. Prüss-Üstün and others (2008).

47. Bradley and others (2010).

48. Maeda and others (2014).

49. Gertler and Vermeersch (2012).

50. Das and others (2016).

51. Betcherman, Dar, and Olivas (2004); Card, Kluve, and Weber (2010).

52. Betcherman (2014).

53. Brudevold-Newman and others (2017).

54. Alfaro, Evans, and Holland (2015).

55. Bussolo, Koettl, and Sinnott (2015).

56. International Monetary Fund (2016a).
57. Barbiero and Cournède (2013).
58. Gupta and others (2005).
59. International Monetary Fund (2016b).
60. Miyazaki (2014); Castro (2011); Afonso and Jalles (2012).
61. Kilic Celik and others, forthcoming.
62. Organisation for Economic Co-operation and Development (2017).
63. Ran and others (2011).
64. Dabla-Norris (2016).
65. World Bank (2008, 2013).
66. International Monetary Fund (2016b).

REFERENCES

Acemoglu, D., and P. Restrepo. 2016. "The Race between Machine and Man: Implications of Technology for Growth, Factor Shares and Employment," NBER Working Paper 22252 (Cambridge, Mass.: National Bureau of Economic Research).

———. 2017a. "Low-Skill and High-Skill Automation," MIT Department of Economics Working Paper 17-12 (Cambridge, Mass.: Massachusetts Institute of Technology).

———. 2017b. "Robots and Jobs: Evidence from U.S. Labor Markets," NBER Working Paper 23285 (Cambridge, Mass.: National Bureau of Economic Research).

———. 2017c. "Secular Stagnation? The Effect of Aging on Economic Growth in the Age of Automation," NBER Working Paper 23077 (Cambridge, Mass.: National Bureau of Economic Research).

Adler, G., and others. 2017. "Gone with the Headwinds: Global Productivity," Staff Discussion Note 17/04 (Washington, D.C.: International Monetary Fund).

Afonso, A., and J. T. Jalles. 2012. "Fiscal Volatility, Financial Crises and Growth," ISEG Economics Working Paper 06/2012/DE/UECE 2012/06 (Lisbon: Lisbon School of Economics and Management, Department of Economics, University of Lisbon).

Ahmed, S., and Cruz, M. 2016. "On the Impact of Demographic Change on Growth, Savings, and Poverty." World Bank Policy Research Paper 7805 (Washington, D.C.: World Bank).

Aiyar, S., and A. Mody. 2011. "The Demographic Dividend: Evidence from the Indian States," IMF Working Paper 11/38 (Washington, D.C.: International Monetary Fund).

Alfaro, P., D. K. Evans, and P. Holland. 2015. "Extending the School Day in Latin America and the Caribbean," Policy Research Working Paper 7309 (Washington, D.C.: World Bank).

Asian Development Bank. 2016. *Asian Development Outlook 2016: Asia's Potential Growth*. Report. Manila.

Baily, M. N., and N. Montalbano. 2016. "Why Is U.S. Productivity Growth So Slow? Possible Explanations and Policy Responses," Hutchins Center Working Paper 22 (Brookings Institution), September.

Banerji, A., and others. 2017. "Labor and Product Market Reforms in Advanced Economies: Fiscal Costs, Gains, and Support," IMF Staff Discussion Note 17/03 (Washington, D.C.: International Monetary Fund).

Bank of Korea. 2017. "Estimation of Korean Economy's Potential Growth Rate," Bank of Korea Monthly Bulletin (August).

Barbiero, O., and B. Cournède. 2013. "New Econometric Estimates of Long-Term Growth Effects of Different Areas of Public Spending," OECD Economics Department Working Paper 1100 (Paris: Organisation for Economic Co-operation and Development).

Barro, R. 2000. "Inequality and Growth in a Panel of Countries." *Journal of Economic Growth* 5, no. 1, pp. 5–32.

Betcherman, G. 2014. "Labor Market Regulations: What Do We Know about Their Impacts in Developing Countries?" *World Bank Research Observer* 30, no. 1, pp. 124–53.

Betcherman, G., A. Dar, and K. Olivas. 2004. "Impacts of Active Labor Market Programs: New Evidence from Evaluations with Particular Attention to Developing and Transition Countries," Social Protection and Labor Policy and Technical Note 29142 (Washington, D.C.: World Bank).

Bloom, D. E., and D. Canning. 2004. "Global Demographic Change: Dimensions and Economic Significance," NBER Working Paper 10817 (Cambridge, Mass.: National Bureau of Economic Research).

Bloom, D. E., D. Canning, and G. Fink. 2010. "Implications of Population Ageing for Economic Growth." *Oxford Review of Economic Policy* 26, no. 4, pp. 583–612.

Bloom, D. E., D. Canning, and P. Malaney. 2000. "Population Dynamics and Economic Growth in Asia." *Population and Development Review*, 26(Supplement), 257–90.

Bloom, D. E., and others. 2007. "Fertility, Female Labor Force Participation, and the Demographic Dividend," NBER Working Paper 13583 (Cambridge, Mass.: National Bureau of Economic Research).

Bloom, D. E., and others. 2010. "The Contribution of Population Health and Demographic Change to Economic Growth in China and India." *Journal of Comparative Economics* 38, pp. 17–33.

Bloom, D. E., and J. Williamson. 1998. "Demographic Transitions and Economic Miracles in Emerging Asia." *World Bank Economic Review*, 12(3), 419–55.

Bradley, E. H., and others. 2010. "Developing Strategies for Improving Health Care Delivery: Guide to Concepts, Determinants, Measurement, and Intervention Design," Health, Nutrition and Population Discussion Paper 59885 (Washington, D.C.: World Bank).

Brudevold-Newman, A., and others. 2017. "A Firm of One's Own: Experimental Evidence on Credit Constraints and Occupational Choice," IZA Discussion Paper 10583 (Bonn: IZA Institute for Labor Economics).

Bussolo, M., J. Koettl, and E. Sinnott. 2015. *Golden Aging: Prospects for Healthy, Active, and Prosperous Aging in Europe and Central Asia* (Washington, D.C.: World Bank).

Calderón, C., and L. Servén. 2010a. "Infrastructure and Economic Development in Sub-Saharan Africa." *Journal of African Economies* 19, no. S1, pp. i13–87.

———. 2010b. "Infrastructure in Latin America," Policy Research Working Paper 5317 (Washington, D.C.: World Bank).

———. 2014. "Infrastructure, Growth, and Inequality: An Overview," Policy Research Working Paper 7034 (Washington, D.C.: World Bank).

Card, D., J. Kluve, and A. Weber. 2010. "Active Labour Market Policy Evaluations: A Meta-Analysis." *Economic Journal* 120, no. 548, pp. F452–77.

Castro, V. 2011. "The Impact of the European Union Fiscal Rules on Economic Growth." *Journal of Macroeconomics* 33, no. 2, pp. 313–26.

Cette, G., J. Fernald, and B. Mojon. 2016. "The Pre-Great Recession Slowdown in Productivity." *European Economic Review* 88, pp. 3–20.

Cirera, X., and W. F. Maloney. 2017. *The Innovation Paradox* (Washington, D.C.: World Bank).

Connelly, R. 1992. "The Effect of Child Care Costs on Married Women's Labor Force Participation." *Review of Economics and Statistics* 74, no. 1, pp. 83–90.

Corrado, C., and C. Hulten. 2010. "How Do You Measure a 'Technological Revolution'?" *American Economic Review* 100, no. 2, pp. 99–104.

Dabla-Norris, E. 2016. Structural Reforms and Productivity Growth in Emerging Market and Developing Economies. Washington, D.C.: International Monetary Fund.

Dabla-Norris, E., G. Ho, and A. Kyobe. 2015. "Structural Reforms and Productivity Growth in Emerging Market and Developing Economies," IMF Working Paper 16/15 (Washington, D.C.: International Monetary Fund).

Dabla-Norris, E., and others. 2015. "The New Normal: A Sector-Level Perspective on Productivity Trends in Advanced Economies," IMF Staff Discussion Note (Washington, D.C.: International Monetary Fund).

Das, J., and others. 2016. "The Impact of Training Informal Health Care Providers in India: A Randomized Controlled Trial." *Science* 354, no. 6308, p. 7384.

Devarajan, S., V. Swaroop, and H. F. Zou. 1996. "The Composition of Public Expenditure and Economic Growth." *Journal of Monetary Economics* 37, no. 2, pp. 313–44.

Dollar, D., T. Kleineberg, and A. Kraay. 2013. "Growth Is Still Good for the Poor," Policy Research Working Paper 6568 (Washington, D.C.: World Bank).

Eastwood, R., and M. Lipton. 2011. "Demographic Transition in Sub-Saharan Africa: How Big Will the Economic Dividend Be?" *Population Studies* 65, pp. 9–35.

European Bank for Reconstruction and Development. 2014. *Transition Report.* London (https://www.ebrd.com/publications/transition-report-2014-english .pdf).

European Commission. 2015. *The 2015 Aging Report: Economic and Budgetary Projections for the 28 EU Member States (2013–2060).* Report. Brussels.

Evans, D. K., and A. Popova. 2016. "What Really Works to Improve Learning in Developing Countries? An Analysis of Divergent Findings in Systematic Reviews." *World Bank Research Observer* 31, no. 2, pp. 242–70.

Gertler, P., and C. Vermeersch. 2012. "Using Performance Incentives to Improve Health Outcomes," Policy Research Working Paper 6100 (Washington, D.C.: World Bank).

Glewwe, P., and K. Muralidharan. 2015. "Improving School Education Outcomes in Developing Countries: Evidence, Knowledge Gaps, and Policy Implications," Research on Improving Systems of Education (RISE) Working Paper 15/001 (University of Oxford).

Goldin, C. 1994. "The U-Shaped Female Labor Force Function in Economic Development and Economic History," NBER Working Paper 4707 (Cambridge, Mass.: National Bureau of Economic Research).

Gordon, R. 2013. "U.S. Productivity Growth: The Slowdown Has Returned after a Temporary Revival." *International Productivity Monitor* 25, pp. 13–19.

Gould, E. D. 2007. "Cities, Workers, and Wages: A Structural Analysis of the Urban Wage Premium." *Review of Economic Studies* 74, no. 2, pp. 477–506.

Greenwood, J., Z. Hercowitz, and P. Krusell. 1997. "Long-Run Implications of Investment-Specific Technological Change." *American Economic Review* 87, no. 3, pp. 342–62.

Grossman, G. M., and E. Helpman. 1991. "Quality Ladders in the Theory of Growth." *Review of Economic Studies* 58, no. 1, pp. 43–61.

Gupta, S., and others. 2005. "Fiscal Policy, Expenditure Composition, and Growth in Low-Income Countries." *Journal of International Money and Finance* 24, no. 3, pp. 441–63.

Hanushek, E. A., and L. Woessmann. 2008. "The Role of Cognitive Skills in Economic Development." *Journal of Economic Literature* 46, no. 3, pp. 607–68.

Higgins, M., and J. G. Williamson. 1997. "Age Structure Dynamics in Asia and Dependence on Foreign Capital." *Population and Development Review* 23, no. 2, pp. 261–93.

Hill, M. A. 1983. "Female Labor Force Participation in Developing and Developed Countries—Consideration of the Informal Sector." *Review of Economics and Statistics* 65, no. 3, pp. 459–68.

Huidrom, R., M. A. Kose, and F. Ohnsorge. 2017. "Spillovers from Major Emerging Markets," Policy Research Working Paper 8093 (Washington, D.C.: World Bank).

International Monetary Fund. 2004. "How Will Demographic Change Affect the Global Economy?" in *World Economic Outlook September 2004*. Report. Washington, D.C.

———. 2015. "Where Are We Headed? Perspectives on Potential Growth," in *World Economic Outlook April 2015*. Report. Washington, D.C.

———. 2016a. "Fiscal Policies for Innovation and Growth," in *Acting Now, Acting Together, Fiscal Monitor April 2016*. Report. Washington, D.C.

———. 2016b. "Time for a Supply-Side Boost? Macroeconomic Effects of Labor and Product Market Reforms in Advanced Economies," in *World Economic Outlook April 2016*. Report. Washington, D.C.

———. 2018. "A New Strategy for Korea's Fiscal Policy in a Low-Growth Environment," in *Republic of Korea, Selected Issues. February 2018*. IMF Country Report No. 18/41. Washington, D.C.

Jones, Charles. 2016. "The Facts of Economic Growth," in *Handbook of Macroeconomics*, vol. 2A, edited by J. Taylor and H. Uhlig (Amsterdam: Elsevier).

Kelley, A. C., and R. M. Schmidt. 1995. "Aggregate Population and Economic Growth Correlations: The Role of the Components of Demographic Change." *Demography* 32, no. 4, pp. 543–55.

———. 2005. "Evolution of Recent Economic Demographic Modelling: A Synthesis." *Journal of Population Economics* 18: 275–300.

———. 2007. "A Century of Demographic Change and Economic Growth: The Asian Experience in Regional and Temporal Perspective," in *Population Change, Labor Markets and Sustainable Growth: Towards a New Economic Paradigm*, edited by A. Mason and M. Yamaguchi (Amsterdam: Elsevier).

Kilic Celik, S., and others. Forthcoming. "A Cross-Country Database of Potential Growth." Washington, D.C.: World Bank.

Killingsworth, M. R., and J. J. Heckman. 1986. "Female Labor Supply: A Survey." *Handbook of Labor Economics* 1, pp. 103–204.

Kose, M. A., and others. 2017. "Weakness in Investment Growth: Causes, Implications and Policy Responses," Policy Research Working Paper 7990 (Washington, D.C.: World Bank).

Kremer, M., C. Brannen, and R. Glennerster. 2013. "The Challenge of Education and Learning in the Developing World." *Science* 340, no. 6130, pp. 297–300.

Lucas, R. E., Jr. 1988. "On the Mechanics of Economic Development." *Journal of Monetary Economics* 22, no. 1, pp. 3–42.

Maeda, A., and others. 2014. *Universal Health Coverage for Inclusive and Sustainable Development: A Synthesis of 11 Country Case Studies*, Directions in Development 88862 (Washington, D.C.: World Bank).

Maestas, N., K. Mullen, and D. Powell. 2016. "The Effect of Population Aging on Economic Growth, the Labor Force and Productivity," NBER Working Paper 22452 (Cambridge, Mass.: National Bureau of Economic Research).

Mincer, J. 1962. "Labor Force Participation of Married Women: A Study of Labor Supply," in *Aspects of Labor Economics* (Princeton University Press).

Miyazaki, T. 2014. "Fiscal Reform and Fiscal Sustainability: Evidence from Australia and Sweden," Graduate School of Economics Discussion Paper 1407 (Kobe University).

———. 2017. *Going for Growth* (Paris).

———. 2018a. *The Future of Education and Skills: Education 2030* (Paris).

———. 2018b. *OECD Economic Surveys: Korea* (Paris).

Ollivaud, P., Y. Guillemette, and D. Turner. 2016. "The Links between Weak Investment and the Slowdown in OECD Productivity and Potential Output Growth," OECD Economics Department Working Paper 1304 (Paris: Organisation for Economic Co-operation and Development).

Organisation for Economic Co-operation and Development. 2014. "Growth Prospects and Fiscal Requirements over the Long Term," in *OECD Economic Outlook*, vol. 2014/1 (Paris).

Prati, A., M. G. Onorato, and C. Papageorgiou. 2013. "Which Reforms Work and under What Institutional Environment?" *Review of Economics and Statistics* 95, no. 3, pp. 946–68.

Presbitero, A. F. 2016. "Too Much and Too Fast? Public Investment Scaling-Up and Absorptive Capacity." *Journal of Development Economics* 120, pp. 17–31.

Prüss-Üstün, A., and others. 2008. Safer Water, Better Health: Costs, Benefits and Sustainability of Interventions to Protect and Promote Health (Geneva: World Health Organization).

Ran, T., and others. 2011. "Paradox of 'Lewis Turning Point' and Coordinated Reforms of China's Hukou-Land-Fiscal System." *International Economic Review* 3, pp. 120–48.

Ravallion, M., and G. Datt. 2002. "Why Has Economic Growth Been More Pro-Poor in Some States of India than Others?" *Journal of Development Economics* 68, no. 2, pp. 381–400.

Romer, P. M. 1986. "Increasing Returns and Long-Run Growth." *Journal of Political Economy* 94, no. 5, pp. 1002–37.

Sakeflaris, P., and D. J. Wilson. 2004. "Quantifying Embodied Technological Change." *Review of Economic Dynamics* 7, no. 1, pp. 1–26.

Solow, R. M. 1962. "Technical Progress, Capital Formation, and Economic Growth." *American Economic Review* 52, no. 2, pp. 76–86.

Tsimpo Nkengne, C., A. Etang Ndip, and W. T. Wodon. 2017. "Education and Health Services in Uganda: Quality of Inputs, User Satisfaction, and Community Welfare Levels," Policy Research Working Paper 8116 (Washington, D.C.: World Bank).

United Nations. 2017. *World Population Prospects: The 2017 Revision.* Department of Economic and Social Affairs, Population Division Report. New York. [DVD edition]

United Nations Conference on Trade and Development. 2014. "Investment in SGDs: An Action Plan," in *World Investment Report.* Report. New York.

Vashakmadze, E. T., and others. 2017. "Regional Dimensions of Recent Weakness in Investment: Drivers, Investment Needs and Policy Responses," Policy Research Working Paper 7991 (Washington, D.C.: World Bank).

World Bank. 2008. *The Road Not Travelled: Education Reform in the Middle East and Africa* (Washington, D.C.).

———. 2013. *Jobs for Shared Prosperity: Time for Action in the Middle East and North Africa* (Washington, D.C.).

———. 2015. *Global Economic Prospects: Having Fiscal Space and Using It* (Washington, D.C.).

———. 2017a. *Global Economic Prospects: Weak Investment in Uncertain Times* (Washington, D.C.).

———. 2017b. *Global Economic Prospects: A Fragile Recovery* (Washington, D.C.).

———. 2017c. *World Development Report: Learning to Realize Education's Promise* (Washington, D.C.).

World Economic Forum. 2016. *The Future of Jobs Employment, Skills and Workforce Strategy for the Fourth Industrial Revolution.* Report. Geneva, January.

Yankow, J. J. 2006. "Why Do Cities Pay More? An Empirical Examination of Some Competing Theories of the Urban Wage Premium." *Journal of Urban Economics* 60, no. 2, pp. 139–61.

THREE

Stagnation vs. Singularity

The Global Implications of Alternative Productivity Growth Scenarios

WARWICK J. McKIBBIN AND ADAM TRIGGS

In 1978, the first Superman film was released. Starring as Superman, Christopher Reeve fought foes and vanquished villains in an action-packed battle between good and evil. Four decades later, Superman continues to feature in films. But he is often not alone. Superman now stars alongside Batman, Wonder Woman, the Flash, Aquaman, Cyborg, and many other superheroes. For the fans of DC Comics, it is a delightful coming together of childhood favorites. But for economists, it symbolizes a worrying decline in productivity. Where once a single superhero was able to save the world, now two or more are required to complete the same task (although the increase in superheroes needs to be adjusted by any change in crime rates).

As Oscar Wilde once said, life often imitates art. When the first Superman film was released, average annual total factor productivity (TFP) growth among advanced economies was almost ten times what it was in 2016 (figure 3-1; note that all figures are presented in the appendix at the end of this chapter). The emerging markets have fared a little better but have similarly struggled to replicate the productivity growth enjoyed in the recent past. Other measures show the same pattern. Cyclically adjusted TFP and labor-based measures show that productivity growth is not what it used to be.[1]

The world has a productivity problem. The problem is that there is not enough of it. Productivity growth is the fundamental driver of long-run living standards.[2] Weak productivity growth has been linked to poorer fiscal outcomes, weaker export competitiveness, lower wages, and higher income inequality, to name a few issues.[3]

But what is most striking about these data is the time period they cover. The period from 1990 to 2016 saw extraordinary advances in technology. An additional 3.5 billion people gained access to the internet. The processing power of computers increased exponentially. Their cost and size plummeted. Smartphones were invented. Online businesses flourished. Email, GPS, and advanced software became widespread. The sharing economy unlocked the full potential of our idle cars, unused bicycles, and empty rooms and houses. Information and communications technology (ICT) and artificial intelligence (AI) reshaped our industries. The accumulated history of human knowledge is now at our fingertips.

But where is the increase in productivity? Robert Solow famously remarked in the 1980s that "you can see the computer age everywhere but in the productivity statistics."[4] This anomaly, which has become known as the Solow paradox, continues to plague economists to this day.

Economists put forward a variety of explanations for this paradox. Some, like 2018 Nobel laureate William Nordhaus, point to historical data showing long lag times between technological advances and increases in productivity.[5] For these economists, a large surge in productivity is just around the corner (ten years away, wrote Iraj Saniee and his coauthors in 2017).

Other economists, such as Harvard's Martin Feldstein, argue that the paradox is driven by measurement failures. They argue that productivity has increased but our flawed statistical methods fail to detect it. They show how productivity statistics can struggle to measure changes in the quality of goods and services and the value created by new goods and services, particularly those in the digital space.[6] For these economists, the productivity slowdown is either partly or entirely an illusion.

Others argue that although technological advances have increased productivity, these benefits have been crowded out by other factors, including the aftershocks of the global financial crisis and "TFP hysteresis,"[7] weak demand and investment,[8] slowing trade and stalling growth in global value chains,[9] aging populations and demographic factors,[10] reduced investment in education,[11] the effects of automation on demand and inequality,[12] and weakening competition and business dynamism.[13]

Harvard's Marc Melitz suggests that the explanation for the paradox lies at the firm level. Some firms have been highly productive and contributed to strong, positive statistics, but their effects have been dragged down by laggard firms.[14] The Organisation for Economic Co-operation and Development (OECD) found that "frontier firms" have consistently achieved high rates of productivity since 2000, more than six times that of laggard firms, which have dragged down the average.[15] Some economists attribute this to the increased prevalence of "zombie firms"—unproductive firms kept alive by cheap money, low interest rates, and risk-averse investors.[16] There is similar evidence at the industry level. John Fernald of the Federal Reserve Bank of San Francisco shows that ICT productivity gains have been concentrated in specific industries, while other industries have failed to adopt these technologies.[17]

Some economists, notably Northwestern University's Robert Gordon, see no paradox at all. Gordon argues that the technological advances in recent decades are simply no match for the inventions of the previous century. Given the life-altering scale of the innovations between 1870 and 1970—such as electricity and the automobile—we should not be surprised that the relatively meager inventions since then have failed to register in the statistics.[18]

Others go further. Some point to evidence that recent technological advances are not just benign but may be reducing our productivity by distracting employees and reducing our attention span.[19] Others are less pessimistic about the impact of new technologies but still warn that the extent to which firms adopt ICT might be subject to diminishing returns over time.[20]

In short, there are many explanations for why recent advances in technology have not translated into increases in productivity. The upshot is that the future path of productivity is highly uncertain.

This uncertainty poses several challenges. The future path of productivity will have profound implications, not just for individual economies but for the global economy. It is possible, even likely, that individual economies and individual sectors could follow different productivity paths, with significant implications for trade flows, capital flows, the adjustments of real exchange rates, and global imbalances. For policymakers, this uncertainty raises challenging questions about the appropriate course of monetary, fiscal, and structural policies and whether there is a case for cooperation between countries.

These are the issues explored in this chapter. The chapter applies a global economic model to explore the implications of four alternative future productivity scenarios for the global economy, trade flows, capital flows, the adjustments of macroeconomic variables, the effects on individual economies, and what these alternative scenarios mean for policymakers. Each scenario is detailed in the next section, followed by a summary of the general equilibrium framework: the G-Cubed (G20) model of the global economy. The final two sections model the outcomes of each scenario and consider the policy implications that flow from this analysis, as well as possible extensions to the analysis.

Four Possible Paths of Productivity

The literature reviewed in the preceding suggests at least four possible paths for future productivity growth.

The first path is one where the weak productivity growth experienced by the advanced economies in recent years persists into the future. Under this scenario, there is a gradual catch-up in productivity growth by the emerging economies, but they are catching up to a more slowly growing frontier. This is the path predicted by Robert Gordon—who argues that today's technological advances are no match for those of the past[21]—and by those economists who argue that any recent improvements in productivity have been (and will continue to be) crowded out by other long-term structural factors, such as aging populations.

The second path is one where there is a global takeoff toward singularity, with all countries adopting the new technologies simultaneously. This is the path predicted by William Nordhaus and others, who believe the paradox is explained by a time lag between technological advances and increases in productivity.[22]

The third and fourth scenarios consider productivity paths that exhibit more asymmetry.

The third scenario explores the implications of a takeoff in productivity toward singularity that occurs only in economies that have invested in research and development of artificial intelligence. As in the first scenario, the other advanced and emerging economies are playing catch-up, but to the original productivity frontier. This scenario is consistent with analysis that shows sharp differences in the levels of investment between countries in research and development, particularly in artificial intelligence,[23] and studies that show that the rate of technological diffusion can vary widely between countries.[24]

The fourth scenario explores a takeoff in productivity across all countries but only in specific sectors. Under this scenario, the sectors that have invested the most heavily in research and development experience the largest increase, with other sectors playing catch-up. This is consistent with the predictions of John Fernald, who observes sharp differences in the productivity paths between industries, and Marc Melitz and the OECD, who observe significantly different productivity paths between firms.[25]

While there has been much research exploring why recent advances in technology have not translated into increases in productivity, there has been less research on the focus of this chapter: what these alternative paths might mean for the global economy. There are, however, some exceptions.

PwC used a spatial computable general equilibrium model to estimate the impact of AI on the global economy up until 2030. They found that 55 percent of the GDP benefits would be due to productivity increases and that North America and China stand to see the biggest economic gains, primarily due to their larger investment in AI technologies.[26] They found that the services industry benefited more than others.

Avi Goldfarb and Dan Trefler explored some of the factors that shape how AI influences the composition of global trade flows.[27] These include economies of scale and scope in the development of the technologies (for example, knowledge clusters), the extent of competition between firms, the extent and geography of knowledge diffusion and externalities, the role of behind-the-border domestic regulations (for example, regulations around privacy, cross-border data flows, competition, and consumer protection), and the impact of international agreements constraining AI, such as the North American Free Trade Agreement (NAFTA) and the Transpacific Partnership-11 (TPP-11).

Similarly, Laura Márquez-Ramos and Immaculada Martínez-Zarzoso use a gravity model to estimate the relationship between technological innovation and international trade.[28] They find a U-shaped relationship between exports and the creation of technology and between exports and diffusion of old innovations, whereas an inverted U-shaped relationship is found between exports and diffusion of recent innovations and between exports and human skills.

It should also be noted that many studies look in the opposite direction—exploring the role of trade and capital flows in boosting productivity, rather than the role of productivity in shifting flows of trade and capital.[29] The potential for a sharp increase in productivity from singularity makes this a pertinent time to explore this question.

The G-Cubed Model

The G-Cubed (G20) model is a multicountry, multisector, intertemporal general equilibrium model. It is designed to bridge the gaps between three areas of research—econometric general equilibrium modeling, international trade theory, and modern macroeconomics—by incorporating the best features of each.

Several versions of the model have been developed, which have been incrementally improved and built on over many years. The version presented in this chapter is the newest, and largest, version of the G-Cubed model, designed specifically to study the G20 nations (nineteen countries plus the EU) and the implications of its policy agenda. Previous versions of G-Cubed have been used to study a range of policy areas, including macroeconomic cooperation, international trade, monetary policy, fiscal policy, tax reform, and environmental regulation. Studies have shown the effectiveness of G-Cubed in explaining the adjustment process in many historical episodes, including Reaganomics, German reunification, European fiscal consolidation in the 1990s, the formation of NAFTA, and the Asian financial crisis. G-Cubed has also proven successful in helping to explain the "six major puzzles in international macroeconomics" highlighted by Maurice

Table 3-1. *Overview of the G-Cubed (G20) Model*

Countries (20)	Regions (4)
Argentina	Rest of the OECD
Australia	Rest of Asia
Brazil	Other oil-producing countries
Canada	Rest of the world
China	
Rest of eurozone	**Sectors (6)**
France	Energy
Germany	Mining
Indonesia	Agriculture (including fishing and hunting)
India	Durable manufacturing
Italy	Nondurable manufacturing
Japan	Services
Korea	
Mexico	**Economic Agents in Each Country (3)**
Russia	A representative household
Saudi Arabia	A representative firm (in each of the six production sectors)
South Africa	Government
Turkey	
United Kingdom	
United States	

Obstfeld and Kenneth Rogoff in a 2000 paper. It has also proven useful in understanding the 2009 global financial crisis.[30]

The G-Cubed (G20) model represents the world as twenty-four autonomous blocks: one for each G20 economy (including the rest of the eurozone) and four regions that represent the world's non-G20 economies. These regions are: the other economies of the OECD, the other economies of Asia, the other oil-producing economies, and a catch-all "rest of the world" (table 3-1). Each region in G-Cubed is represented by its own multisector econometric general equilibrium model with highly disaggregated, multi-sectoral flows of goods and assets between them.

Each region has six industries, which correspond to the production of six goods: energy, mining, agriculture (including fishing and hunting), durable manufacturing, nondurable manufacturing, and services. Each good in a region is an imperfect substitute for goods from other regions. Thus there are effectively 144 goods.

Each country consists of six representative firms, a representative household, and a government. The model also includes markets for goods and services, factors of production, money, and financial assets (bonds, equities, and foreign exchange). Finally, each country is linked through the flows of goods and assets. Some of the key features of the G-Cubed (G20) model are:

- specification of the demand and supply sides of economies
- integration of real and financial markets of these economies with explicit arbitrage linking real and financial rates of return
- intertemporal accounting of stocks and flows of real resources and financial assets
- imposition of intertemporal budget constraints so that agents and countries cannot borrow or lend forever without undertaking the required resource transfers necessary to service outstanding liabilities
- short-run behavior as a weighted average of neoclassical optimizing behavior based on expected future income streams and Keynesian current income
- a disaggregated real side of the model to allow for production of multiple goods and services within economies
- international trade in goods, services, and financial assets
- full short-run and long-run macroeconomic closure with macro-dynamics at an annual frequency around a long-run Solow-Swan-Ramsey neoclassical growth model
- full rational-expectations equilibrium (consisting of a mix of rational and rule-of-thumb agents) annually from 2015 to 2100.

The rules for monetary and fiscal policies in the model are important for the results. Central banks in each economy follow a Henderson-McKibbin-Taylor rule with weights on output growth relative to trend, inflation relative to target, and in some cases weights on nominal exchange rates relative to target. Some countries such as Saudi Arabia peg exactly to the U.S. dollar so the weights on inflation and output growth are zero and the weight on the exchange rate is very large. Other countries such as China follow a crawling peg with some weight on inflation and the output gap but additional weight on change in the yuan/$US exchange rate. Within the eurozone, a single central bank sets monetary policy with weights on eurozone-wide output growth relative to target and eurozone-wide inflation. The nominal policy interest rate is equal across Germany, France,

Italy, and the rest of the eurozone. Further details can be found in the model documentation in the accompanying working paper.[31] The fiscal rules followed by each country are standardized across countries. Government spending is set at a constant share of baseline GDP with tax rates on households and firms and tariff rates of trade constant at the rates in 2015. There is a lump-sum tax on households that changes in response to changes in the interest payments on government debt.[32] Budget deficits are endogenous given these assumptions, but fiscal sustainability is assured by the fiscal rule that sets lump-sum taxes as equal to the change in servicing costs on government debt. After a shock, in the long run the stock of debt to GDP will stabilize at the long-run primary fiscal deficit divided by the real growth rate of the economy. This implies that a fall in productivity will lead to a permanently higher stock of government debt to GDP, and a rise in productivity will lead to a permanently lower stock of debt to GDP. Alternative fiscal closures can significantly change the results described in this chapter. Future research will explore the interaction of the fiscal closure assumption and changes in productivity growth.

The following simulations elaborate further on some of these key features of the model.[33]

The Global Implications of Four Alternative Productivity Growth Scenarios

We first solve the model from 2016 to 2100 to create a baseline scenario. Our approach to generating a baseline projection is outlined in detail by Warwick McKibbin, David Pearce, and Alison Stegman.[34] This is a complicated procedure in a model such as G-Cubed where some economic agents have rational expectations. Stegman and McKibbin provide a comparison of the long-term projections with other global economic models in an earlier exercise.[35]

The key inputs into the baseline are the initial dynamics leading into 2016 (that is, the evolution of the economy from 2015 to 2016) and subsequent projections from 2016 onward for labor force growth and productivity growth (defined as labor augmenting technical change) by sector and by country. We take labor force growth from the United Nations population projections.[36] The productivity projections are generated following the approach of Robert Barro.[37] Over long periods of time, Barro estimates that the average catch-up rate of individual countries to the worldwide productivity frontier is 2 percent per year. We assume each sector in the United States has labor productivity growth of 1.4 percent per year. We use the Groningen Growth and Development ten-sector database, as outlined by Marcel Timmer and his coauthors to estimate the initial level of productivity in each sector of each region in the model in 2010.[38] Given this initial productivity, we then take the ratio of this productivity to the equivalent sector in the United States, which we assume is the frontier. Given this initial gap in sectoral productivity, we then use the Barro catch-up model to generate long-term projections of the productivity growth rate of each sector within each country. In the case where we expect that economic reforms will allow regions to catch up more quickly to the frontier (for example, in China) or that institutional rigidities will slow them down (for example, in Russia), we vary the catch-up rate over time.

The exogenous sectoral labor productivity growth rate, together with the economy-wide growth in labor supply, is the exogenous driver of sector growth for each country. The growth in the capital stock in each sector in each region is determined endogenously within the model.

Given assumptions about monetary policy rules, fiscal rules, and other institutional rigidities in the model (including labor markets), we solve for a path for the world economy from 2016 to 2100. We then explore each of the scenarios on productivity by rolling the model forward to 2019 and beginning the shocks as surprise events all commencing in 2019.

In the results that follow, all variables are plotted relative to the baseline projection. Some variables, such as GDP, investment, consumption, and real effective exchange rates, are presented as a percentage change relative to the baseline. The trade balance is a percentage of baseline GDP change. Inflation and interest rates are percentage differences from the baseline. Any variable that is zero in the scenario means that the variable is unchanged relative to baseline values. A negative outcome is a variable below the baseline.

Persistently Weak Productivity Growth in the Advanced Economies, with Gradual Catch-up by the Emerging Markets

The first scenario is one in which the weak productivity growth experienced by the advanced economies in recent years persists into the future. While there is a gradual catch-up of productivity growth by the emerging economies (and advanced economies that are not at the frontier), the emerging economies are catching up to a more slowly growing frontier. This is the path predicted by Gordon and by those economists who argue that any recent improvements in productivity have (and will continue to be) crowded out by other long-term structural factors, such as aging populations.[39]

The underlying productivity growth in the frontier economy of the United States is assumed to be 1.4 percent per year in the baseline. Other countries will experience faster productivity growth in each sector depending on how far from the frontier each sector is located relative to the U.S. sector. The shock is illustrated in figure 3-2. This plots the level of labor productivity relative to the baseline in each year. The slope of the curve is the change in the growth rate.

In this section we assume that, commencing in 2019, it is discovered that there is weaker labor augmenting technical change in each sector in each advanced economy than was expected and that this downward revision will continue for the remainder of the century. The assumption that is implemented is a uniform reduction in productivity growth in each sector of 0.5 percent per year from 2019 to 2043. The decline in the growth rate eventually returns to zero, commencing in 2044 with the rate calculated as −0.5 plus 0.98 multiplied by the productivity decline in the previous year. This can be considered a permanent decline in productivity over the period we are considering, even though, for technical reasons, the steady state rate of productivity growth eventually returns to 1.4 percent in all economies.

The results for the surprise fall in productivity are contained in figure 3-3 through figure 3-13 for a selection of advanced economies (the United States, Japan, Germany, and Australia) and a selection of emerging economies (South Korea, China, and India). In figure 3-12 and figure 3-13 we show sectoral results for the United States and for South Korea to give some insight into the changes in sectoral outcomes that lie behind the macroeconomic adjustments. Recall again that all results are expressed as relative to baseline values.

Figure 3-3 shows the results for the economy-wide GDP growth rate for a range of countries. As expected, the uniform fall in sectoral labor productivity growth of 0.5 percent per year eventually leads to a sustained fall in GDP growth of 0.5 percent for each of the advanced economies. The short-term results also reflect the fact that the accumulation of capital in the model is endogenous. The surprise realization that productivity growth will be lower for longer causes forward-looking firms to reassess their investment decisions. Owing to the adjustment costs in capital accumulation, firms do not immediately reduce their capital stocks. They run them down smoothly over time, but the adjustment is front-loaded. Investment falls sharply in the advanced economies (figure 3-4), which causes GDP growth to fall more than the decline in trend growth for four years.

The sectoral disaggregation of the model shows some important macroeconomic differences across countries. The investment good that firms buy to build the capital stock largely comes from the durable goods sector, mining, and energy. When investment falls, the demand for durable goods falls by more than the demand for goods from other sectors. Economies that produce a large share of global investment goods (Germany, Japan, Korea) or rely on durable goods exports for income generation will be most affected by the fall in demand for investment in advanced economies. This will be offset to some extent by increased demand from emerging economies, but it depends on the country investing and the trade shares with the country exporting durable goods. The differential response to investment shown in figure 3-4 shows this clearly for Germany and Japan, who experience a much larger investment decline than either the United States or Australia.

Note that GDP growth rises in the emerging countries. There are two offsetting effects of the productivity slowdown in advanced economies: international trade and financial capital flows.

A decline in growth in the advanced economies means reduced demand for the exports from the emerging economies. However, the weaker growth prospects in the advanced economies also implies a higher relative return to investment in emerging economies. As a result, financial capital flows out of the advanced economies into emerging economies. This drives down the real interest rate globally and increases investment in the emerging countries. The role of advanced economy financial conditions in driving capital into the emerging markets has been well documented in the literature on the push and pull factors associated with capital flows.[40] Thus, while the trade effects are a negative demand shock for the emerging economies, the capital flow effect is a positive stimulus to their GDP.

In some countries the weakening on the U.S. dollar as capital flows out of the United States causes economies pegging to the U.S. dollar or leaning against currency appreciation to loosen monetary policies to soften their own currency appreciation. This is clear in figure 3-3 as China has a large monetary stimulus that temporarily raises GDP growth as it loosens monetary policy in response to an appreciating renminbi.

The results for consumption are shown in figure 3-5. Consumption rises in all emerging economies as capital flows in, real interest rates fall, and incomes rise. In advanced economies, the consumption profile is more complex. In the longer term, consumption falls along with the decline in real GDP. But for the first decade, consumption is above baseline. This shift reflects several interesting dynamics.

The first is that the lower rate of labor productivity growth acts to reduce the marginal product of capital. Real interest rates fall in parallel to the decline in the marginal product of capital (see figure 3-6). Lower real interest rates increase the human capital of households as they discount the lower future streams of income at a lower interest rate. This implies, initially at least, that human capital rises.

The second and more important channel is the realization by firms that they no longer need to invest as much as previously expected. Over time, firms return the funds that would have been used for real investment to shareholders as net transfers (that is, higher dividends and share buybacks). Thus, initially consumers' cash flow rises and backward-looking households (70 percent of all households) consume this windfall and sustain consumption for a decade, even though wealth is ultimately declining.

Figure 3-7 shows the trade adjustment that occurs globally. This reflects the reallocation of global capital as well as changes in the relative prices of traded goods. As capital flows out of the advanced economies, the real effective exchange rate depreciates. The emerging economies receiving the capital inflow experience an appreciation of their real effective exchange rates (figure 3-8). Thus, the trade balances of the United States, Germany, Japan, and Australia improve while the trade balances of the emerging economies deteriorate. The extent to which the trade balance changes also depends on the composition of exports and imports for each country. Countries such as Japan and Germany, although exporters of capital goods whose demand has fallen by more than other types of goods, experience larger investment declines and therefore a larger capital outflow than other countries. Thus their trade balances improve by more and their real exchange rate depreciates by more than those of other advanced economies.

Figure 3-8 shows that exchange rates in the long term move in the opposite direction in the short term. This reflects the consumption side of the model. Consumers in all countries consume goods from all countries. But these goods are imperfect substitutes. Thus, if goods from the United States are less available over time, their relative price will eventually rise. It also reflects the imposition of the intertemporal budget constraint on all countries that the present value of all future trade surpluses must equal the initial value of foreign debt. To the extent that relative incomes do not achieve this outcome, the real exchange rate will adjust to ensure solvency.

Figure 3-9 shows the results for inflation. It is clear from the figure that the shift in productivity growth has led to an inflation bias in the advanced economies. This is because it is assumed that the central banks do not adjust their estimates of productivity growth when the shock occurs. Thus they are continually trying to return the economy to the long-term growth path that existed before the decline in productivity. Since monetary policy cannot achieve this, inflation is permanently higher. These circumstances are assumed intentionally in this scenario to illustrate the importance of the monetary rule (discussed later in the chapter). In the remainder of the scenarios in this chapter we assume that the central banks know about the productivity shocks and revise their estimates of potential growth.

The outcomes for employment and real wages are shown in figure 3-10 and figure 3-11. The assumption in the model is that wages are sticky in all economies. This is because wages are based on wage contracts driven by past inflation, expected inflation, and the aggregate labor market condition. Firms in each sector hire workers to the point where the marginal product of the worker in that sector equals the nominal wage less the output price of that sector. Over time, the aggregate unemployment (or overemployment) will drive the economy-wide nominal wage to return to full employment.

In advanced economies, the persistent decline in productivity implies that the real wage stays above market clearing levels for many decades, leading to persistent unemployment. Eventually full employment will occur, but it is well past the period being considered. There is a persistent decline in real wages in advanced economies as a result of the decline in labor productivity.

The adjustment in emerging economies is very different. Financial capital flowing into these economies leads to higher investment and a larger physical capital stock. This increases the marginal product of workers and leads to higher real wages and more employment. Employment eventually returns to the baseline by assumption, but the rise in real wages persists.

Finally, it is useful to dig down into the sectoral adjustment that under-lies the macroeconomic adjustment. It differs across economies; owing to space limitations, we consider only two economies in detail. The sectoral output results for the United States are shown in figure 3-12. While the decline in productivity is uniform across sectors, the endogenous adjust-ment of output differs across sectors. There are several reasons for this. The clearest, as noted earlier, is the large decline in the demand for durable goods that would normally go into investment. This is followed by the de-mand for energy and mining goods.

Figure 3-13 shows the sectoral results for Korea. Korea does not expe-rience a decline in productivity, although the spillovers to Korea differ by sector. In particular, notice the decline in output of durable goods imme-diately and the gradual decline in the demand for energy goods due to the shocks in the advanced economies.

Overall, this simulation shows that a lower-productivity growth future for the advanced economies means weaker growth, investment, wages, and employment, particularly for those economies that export investment goods. But the financial side of the model is critical in showing how a re-duction in the productivity differential between the emerging economies and the advanced economies is a boom for the emerging markets through capital flows and lower global interest rates. While the advanced economies suffer, the emerging economies benefit. This is a timely reminder of the incentives to undertake productivity-enhancing reforms and to boost in-vestment in infrastructure. An economy that undertakes productivity-enhancing reforms will reap the domestic economic dividends from those reforms and, if their trading and investment partners are not undertaking reforms, they will also reap a global benefit, too, through shifts in capital. This highlights the prisoner's-dilemma incentive for countries to out-reform one another.

There are also some important lessons in these simulation results on trade. Productivity differentials between the advanced and the emerging economies play an important role in global trade and current account im-balances. A fall in productivity in advanced economies helps correct these imbalances. Conversely, a rise in productivity in the emerging economies would also help to correct these imbalances. It follows that, if advanced economies are primarily concerned about global trade imbalances, these re-sults suggest that they would be wise to share their technologies with the emerging markets to help them raise productivity.

Productivity Takeoff in All Countries

In this section we consider the opposite scenario to that above: one in which productivity growth takes off rapidly. This is the path predicted by Nordhaus and others, who believe the productivity paradox is explained by a time lag between technological advances and increases in productivity.[41]

Although we refer to the simulation as "the takeoff toward singularity," we cannot technically model true singularity in the model because this implies productivity rising to infinity. Instead, we implement a form of the experience in which the widespread penetration of a range of digital networks (energy, health and sanitation, transportation, communication and production) leads to a surge in economy-wide productivity growth.[42] We assume that the widespread penetration of the digital technologies that have been emerging since 2000 leads to a sharp increase in productivity growth, beginning in 2019. Figure 3-14 shows the shock that we implement in the model, based on the findings of Saniee and coauthors.

As with historical productivity growth experience, the growth rate surge is ultimately temporary. But it leaves the economy at a much higher level of productivity. True singularity, such as that modeled by Nordhaus,[43] would have ever-rising productivity growth. However, for the purpose of the modeling exercise in this chapter, the surge in productivity from 2019 to mid-century would be similar to singularity over the initial decades on which we focus.

The results for this scenario are shown in figures 3-15 to 3-25.

There are three main differences between the productivity surge in this section and the decline in productivity in the previous section. The first is the sign of the change: positive versus negative. The second is the coverage of the shock. In this section the shock is assumed to be global, whereas in the previous section the decline in productivity only occurred in a group of advanced economies. The third is the nature of the future expected adjustment. In this section a large part of the productivity boom is expected to be in the future—the period between 2040 and 2060.

Figure 3-15 shows the change in the real GDP growth rate of a selection of economies. We have included Italy in place of Indonesia in the figures in this section and the following sections because it illustrates the importance of the eurozone common currency. The longer-run growth in figure 3-15 clearly reflects the surge in productivity. But when the shock is global rather than asymmetric, endogenous capital accumulation needs to ramp up as labor productivity rises. Since all countries are having the same adjustment, any resources that will be used to build the capital stock will have to come from increased output due to the shock, from current consumption or from changes in government savings, because the global economy is a closed system. In the previous scenario, where the coverage of the shock was not global, it was possible for savings to flow from countries outside the group of countries experiencing the shock to the booming economies.

In the first year, growth declines in most economies as consumers experience a fall in human wealth since interest rates rise before future income rises. The resulting reduction in consumption enables the investment buildup to begin immediately. The anticipation of higher future growth causes investment to rise in the short term. Countries that supply investment goods such as durable manufacturing, energy, and mining experience a much more rapid investment boom. The expected boom leads to a global reallocation of capital. Countries attracting capital such as Australia, the United States, and Germany experience some deterioration in the trade balance.

Real interest rates rise (see figure 3-19) over time, reflecting the increase in the marginal product of capital driven by higher labor productivity. By 2040, global real interest rates are between 4 percent and 7 percent higher. Higher interest rates dampen the investment response and increase savings in order to maintain the saving–investment balance. Interest rates eventually return close to baseline, driven back to the rate of time preference. This occurs well outside the period of focus, once the capital stock reaches a higher level through reduced consumption, which allows the substantial expansion. The higher productivity growth rate lasts until the end of the century.

Employment and real wages are driven higher (figures 3-22 and 3-23). The rise in labor productivity increases the marginal product of labor, which drives wages higher. Substantial sectoral changes cause job turnover. But the aggregate employment effects of labor augmenting technical change are significant. Over time, employment will return to baseline as real wages eventually eliminate the excess demand for labor in the booming global economy.

The sectoral output results for the United States are shown in figure 3-24 and for Korea in figure 3-25. The broad pattern is similar across countries. The expected future productivity surge leads to an investment response in all countries. The demand for goods that feed into creating capital goods rises sharply. The sectors that benefit most are durable goods, energy, and mining. No sectoral outputs fall since the inputs that are needed to expand global economic output are labor productivity, longer working hours for workers, and a rising capital stock.

In sum, this section shows that a global surge in labor productivity comes with substantial benefits in the form of growth, employment, and investment. But there are factors that can prevent economies from reaping the full benefits of the productivity boom. The first is that interest rates increase significantly because all countries call on the same pool of global savings. As a result, consumption is reduced as savings increase to finance the investment. If consumption is used as a measure of welfare, then the welfare benefits of this boom are reduced. For policy, this highlights the critical importance of having flexible financial markets, being open to global capital flows, and having a deep financial system, all of which improve an economy's access to much needed savings during the boom period.

The second factor that can prevent economies from reaping the full benefits of the productivity boom relates to labor markets. The results for this scenario show that the productivity boom increases both wages and employment. But the extent to which this occurs depends on the stickiness of wages (where the model assumes some nominal wage rigidity), the extent to which labor is mobile (the model assumes perfect labor mobility within, but not across, countries and regions), and the extent to which these technological advances are labor saving. If labor market rigidities are strengthened, the extent to which the benefits of the productivity boom are shared with labor is therefore reduced, highlighting the critical importance of flexible labor markets.

The third factor that can prevent economies from reaping the full benefits of the productivity boom relates to product markets. The productivity boom shifts relative prices between sectors and results in substantial reallocation of resources within and across economies. If there is inadequate competition between firms, or if there are government regulations that protect particular industries from competition, then this reallocation of resources will not occur as easily and the full potential of the boom may not be realized.

The critical policy insight in this simulation, therefore, is around the importance of economic flexibility. There is a lot of fear in the literature that technological advances will cause more pain than good. The two main dimensions that are important are (1) the issue of substitution of factors of production and (2) the greater wealth generated by greater labor productivity. This simulation shows that the negative outcomes that many people fear need not be realized, provided policymakers invest in flexible capital, labor, and product markets and remain open to capital and trade flows.

Takeoff toward Singularity in Some Technologically Advanced Economies While Other Economies Are Slow to Adapt

Given some of the challenges posed by a productivity surge that is global in nature, in this section we consider a more asymmetric scenario. We assume that the productivity surge implemented in the previous section is restricted to a small group of countries. This scenario is consistent with analysis that shows sharp differences in the levels of investment between countries in research and development, particularly in artificial intelligence,[44] and studies that show that the rate of technological diffusion can vary widely between countries.[45] Of key interest is not only what happens to the countries that have invested heavily but also what happens to the countries that have not.

The countries that experience the productivity surge are assumed to be the United States, Japan, Germany, France, the United Kingdom, China, and Korea. The results are shown from figures 3-26 to 3-36.

The real GDP growth rate of the booming economies (figure 3-26) follows a similar path as in the case of a global boom. Other economies experience declining GDP growth and capital moves from these economies to more innovative economies. A third group of countries, including Australia, produce goods such as mining and energy that are in rising demand in the booming economies, and they receive higher income as an indirect benefit of the boom.

Figure 3-27 shows the surge of investment in the booming economies. Japan and Germany in particular benefit from their expertise in producing capital goods that are in demand for investment purposes. Italy experiences a particularly large fall in investment. While Germany and France are booming, the strength of the euro causes a large contraction in Italy. Eurozone monetary policy targets Europe-wide growth as well as average inflation. Thus, Italy experiences a tightening of monetary policy and a strengthening of the euro. This is much like the experience under the

European Monetary System (EMS) that occurred during German reunification in the early 1990s. The internal contradictions of a fixed exchange rate within a monetary union with an asymmetric shock drove Italy out of the EMS at that time. The pressures in this scenario are also clear.

The asymmetric boom has an impact on the levels of global investment as well as the distribution of global investment. The extent of capital outflow from economies not directly experiencing the productivity boom is shown in the movement of trade balances in figure 3-29. Countries not experiencing the productivity boom, such as India and Australia, experience an outflow of capital. Global real interest rates rise by less than the global boom, but all countries, both booming and nonbooming economies, experience higher interest rates because strong global investment needs to be funded by higher global savings.

The employment outcomes differ across economies. While booming economies experience rising employment, the other economies experience only a small fall in employment, except Italy, which has a deep recession as the constraints of the euro fall on the Italian economy.

Real wages rise in the booming economies but fall in the other economies, reflecting the global reallocation of global capital, which reduces the return to labor in economies that lose capital. The nonbooming economies have different experiences based on their economic structure and the composition of exports. Real wages fall by less in Australia than in other economies because of the global demand for energy and mining goods. The results for sectoral output for Australia are shown in figure 3-36.

Overall, economies that have invested less in research and development are typically warned that they will be left behind by those that have invested more. The results in this section suggest a more complex story. Countries whose exports feed into the increase in investment and demand in the booming economies tend to benefit, even though their own productivity has not increased. The results depend on the characteristics of individual economies. Some, like Australia, benefit significantly while others are left with lower real wages as capital leaves their economies.

This section also highlights the importance of exchange rate and monetary policy frameworks. It provides a particular warning for the eurozone. A productivity surge in Germany creates significant strain on other countries in the eurozone that are not experiencing the shock. This underscores the importance of building more flexibility into the eurozone's macroeconomic frameworks and promoting increased labor mobility within the region.

Asymmetry in Sectors: Where the Service Sector Takes Off toward Singularity

The final scenario is a global productivity surge that is confined to the service sector—a sector that stands out globally as having invested significantly in technologies such as ICT and AI. This scenario illustrates the impact of differential sectoral productivity growth. It shows what productivity advances in one sector might mean for the lagging sectors of an economy. This scenario is consistent with the predictions of John Fernald, who observes sharp differences in the productivity paths between industries, and Marc Melitz and the OECD, who observe significantly different productivity paths between firms.[46]

This is a pertinent issue to explore. Warnings often appear in the popular media that industries that are failing to invest in emerging technologies will fall behind the soon-to-be frontier industries. The results in this section do not contradict these warnings. But they do show that such warnings are incomplete. Although sectors experiencing a productivity surge benefit more than their peers, other sectors that feed inputs into the surging sectors (and the countries in which those sectors are dominant) also experience important benefits.

The results are shown in figures 3-37 to 3-45.

Although the results for individual economies differ, the overall impact of higher productivity in the service sector is a reallocation of resources between sectors, both domestically and globally. Because of higher productivity growth, service sectors now have a higher return to capital than previously. This leads to an increase in investment and an increase in production in the service sector (figure 3-38).

The increased production in the service sector also benefits other sectors through increased demand and shifts in relative prices. The effect is strongest for those sectors that feed inputs directly into the production processes of the service sector. This is particularly the case for durable manufacturing, which sees an increase in investment and production (figure 3-45). Higher productivity growth also means that the service sector requires less labor, freeing up resources that move into other sectors. The sectors that are less integrated into the service sector also benefit from the higher productivity in services but to a smaller extent than is the case for durable manufacturing. The mining and resource sectors, for example, feed into the production of durable goods, which in turn feed into the surging service sector.

The aggregate effect on the service sector is substantial. Investment increases significantly. Given that the productivity surge is global, countries not only experience the benefits from their own increased domestic production but also enjoy the positive spillovers from increased production in other economies through greater demand for their exports. These benefits, however, are partly offset by shifts in interest rates. With the service sector in all countries experiencing the productivity surge at the same time, there is a substantial call on the global pool of savings, pushing up global interest rates; higher interest rates then constrain investment.

These country-by-country results are largely driven by the relative importance of services in these economies, rather than by any other consideration related to the type of firm heterogeneity you get within sectors and countries. The economies that tend to have the largest service sectors, such as Japan, experience the largest long-run increases in GDP, employment, and investment. Capital inflows to those economies, however, mean that they also experience the largest partially offsetting appreciation in their real effective exchange rates and the largest declines in their trade balance.

Overall, the findings of this scenario at the sectoral level are similar to the findings of the previous scenario at the country level. Even when advances in productivity are asymmetric, either by sector or by country, sectoral and cross-country linkages mean that such advances are not a zero-sum game. Spillovers across countries and sectors mean the benefits of productivity are shared more widely.

Policy Implications and Conclusions

Productivity growth has flatlined in most economies despite rapid advances in technology. Economists suggest competing explanations for this paradox. Some argue that the current stagnation will persist because recent technological advances are no match for those of the past or that deep structural challenges will offset any productivity increases. Others argue that the historical time lag between technological advances and increased productivity means that a productivity surge is just around the corner. This chapter explores the implications of alternative productivity growth scenarios for the global economy, particularly for growth, labor markets, and the flows of trade and capital, as well as the implications for policymakers.

If economists such as Robert Gordon are correct,[47] productivity growth in the advanced economies will remain lackluster for the foreseeable future. The consequences, should this scenario play out, are significant. A slow-down in productivity growth in advanced economies causes real interest rates to fall globally. For advanced economies, it results in a sharp drop in investment. Unemployment increases in the short term and is reduced only once real wages fall. While consumption initially increases in the short term, it is below the baseline in the longer term.

Even if Gordon is correct, there is still substantial productivity growth to be achieved in emerging economies that are behind the current techno-logical frontier. It is common to interpret Gordon's argument as an expla-nation for why global productivity will be weak, but it is a U.S.- and European-centric view that only applies to the economies at the frontier of innovation. Investment rises in the economies not experiencing the decline in productivity. The global reallocation of capital away from slowing econ-omies leads to trade deficits in economies that are receiving capital and to trade surpluses in economies that are losing capital. A reduction in the pro-ductivity differential between the emerging economies and the advanced economies is a boon for the emerging markets through capital flows and lower global interest rates. While the advanced economies suffer, the emerg-ing economies benefit. This is a timely reminder of the incentives to under-take productivity-enhancing reforms. An economy that undertakes productivity-enhancing reforms will reap the domestic economic dividends from those reforms and, if their trading and investment partners are not undertaking reforms, they will also reap a global benefit through shifts in capital. This highlights the prisoner's-dilemma incentive for countries to outreform one another. The chapter also highlights important considerations for central banks. It shows that if central banks do not reevaluate their es-timate of potential growth, their monetary rules can introduce an inflation-ary bias into the economy over time.

Not everyone predicts a bleak future for productivity. If researchers such as Nordhaus and Saniee and colleagues are correct, the future path of pro-ductivity could be much rosier.[48] In the case of the global productivity boom, the results are similar to those for the productivity decline, but with the opposite sign. A big difference in the simulation is the rapid acceleration in the productivity uplift, which front-loads the investment boom. In contrast to popular discussions of the impact of a new industrial revolution that suggest unemployment would rise, we find that the prosperity that is generated by higher labor productivity raises global production and incomes and is shared through intersectoral linkages in the economy as well as through international trade and investment channels.

But this chapter also shows that a large increase in productivity has its costs. The productivity boom leads to sectoral changes, which cause substantial transitions and disruptions in the short term. When all economies boom at the same time, the call on the global pool of savings and labor tends to highlight supply-side constraints. Interest rates rise sharply, acting to offset some of the benefits of the boom. And while employment is boosted, labor markets face significant disruption. The chapter therefore highlights some of the critical factors that can prevent economies from reaping the full benefits of the productivity boom. Having flexible financial markets, being open to global capital flows, and having a deep financial system all improve an economy's access to much needed savings during the boom period. If labor market rigidities are significant, the extent to which the benefits of the productivity boom are shared with labor is therefore reduced, highlighting the critical importance of flexible labor markets. If there is inadequate competition between firms, or if there are government regulations that protect particular industries from competition, then the necessary reallocation of resources within and across economies will not occur as easily and the full potential of the boom will not be realized. The critical policy insight, therefore, is around the importance of economic flexibility. There is a lot of fear in the literature that technological advances will cause more pain than good. This simulation shows that this need not be the case as long as policymakers invest in flexible capital, labor, and product markets and remain open to capital and trade flows.

A globally symmetric boom in productivity, however, is not guaranteed. Some analyses suggest that the levels of investment and the rate of technological diffusion differ greatly between countries.[49] Economies that have invested less in research and development are typically warned that they will be left behind by those that have invested more. The results presented here suggest a more complex story. Countries whose exports feed into the increase in investment and demand in the booming economies tend to benefit, even though their own productivity has not increased. The results depend on the characteristics of individual economies. Some, like Australia, benefit significantly while others bear the brunt of lower real wages as capital leaves their economies. The introduction of asymmetry between countries also finds that the assumption about monetary policy, and particularly on the nature of the exchange rate regime in different countries, matters greatly. For example, in the case where Germany and France experience a productivity boom but Italy does not, the constraints of the euro impose a deep recession on Italy. This underscores the importance of building more flexibility into the eurozone's macroeconomic frameworks and promoting greater labor mobility within the region. When China has a crawling peg against the U.S. dollar, a slowdown in U.S. productivity growth causes a depreciation of the U.S. dollar and induces a relaxation of monetary policy in China, which gives an additional short-term stimulus to the Chinese economy and adds to the flow of capital into the emerging economies seeking higher rates of return.

Whether a productivity takeoff occurs in a particular sector or is economy wide changes the magnitude and the relative economic outcomes; but all sectors eventually gain, whether the higher productivity is localized or broad-based. This outcome is the result of having endogenously determined capital investment. If there is a fixed amount of capital in an economy, the expansion of one sector must imply the contraction of another sector. If the stock of capital can rise either through domestic investment or through the inflow of foreign capital, then it is not necessary for one sector to shrink so another can grow. The intersectoral linkages have important macroeconomic implications. Although this is a positive for sectors within an economy, at the global level some countries can shrink when there is strong productivity growth in some countries and the nonproductive countries' trade is competing with the booming countries rather than being inputs into the production sectors in the booming economies.

The scenarios in this chapter are intended to illustrate some of the main issues that arise from a global general equilibrium perspective on the debate about productivity slowdowns and new industrial revolutions. They explore a small number of the many issues related to this debate. One issue is the importance of the fiscal rule in a world of changing productivity. An

issue that has not been explored but could be a fruitful area of future research with the model used here is the role of public sector infrastructure
investment either to support productivity surges or to dampen productivity slowdowns.[50] The chapter highlights the critical importance of structural reforms that build flexibility into economies, particularly reforms in
labor, capital, and product markets. Such reforms will be key to avoiding
the pitfalls of the Gordon scenario by boosting productivity. Similarly, in
the Nordhaus scenario, increased flexibility will be key to reaping the greatest benefits from the productivity boom. As the Chinese proverb tells us,
"The best time to plant a tree is twenty years ago. The second-best time is
now." The same is true for structural reform.

Appendix: Figures

Introduction

FIGURE 3-1. TFP Growth in Advanced and Emerging Economies[a]

Percent, 5 year average growth rate

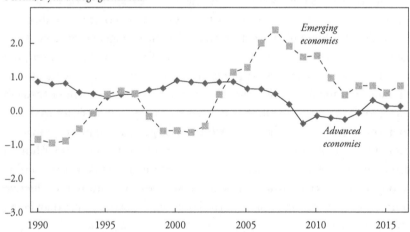

Source: Penn World Table 9.0.

a. Group averages are weighted using purchasing power parity GDP.

Simulation 1: Slowdown in Productivity Growth in Advanced Economies

FIGURE 3-2. **Productivity Growth Slowdown Shock in Advanced Economies**

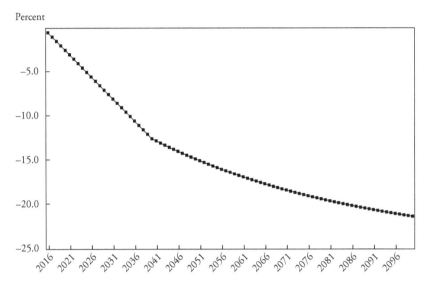

Source: Authors' calculations.

FIGURE 3-3. **Slowdown in Productivity Growth in Advanced Economies: Real GDP Growth**

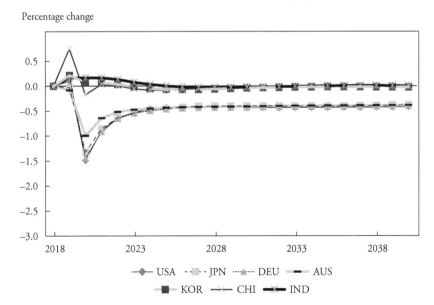

Source: Authors' calculations.

Note: "DEU" is Germany. "IND" is India. "IND" is Indonesia. See Table 3.1 for full list of countries.

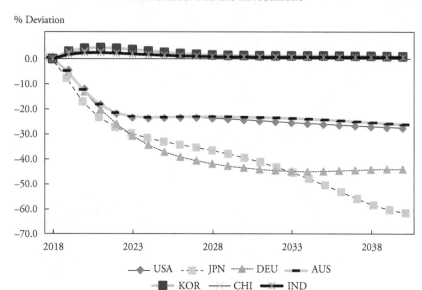

FIGURE 3-4. **Slowdown in Productivity Growth in Advanced Economies: Private Investment**

% Deviation

Source: Authors' calculations.

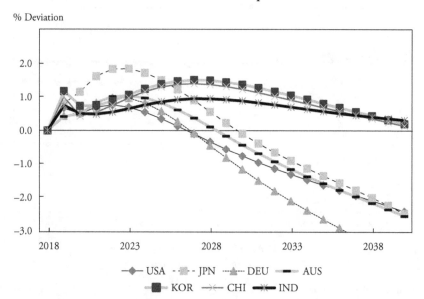

FIGURE 3-5. **Slowdown in Productivity Growth in Advanced Economies: Consumption**

% Deviation

Source: Authors' calculations.

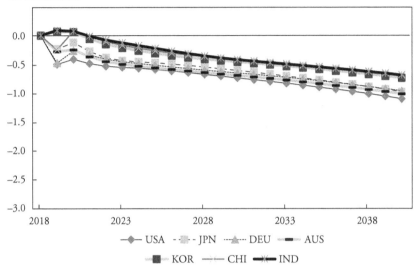

FIGURE 3-6. Slowdown in Productivity Growth in Advanced Economies: Real Interest Rates

% Point deviation

Source: Authors' calculations.

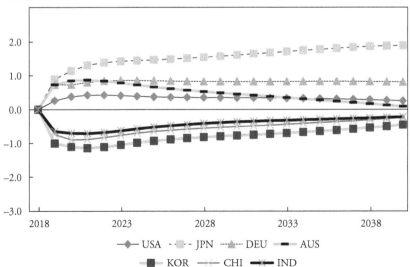

FIGURE 3-7. Slowdown in Productivity Growth in Advanced Economies: Trade Balance

% GDP deviation

Source: Authors' calculations.

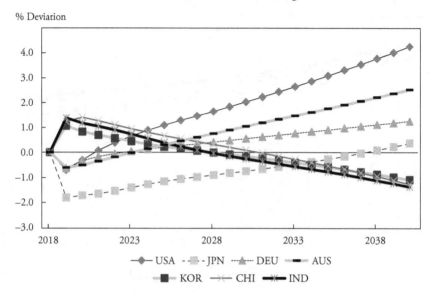

FIGURE 3-8. Slowdown in Productivity Growth in Advanced Economies: Real Effective Exchange Rates

% Deviation

Source: Authors' calculations.

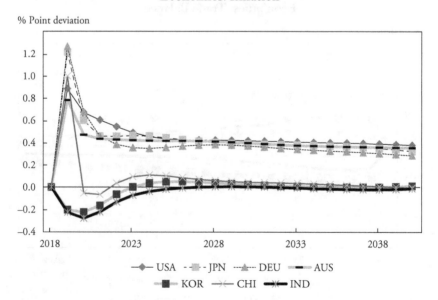

FIGURE 3-9. Slowdown in Productivity Growth in Advanced Economies: Inflation

% Point deviation

Source: Authors' calculations.

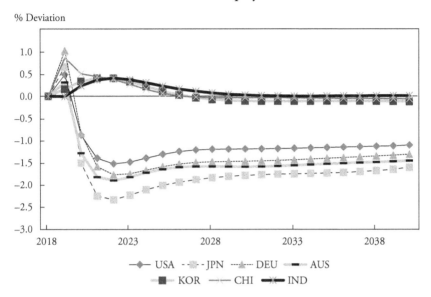

FIGURE 3-10. Slowdown in Productivity Growth in Advanced Economies: Employment

% Deviation

Source: Authors' calculations.

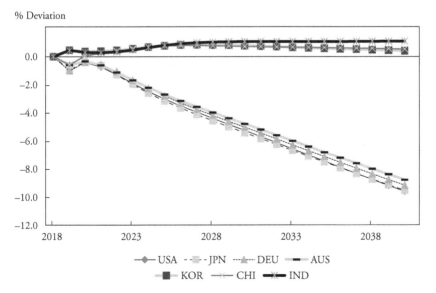

FIGURE 3-11. Slowdown in Productivity Growth in Advanced Economies: Real Wages

% Deviation

Source: Authors' calculations.

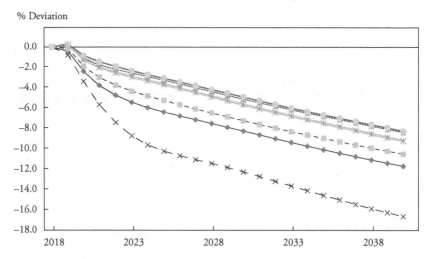

FIGURE 3-12. Slowdown in Productivity Growth in Advanced Economies: U.S. Sectoral Output

Source: Authors' calculations.

FIGURE 3-13. Slowdown in Productivity Growth in Advanced Economies: Korea Sectoral Output

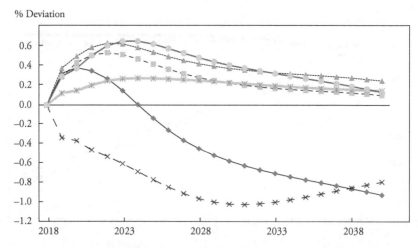

Source: Authors' calculations.

FIGURE 3-14. The "S-Curve": Change in the Growth Rate of Labor Productivity Relative to the Baseline

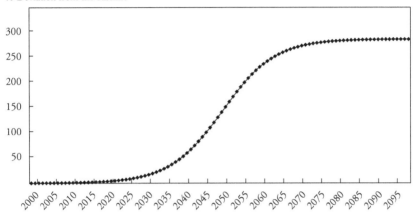

% Deviation from the baseline

Source: Authors' calculations.

FIGURE 3-15. Takeoff in Global Productivity Growth: Real GDP Growth Rate

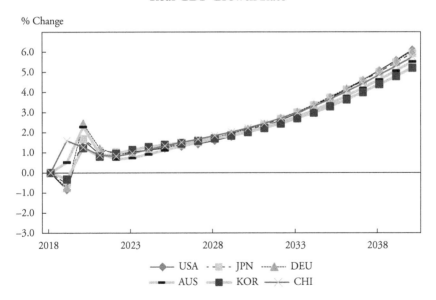

% Change

Source: Authors' calculations.

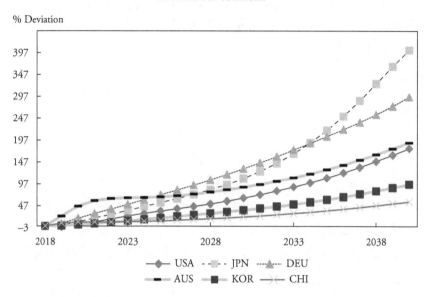

FIGURE 3-16. Takeoff in Global Productivity Growth: Private Investment

% Deviation

Source: Authors' calculations.

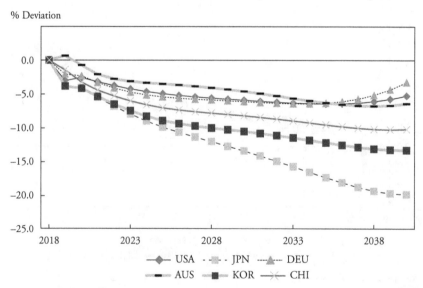

FIGURE 3-17. Takeoff in Global Productivity Growth: Consumption

% Deviation

Source: Authors' calculations.

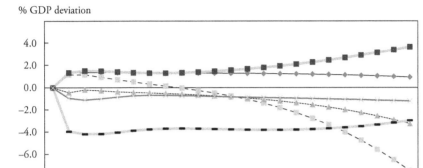

FIGURE 3-18. Takeoff in Global Productivity Growth: Trade Balance

Source: Authors' calculations.

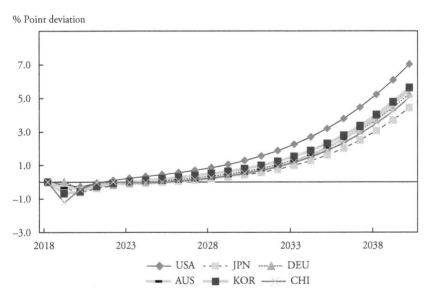

FIGURE 3-19. Takeoff in Global Productivity Growth:
Real Interest Rates

Source: Authors' calculations.

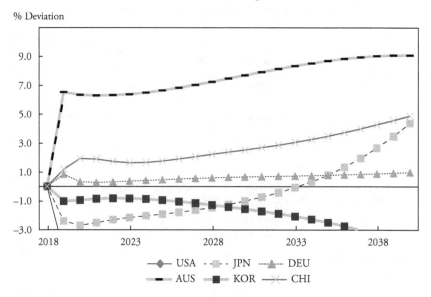

**FIGURE 3-20. Takeoff in Global Productivity Growth:
Real Effective Exchange Rates**

% Deviation

Source: Authors' calculations.

FIGURE 3-21. Takeoff in Global Productivity Growth: Inflation

% Point deviation

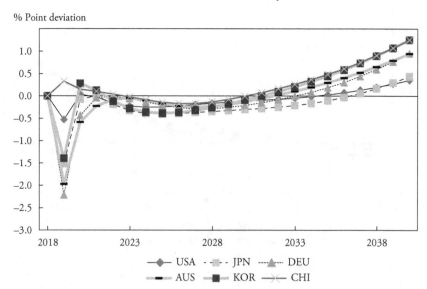

Source: Authors' calculations.

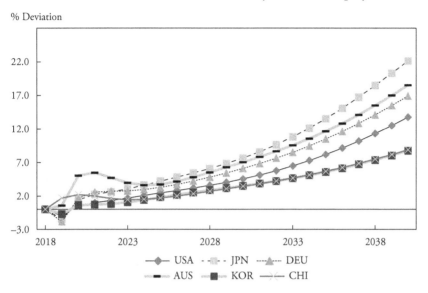

FIGURE 3-22. Takeoff in Global Productivity Growth: Employment

% Deviation

Source: Authors' calculations.

FIGURE 3-23. Takeoff in Global Productivity Growth: Real Wages

% Deviation

Source: Authors' calculations.

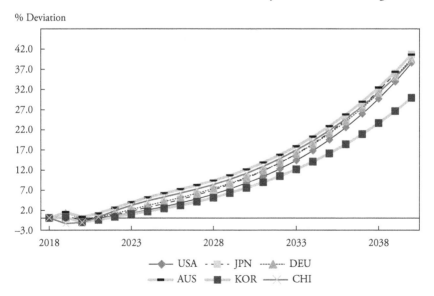

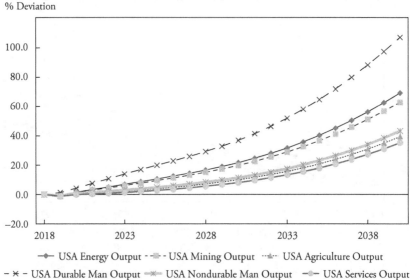

FIGURE 3-24. Takeoff in Global Productivity Growth: U.S. Sectoral Output

Source: Authors' calculations.

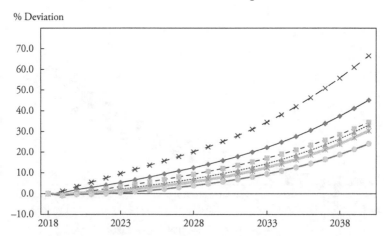

FIGURE 3-25. Takeoff in Global Productivity Growth: Korea Sectoral Output

Source: Authors' calculations.

Simulation 3: Takeoff in Productivity in Select Countries

FIGURE 3-26. Takeoff in Productivity in Select Countries: Real GDP Growth Rate

Percentage change

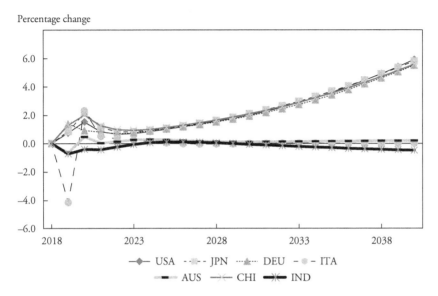

Source: Authors' calculations.

FIGURE 3-27. Takeoff in Productivity in Select Countries: Private Investment

% Deviation

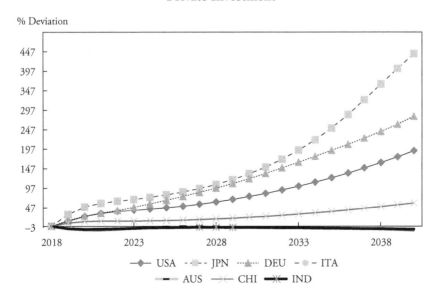

Source: Authors' calculations.

FIGURE 3-28. Takeoff in Productivity in Select Countries: Consumption

% Deviation

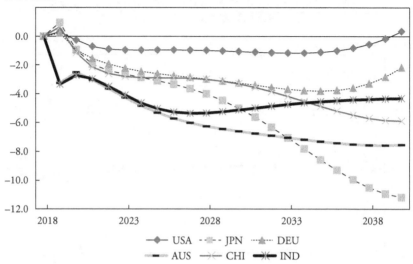

Source: Authors' calculations.

FIGURE 3-29. Takeoff in Productivity in Select Countries: Trade Balance

% GDP deviation

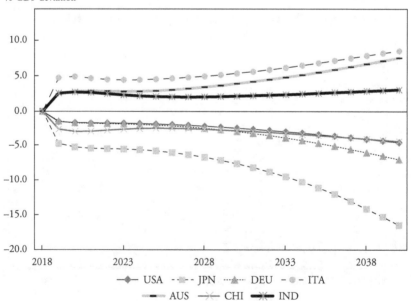

Source: Authors' calculations.

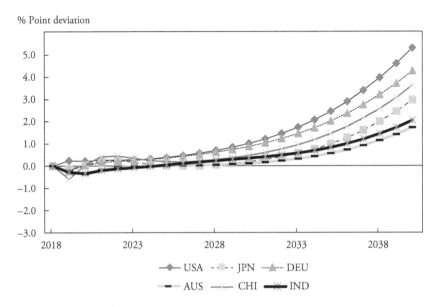

FIGURE 3-30. **Takeoff in Productivity in Select Countries: Real Interest Rates**

% Point deviation

Source: Authors' calculations.

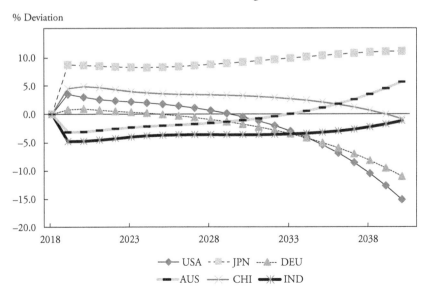

FIGURE 3-31. **Takeoff in Productivity in Select Countries: Real Effective Exchange Rates**

% Deviation

Source: Authors' calculations.

FIGURE 3-32. Takeoff in Productivity in Select Countries: Inflation

% Point deviation

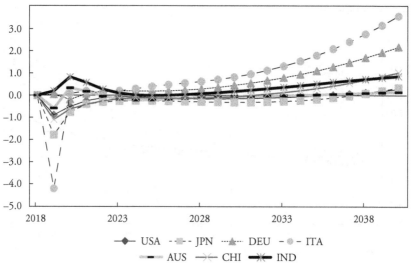

Source: Authors' calculations.

FIGURE 3-33. Takeoff in Productivity in Select Countries: Employment

% Deviation

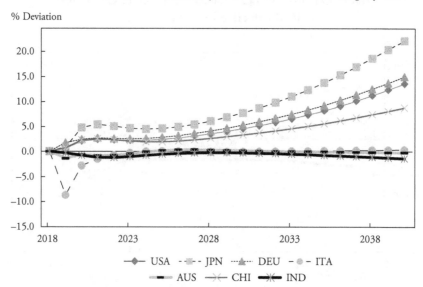

Source: Authors' calculations.

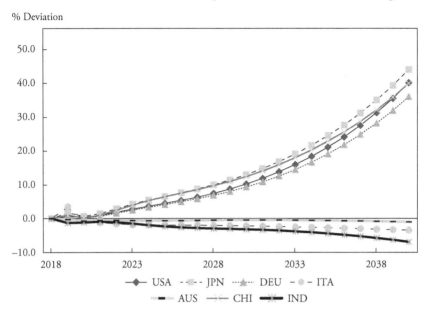

FIGURE 3-34. Takeoff in Productivity in Select Countries: Real Wages

% Deviation

Source: Authors' calculations.

FIGURE 3-35. Takeoff in Productivity in Select Countries: U.S. Sectoral Output

% Deviation

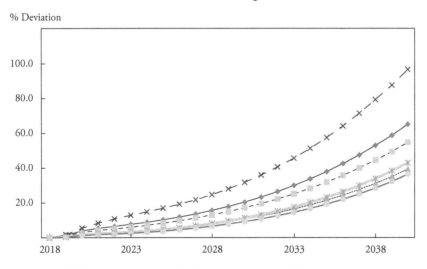

Source: Authors' calculations.

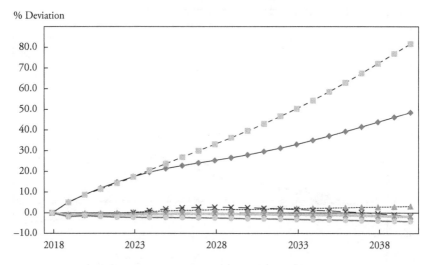

FIGURE 3-36. **Takeoff in Productivity in Select Countries: Australia Sectoral Output**

───◆── AUS Energy Output - -■- - AUS Mining Output ····▲···· AUS Agriculture Output
- ✕ –AUS Durable Man Output ──✕── AUS Non-Durable Man Output ──■── AUS Services Output

Source: Authors' calculations.

Simulation 4: Global Takeoff in Service Sector Productivity Growth

FIGURE 3-37. **Global Takeoff in Service Sector Productivity Growth: Real GDP Growth Rate**

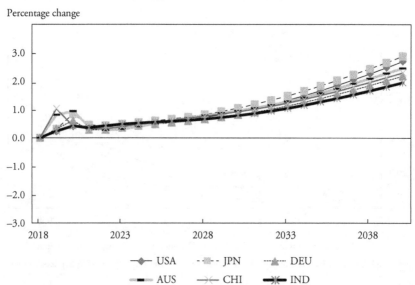

──◆── USA   - -■- - JPN   ····▲···· DEU
──■── AUS   ──✕── CHI   ──✕── IND

Source: Authors' calculations.

FIGURE 3-38. Global Takeoff in Service Sector Productivity Growth: Private Investment

% Deviation

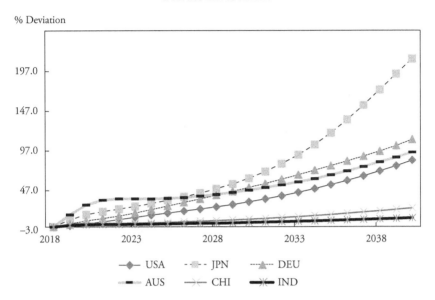

Source: Authors' calculations.

FIGURE 3-39. Global Takeoff in Service Sector Productivity Growth: Trade Balance

% GDP deviation

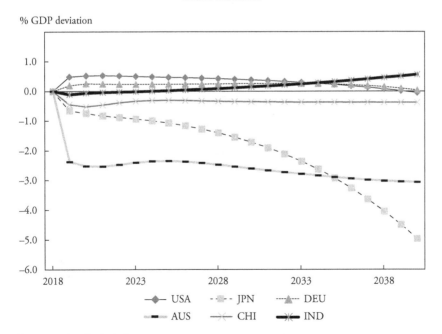

Source: Authors' calculations.

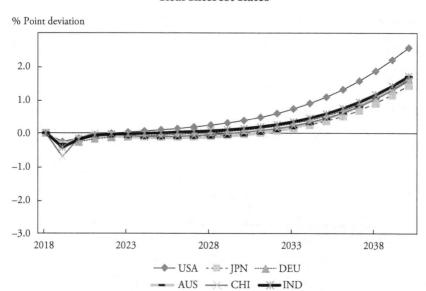

FIGURE 3-40. **Global Takeoff in Service Sector Productivity Growth: Real Interest Rates**

% Point deviation

Source: Authors' calculations.

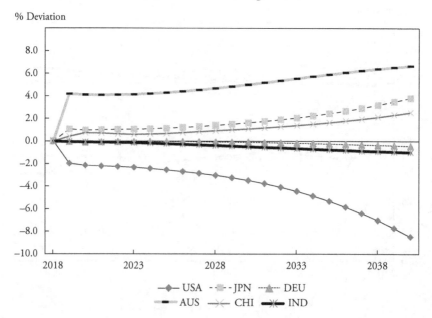

FIGURE 3-41. **Global Takeoff in Service Sector Productivity Growth: Real Effective Exchange Rates**

% Deviation

Source: Authors' calculations.

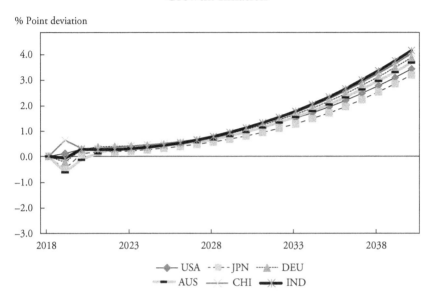

FIGURE 3-42. **Global Takeoff in Service Sector Productivity Growth: Inflation**

% Point deviation

Source: Authors' calculations.

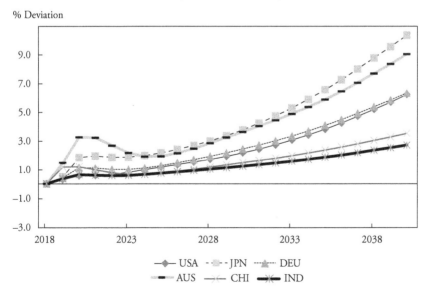

FIGURE 3-43. **Global Takeoff in Service Sector Productivity Growth: Employment**

% Deviation

Source: Authors' calculations.

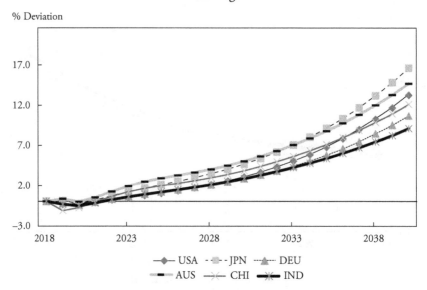

FIGURE 3-44. **Global Takeoff in Service Sector Productivity Growth: Real Wages**

% Deviation

Source: Authors' calculations.

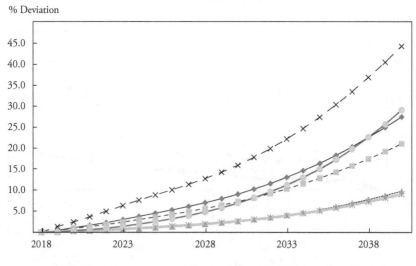

FIGURE 3-45. **Global Takeoff in Service Sector Productivity Growth: U.S. Sectoral Output**

% Deviation

Source: Authors' calculations.

NOTES
The authors thank Peter Wilcoxen for his substantial and ongoing contributions to the modeling research on which this chapter is built and Weifeng Liu for collaboration on model development. The authors also thank participants at the Brookings/KDI workshop held January 7, 2019, particularly Oya Celasun and Zia Qureshi, and participants at a World Bank seminar, particularly Ayhan Kose and Alistair Dieppe, for helpful comments. Renee Fry-McKibbin, Iraj Saniee, and Marcus Weldon also provided very helpful suggestions.

1. See Adler and others (2017).

2. Krugman (1997).

3. See, respectively, Mehrotra (2019); Duggar (2019); Mauro and others (2019); Stansbury and Summers (2019); Furman and Orszag (2019).

4. Solow (1987).

5. Nordhaus (2015); Saniee and others (2017); Basu, Fernald, and Kimball (2006).

6. Feldstein (2017).

7. Byrne, Oliner, and Sichel (2013); Adler and others (2017).

8. United Nations (2016).

9. Lileeva (2008); De Loecker (2007); United Nations (2016); Adler and others (2017).

10. Aiyar and Ebeke (2016).

11. Organisation for Economic Co-operation and Development (2015).

12. Kotlikoff and Sachs (2012); Akst (2013); Brynjolfsson and McAfee (2016); Goldin and Katz (2008).

13. Qureshi (2018); Decker and others (2014).

14. Melitz (2003).

15. Organisation for Economic Co-operation and Development (2015).

16. McGowan, Andrews, and Millot (2017).

17. Fernald (2014).

18. Gordon (2016).

19. See Frankel (2016); and Nixon (2007).

20. Aral, Brynjolfsson, and Van Alstyne (2007).

21. Gordon (2016).

22. Nordhaus (2015); Saniee and others (2017); Basu, Fernald, and Kimball (2006).

23. PricewaterhouseCoopers (2018).

24. See Goldfarb and Trefler (2018).

25. Fernald (2014); Melitz (2003); Organisation for Economic Co-operation and Development (2015).

26. PricewaterhouseCoopers (2018) use the EU and World KLEMS databases, which contain more aggregated data series of capital stock groupings that

contain AI technologies and therefore can capture the potential effect of AI on productivity (assuming the impact of AI is similar to that of other emerging technologies in the grouping).

27. Goldfarb and Trefler (2018).

28. Márquez-Ramos and Martínez-Zarzoso (2010).

29. European Central Bank (2017); Melitz (2003); Lileeva (2008); De Loecker (2007).

30. Obstfeld and Rogoff (2000).

31. McKibbin and Triggs (2018).

32. McKibbin and Sachs (1991) call this an incremental interest payments rule.

33. Further details are available in McKibbin and Triggs (2018).

34. McKibbin, Pearce, and Stegman (2007).

35. Stegman and McKibbin (2013).

36. United Nations (2017).

37. Barro (1991, 2015).

38. Timmer, de Vries, and de Vries (2015).

39. Gordon (2016); Adler and others (2017).

40. Calvo, Leiderman, and Reinhart (1993) and Hannan (2018) for a review of this literature.

41. Nordhaus (2015); Saniee and others (2017); Basu, Fernald, and Kimball (2006).

42. This experience is documented by Saniee and others (2017).

43. Nordhaus (2015).

44. PricewaterhouseCoopers (2018).

45. Goldfarb and Trefler (2018).

46. Fernald (2014); Melitz (2003); Organisation for Economic Co-operation and Development (2015).

47. Gordon (2016).

48. Nordhaus (2015); Saniee and others (2017).

49. PricewaterhouseCoopers (2018); Goldfarb and Trefler (2018).

50. The importance of infrastructure in the impacts of fiscal policy in the G-Cubed (G20) model is explored in McKibbin, Stoeckel, and Lu (2014).

REFERENCES

Adler, G., and others. 2017. "Gone with the Headwinds: Global Productivity," Staff Discussion Note 17/04 (Washington, D.C.: International Monetary Fund), April.

Aiyar, S., and C. H. Ebeke. 2016. "The Impact of Workforce Aging on European Productivity," Working Paper 16/238 (Washington, D.C.: International Monetary Fund), December.

Akst, D. 2013. "What Can We Learn from Past Anxiety over Automation?" *Wilson Quarterly* (Summer) (https://wilsonquarterly.com/quarterly/summer -2014-where-have-all-the-jobs-gone/theres-much-learn-from-past-anxiety -over-automation/).

Aral, S., E. Brynjolfsson, and M. W. Van Alstyne. 2007. "Information, Technology and Information Worker Productivity," National Bureau of Economic Research, No. 13172 (https://www.nber.org/papers/w13172).

Barro, R. J. 1991. "Economic Growth in a Cross Section of Countries." *Quarterly Journal of Economics* 106, no. 2, pp. 407–43.

———. 2015. "Convergence and Modernisation." *Economic Journal* 125, no. 585, pp. 911–42.

Basu, S., J. G. Fernald, and M. S. Kimball. 2006. "Are Technology Improvements Contractionary?" *American Economic Review* 96, no. 5, pp. 1418–48.

Brynjolfsson, E., and A. McAfee. 2016. *The Second Machine Age: Work, Progress, and Prosperity in a Time of Brilliant Technologies* (New York: W. W. Norton).

Byrne, D., S. D. Oliner, and D. Sichel. 2013. "Is the Information Technology Revolution Over?" Divisions of Research & Statistics and Monetary Affairs Finance and Economics Discussion Series 2013-36 (Washington, D.C.: Federal Reserve Board).

Calvo, G. A., L. Leiderman, and C. M. Reinhart. 1993. "Capital Inflows and Real Exchange Rate Appreciation in Latin America: The Role of External Factors," in *IMF Staff Papers* (Washington, D.C.: International Monetary Fund).

Decker, R., and others. 2014. "The Role of Entrepreneurship in U.S. Job Creation and Economic Dynamism." *Journal of Economic Perspectives* 28, no. 3, pp. 3–24.

De Loecker, J. 2007. "Do Exports Generate Higher Productivity? Evidence from Slovenia." *Journal of International Economics* 73, no. 1, pp. 69–98.

Duggar, E. 2019. "Slow Productivity Growth Will Pressure Sovereign Debt Sustainability," in *Facing Up to Low Productivity Growth*, edited by S. Posen and J. Zettelmeyer (Columbia University Press).

European Central Bank. 2017. "Does Trade Play a Role in Helping to Explain Productivity Growth?" *ECB Economic Bulletin* 7, pp. 21–24.

Feldstein, M. 2017. "Underestimating the Real Growth of GDP, Personal Income and Productivity," NBER Working Paper 23306 (Cambridge, Mass.: National Bureau of Economic Research), March.

Fernald, J. 2014. "Productivity and Potential Output Before, During, and After the Great Recession," NBER Working Paper 20248 (Cambridge, Mass.: National Bureau of Economic Research), June.

Frankel, J. 2016. "Is Technology Hurting Productivity?" *Project Syndicate*, March 19 (www.project-syndicate.org/commentary/technological-innovation -hurting-productivity-by-jeffrey-frankel-2018-03?barrier=accesspaylog).

Furman, J., and P. Orszag. 2019. "Are Slower Productivity and Higher Inequality Related?" in *Facing Up to Low Productivity Growth*, edited by S. Posen and J. Zettelmeyer (Columbia University Press).

Goldfarb, A., and D. Trefler. 2018. "AI and International Trade," NBER Working Paper 24254 (Cambridge, Mass.: National Bureau of Economic Research).

Goldin, C., and L. F. Katz. 2008. "The Race between Education and Technology: The Evolution of U.S. Educational Wage Differentials, 1890 to 2005," NBER Working Paper 12984 (Cambridge, Mass.: National Bureau of Economic Research).

Gordon, R. 2016. *The Rise and Fall of American Growth* (Princeton University Press).

Hannan, S. A. 2018. "Revisiting the Determinants of Capital Flows to Emerging Markets—A Survey of the Evolving Literature," IMF Working Paper 18/214 (Washington, D.C.: International Monetary Fund).

Henderson, D. W., and W. McKibbin. 1993. "A Comparison of Some Basic Monetary Policy Regimes for Open Economies: Implications of Different Degrees of Instrument Adjustment and Wage Persistence." *Carnegie-Rochester Conference Series on Public Policy* 39, pp. 221–318.

Kotlikoff, L. J., and J. D. Sachs. 2012. "Smart Machines and Long-Term Misery," NBER Working Paper 18629 (Cambridge, Mass.: National Bureau of Economic Research).

Krugman, P. 1997. *The Age of Diminished Expectations*, 3rd ed. (MIT Press).

Lee, J. W., and W. McKibbin. 2018. "Service Sector Productivity and Economic Growth in Asia." *Economic Modeling* 74, pp. 247–63.

Lileeva, A. 2008. "Trade Liberalization and Productivity Dynamics: Evidence from Canada." *Canadian Journal of Economics* 41, no. 2, pp. 360–90.

Márquez-Ramos, L., and I. Martínez-Zarzoso. 2010. "The Effect of Technological Innovation on International Trade: A Nonlinear Approach." *Open-Access, Open-Assessment E-Journal* 4, pp. 1–37.

Mauro, F., and others. 2019. "Living with Lower Productivity Growth: Impact on Exports," in *Facing Up to Low Productivity Growth*, edited by S. Posen and J. Zettelmeyer (Columbia University Press).

McGowan, M. A., D. Andrews, and V. Millot. 2017. "The Walking Dead? Zombie Firms and Productivity Performance in OECD Countries," OECD Economics Department Working Paper 1372 (Paris: Organisation for Economic Co-operation and Development).

McKibbin, W. J., D. Pearce, and A. Stegman. 2007. "Long Term Projections of Carbon Emissions." *International Journal of Forecasting* 23, pp. 637–53.

McKibbin, W. J., and J. Sachs. 1991. *Global Linkages: Macroeconomic Interdependence and Co-operation in the World Economy* (Brookings Institution).

McKibbin, W. J., A. Stoeckel, and Y. Lu. 2014. "Global Fiscal Adjustment and Trade Rebalancing." *World Economy* 37, no. 7, pp. 892–992.

McKibbin, W. J., and A. Triggs. 2018. "Modelling the G20," Centre for Applied Macroeconomic Analysis Working Paper 17/2018 (Canberra: Australian National University).

McKibbin, W. J., and P. Wilcoxen. 1999. "The Theoretical and Empirical Structure of the G-Cubed Model." *Economic Modelling* 16, no. 1, pp. 123–48.

———. 2013. "A Global Approach to Energy and the Environment: The G-Cubed Model," in *Handbook of CGE Modeling* (Amsterdam: North Holland).

Mehrotra, N. R. 2019. "Implications of Low Productivity Growth for Debt Sustainability," in *Facing Up to Low Productivity Growth*, edited by S. Posen and J. Zettelmeyer (Columbia University Press).

Melitz, M. K. 2003. "The Impact of Trade on Intra-Industry Reallocations and Aggregate Industry Productivity." *Econometrica* 71, no. 6, pp. 1695–1725.

Nixon, D. 2007. "Is the Economy Suffering from the Crisis of Attention?" *Bank Underground* (blog), November 24.

Nordhaus, W. 2015. "Are We Approaching an Economic Singularity? Information Technology and the Future of Economic Growth," NBER Working Paper 21547 (Cambridge, Mass.: National Bureau of Economic Research).

Obstfeld, M., and K. Rogoff. 2000. "The Six Major Puzzles in International Macroeconomics: Is There a Common Cause?" NBER Working Paper 7777 (Cambridge, Mass.: National Bureau of Economic Research).

Organisation for Economic Co-operation and Development. 2015. *The Future of Productivity* (Paris).

PricewaterhouseCoopers. 2018. *The Macroeconomic Impact of Artificial Intelligence.* PwC Technical Report (www.pwc.co.uk/economic-services/assets/macroeconomic-impact-of-ai-technical-report-feb-18.pdf), February.

Qureshi, Z. 2018. "Today's Economic Puzzles: A Tale of Weakening Competition." *Up Front* (blog), Brookings Institution, April 5.

Saniee, I., and others. 2017. "Will Productivity Growth Return in the New Digital Era?" *Bell Labs Technical Journal* 22, pp. 1–18.

Solow, R. 1987. "We'd Better Watch Out," review of *The Myth of the Post-Industrial Economy*, by Stephen S. Cohen and John Zysman. *New York Times*, July 12.

Stansbury, A., and L. Summers. 2019. "Productivity and Pay: Is the Link Broken?" in *Facing Up to Low Productivity Growth*, edited by S. Posen and J. Zettelmeyer (Columbia University Press).

Stegman, A., and W. McKibbin. 2013. "Long Term Projections of the World Economy: A Review," Centre for Applied Macroeconomic Analysis Working Paper 14/2013 (Canberra: Australian National University).

Taylor, J. B. 1993. "Discretion versus Policy Rules in Practice." *Carnegie-Rochester Conference Series on Public Policy* 39, no. 1, pp. 195–214.

Timmer, M. P., G. J. de Vries, and K. de Vries. 2015. "Patterns of Structural Change in Developing Countries," in *Routledge Handbook of Industry and Development*, edited by J. Weiss and M. Tribe (London: Routledge).

United Nations. 2016. "The Slowdown in Productivity Growth: A View from International Trade." *Development Issues* 11 (April 21) (www.un.org /development/desa/dpad/wp-content/uploads/sites/45/publication/dsp _policy_11.pdf).

———. 2017. *2017 Revision of World Population Prospects.* Report. New York (https://www.un.org/development/desa/publications/world-population -prospects-the-2017-revision.html).

FOUR

The Future of Global Manufacturing

BRAHIMA COULIBALY AND KARIM FODA

Manufacturing-led development has historically been the most domi-nant economic development paradigm. Since the first Industrial Revolu-tion in the eighteenth century, manufacturing has helped transform most of today's advanced and richest economies and, more recently, has been the catalyst of the East Asian miracle. Three salient features of manufacturing made it an effective development escalator. First, manufacturing goods are tradeable, which provide possibilities for countries to scale up production be-yond the consumption capacity of local economies and boost national in-come. Second, manufacturing benefits from technological transfers, which allow productivity of local production to converge with that of global pro-duction. Third, importantly, manufacturing could absorb large numbers of moderately skilled labor at a productivity premium, delivering sustained ag-gregate productivity gains and driving structural economic transformation.

However, some global trends in manufacturing activity suggest that without more proactive policies, manufacturing-led growth may no longer serve as a viable development model for current developing countries, as in the past. First, the "Great Convergence" between the 1990s and 2010, which resulted in a declining share of advanced economies and a rising share of major emerging market economies in global manufacturing, appears to have stalled. Second, as documented by Dani Rodrik,[1] the hump-shaped relationship between industrialization (measured by national employment or output shares) and income has shifted downward.[2] In other words, the shares of manufacturing output and employment in aggregate output and employment are declining. The final trend explored is the increasingly higher value added contribution of upstream and downstream activities along manufacturing value chains and the growing importance of high skills and services in manufacturing.

Although these trends have been around for some time, the pace appears to have accelerated with the increasingly rapid pace of technological progress. Both technology and globalization have shaped the global manufacturing landscape since the first Industrial Revolution, but the balance of influence is shifting toward technology. The diffusion of labor-saving technologies is raising the capital intensity of manufacturing and reducing demand for less-skilled labor. In the process it is altering countries' comparative advantages in global manufacturing. Newer technologies like advanced robotics, artificial intelligence, 3-D printing, and the internet of things—often referred to as "Industry 4.0" technologies, in reference to today's "fourth Industrial Revolution"—are poised to reshape the global manufacturing landscape with important consequences for the traditional role of manufacturing in economic development.

Against this background, this chapter first explores the fundamental drivers of four key trends in global manufacturing activity—geographical distribution, importance in gross domestic product, ability to generate large-scale employment, and increasing high skills and servicification of manufacturing—with a special focus on the role of technology. Understanding the drivers of these trends allows for formulation of a view on the future of global manufacturing as well as on the implications for economic development.

Trend 1: The geographic distribution of manufacturing output. Following the Industrial Revolutions of the late eighteenth and nineteenth centuries, a "Great Divergence" took hold in the global economy,[3] where industrialized nations (G-7) increased their shares of global manufacturing to 68 percent by the late 1980s,[4] even though they accounted for only around 15 percent of the world's population. As these nations continued to advance the tech-

FIGURE 4-1. **Geographical Distribution of Global Manufacturing
Output Shares, 1970–2016**[a]

Percent

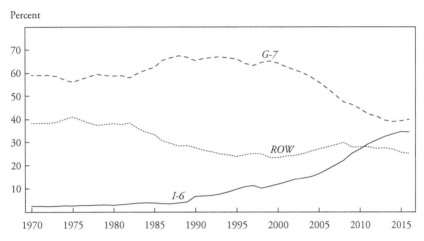

Source: UNCTAD National Accounts Data.

a. G-7 includes Canada, France, Germany, Italy, Japan, the United Kingdom, and the United States. I-6 includes China, India, Indonesia, Korea, Poland, and Thailand.

nological frontier, the production of lower-skilled and labor-intensive manufactured goods shifted to developing economies with lower labor costs, mainly in Asia. In the 1990s the spread of information and communications technology (ICT) gave rise to a third Industrial Revolution that heralded what is often referred to as the "Great Convergence."[5] ICT made information sharing and communication across longer distances more effective and cost efficient, enabling the fragmentation and coordination of production across different geographical regions. In just two and a half decades between 1990 and 2015, developing economies increased their share of global manufacturing from 7 percent to 35 percent, largely reflecting the offshoring of production from developed countries, facilitated by the emergence of more global value chains (GVCs), to lower-cost locations or local markets.[6] These offshore locations, however, were not significantly spread across emerging and developing economies. Only six industrializing nations (China, India, Indonesia, Poland, South Korea, and Thailand) increased their shares of global manufacturing since 1990 (figure 4-1).[7] Led by China, these six nations account for the vast majority of the "Great Convergence" in global manufacturing output in recent decades. China alone has become the single largest manufacturer in the world, surpassing the United States

FIGURE 4-2. Geographical Distribution of Global Manufacturing Employment Shares, 1970–2009[a]

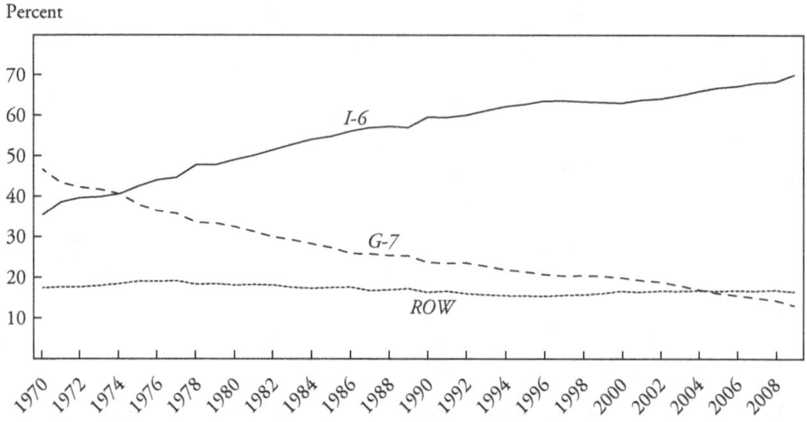

Percent

a. G-7 includes Canada, France, Germany, Italy, Japan, the United Kingdom, and the United States. I-6 includes China, India, Indonesia, Korea, Poland, and Thailand. Our data include employment statistics for fifty-four countries.

in 2010 and accounting for a quarter of the world's manufacturing as of 2016. All of the G-7 economies have seen their manufacturing shares steadily decline over this time period.

Why has the shift away from G-7 dominance in global manufacturing been so concentrated across just six developing economies? One prevailing explanation is provided by the "flying geese" theory of economic development,[8] suggesting that as countries move up the value chain and wages rise, lower-skill tasks shift to nearby locations with lower unit labor costs and low transportation or trade costs.[9] The proximity of the "Industrializing 6" (I-6) nations to the world's largest manufacturers, or manufacturing hubs, in Europe, the United States, and East Asia aligns with the flying geese paradigm, but the persistent dominance of the world's leading manufacturers points to frictions in the paradigm. For example, seven of the world's top ten exporters of low-skill, labor-intensive tradables in 2011 were still high-income economies.[10]

As developing economies grew their share of global manufacturing value added, they also grew their share of global manufacturing employment (see figure 4-2). The labor share of global manufacturing is declining across all G-7 countries and rising across all I-6 countries. In each G-7 country the

FIGURE 4-3. **Trends in Manufacturing Value Added as Percent of GDP, 1970–2016**[a]

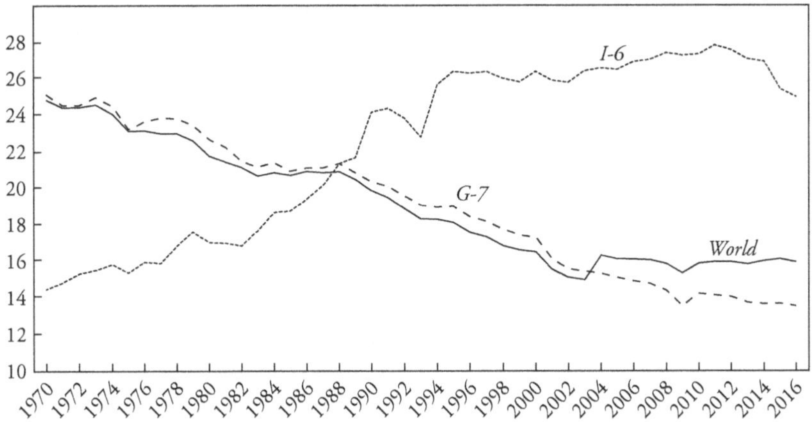

Source: UNCTAD National Accounts.

a. For I-6 countries, data for China start in 1990 and for Poland in 1994.

employment share in global manufacturing has fallen below 5 percent. This shift in shares of global manufacturing employment from developed to developing countries began much earlier than the shift in value added, suggesting that these shifts were largely in labor-intensive manufacturing.

Trend 2: Global manufacturing output. The contribution of manufacturing to world output has been declining. At the global level, the world economy had been steadily deindustrializing (declining manufacturing share of output) since the 1970s, when manufacturing accounted for nearly a quarter of world GDP, until the early 2000s, when it stabilized at about 16 percent of world GDP (figure 4-3).

The steady relative decline was first driven by deindustrialization in developed economies. With technological progress and rapid productivity growth in manufacturing, the industrialized nations moved further up the value chain into higher-skilled and capital-intensive manufacturing as lower value added, labor-intensive production shifted overseas. While this is consistent with the conventional structural change process of economic growth and development, the shares of GDP for higher-skill manufacturing subsectors have also declined over the last twenty years.[11] Meanwhile, manufacturing value added in absolute levels continued to rise. For example, between 1970 and 2016 manufacturing output tripled in Japan and the United States and rose by 40 percent in the United Kingdom.

In the I-6 countries, the GDP share of manufacturing increased through around 2010 but also began to experience an overall trend of decline since then. Among a broader range of developing economies, domestic shares of manufacturing value added have declined even as shares of global manufacturing value added have risen. Around half of all countries with rising global shares in manufacturing value added between 1994 and 2014 are deindustrializing domestically.[12]

While peak GDP shares of manufacturing value added occurred later in many developing economies than in developed economies, peaks are happening at increasingly lower levels of economic development. This stylized fact is often referred to as "premature" deindustrialization,[13] where the role of manufacturing as a development escalator fades too soon, before the opportunity to increase incomes and employ more people is actualized.

Trend 3: Global manufacturing employment intensity. Historically, manufacturing's ability to hire large numbers of low-skilled and middle-skilled workers into higher productivity jobs has made it a critical driver of economic development and growth. The transition of labor from agriculture to labor-intensive manufacturing helped spur sustained periods of both employment and productivity growth. Higher up the value chain, skills requirements and capital intensity of manufacturing grow and reduce the scope for large-scale employment. Over the last several decades, however, countries have been experiencing peak national shares of employment in manufacturing at lower levels of national income, before having developed a comparative advantage in higher value added manufacturing activities. Dani Rodrik shows this stylized fact indicating increasing productivity and capital intensity of manufacturing (figure 4-4a).[14]

Globally, the share of total employment in manufacturing has been roughly steady between 1970 and 2010; it has declined in the advanced economies, but this decline was offset by increases in the I-6 countries, notably China (figure 4-4b). In the United States the labor share of manufacturing fell from around 25 percent between 1950 and 1970 to around 5 percent in 2010, and similar declines in labor shares and levels occurred in the United Kingdom, Germany, Japan, and France. In absolute terms, the total number of workers in manufacturing fell in the advanced economies by roughly one-third between 1970 and 2010. Globally, the total number of workers in manufacturing more than doubled between 1970 and 2010, from 132 million to 326 million, driven mainly by China and, to a lesser extent, other I-6 countries. China now employs close to half of the world's manufactur-

FIGURE 4-4A. **Premature Deindustrialization, 1950–2012**[a]

Peak manufacturing share of total employment

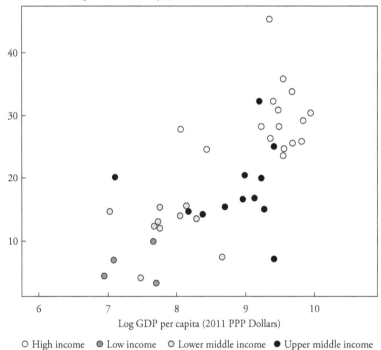

Log GDP per capita (2011 PPP Dollars)

○ High income   ◉ Low income   ○ Lower middle income   ● Upper middle income

Source: Groningen Growth and Development Center ten-sector database and Penn World Tables.

a. Peak manufacturing share of total employment by country income level.

ing workers or nearly one-fifth of employment in its own economy. After China's accession into the World Trade Organization (WTO) in 2001, the share of Chinese workers in manufacturing jumped by over 5 percentage points in less than ten years. Meanwhile, the share of workers in manufacturing in the other I-6 economies peaked and began to decline around 2000.

Trend 4: Increasing high-skills and servicification of manufacturing. The manufacturing employment challenge is real in many advanced economies, and it is primarily reflected in declining middle-skill manufacturing jobs that have either been offshored to lower-wage developing countries or replaced by machinery. In nearly all industries across OECD economies from 1995 to 2015, middle-skill jobs have declined while high-skill jobs have grown, due in part to their complementarity with ICT and newer technologies.[15] Low-skill jobs

FIGURE 4-4B. **Share of Manufacturing Employment in Total Employment, 1970–2010**

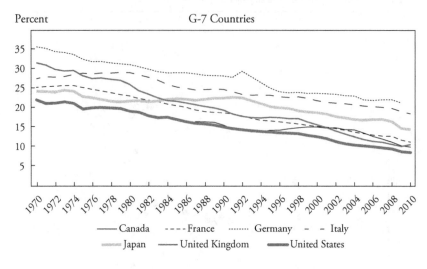

Percent   G-7 Countries

——— Canada   - - - - France   ········ Germany   – – Italy
        Japan   ——— United Kingdom   United States

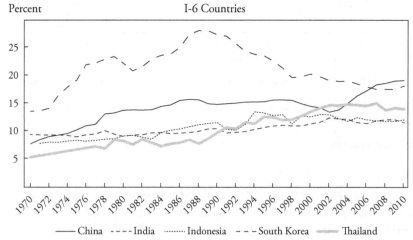

Percent   I-6 Countries

——— China   - - - - India   ········ Indonesia   – – South Korea   Thailand

Source: Groningen Growth and Development Center ten-sector database and OECD employment statistics.

Note: Poland is not shown in this chart as available data cover only a short part of the relevant period.

have also grown on aggregate as middle-skill workers have increasingly been pushed into lower-wage service sectors, resulting in increasingly polarized labor markets.[16] Manufacturing has seen one of the largest declines in middle-skill jobs and, conversely, all manufacturing job growth is occurring among high-skill positions. Figure 4-5 illustrates this labor market polariza-

FIGURE 4-5. Job Polarization and Decline in Manufacturing Jobs, 1995–2015[a]

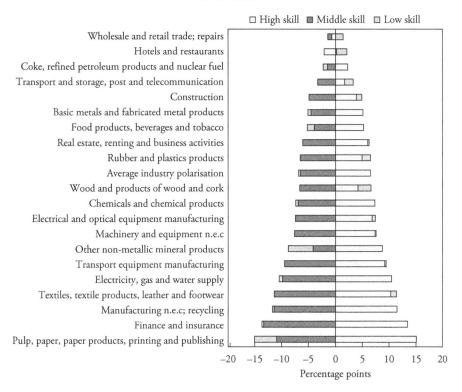

□ High skill   ■ Middle skill   □ Low skill

Wholesale and retail trade; repairs
Hotels and restaurants
Coke, refined petroleum products and nuclear fuel
Transport and storage, post and telecommunication
Construction
Basic metals and fabricated metal products
Food products, beverages and tobacco
Real estate, renting and business activities
Rubber and plastics products
Average industry polarisation
Wood and products of wood and cork
Chemicals and chemical products
Electrical and optical equipment manufacturing
Machinery and equipment n.e.c
Other non-metallic mineral products
Transport equipment manufacturing
Electricity, gas and water supply
Textiles, textile products, leather and footwear
Manufacturing n.e.c; recycling
Finance and insurance
Pulp, paper, paper products, printing and publishing

−20 −15 −10 −5   0   5   10   15   20

Percentage points

Source: Organisation for Economic Co-operation and Development (2017).

a. Percentage point change in share of industry employment for select OECD countries.

tion for OECD countries. Overall, however, manufacturing jobs on aggregate have been declining across the majority of manufacturing subsectors in developed economies between 1995 and 2015, as the growth in high-skill jobs only partially offset the reduction in lower-skill jobs.

Lower trade and information costs as a result of the ICT revolution in the 1990s enabled complex GVCs to take shape, where intermediate inputs could cross more than one border before final assembly and consumption. From 1995 until the global financial crisis in 2008, GVC trade production grew faster than traditional trade (where a good is produced in one country and exported to another for consumption), with complex GVCs growing the fastest. In the post-crisis period since 2011, however, growth of GVCs has stalled.[17]

As labor-intensive activities shifted to developing countries and developed economies moved further up the value chain into higher-skill activities, income inequality and development concerns began to arise. In developed economies, the decline in lower-skill manufacturing jobs and the rising wage premium for higher-skill workers contributed to rising income inequality. In developing economies participating in GVCs there is the risk that the increasing skills requirements will contribute to raising the bar for greater participation or that their participation would be confined to lower value added activities with limited opportunity to move up the value chain.

Indeed, along the GVCs, the distribution of value addition mimics a "smile curve," a term coined by Stan Shih to reflect the higher value added contribution of upstream and downstream activities relative to assembly and production activities.[18] For example, if one considers the production of an iPhone, high value added activities like research and development, design, and other high-skill activities occur in the United States while capital-intensive components such as the production of advanced computing chips occur in other high-skill locations such as Japan and Taiwan. Lower value added activities, including assembly, take place in China. The assembled iPhone is then exported back to the United States, where higher value added postproduction activities, including branding, embedded services, and marketing, take place. The upstream and downstream activities are more skill and capital intensive, thereby enjoying a higher wage premium and value addition.[19]

A noteworthy trend in smile curves of manufactured products is their steepening over time, with value added during the production phase accounting for a smaller share of the final product's total value (as illustrated in figure 4-6). Meng and coauthors estimated the smile curve for China's exports of electrical and optical equipment in 1995 and in 2009.[20] The results indicate that the curve steepened over time, reflecting faster growth in compensation per hour for higher-skilled workers in the United States, Europe, and Japan working in pre- and postproduction service-based activities and more moderate growth in China, where assembly and production took place. The authors found that aggregate value added gains in China reflect the large amount of labor it employed in this sector, but labor compensation per hour only slightly increased from $0.60 in 1995 to $1.60 in 2009. By contrast, labor compensation per hour for U.S. ICT workers in this value chain soared from $18.10 in 1995 to $52.20 in 2009.

FIGURE 4-6. **Smile Curve in Global Value Chains**

Share of product's total value added

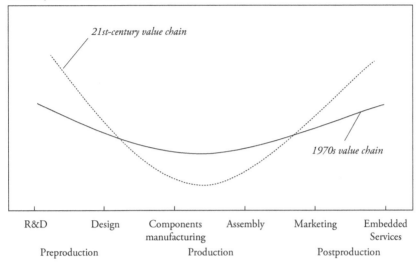

R&D	Design	Components manufacturing	Assembly	Marketing	Embedded Services
Preproduction		Production		Postproduction

Source: Authors.

As a whole, the rising service content in manufacturing is leading to a rising share of service value added in manufacturing output. Between 1995 and 2011 the share of service inputs in aggregate manufacturing value added increased by about 6 percentage points on average across countries (figure 4-7).[21] This can be attributed to increased demand for goods that require greater service input, such as design, software, or branding, or greater service delivery for manufactured products, such as logistics, e-commerce, or communications.[22] Such services are considered "embodied" in manufacturing products. On the other hand, there are also services that are "embedded" in manufactured products, such as mobile phones that require telecommunications services and enable the use or purchasing of applications that offer additional services like messaging, video gaming, or mobile banking. Embedded services can also include warranties, customer servicing to drive brand loyalty, and other services that may deliver strategic benefits to manufacturing firms.[23] The rising share of service value added reflects the higher skills content and skills premium that is increasingly required in manufacturing and has been a key driver of steeper smile curves across domestic or global value chains.

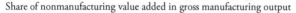

FIGURE 4-7. **Nonmanufacturing Content in Gross Manufacturing Output, 1995–2011**

Share of nonmanufacturing value added in gross manufacturing output

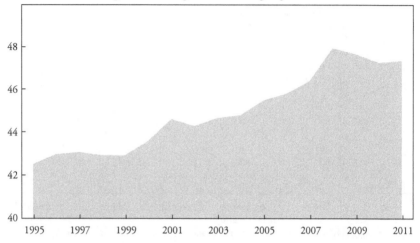

Source: International Monetary Fund (2018b).

In sum, the global manufacturing landscape has been characterized by these important trends: (1) convergence in global manufacturing shares between major developed and developing economies and the spread of GVCs, (2) declining manufacturing shares in GDP, (3) declining manufacturing labor shares, and (4) greater servicification and skill content of manufacturing.

Globalization and technology have been the primary drivers of these trends. Globalization has played a key role in bringing developing countries into the global manufacturing process, often in lower-skilled and labor-intensive manufacturing. Technological progress has enabled the specialization of discrete activities that allow countries to participate in GVCs. Over the last few years, however, growth in GVCs and the Great Convergence have stalled. Drivers of globalization appear to have run their course, though technological change continues to speed ahead. In the next section, we turn to the importance of technology in manufacturing and its growing role in shaping comparative advantages in manufacturing in the twenty-first century. We then turn to our predictions on how the key trends in manufacturing over recent decades will evolve into the future and how low- and middle-income countries can respond.

Manufacturing Technologies and Shifting Comparative Advantages

For nearly two centuries since the Industrial Revolution, the technological breakthroughs that allowed for the separation of geographic locations of production and consumption, and subsequently the fragmentation of production itself, facilitated the growing role of developing countries with a comparative advantage in labor-intensive manufacturing. An abundant supply of low-cost labor in developing countries, coupled with policies to lower trade barriers and promote industrial zones, was able to meet demand by firms in developed economies for labor-intensive manufacturing activities along GVCs. However, the growth in GVCs and the convergence in global manufacturing shares have stalled in recent years; technological change is marching on and shifting the comparative advantages of nations.

Notably, labor cost competitiveness is becoming relatively less important across the manufacturing sector. The McKinsey Global Institute (MGI) estimates that only 18 percent of total goods trade is based on "labor-cost arbitrage" (or the export of goods from low-wage to high-wage countries).[24] The share for labor-intensive goods trade that is based on labor-cost arbitrage declined from 55 percent in 2005 to 43 percent in 2017. The factors that drive competitiveness in manufacturing are expanding beyond low labor costs in production. New technologies are raising the capital intensity of production, elevating the importance of skills and proximity to consumers, and requiring sufficient digital infrastructure and readiness for manufacturers to be competitive. The countries that currently possess and are investing in the capital, skills, and infrastructure of the future are well positioned to dominate global manufacturing in the years ahead. Indeed, factors that are becoming more important include advanced robotics, supply of high skills, innovation ecosystems, digital readiness, and overall competitiveness.

First, the stock and investment in advanced robotics is becoming increasingly prevalent in manufacturing. The adoption of automation capabilities drives operating efficiencies and boosts productivity, particularly with increasingly smart machines in the internet of things (IoT) ecosystems where capital inputs transmit product, user, logistics, and other data directly to each other throughout the production process. As the cost of capital declines and as demand for customizable products grows, robotics and additive manufacturing capabilities (for example, 3-D printing) will grow as an important factor for manufacturing competitiveness.

Second, the complementarity of manufacturing technologies and high skills is growing. As increasingly sophisticated and new technologies are embodied in the production process, and as a growing share of manufacturing value added is captured by high-skill services content in upstream and downstream activities, the supply of high-skilled labor is an increasingly important factor. MGI estimates that spending on research and development and knowledge-based assets (such as intellectual property, software, organization design, and so forth) is growing across manufacturing value chains from 5.4 percent of revenue in 2000 to 13.1 percent in 2016.[25] In addition to the supply of skills, other factors, including intellectual property frameworks, innovation policies, and public spending on basic research, are also increasingly important.[26]

Third, physical infrastructure that supports the reliable and secure transmission of data is a prerequisite for manufacturing competitiveness. While individual firms can often bypass the high fixed costs associated with setting up their own data servers through cloud-computing and open-source systems, they still need to operate in an environment with access to reliable high-speed broadband. For manufacturers, equipping factories with IoT technologies and advanced robotics relies on the flow of data and information across devices and, in some cases, device operators who may be located in separate geographies. On the demand side, an e-commerce presence and advanced data analytics capabilities to meet consumer expectations in the digital age also requires an underlying digital infrastructure with wide internet access and penetration.

Finally, manufacturing competitiveness will continue to rely on a country's overall regulatory and policy frameworks, trade logistics, contract enforcement capacity, and other traditional measures of competitiveness. In the rapidly evolving digital age, these factors will tend to become more important as legal and regulatory issues around data governance or privacy come to the fore and as consumer expectations around speed of delivery and product customization place more emphasis on streamlining processes.

Countries that are strong in these areas are poised to lead or successfully develop twenty-first-century manufacturing sectors. Given the declining relative importance of low wages and the rising capital intensity, skills requirements, and infrastructure prerequisites, the bar is rising for today's developing and low-income countries to develop competitive manufacturing sectors. On the other hand, the world's manufacturing hubs in North America, East Asia, and Europe stand to gain as they generally score higher in these areas. Figure 4-8 shows how different countries generally stack up in these factors of future manufacturing competitiveness. Of particular note is China's rapid investment in industrial robots. Between 2010 and 2018 the stock of industrial robots operating in China's manufacturing sector jumped from around 25,000 to over 400,000, doubling in size in just the three years from 2015 to 2018, more than the level in other global manufacturing hubs.

Across all dimensions, it is clear that today's global manufacturing hubs lead and low-income countries lag, most notably in measures of internet access (percent of population using the internet) and digital readiness. Middle-income countries, particularly many emerging Asian economies, have scope to develop comparative advantages in an increasingly technology-led manufacturing sector, as shown by their relatively high scores on key competitiveness factors along with growing domestic supply chains and growing consumer markets, as discussed in the following section. Indonesia, Malaysia, Thailand, and Vietnam stand out among emerging Asian economies as countries with relatively favorable conditions to support more technologically enabled manufacturing sectors, while others face larger needs in developing higher skills among their workforces, more accommodative business environments, and wider access to the internet.

East Asia, Europe, and the United States, which already dominate global manufacturing, are making the greatest investments in robotics and other Industry 4.0 technologies and thereby raising the prospect for further concentration of manufacturing activity in these regions. In 2017 around 75 percent of the volume of robot sales were concentrated in the world's manufacturing hubs of Asia (China, Korea, and Japan), the United States, and Germany.[27] The Asia-Pacific region, Western Europe, and the United States make up the majority of the investment in internet of things technologies, a market projected to grow from $737 billion in 2015 to $1.5 trillion in 2021 and most widely adopted in manufacturing.[28] In 2016, 95 percent of investments in 3-D printing were made by North America (39 percent), Asia-Pacific (29 percent), and Europe (28 percent).[29] China and the United States are leading in investment in both artificial intelligence research and development and its deployment in manufacturing. Between 2016 and 2021 the artificial intelligence market is projected to grow by 55 percent a year, from $8 billion to $72 billion.[30] Pricewaterhouse

FIGURE 4-8. Strength in Competitiveness Factors for Manufacturing

A. Operational Stock of Industrial Robots in Manufacturing Sector, 1995–2018

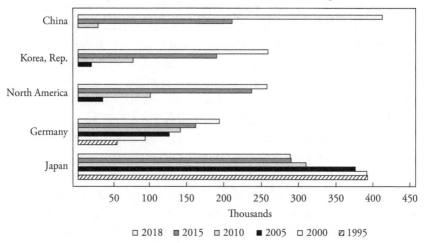

B. Skills, Digital Readiness, and Competitiveness Indexes
Global View by Income Level

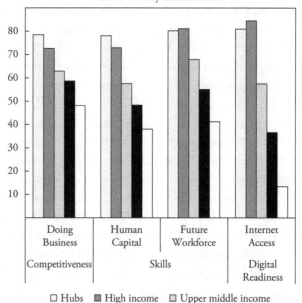

Source: Panel A from Hallward-Dreiemer and Nayyar (2018), using data from International Federation of Robotics; Panel B World Bank Doing Business Index (for Doing Business (Overall)); World Bank Human Capital Index (for Human Capital); World Economic Forum Competitiveness Index (for Future Workforce); International Telecommunication Union (for Internet Access).

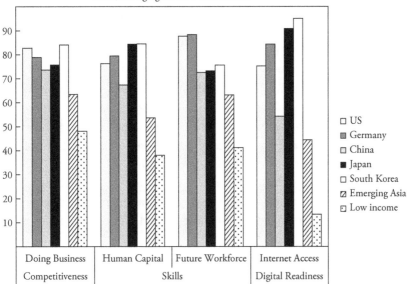

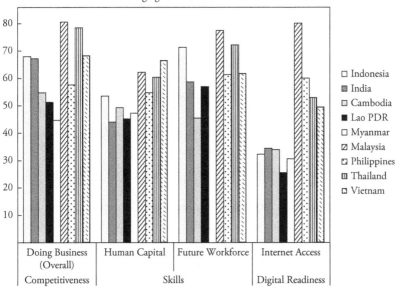

Coopers estimates that the deployment of artificial intelligence will contribute $15.7 trillion to global GDP by 2030, with China and the United States accounting for $7 trillion and $3.7 trillion, respectively, roughly 70 percent of the total (figure 4-9).[31]

Low-cost production networks will continue to be an important factor in firms' decisions and technology will further enable greater coordination of discrete tasks across GVCs. But as the cost of capital declines more rapidly, the comparative advantage of developing countries in labor-intensive manufacturing will continue to erode in the absence of proactive policies to invest in the skills and infrastructure of the future.

In the following section we discuss how the key trends of global manufacturing—changing geographical distribution, manufacturing output and servicification, and employment—could play out in the future in the context of technological change.

The Future of Global Manufacturing

While globalization and technology will continue to shape the future of manufacturing, technology will play a predominant role, given the rapid pace of technological innovations and adoption. As pointed out by Canadian prime minister Justin Trudeau, "The pace of [technological] change has never been this fast, yet it will never be this slow again."[32] To assess the future of global manufacturing, it is useful to analyze how the four major trends explored earlier will evolve in the context of rapid technological progress and shifting comparative advantages.

The Geography of Global Manufacturing: Poised for Divergence

In the coming decades, not only is the Great Convergence unlikely to broaden to many more countries, it could stall or even reverse as manufacturing hubs consolidate their dominant position thanks to greater investment in competitiveness technologies and infrastructure. Three reasons help support this view: First, technology is boosting productivity in current manufacturing centers, largely offsetting the effect of rising wages. Second, technology is making production more capital- and less labor-intensive, reducing the attractiveness of developing countries as production centers. As the cost of capital falls further, reshoring could accelerate and

FIGURE 4-9. Projected Shipments of Industrial Robots and Gains from AI Investment

Projected Annual Shipments of Industrial Robots, 2019–21

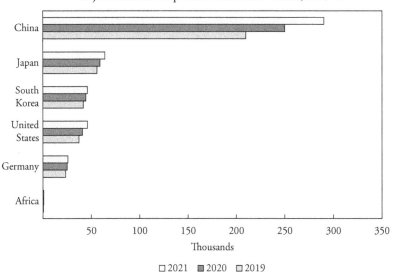

□ 2021 ■ 2020 □ 2019

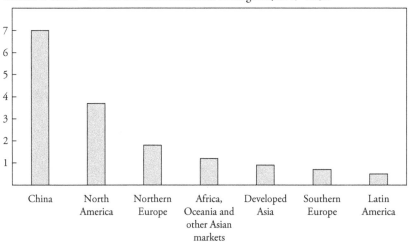

Trillions of dollars   Global Gains from Artificial Intelligence, 2017–2030

Source: Top, International Federation of Robotics; bottom, PricewaterhouseCoopers Global Artificial Intelligence Study: Exploiting the AI Revolution (2018, bottom panel).

lead to further concentration of global manufacturing. Third, entry in global value chains, which allowed many low-income countries to develop local manufacturing sectors, will become difficult, as reflected in the likely structural slowdown in GVC growth. Moreover, standards, skills, and infrastructure requirements in GVCs are raising the bar for participation by low-income countries.

TECHNOLOGY AND LABOR COST COMPETITIVENESS. Factors like proximity to manufacturing hubs, trade costs, and export zones that traditionally drive globalization have influenced trends in global manufacturing,[33] but the role of technology, particularly as it relates to efficiency and productivity, has been instrumental in explaining the geographical distribution of global manufacturing activity and the Great Convergence.[34]

Along with proximity and low transportation and trade costs, wage competition is commonly thought to be a major determinant in the participation of developing countries in global manufacturing. However, low wages are only part of the story. Many developing countries, including those that are relatively close to the world's manufacturing hubs, have low wages but only a few are involved in GVCs. Low unit labor costs—the ratio of average wages to per capita GDP—have been a far more important driver, reflecting the importance of labor productivity. Countries more deeply involved in global manufacturing have low unit labor costs but not necessarily low wages.[35]

The case of China helps to illustrate the declining relative importance of labor cost competitiveness in manufacturing. Between 2003 and 2010, average wages in China rose by 281 percent and, although labor productivity also increased, average unit labor costs rose relative to other developing economies (figure 4-10). Yet, despite the decline in Chinese labor cost competitiveness, its share of global manufacturing continued to rise, from 8 percent to 18 percent over the same period, faster than any other country in the world. China remains the world's largest exporter and is among the world's export leaders across low-, medium- and high-skill manufacturing subsectors.[36]

While China's upgrading of its economy toward higher value added production has generated some opportunities to absorb low-skill production activities for neighboring low-income economies with complementary production structures,[37] China is increasingly developing its own industries and capacity to substitute imported intermediate inputs by domestic firms.

FIGURE 4-10. Change in Manufacturing Wages and Relative Unit Costs between China and Select Developing Countries, 2003–2010

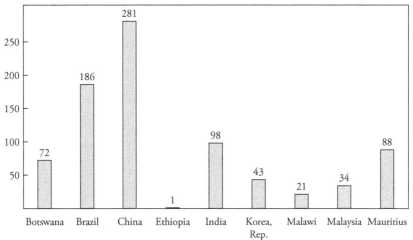

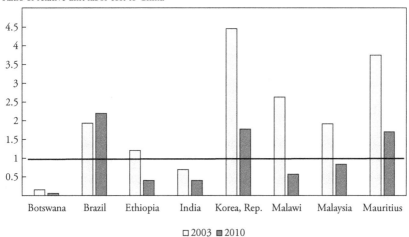

Source: From Hallward-Dreiemer and Nayyar (2018).

Figure 4-11 illustrates how China has increased the domestic value added component of its manufacturing exports across subsectors, from more labor-intensive textiles to higher-technology electrical and optical equipment.

In a recent survey of Chinese light manufacturing firms by Jiajun Xu and coauthors, 28 percent of firms declared rising wages in China to be the

FIGURE 4-11. **Change in Domestic Value Added of Manufacturing Sectors, China, 1995–2011**

Share of domestic value added in gross exports, percent

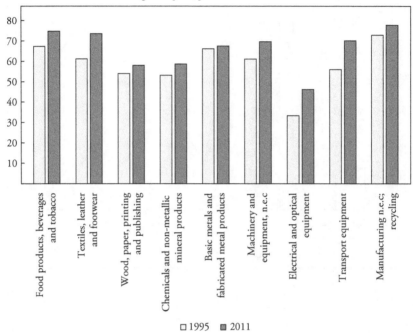

□ 1995   ■ 2011

Source: From Hallward-Dreiemer and Nayyar (2018).

greatest challenge in firm operations, and 31 percent identified "technology upgrading" as the preferred response to rising labor costs, as opposed to investing abroad in regions where labor is cheaper.[38] In other emerging Asian economies, domestic supply chains have also grown as they have become less reliant on importing intermediate inputs for goods production compared to the rest of the developing world. According to MGI, 8.3 percent of total value added for the production of goods in emerging Asia in 2017 came from imported intermediate inputs, compared to 15.1 percent in the rest of the developing world.[39]

RESHORING OF PRODUCTION. Greater investment in Industry 4.0 technologies will continue to push down the cost of capital to eventually fall below unit labor costs across countries, helping to accelerate reshoring of production. For example, though still relatively expensive, the average cost of a 3-D

Table 4-1. *Most Often Cited Reasons for Reshoring by U.S. Firms,*
2010–2017

Factors, Reshoring + FDI, 2010–2017					
Rank	Negative Offshore Factor	Citings	Rank	Positive Domestic Factor	Citings
1	Quality/rework/ warranty	292	1	Government incentives	527
2	Freight cost	196	2	Proximity to customers/ market	493
3	Total cost	147	3	Skilled workforce training/availability	446
4	Delivery	100	4	Image/brand	398
5	Inventory	91	5	Eco-system synergies	336
6	Rising wages	88	6	Lead time/Time to market	251
7	Supply chain interruption risk/ Natural disaster risk/ Political instability	78	7	Infrastructure	239
8	Intellectual property risk	64	8	Automation/technology	211
9	Communications	61	9	Manufacturing/ engineering joint innovation (R&D)	155
10	Green considerations	53	10	Higher productivity	141

Source: Reshoring Initiative (2018).

printer declined 4.7 percent between 2012 and 2015 and 5.5 percent between 2015 and 2018.[40] Box 4-1 discusses the "inflection point" at which
the cost of capital and labor will meet in the case of furniture manufacturing. It suggests that at around 2033 the cost of robots used to manufacture
furniture in the United States will fall below wages in Kenya.

Other critical factors such as proximity to consumers and the supply of
skilled labor also portend rapid reshoring of production. A survey of U.S.
manufacturers by the Reshoring Initiative indicated that government policy, proximity to consumers, the supply of skilled labor, and ecosystem synergies are more commonly cited drivers for reshoring than automation
technologies (see table 4-1).[41]

BOX 4-1. Window of Opportunity for Developing Countries Is Narrowing

Greater adoption of and investment in robots and other labor-saving technologies will continue to reduce the cost of capital and lead it lower than the cost of labor. While the growing use of robots in manufacturing in developed countries could place downward pressure on wages in developing countries to maintain competitiveness, the growing use of robots in developing countries themselves in order to remain competitive adds further pressure on the attractiveness of labor. For example, while Africa accounted for 0.05 percent of global robot sales in the early 2000s, that share has risen to 0.2 percent to 0.5 percent in recent years. The robot intensity of production in Africa remains low in part because of low labor costs, but as the cost of robots declines, manufacturers will find it profitable to further automate production. For furniture manufacturing in Kenya, for example, the inflection point—when it becomes more profitable to substitute robots for labor—is estimated to occur in 2034 (Figure B 4-1; Banga and Velde 2018).

FIGURE B 4-1. Robot Costs and Wages in Kenya and the United States: The Case of Furniture Manufacturing

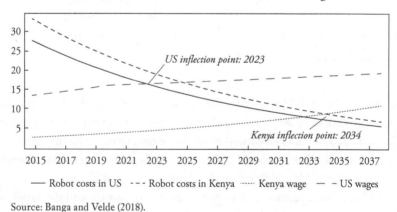

Source: Banga and Velde (2018).

Moreover, as the complementarity of ICT and newer technologies with high skills increases, the importance of the availability of skills in firm location decisions is likely to grow and, therefore, support reshoring of production. Ongoing research at the OECD finds a negative link between robot use and offshoring across countries and industries.[42] Currently, the pace of reshoring is slow. For example, between 2010 and 2012 there were about three offshoring companies for every one reshoring company.[43] But the nature of technological progress, the importance of high-skilled workers, and increasingly sophisticated consumer tastes support the potential for the pace of reshoring to accelerate in the future.

GROWTH IN GLOBAL VALUE CHAINS TO STALL. Another observation that supports the view that convergence will likely stall and possibly reverse is the slowdown in GVC growth since 2011. This slowdown appears to be structural. The length of production chains, or the number of times value added is counted as an output in the full production chain,[44] has been declining for GVCs between 2011 and 2015 in emerging and advanced economies and across both manufacturing and services (figure 4-12).

The decline in production lengths for manufacturing was greater in emerging economies while the decline for services was greater in advanced economies, both driven by a declining number of national border crossings in complex GVCs.[45] Meanwhile, the production length of simple GVCs rose in both groups of countries, with the rise more notable for emerging economies. The increase in production lengths before and after national border crossings suggests a shift toward division of labor *within* as opposed to across national borders.

Further, the complementarity of production and higher-skilled labor increases with the adoption of new technologies and thereby reduces the comparative advantage of developing countries in labor-intensive manufacturing. The standards, skills, and infrastructure requirements in GVCs raise the bar for low-income countries to participate[46] and provide less scope to develop manufacturing in these countries.

In the coming decades the pace and nature of technological progress will add further frictions in the flying geese paradigm. Greater division of labor within countries and increasing complementarity between newer technologies and high skills make it difficult for developing countries to participate in GVCs and increase their share of global manufacturing activity. Declining costs of labor-saving technologies and more investment

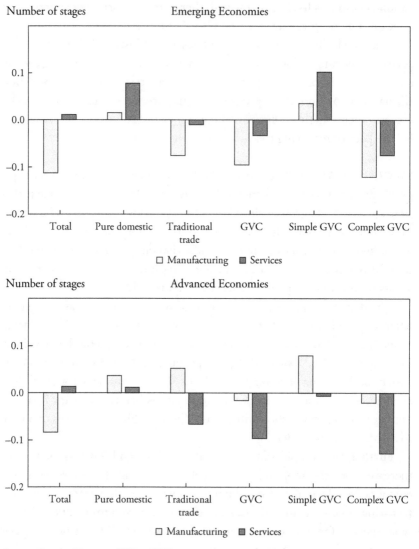

FIGURE 4-12. **Change in Production Length by Value Added Activity, 2011–2015**

Source: Degain, Meng, and Wang (2017).

in technological innovations in today's manufacturing centers will likely lead to an even greater concentration of global manufacturing activity.

The Outlook for Manufacturing Output and Servicification

In the coming decades the share of manufacturing value added in GDP will likely continue to decline globally. In developed economies, where the prospects for manufacturing value added to grow are stronger, rising contributions from services as well as higher income elasticities for services could keep manufacturing shares of GDP from rising. In developing economies, as technological progress erodes comparative advantages in low-cost production and raises the bar for participation in GVCs, peak shares of manufacturing value added in GDP will continue to decline.

The smile curve and the rising value added contributions of service activities in manufacturing is a useful starting point to illustrate these tendencies. Higher income elasticity of services and greater adoption of increasingly sophisticated products by consumers raise the potential for higher value additions in postproduction service activities like product servicing, customer service, marketing, outreach, copyright, and branding. With growing embedded services in manufactured goods, including applications and add-on services, the capability for postproduction service value addition will increase. At the front end of the value chain, product design, research and development, software development, and professional business services like market research are increasingly important in value addition and in the competitiveness of manufactured products. Overall, the rising value added contributions in pre- and postproduction service activities and the declining relative importance of the production phase of the value chain will result in steeper smile curves (see figure 4-13 for an illustration). At the extreme, the value added during the production phase could become so insignificant that its activities will be reshored and conducted by advanced economies.

In the future, comparative advantages at the technological frontier—advanced robotics, high skill availability, digital infrastructure, and modern regulatory frameworks—and significantly higher investment in Industry 4.0 technologies—are supportive of rising manufacturing production in developed economies. However, it remains uncertain whether this increase will result in a higher share of manufacturing value added in GDP. In addition to rising shares of services in manufacturing, income elasticities in advanced economies for services are higher than those for manufacturing.

FIGURE 4-13. Greater Intensification of Servicification in the Future

Share of product's total value added

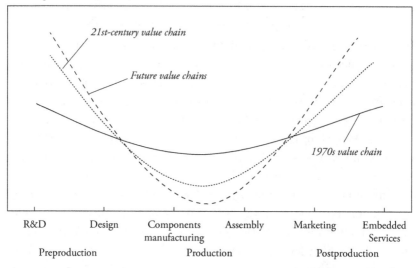

| R&D | Design | Components manufacturing | Assembly | Marketing | Embedded Services |

Preproduction   Production   Postproduction

Source: Authors.

As such, the demand for services could rise faster and, from an accounting standpoint, restrain the increase in the share of manufacturing or even cause it to fall. For these reasons, the outlook of the manufacturing share of GDP in advanced economies remains ambiguous.

In developing countries the outlook for manufacturing to play its traditional role as an escalator industry that drives sustained aggregate growth—a function that had already been elusive for most developing countries over the last few decades—is not particularly bright. With steeper smile curves, the production or assembly phases of value chains, where developing countries have typically contributed, are likely to contribute less and have lower potential to drive structural transformation.

Moreover, as manufacturing processes adopt new technologies, it will become more difficult for lower-skilled labor in developing countries to substitute for capital and attract more value additions in a value chain. Aside from any differences in the marginal costs of labor and capital, the range of production techniques that yield the same output will decline.[47] In other words, the elasticity of substitution between unskilled labor and other factors of production (including skilled labor and capital) declines as newer technologies become embodied in production. Higher quality standards, greater precision, and rising skill requirements from newer technologies make it difficult to use unskilled labor as a substitute for capital or skilled labor. Along GVCs, the substitutability of low-skill labor for other production inputs is even less likely given the standards imposed by global firms.[48]

Not all trends directly suggest lower manufacturing output shares in GDP for developing countries, but, as discussed in the next section, the upside will still require significant investment in skills and soft and hard infrastructure and that these countries adopt a multifaceted approach to industrial development and structural transformation.

Outlook for Manufacturing Employment: For Machines and the Skilled Worker

The future of manufacturing will see continuing declines in employment shares of manufacturing in both industrial and developing countries. The increasing adoption of Industry 4.0 technologies will lead to higher productivity in manufacturing but will likely put downward pressure on the labor share of manufacturing. The skill bias of technological progress and the increased capital intensity of production with labor-saving technologies will continue to reduce the need for less-skilled workers and, by polarizing the job market and placing a premium on high skills, contribute to rising income inequality.

The adoption of robots and machines to automate routine tasks, which tend to be clustered at the mid-level of the skills spectrum, is contributing to greater polarization between high- and low-skill jobs.[49] In the United States, for example, employment growth in routine manual and cognitive occupations has been slowing since the 1990s and has turned negative since 2007, while nonroutine manual and cognitive employment grew faster and continues to grow (figure 4-14). Higher adoption of labor-saving technologies and production techniques has reallocated some middle-skilled labor into lower-wage service sectors while increasing the demand for high-skilled labor.[50]

Further, developments in artificial intelligence and machine learning are expanding the scope of automatable activities beyond strictly routine activities and into higher value added professional functions like legal services, investment advice, and medical imaging. While automation and artificial intelligence may also generate demand for labor in nonautomated tasks, they will likely not offset the jobs lost. Reshoring of production back to advanced economies will provide some offset for those countries, but these will be limited in scale given the capital intensity of production, which drove

FIGURE 4-14. U.S. Employment Growth by Broad Occupation Category,
Subperiods from 1983–2015

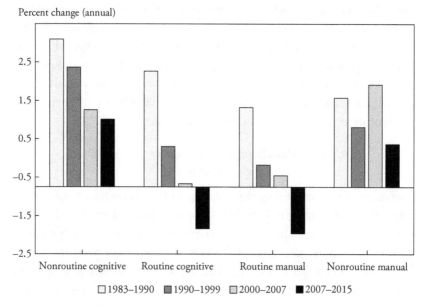

Percent change (annual)

□ 1983–1990   ■ 1990–1999   □ 2000–2007   ■ 2007–2015

Source: Valletta (2016).

the decision to reshore production. For example, data on U.S. multinationals indicate that despite the growing share of capital investment deployed in the United States in low and medium-low technology manufacturing industries, the share of employment has not increased.[51] This increasing capital intensity is consistent with the prediction that firms will continue shifting manufacturing activity back to developed economies, though with less potential to drive a rebound in labor shares, as fewer but higher-skilled workers could satisfy labor demand.

Another factor that supports the reduction in a share of manufacturing employment is population aging in developed economies, like South Korea and Singapore, and developing economies, like China. As population aging weighs on the labor force and pushes up labor costs, firms will have greater incentives to make production processes even more capital intensive, particularly in industries that rely on middle-aged workers.[52]

In developing economies the baseline outlook for employment shares in manufacturing is also downward trending but with potentially more severe consequences than in advanced economies. Lower peak shares of manufacturing employment than experienced by higher income countries will likely be exacerbated by technological innovations and increasing capital intensity of production. In the early 1990s, average exposures of employment activities to automation were higher in developed economies, leaving workers at higher risk of being substituted by ICT and machines than in developing economies. By the early 2010s, however, average exposures in developing countries had overtaken those in developed economies in about half of all industries, including manufacturing.[53]

With peak manufacturing shares of labor already declining, the economics of technology adoption by firms will lead to further declines. Lower costs of capital will add further wage pressures on low-skilled labor performing routine and automatable tasks to maintain competitiveness, resulting in greater labor market polarization over the coming decades.[54]

To be sure, there remains a window of opportunity in industrial economies to capture manufacturing jobs, but there is urgency to act, as this window of opportunity is narrowing fast. Moreover, as the cost of capital falls further, industrial economy firms will have greater incentives to reshore the manufacturing production currently located in developing economies and contribute to lower manufacturing employment shares. In many industrial economies, rapidly aging population and declining labor force growth helps to cushion the effect of automation. In developing economies, however, where populations are young and the labor force is growing rapidly, lower growth in manufacturing employment poses a stark challenge.

New demand for labor and unforeseen occupations may emerge in the future. In low- and middle-income countries, many workers are employed in occupations that did not exist three decades ago, including 4 million app developers in India or 100,000 data labelers in China, while many other occupations evolved to require new skills, like marketing professionals who may also need to write algorithms.[55] As technological change and automation reshape demand for labor, particularly in manufacturing and other sectors with high exposure to automation, the demand for new and high skills is likely to continue to grow. In developing economies employment growth in high-skilled jobs has also tended to outpace employment growth in middle- and low-skilled jobs in the fifteen years between 2000 and 2015 (figure 4-15). During this time, labor shares of manufacturing have continued to decline, suggesting reduced employment elasticity in manufacturing.

In addition to lowering labor shares in manufacturing, technological innovation will contribute to higher income inequality. By replacing

FIGURE 4-15. Increasing Share of High-Skilled Employment in
Developing Countries, circa 2000–15

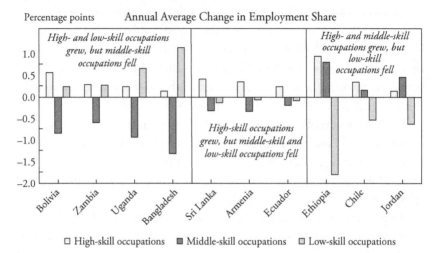

Source: World Bank (2019), *World Development Report*.

low- and middle-skill manual jobs while acting as a complement to high-skilled workers, modern technologies raise skill premium. The pressure on wider income inequality will be felt in both industrial and developing economies, with the extent of the inequality dependent on remedial policy measures, including adapting educational systems, reskilling the workforce, and enhancing worker or social protection systems.

Structural Transformation and Economic Development Reconsidered

As noted earlier, not all global trends suggest reduced ability of developing countries to develop manufacturing, but the upside will be more limited and require significant investment in skills and infrastructure. In what follows, we explore some of the viable options.

Opportunities for Industrialization Still Exist

First, a rising middle class in the developing world could lead manufacturers to locate closer to fast-growing consumer markets. Recent estimates suggest that by the end of 2018 the majority of the world became "middle

FIGURE 4-16. Projections for Shares of Global Consumption by Region

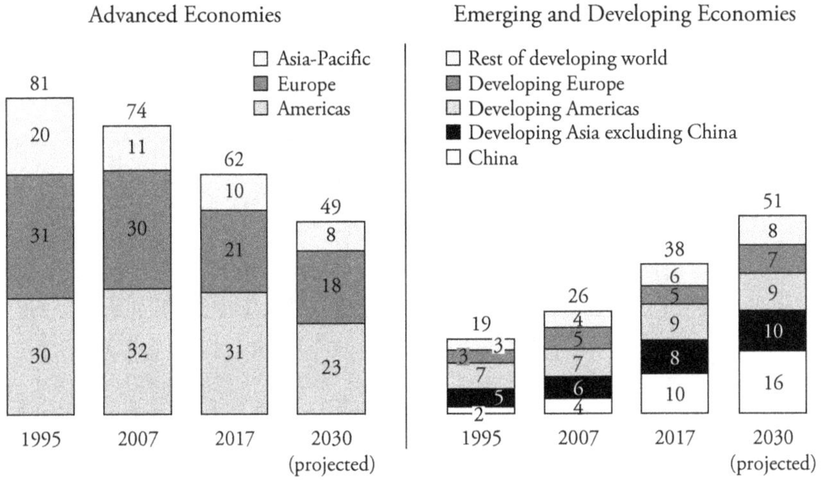

Advanced Economies

- ☐ Asia-Pacific
- ■ Europe
- ☐ Americas

Emerging and Developing Economies

- ☐ Rest of developing world
- ■ Developing Europe
- ☐ Developing Americas
- ■ Developing Asia excluding China
- ☐ China

Source: Lund and others (2019).

a. Asia-Pacific incudes Australia, Hong Kong, Japan, Singapore, South Korea, and New Zealand.

class" or "rich" for the first time in human civilization and that by 2030 there will be over 2 billion more people in the global middle class (5.3 billion) than are vulnerable (2.3 billion), poor (450 million), or rich (300 million), making it the fastest growth segment. The majority of the global middle class will be in developing countries, with purchasing power particularly concentrated in Asia, where over 1 billion millennials currently live.[56]

The greater emphasis on speed to market coupled with the ability to produce smaller quantities of goods at lower costs thanks to newer technologies has increased the scope and demand for production to move closer to the consumer,[57] along with the incentive for countries to invest in the requirements for modern manufacturing. Proximity to consumers has motivated multinational firms to move production back onshore and could therefore drive potential to move closer to where consumer markets are most rapidly growing.

McKinsey Global Institute projects that by 2030 the developing world (excluding China) will account for 35 percent of global consumption, with emerging Asian countries like Thailand, Malaysia, and the Philippines leading the way, and that by 2025 emerging markets will consume two-thirds of the world's manufactured goods.[58] Figure 4-16 breaks these projections down by region.

FIGURE 4-17. **Share of Intra-African Exports in Total Exports, Manufacturing Sectors, 2000–13**

Share of intra-Africa exports in total exports

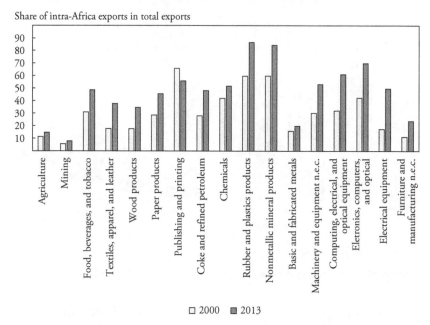

□ 2000   ■ 2013

Source: Nayyar and Nee (2016); from Hallward-Driemeier and Nayyar (2018).

In Africa the market size is rapidly growing along with the middle class. Africa's current population of 1.2 billion people is projected to double in the next thirty years, and the region's middle class will experience the second-highest growth rate (66 percent) by 2030. Urbanization is also very rapid. Between 2015 and 2030, the number of African cities with more than 5 million residents will jump from six to seventeen, faster than any other region. In just seven years, from 2015 to 2022, the number of active smartphone users in Africa will double to 636 million, twice the projected number in North America. Chinese firms relocating to Africa serve primarily local markets. Unlike their activities in China, which are destined for exports, 93 percent of their African production is sold locally.[59] Figure 4-17 helps to illustrate the growing role of manufacturing to service local and regional markets in Africa. Between 2000 and 2013 most manufacturing industries in sub-Saharan Africa increased the share of their intra-African exports in their total exports.

Still, the promise of the African market will remain smaller in scale compared with the global markets that industrialized economies served during their export- and manufacturing-led development paths. Importantly, the rising capital intensity of manufacturing will make it difficult to generate large-scale creation of formal-sector jobs for the estimated 10–12 million African young people entering the job market every year.[60]

Second, there is still scope to boost further manufacturing activity across emerging and developing economies (EMDEs). Among emerging market economies where manufacturing has played a key role in driving structural economic transformation over recent decades, persistent productivity gaps with the world's industrialized economies suggest that there is scope for further gains in these economies. For example, in emerging Asia, labor productivity falls significantly short of the OECD average. In Malaysia, for example, the productivity gap in industry with the OECD increased by over one-half between 1975–79 and 2015–16.[61] These productivity gaps with the frontier suggest that there is scope to make further, productivity-enhancing investments in infrastructure and skills to avoid falling behind or to maintain current levels of competitiveness.

Among developing countries there is still time to enter GVCs or further develop their manufacturing sectors as well. In response to rising labor costs, many Chinese firms are choosing to upgrade production technologies by automating. But many are also looking to relocate to areas where labor costs are more competitive both within and outside of China. Developing countries can attract these industries, and some countries, including Vietnam, Bangladesh, and Ethiopia, have all benefited from offshoring by Chinese firms.

Commodity producers in EMDEs also have a comparative advantage to develop commodity-based manufacturing and move up the industrial value chain. For example, Africa produces around 75 percent of the world's cocoa but accounts for just 5 percent of the global chocolate market,[62] suggesting great scope to move up the value chain through industrialization. From a jobs perspective, some commodity-based manufacturing—food-processing, for example—accounts for around 13 percent of global manufacturing employment, second only to textiles and apparel in global manufacturing employment intensity, and could still drive employment gains. In the future of manufacturing, industrial economies may have the technologies and the skills but still will not have the natural resource endowments of commodity producers. This presents perhaps a unique opportunity for commodity-rich developing countries to industrialize in these subsectors and help drive structural transformation.

Beyond some commodity-specific manufacturing subsectors, however, harnessing the opportunities for industrialization at large in the twenty-first century requires countries to act with greater urgency to improve business environments and invest heavily in digital infrastructure and skills to make their economies attractive. For example, the cost of ICT capital—which is instrumental in enabling the adoption of manufacturing technologies and in participating in GVCs with global firms—in Africa is more than three times that in lower-middle income countries and nearly eighteen times that in Brazil, India, and China.[63] The countries that will achieve better infrastructure, skills, and business environments will attract manufacturing industries looking for entry points to serve regional markets.

While opportunities still exist to develop traditional manufacturing industries to serve the local and global market, their limited scope for large-scale employment and structural transformation will remain a challenge for EMDEs. In this context, a third, nonmutually exclusive, option is to develop industries that share the tradability and higher productivity features of manufacturing but have great scope to generate employment.

The Rise of New Industries

New research by the Africa Growth Initiative at Brookings and UNU Wider identified a set of "industries without smokestacks," including horticulture, agro-processing, tourism, and some ICT-based services, that fit the bill for driving structural transformation. The study found that these industries share three key characteristics with traditional manufacturing: (1) they are tradable, (2) productivity in these sectors is higher than that of agriculture, and, importantly, (3) they have demonstrated the capacity to absorb large numbers of moderately skilled workers. The results, published in the volume *Industries Without Smokestacks*,[64] document a new pattern of structural change emerging in Africa spurred by industries without smokestacks, a pattern different from that of the manufacturing-led transformation of East Asia.

ICT-based services, tourism, and transport are outpacing the growth of manufacturing in many African countries. Between 1998 and 2015, services exports grew more than six times faster than merchandise exports. Kenya, Rwanda, Senegal, and South Africa have vibrant ICT-based services sectors. Tourism is Rwanda's largest single export activity, accounting for about 30 percent of total exports. In 2014, 9.5 million tourists visited South

Africa, contributing 3 percent to its GDP. Ethiopia, Ghana, Kenya, and Senegal all actively participate in global horticultural value chains. Ethiopia has achieved extraordinary success in flower exports, so much so that the country is now a global player in the sector.

These findings suggest that it is possible to develop a strategy for structural transformation based on the development of these industries. Like traditional manufacturing, these smokestackless industries benefit from technological change, economies of scale, and agglomeration. Moreover, they have the added advantage of being less exposed to automation, which, notwithstanding its many benefits, presents challenges for countries where the overriding priority is to create a sufficient number of formal-sector jobs.

If properly stewarded, smokestackless industries could play the same role in Africa's development, as well as in that of many developing Asian economies, as manufacturing did in the industrialized economies. Strategies to develop these sectors should emphasize three interrelated factors: (1) infrastructure and skills development; (2) the capacity to export, including infrastructure; and (3) agglomeration. For example, tradable services require reliable infrastructure for export through high-speed data transmission (particularly ICT services) while trade logistics matter for agro-processing and horticulture exports. Skills are important inputs for all three industries, as for manufacturing. The capacity to export is critical for these sectors to benefit from technology transfer from the global frontier and to enhance productivity, a key ingredient in structural transformation. Agglomeration is also important due to the role of geography and clustering for skills transfer, scale, or benefiting from special economic zones.[65]

Fortunately, the choice is not between traditional manufacturing industries and industries without smokestacks. Developing countries should adopt a multifaceted approach to economic development based on traditional manufacturing, where opportunities exist to do so, alongside industries without smokestacks to accelerate structural transformation.

Conclusion

The global economy and the global manufacturing landscape are shifting. Technological change is disrupting virtually all sectors and no country is immune to its challenges, nor is any country barred from realizing its opportunities. Over the last two centuries of industrial revolutions and technological unemployment, societies around the world have found a way forward. Today, the global economy is at another juncture where technology is shifting nations' comparative advantages in manufacturing and changing traditional pathways of development.

While it is difficult to predict with certainty the future of global manufacturing, our analysis of trends and the fundamental drivers lead us to the following projections. The Great Convergence we observed over the past decades will stall and possibly reverse as current global manufacturing hubs consolidate their positions, and the increasing skills content and infrastructure and standard requirements will make it harder for developing countries to participate in global value chains. The value added of manufacturing as a share of GDP, particularly during the production phase, will continue to decline with the increasing importance of high-skill services in manufacturing products. Importantly, the job creation capacity of manufacturing will continue to fall as competition with the adoption of labor-saving technologies and increasing capital intensity of production rises.

For industrialized economies, comparative advantages for manufacturing are shifting in their favor. Their competitiveness in skills, digital readiness, infrastructure, and overall regulatory frameworks give them an advantage, and their sizable investments in research and development and cutting edge technologies are positioning them for an even greater share in global manufacturing. While population aging in many of the industrialized economies might help to partially cushion the effect of labor-saving technologies on employment, inequality arising from skill premiums and the hollowing out of middle-skill occupations will be increasingly important challenges that have broad social, political, and economic implications for policymakers to address.

For developing countries, the bar for manufacturing-led development is higher than it was for most of today's industrialized nations. Increasingly efficient and cheap machines that can automate tasks are being adopted in manufacturing at higher rates than other sectors, eroding the large-scale job-creation benefit of manufacturing and raising the bar for developing countries to participate in global manufacturing. With further advancements in Industry 4.0 and future technologies, the rising complementarity of skills and technology will place greater pressure on education systems and skill development to keep up with future production technologies.

In this context, some of the same technologies that are closing the window of opportunity for industrialization in developing economies are also facilitating the growth of industries without smokestacks and a new kind of structural transformation in developing countries. Both manufacturing and smokestackless industries should anchor policies that promote a broader view of structural transformation.

For all economies, with the right skills, infrastructure, and regulatory or policy frameworks in place, it will be easier to navigate toward inclusive growth and greater well-being. Investments in skills for the jobs of the future, infrastructure that supports digitization and trade logistics, regulatory frameworks suitable for the digital age, and improvements in the ease of doing business and private investment cut across smokestack and smokestackless industries. They offer the potential to travel down multiple paths toward development in the twenty-first century.

NOTES

We acknowledge excellent research support by Dhruv Gandhi for which we are very grateful.

The views expressed in this paper are those of the authors and do not necessarily represent the views of the IMF, its Executive Board, or IMF management.

1. Rodrik (2015).

2. More than three-quarters of all countries are experiencing declines in their manufacturing value added in GDP, with Africa's manufacturing as a share of total economic activity stagnating at around 10 percent.

3. Pritchett (1997).

4. The year 1970 is the earliest for which data are available across countries, though peak manufacturing shares may have occurred prior to 1970.

5. Baldwin (2016).

6. Hallward-Dreiemer and Nayyar (2018).

7. Baldwin (2016).

8. Akamatsu (1962).

9. This can also include information costs, trade governance, insecure contracts, and so forth.

10. Hallward-Dreiemer and Nayyar (2018).

11. Hallward-Dreiemer and Nayyar (2018).

12. Hallward-Driemeier and Nayyar (2018).

13. Rodrik (2015).

14. For countries that reached peak shares after 1990, employment shares peaked at around a third of the ratios experienced before 1990 for other countries, while the corresponding ratio for value added shares was almost one-half (Rodrik 2015).

15. Organisation for Economic Co-operation and Development (2017).

16. Acemoglu and Autor (2011).

17. Degain, Meng, and Wang (2017).

18. Shih (1996).

19. Ali-Yrkkö and others (2011) estimated the value added contributions of upstream and downstream activities in the production of a Nokia N95 phone, released around the same time as the original iPhone. They found that the parts (processors, memories, integrated circuits, displays, and cameras) accounted for one-third of the product's value, and assembly only accounted for 2 percent. The remaining two-thirds of the product's value came from related services, including internal support services (30 percent), licenses (4 percent), distribution (4 percent), retailing (11 percent), and operating profit (16 percent) (Hallward-Driemeier and Nayyar 2018).

20. Meng, Ye, and Wei (2017).

21. On the other hand, services value added in manufacturing output accounts for just 12 percent of total value added in the services sector, and the share of final expenditures that went to manufactured goods has been steadily declining over the 1995–2011 period (International Monetary Fund 2018b).

22. An interpretation of rising services content of manufacturing (and declining manufacturing) is that it reflects better accounting of services previously performed by manufacturing and incorrectly classified as services. As manufacturers began to outsource their services needs, it has resulted in a decline in manufacturing and an increase in services. Hallward-Driemeier and Nayyar (2018) estimate that this accounts for only 10 percent of the decrease in manufacturing.

23. Gebauer, Fleisch, and Friedli (2005); Hallward-Dreiemer and Nayyar (2018).

24. Lund and others (2019).

25. Lund and others (2019).

26. Bahar and Foda (2019).

27. International Federation of Robots (2017); Banga and Velde (2018).

28. Deloitte (2018).

29. ING (2017); Banga and Velde (2018).

30. Deloitte (2018).

31. Potential contributions to global GDP through productivity gains and product enhancements that stimulate consumer demand include increased product variety, personalization, and affordability (PricewaterhouseCoopers 2018).

32. Trudeau (2018).

33. This includes both the monetary dimension (transportation, insurance, other fees, and so forth) and the nonmonetary dimension (regulation, licensing, trade governance, and so forth) of trade costs.

34. Baldwin (2016).

35. Ceglowski and others (2015).

36. Hallward-Dreiemer and Nayyar (2018).

37. Boffa, Santoni, and Taglioni (2017); Hallward-Dreiemer and Nayyar (2018).

38. Xu and others (2017).

39. Lund and others (2019).

40. Banga and Velde (2018).

41. "Reshoring Initiative" (2018).

42. Organisation for Economic Co-operation and Development (2016).

43. De Backer and others (2016).

44. Wang and others (2017).

45. Degain, Meng, and Wang (2017).

46. Rodrik (2018).

47. Rodrik (2018).

48. Rodrik (2018).

49. On the lower end, examples include care-taking or janitorial functions that require spontaneous movements, picking up random objects, and other physical activities that are more difficult for a robot to automate without specific, predictable, and codified instructions. On the higher end, examples include design and managerial functions that require expertise and other nonroutine cognitive activities that are difficult to automate with today's technologies (Chui, Manyika, and Miremadi 2016).

50. Acemoglu and Autor (2011); Autor and Dorn (2013).

51. De Backer and others (2016).

52. Acemoglu and Restrepo (2018).

53. Das and Hilgenstock (2018).

54. Das and Hilgenstock (2018).

55. World Bank (2019).

56. Kharas and Hamel (2018); Hamel, Fenz, and Hofer (2018); World Data Lab (2018).

57. De Backer and others (2016).

58. Lund and others (2019).

59. Leke, Chironga, and Desvaux (2018).

60. African Development Bank Group (2018).

61. Felipe (2018).

62. Adesina (2018).

63. Banga and Velde (2018).

64. Newfarmer, Page, and Tarp (2019).

65. Page (2018); Coulibaly (2018).

REFERENCES

Acemoglu, Daron, and David Autor. 2011. "Skill, Tasks and Technologies: Implications for Employment and Earnings," in *Handbook of Labor Economics*, vol. 4 (Amsterdam: Elsevier).

Acemoglu, Daron, and Pascual Restrepo. 2018. "Demographics and Automation," NBER Working Paper 24421 (Cambridge, Mass.: National Bureau of Economic Research).

Adesina, Akinwumi. 2018. "A Roadmap for African Industrialization." *Project Syndicate*, May 31 (www.project-syndicate.org/commentary/africa-industri alization-roadmap-by-akinwumi-adesina-2018-05?barrier=accesspaylog).

African Development Bank Group. 2018. *Jobs for Youth in Africa*. Report. Abidjan, Côte d'Ivoire.

Akamatsu, Kaname. 1962. "A Historical Pattern of Economic Growth in Developing Countries." *The Developing Economies* 1, s. 1, pp. 3–25.

Ali-Yrkkö, Jyrki, and others. 2011. "Who Captures Value in Global Supply Chains? Case Nokia N95 Smartphone." *Journal of Industry, Competition and Trade*, 11, no. 3, pp. 263–78.

Autor, David H., and David Dorn. 2013. "The Growth of Low-Skill Service Jobs and the Polarization of the US Labor Market." *American Economic Review*, 103, no. 5, pp. 1553–97.

Bahar, Dany, and Karim Foda. 2019. "The Technology-Productivity Paradox: Why Has Productivity Growth Slowed?" in *Productive Equity: The Twin Challenges of Reviving Productivity and Reducing Inequality*. Report. Washington, D.C.: The Brookings Institution and the Chumir Foundation for Ethics in Leadership.

Baldwin, Richard. 2016. *The Great Convergence: Information Technology and the New Globalization* (Harvard University Press).

Banga, Karishma, and Dirk Willem te Velde. 2018. Supporting Economic Transformation: Digitalization and the Future of Manufacturing in Africa. Report. London: Overseas Development Institute.

Boffa, Mauro, Gianluca Santoni, and Daria Taglioni. 2017. "From China with Love," Unpublished manuscript (Washington, D.C.: World Bank). [Cited in Hallward-Dreiemer and Nayyar 2018]

Ceglowski, Janet, and others. 2015. "Can Africa Compete with China in Manufacturing? The Role of Relative Unit Labor Costs," Development Policy Research Unit Working Paper 201504 (University of Cape Town).

Chui, Michael, James Manyika, and Mehdi Miremadi. 2016. "Where Machines Could Replace Humans—and Where They Can't (Yet)." *McKinsey Quarterly* (July).

Coulibaly, Brahima. 2018. "Africa's Alternative Path to Development." *Project Syndicate*, May 3.

———. 2019. "The Future of Work in Africa: What Strategies for Jobs in the Digital Age?" In *Creating Decent Jobs: Strategies, Policies, and Instruments*. Report. (Abidjan, Côte d'Ivoire: African Development Bank Group).

Das, Mitali, and Benjamin Hilgenstock. 2018. "The Exposure to Routinization: Labor Market Implications for Developing Countries," IMF Working Paper 18/135 (Washington, D.C.: International Monetary Fund).

De Backer, Kohn, and others. 2016. "Reshoring: Myth or Reality?" OECD Science, Technology and Industry Policy Papers, no. 27 (Paris: Organisation for Economic Co-operation and Development).

Degain, Christophe, Bo Meng, and Zhi Wang. 2017. "Recent Trends in Global Trade and Global Value Chains," in *Global Value Chain and Development Report 2017*. Report. Washington, D.C: World Bank.

Deloitte. 2018. *Exponential Technologies in Manufacturing*. Report. Council on Competitiveness, Deloitte and Singularity University.

Felipe, Jesus. 2018. "Asia's Industrial Transformation: The Role of Manufacturing and Global Value Chains (Part 1)," Economics Working Paper Series 549 (Manila: Asian Development Bank), July.

Gebauer, Heiko, Elgar Fleisch, and Thomas Friedli. 2005. "Overcoming the Service Paradox in Manufacturing Companies." *European Management Journal* 23, no. 1, pp. 14–26.

Hallward-Driemeier, Mary, and Gaurav Nayyar. 2018. Trouble in the Making? The Future of Manufacturing-Led Development (Washington, D.C.: World Bank).

Hamel, Kristofer, Katharina Fenz, and Martin Hofer. 2018. "How to Harness the Spending Power of Millennials: Move beyond the US." *Future Development* (blog), Brookings Institution, April 30.

ING. 2017. *3D Printing: A Threat to Global Trade*. Report. London.

International Federation of Robots (IFR). 2017. IFR Database (www.ifr.org).

International Monetary Fund. 2018a. "Is Productivity Growth Shared in a Globalized Economy?" *World Economic Outlook* (April), pp. 173–214.

———. 2018b. "Manufacturing Jobs: Implications for Productivity and Inequality." *World Economic Outlook* (April), pp. 129–72.

"Job Creation Lessons from Kenya," Africa Growth Initiative Working Paper 20 (Brookings Institution).

Kharas, Homi, and Kristofer Hamel. 2018. "A Global Tipping Point: Half the World Is Now Middle Class or Wealthier." *Future Development* (blog), Brookings Institution, September 27.

Leke, Acha, Mutsa Chironga, and Georges Desvaux. 2018. Africa's Business Revolution: How to Succeed in the World's Next Big Growth Market (Harvard Business Review Press).

Lund, Susan, and others. 2019. *Globalization in Transition: The Future of Trade and Value Chains*. Report. McKinsey Global Institute, January.

Meng, Bo, Ming Ye, and Shang-Jin Wei. 2017. "Value-added Gains and Job Opportunities in Global Value Chains." IDE Discussion Paper No. 668, IDE–JETRO, Chiba City, Japan.

Newfarmer, Richard, John Page, and Finn Tarp. 2019. *Industries Without Smokestacks: Industrialization in Africa Reconsidered* (Oxford University Press).

Organisation for Economic Co-operation and Development. 2016. "Skills for a Digital World," Policy Brief on the Future of Work (Paris), December.

———. 2017. *Employment Outlook 2017*. Report. Paris.

Page, John. 2018. "Structural Transformation in Africa: The Road Not Taken," in *Foresight Africa: Top Priorities for the Continent in 2018*. Report. Brookings Institution.

PricewaterhouseCoopers. 2018. *Sizing the Prize: What's the Real Value of AI for Your Business and How Can You Capitalise?* Report. London.

Pritchett, Lant. 1997. "Divergence, Big Time." *Journal of Economic Perspectives*, 11, no. 3, pp. 3–17.

"Reshoring Initiative 2017 Data Report: Reshoring Plus FDI Job Announcements up 2,800% Since 2010." 2018. *Reshoring Initiative* (blog), April 10.

Rodrik, Dani. 2015. "Premature Deindustrialization," NBER Working Paper 20935 (Cambridge, Mass.: National Bureau of Economic Research).

Shih, Stan. 1996. *Me-too Is Not My Style: Challenge Difficulties, Break through Bottlenecks, Create Values* (Taipei: The Acer Foundation).

Tan, Kim Song, and James Tang. 2016. *Managing Skills Challenge in ASEAN-5*. Executive Summary. Singapore Management University.

Trudeau, Justin. 2018. "Justin Trudeau's Davos Address in Full." Address at the World Economic Forum, Davos, Switzerland, January 23 (www.weforum.org/agenda/2018/01/pm-keynote-remarks-for-world-economic-forum-2018/).

Valletta, Robert. 2016. "Recent Flattening in the Higher Education Wage Premium: Polarization, Skill Downgrading, or Both?" NBER Working Paper 22935 (Cambridge, Mass.: National Bureau of Economic Research).

Wang, Zhi, and others. 2017. "Measures of Participation in Global Value Chains and Global Business Cycles," NBER Working Paper 23222 (Cambridge, Mass.: National Bureau of Economic Research).

World Bank. 2019. *World Development Report 2019: The Changing Nature of Work*. Report. Washington, D.C.: World Bank.

World Data Lab. 2018 (www.worlddata.io/).

Xu, Jiajun, and others. 2017. "Adjusting to Rising Costs in Chinese Light Manufacturing—What Opportunities for Developing Countries?" SET Report. London: Overseas Development Institute.

FIVE

The Digital Transformation of International Trade

JOSHUA P. MELTZER

Data is driving innovation, with opportunity for a new wave of productivity growth. Global data flows are also transforming international trade, increasing trade in services, and providing opportunities for small business and developing countries to participate in the global economy. The digital opportunity is also economy-wide, as data-driven innovation can be deployed across economic sectors.

Access to data including global data flows supports cloud computing, digital platforms, and access to information. Yet governments are grappling with how to balance the opportunities from global data flows and digital trade with the need to achieve domestic goals such as protection of privacy, strengthening cybersecurity, or ensuring effective access to data for law enforcement purposes. In many cases governments are restricting data flows and requiring data be localized, often taking the view that such action is needed to address regulatory challenges raised by digital trade. Yet such data restriction risks reducing many of the economic and productivity enhancing opportunities from digital trade.[1]

Government regulation of data also often discriminates against foreign entities and is inconsistent with international trade law commitments under the World Trade Organization (WTO) or in Free Trade Agreements (FTAs).[2]

Part two of this chapter looks at the importance for economic growth and trade of cross-border data flows and assesses the arguments for and against the impact of data on innovation and productivity, including the impact of digital technologies on competition. Part three discusses how the internet and data are transforming international trade. Part four provides an overview of barriers to digital trade. Part five discusses the relevance of the WTO and FTAs to digital trade. Part six concludes.

Measuring Data in Economic Growth and International Trade

Currently, approximately half of the world is online. Between 2005 and 2021, global internet traffic will increase 127-fold. Internet access is also increasingly happening using mobile devices. By 2021 the number of devices connected to the internet will be triple the global population.[3] Digital opportunity has also expanded beyond ICT to become an input into the economy broadly. For instance, the U.S. International Trade Commission (ITC) found that digitally intensive industries in the United States include content industries; communications; finance and insurance; retail; health care, education, and manufacturing.[4]

The digitization of economies and trade should improve efficiency, innovation, and increase productivity.[5] Yet measurement of the impact of the internet and data flows on economic growth and international trade are limited. For one, measurement is made difficult by their general and transformational economic effects.[6] Similar to electricity, the internet is a "horizontal" enabler, making it hard to delineate its economic benefits.

Governments and international organizations also do not collect regular and comprehensive data on the impact of the internet and data on growth, jobs, and trade. Official statistics that do capture cross-border data flows are often limited to tech-related sectors of the economy. There is also the challenge of quantifying the role of data in trade, given that many cross-border data transfers do not involve money changing hands as information moves from one country to another. Movement of data from Country A to Country B is usually accomplished by copying the data, which makes cross-border data flows hard to count in traditional trade statistics based on imports and exports.[7]

Some studies have estimated the economic importance of the internet for growth and trade using economic models. For instance, McKinsey Global Institute estimated that in 2014 global data flows contributed $2.8 trillion to the global economy,[8] a figure that could reach $11 trillion by 2025.[9] A study by the U.S. ITC found that in the United States in 2014, digital trade (within the United States and globally) raised U.S. GDP by 3.4 percent to 4.8 percent by increasing productivity and lowering the costs of trade; it has also increased wages and likely contributed to as many as 2.4 million new jobs.[10] A 2018 study by the U.S. Bureau of Economic Analysis concluded that from 2006–16 the U.S. digital economy grew at an average annual rate of 5.6 percent, outpacing the average annual rate of growth of 1.5 percent for the overall U.S. economy, and accounted for 6.5 percent of U.S. output, 3.9 percent of employment, and 6.7 percent of employee compensation.[11]

Another approach to getting a sense of the importance of data for trade has been to determine which services are "digitally deliverable"—services that could be provided online. The United Nations Conference on Trade and Development (UNCTAD) found that some 50 percent of all traded services are enabled by the technology sector, including cross-border data flows.[12] Somewhat similarly, the U.S. ITC estimated that, by the early part of this decade, U.S. exports globally of digitally deliverable services were already 61 percent of total U.S. services exports and 53 percent of services imports.[13] EU exports and imports of digitally deliverable services were at similar levels.[14]

Digital Innovation but Low Productivity?

The development of a global internet, growing broadband access, and the ubiquity of smartphones have enabled the collection and use of data to drive innovation. Two-sided digital platforms such as Uber and Airbnb have created new markets, putting idle assets to work. Platforms such as Kickstarter and GoFundMe are enabling crowdfunding for entrepreneurs, improving the operation of capital markets; Kaggle is crowdsourcing ideas to solve hard problems; businesses are using open innovation platforms to solicit solutions to design challenges from cars to pharmaceuticals; and eBay and Alibaba are matching small businesses with consumers globally.

Yet, despite these developments, productivity growth in the United States remains stubbornly low. U.S. productivity growth over the last eighty-odd years can be divided into four stages. From 1948–73 the United States experienced a productivity surge, with labor productivity growth of 3.3 percent annually and multifactor productivity (MFP) growth of 2.1 percent. Between 1973–95 labor productivity growth declined to 1.5 percent and MFP growth to 0.5 percent. There was a surge between 1995–2004, when labor productivity growth increased back to 3.2 percent and MFP growth increased to 1.7 percent. Since 2004 labor productivity growth has declined to 1.3 percent and MFP growth to 0.5 percent.

In terms of the contribution of specific economic sectors to the most recent productivity surge and then decline, manufacturing, information and communications technology (ICT), and services were the largest contributors, and manufacturing and retail/wholesale trade were also responsible for much of the slowdown post-2004.[15] As Martin Neil Baily and Nicholas Montalbano note, this points to a productivity shock to the U.S. economy in the mid-1990s that was over by the early 2000s, with industries returning to normal rates of productivity growth.[16]

There are two main explanations for slow productivity. One is that productivity is being mismeasured. According to this view, the statistics are failing to capture the gains from new digital technologies. Here, there are two forms of possible mismeasurement. One derives from consumers and businesses obtaining greater value from products than is embodied in prices. The other mismeasurement could stem from using inaccurate price deflators. The second explanation for low productivity is that the period of significant innovation driving productivity is over. For instance, Robert Gordon argues that the current space of digital invention is not as significant as earlier key innovations such as the electric light bulb, the internal combustion engine, and the wireless signal, all of which drove U.S. productivity growth out to 1973.[17] In his view, all the most significant innovations have happened and there is no obvious prospect for them to be repeated, condemning the United States and the world to lower levels of productivity growth.

Is Digital Being Mismeasured?

The growth in the internet and provision of free services is likely to have led to some incremental mismeasurement of their impact on productivity. Yet the size of the mismeasurement seems too small to explain the productivity slowdown.[18] In order to account for the lower productivity since 2004, mismeasurement would need to account for $2.5 to $2.7 trillion of additional output—what the U.S. economy would have produced in the absence of the productivity slowdown.[19]

There are various estimates of the potential size of productivity mismeasurement, ranging from $54 billion to $96 billion in 2015, which does not come close to accounting for even a substantial share of the lost output.[20] Even calculating mismeasured value using time spent online generates an incremental surplus of $842 billion since 2004—less than one-third of the $2.5 to $2.7 trillion of lost income from the productivity slowdown.[21]

Another approach is to assess whether the real value added of ICT was understated. This is even more challenging given the decline in ICT production in the United States. According to Chad Syverson, there would need to be an additional 440 percent in real value added from ICT that has been missed.[22] Alternatively, if the argument is that price deflators have failed to account for quality improvements, the price fall would need to have been seven times larger. Other factors that support the conclusion that the productivity slowdown is not a mismeasurement problem is that the slowdown is global and is not related to the size of the ICT sector.[23]

Is Digital Not that Innovative?

There are a number of good reasons for rejecting the view that there are no longer significant new innovations that could drive high productivity growth going forward. To start, Robert Gordon, in his pessimistic assessment of current digital technologies, seems unwilling to recognize the time delay for the diffusion of digital technologies, while clearly recognizing the time it took for, say, the electric light bulb to have an impact on economic growth. As Gordon himself notes, while the electric light bulb was first invented in 1879, electricity had little impact before 1900 (2014, p. 23). Moreover, the impact of electricity through the development of lights, elevators that enabled high-rise buildings, power tools, air conditioners, home appliances, and so forth took time to diffuse and supported productivity growth for the next seventy-odd years.

Yet, in Gordon's accounting the digital revolution started in the 1980s and finished in the early 2000s.[24] He seems unwilling to apply the same standard used for the inventions of the Second Industrial Revolution (such as electricity) to the diffusion of the current wave of innovation, and to allow for the possibility that these technologies are still in their infancy, are still being developed, and will take time to disperse across the economy and be used effectively. Consider that internet penetration globally is only 50 percent, and much of the connected world still does not have access to broadband networks. Even in advanced economies where connectivity and development and use of digital technologies is advanced, the McKinsey Global Institute estimates that the United States, for instance, is only at around 18 percent of its digital potential.[25] Moreover, the next generation of 5G connectivity will offer speeds ten to one hundred times faster than 4G, underpinning the next wave of digitally driven innovation.

In addition, there is arguably a large pipeline of inventions. Take artificial intelligence (AI), which is not a single technology and has the potential to make an economy-wide impact, including in low-productivity services such as health and education. Yet, as Erik Brynjolfsson notes, it takes time for an economy to incorporate and make effective use of new technologies, particularly complex ones with economy-wide impacts such as AI.[26] This includes time to build a large enough capital stock to have an aggregate effect and for the complementary investments needed to take full advantage of AI investments, including access to skilled people and business practices.[27] AI is already being used to enhance medical diagnostics and build self-driving cars. AI translation services are also enabling international trade. For example, as a result of eBay's machine translation service, eBay-based exports to Spanish-speaking Latin America increased by 17.5 percent (value increased by 13.1 percent).[28] To put this growth into context, a 10 percent reduction in distance between countries is correlated with increased trade revenue of 3.51 percent—so a 13.1 percent increase in revenue from eBay's machine translation is equivalent to reducing the distance between countries by over 35 percent. This scope for innovation to propel productivity is also revealed in the divergence in performance between the global frontier and the laggards.[29] McKinsey Global Institute finds that in the United States most sectors across the economy are less than 15 percent as digitized as the leading sectors.[30]

One driver of this divergence is the growing productivity of frontier firms as they most effectively use data and develop the know-how to innovate.[31] In addition, when it comes to digital platforms, there are network effects and winner-take-all dynamics that create large wins for the largest firms. Digital trade can reinforce these dynamics by expanding potential market size.[32] Yet this is not the full story. There is evidence that MFP performance is weaker in industries where MFP divergence was greatest, which suggests a breakdown in the mechanisms by which technology is diffused throughout an economy.[33] For instance, a slowdown in technology diffusion could be caused by less competition in key markets. The costs and difficulties of going digital could also be a factor. For instance, the need to train workers, develop tacit knowledge, and develop new business models could slow the pace at which laggards adapt to an economy that increasingly values ideas.[34]

Competition, Productivity, and the Digital Economy

The growing divergence among firm productivity and the trend toward lower levels of new firm creation puts a spotlight on whether there is an absence of competition caused by rising market power and barriers to entry which is entrenching dominant firms and preventing laggard firms from catching up. For instance, there is evidence of declining business dynamism in digitally intensive sectors.[35] However, this could be a symptom of a maturing industry rather than anticompetitive barriers to entry.

In fact, the impact of large technology firms on competition is unclear. On the one hand, Google does have high levels of market share in search—its global market share in online search is over 88 percent.[36] Such a market profile would typically raise competition concerns. One view is that the digital space remains characterized by low barriers, making concentration more ephemeral than it appears.[37] That there remains a real threat of competition continues to drive innovation and increases in consumer welfare.[38] This could mean that market concentration does not necessarily lead to the types of outcomes that competition law seeks to prevent, such as monopolistic pricing, a lack of choice, and less innovation. In the case of platforms, below-cost pricing by one side of a multisided market may help internalize cross-platform network externalities.[39] Yet even here, below-cost pricing could also be predatory if prices were lowered to weaken competition by preventing rivals from building their own user base.[40]

A related question is whether competition concerns arise from large tech firms' collection and use of data. One view is that "big data" itself does not confer strategic advantages. Instead, it is the ability to generate actionable insights from the data that matters.[41] Moreover, generating big data and the ability to collect big data is not itself costly. In support of this view are those companies that succeeded not through their possession or use of big data but by offering a superior proposition to consumers. For example, Uber disrupted the taxi market not with any trove of big data but by offering a cheaper and better user experience than taxis. KAYAK has become a successful travel search engine without any initial big data holdings, whereas Google's purchase of ITA Software, along with its flight data and data processing capabilities, has yet to lead to Google establishing a significant presence in the flight search market.[42]

There is a related question as to whether big data and network effects make switching costs high enough to give incumbents significant market power.[43] There is evidence of firms with large amounts of data not being protected from disruption, such as the success of Myspace over Friendster, which was subsequently eclipsed by Facebook. An alternative view is that a company such as Facebook presents exactly these network effects and switching costs, as moving to another social networking site would require not only uploading new photos and reauthenticating sites that use a Facebook login but—perhaps most important—convincing a critical mass of friends to follow to the new social networking site.[44]

A further issue is whether companies can use big data and business insights to exercise market power acquired in one market to extend dominance in ancillary markets. For example, Google's dominance in internet search could allow it to also dominate the market for broadband networked-delivered advertising.[45]

The aim here is not to draw specific conclusions about the impact of large technology firms on competition but to underscore that the market is dynamic and that technology is changing rapidly. For instance, while Google dominates search, its biggest competitor may not be Bing but Amazon, as consumers increasingly use Amazon to compare prices, read reviews, and purchase online.[46] This underscores that forces of technological convergence can generate competition. From a regulatory perspective, it suggests that competition regulators should be cautious about overreaching and the risk to innovation.

The other dimension of the competition issue is the scope for digital platforms to increase competition. Digital platforms create opportunities for competition across sectors. For instance, innovation in financial technology services could challenge big bank dominance in some areas, online retailers can increase competition with brick and mortar stores, and Amazon will compete with incumbent supermarkets. The regulatory challenge is to ensure that these opportunities for competition across digital platforms are maximized while ensuring that underlying regulatory goals such as consumer health and safety are achieved. In some cases, competition law may be best suited to opening markets and in other cases providing regulatory relief—such as by reducing financial licensing requirements for Fintech or avoiding the need for Uber drivers to have a taxi license to operate—which may be enough to spur competition.

As digital technologies allow for competition across markets, regulation needs to be assessed to ensure that it is achieving its primary aims— protecting consumer health and safety, reducing information asymmetries, limiting abuse of markets, and addressing externalities.[47] As such, existing laws need to be examined to determine whether automatic application to emerging digital businesses is always appropriate. For instance, it needs to be asked whether the social and other regulatory goals that underpin such regulation would be compromised in the absence of the full or partial application of the regulation, while also taking into account the missed opportunities in terms of competition, lower prices, and greater choice should the full application of regulation in effect prevent these businesses from forming.

Digital Trade

According to the McKinsey Global Institute, "virtually every type of cross-border transaction now has a digital component."[48] The open nature of the internet and the ability to move data globally means that even when an activity appears local, cross-border data flows may still be involved. For instance, data stored in a data facility in Chile might still be backed up in the United States.[49]

In important ways, the impact of the global internet and cross-border data flows has the potential to transform international trade, creating new avenues for growth and productivity gains.

Defining Digital Trade

There is no specific definition of digital trade. The WTO Work Programme on Electronic Commerce limited its consideration to "the production, distribution, marketing, sale or delivery of goods and services by electronic means."[50] The United States International Trade Commission (USITC) developed a broader definition of digital trade as "U.S. domestic commerce and international trade in which the internet and internet-based technologies play a particularly significant role in ordering, producing, or delivering products and services."[51] An even broader definition includes how cross-border data flows enable digital trade, either through the cross-border movement of data flows themselves as a form of trade or through productivity gains from using digital services that make firms more competitive domestically and overseas.[52] Taking a broad approach to what constitutes digital trade, the following identifies four key developments.

International E-commerce Opportunities

Already, around 12 percent of global goods trade is via international e-commerce.[53] Businesses can have their own website or use digital platforms to become global. This is about purchasing online and having the good delivered offline. Trade in digital services is also relevant here. For instance, for e-commerce to work, international payments systems are required. In addition, efficient logistics and delivery services are also needed to manage warehousing and transportation. Some trade in goods could decline as 3-D printing becomes more widely used.

E-commerce provides a potentially significant opportunity to increase small businesses' participation in international trade.[54] For instance, having a website gives small businesses an instant international presence without having to establish a physical presence overseas—often not an economic option. In addition, the internet provides access to advertising and communication services as well as information on foreign markets, all of which help small businesses participate in international trade.[55] Figure 5-1 shows the potential for internet platforms to enable digital trade for small businesses. Using eBay data, figure 5-1 shows that in Korea, for instance, 100 percent of firms on eBay have cross-border sales, compared with 20 percent of offline firms.[56]

Digital Services Trade

Services can increasingly be purchased and consumed online. This is particularly true for information technology (IT), professional, financial, retail, and education services.[57] New digital services, such as cloud computing, have been developed and are becoming crucial business inputs.[58] Moreover, some goods imports have been transformed into a trade in a service, such as software, books, and movies.

Figure 5-2 shows opportunities for exports of digitally deliverable services (DDS)—those services that could be delivered online. As can be seen, in the United States, DDS could be as high as 23 percent of total exports

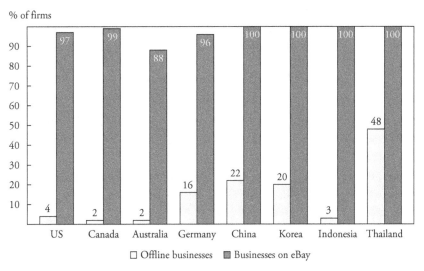

FIGURE 5-1. Share of eBay-Enabled SMEs Exporting vs. Traditional Businesses, 2014

% of firms

□ Offline businesses ■ Businesses on eBay

Source: eBay (2016, p. 26).

FIGURE 5-2. Digitally Deliverable Services Exports, 2011

% Total exports

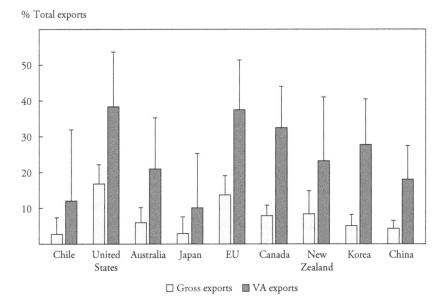

□ Gross exports ■ VA exports

Source: OECD TiVA Database, author's calculations.

Note: The lines on top of the bars show upper ranges of what could be digitally deliverable services.

and, taking into account DDS embodied in goods exports, could reach 55 percent of total exports. South Korea also shows significant exports of DDS, particularly when taking into account the use of DDS in goods exports, underscoring the importance of digital services in Korea's goods exports in areas such as automobiles, IT, and telecommunications products.

The Digitization of Goods Exports

As noted, data collection and analysis allows new digital services (often also provided online) to add value to goods exports. For example, data collected from sensors on mining and farming equipment allows businesses to improve their operations and thereby the value from the use of such equipment. Digital services are also increasingly key inputs into manufacturing processes. This includes commercial services such as research and development, design, marketing, and sales. A 2016 PricewaterhouseCoopers survey of more than 2,000 companies identified data and data analytics as the key for successful transformation to smart manufacturing.[59] This reflects the importance of digital services in manufacturing for increasing productivity, which affects the capacity of firms to compete domestically and overseas.[60]

Increased Participation in Global Value Chains

Global data flows underpin global value chains (GVC), creating new opportunities for participation in international trade.[61] The global internet and data flows enable businesses to plug into these GVCs to offer their own specific service.

For many economies, participation in global value chains (GVCs) is an important avenue for engaging in international trade. More than 50 percent of trade in goods and over 70 percent of trade in services is in intermediate inputs.[62] Figure 5-3 provides one measure of integration into GVCs. In figure 5-3, the backward linkages point to use of imports in the production of additional goods for export, and forward linkages show where exports are further processed in other countries. As is to be expected, Korea has particularly strong backward linkages, highlighting its integration into regional GVCs and the importance of imports for its manufacturing sector in particular.

Data and digital technologies are affecting GVC participation in several ways. As noted, in many respects the development of global value chains has been made possible by global connectivity and cross-border data flows that enable communications and can be used to coordinate logistics.[63] Dig-

FIGURE 5-3. **Integration into Global Value Chains, 2011**

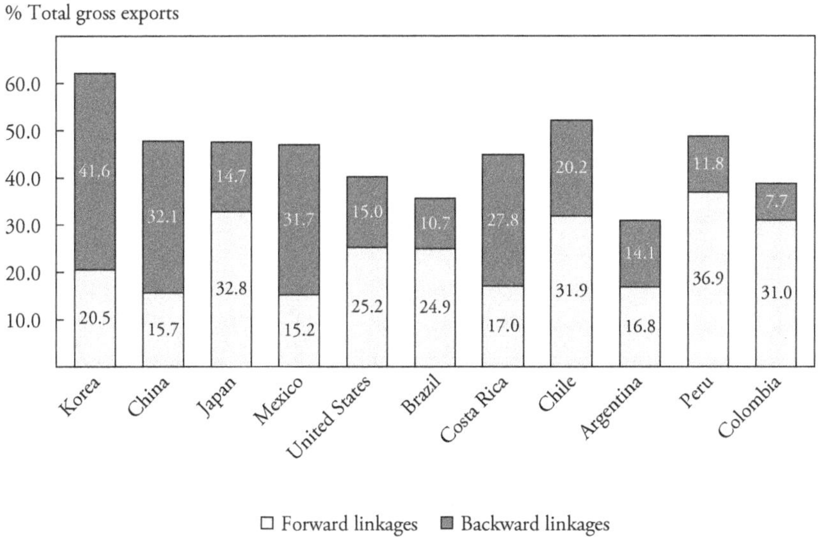

% Total gross exports

□ Forward linkages   ■ Backward linkages

Source: OECD TiVa Database.

ital services are themselves part of global value chains. There is also a trend toward increasing the use of imported services inputs in manufactured goods exports, suggesting that digital services are also being traded within GVCs.[64] At the same time, digital technologies, such as 3-D printing, could also lead to some relocalization of production, reducing the length and complexity of GVCs.[65]

Digital Trade Barriers

As the opportunities presented by digital technologies grow, governments and regulators have to determine how to benefit from going digital while maintaining the integrity of their domestic regulations. Against this backdrop, there has been significant growth in data localization measures globally.[66] Figure 5-4 shows exponential growth in the number of restrictions on cross-border data flows globally.

There are various forms of restrictions on data flows. They include measures that disallow the transfer of data outside national borders; measures that allow cross-border transfers but require a copy to be maintained

FIGURE 5-4. Cumulative Number of Restrictions on Cross-border Data Flows, 1960–2017

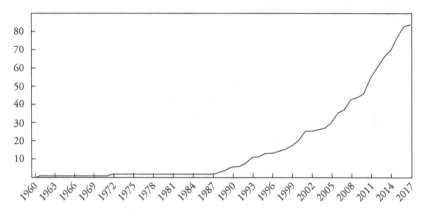

Source: Ferracane (2017, p. 2).

Note: Calculations based on data from Digital Trade Estimates database and legal texts.

domestically; and requirements of prior consent before data can be transferred overseas. There are also data localization restrictions that often also include restrictions on data flows. Figure 5-5 provides a taxonomy of local storage requirements and their impacts on cross-border flows.

Measures that restrict data flows and require data to be localized are implemented for a range of reasons. One reason, which is the case with privacy regulations, prevents data flows to jurisdictions with lower levels of privacy protection where this undermines domestic privacy protections. For example, the EU General Data Protection Regulation (GDPR), which came into effect in April 2018, prohibits businesses that collect personal data in the EU from transferring it outside the EU unless the receiving country has an equivalent level of privacy protection.[67]

Governments can also require data to be localized on the grounds that regulators need access to data in order to perform their regulatory functions. The most common of these is in the financial services sector, where data localization requirements are justified on the basis that financial regulators require financial data to remain local in case they need access to the data for regulatory purposes. For instance, in 2018 India introduced a requirement that payment system operators store data locally in order to allow financial regulators to effectively perform their supervisory function.[68]

FIGURE 5-5. Taxonomy of Data Localization Requirements

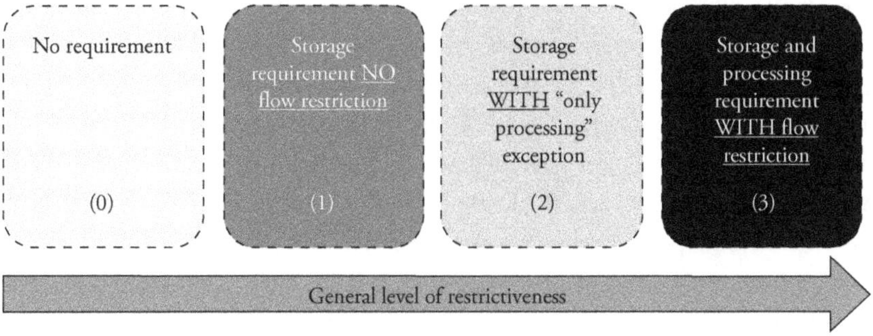

No requirement	Storage requirement NO flow restriction	Storage requirement WITH "only processing" exception	Storage and processing requirement WITH flow restriction
(0)	(1)	(2)	(3)

General level of restrictiveness

Source: Casalini and Lopez Gonzalez (2019, p. 23).

China requires that insurers localize data in order for the insurance regulatory authorities to perform their regulatory responsibilities.

Ensuring cybersecurity is another rationale for requiring data to be local. The view here is that having data localization decreases the risks of unauthorized access. Cybersecurity is another reason India provided for requiring financing data to be localized. China's cybersecurity law requires data localization and access to source code for "critical information infrastructure," which is yet to be well defined.[69]

Another reason for data flow restrictions is to control access to what content can be accessed online, usually on moral, religious, or political grounds. For example, Iran censorship aimed at creating the "Halal internet" limits access to content deemed offensive to Islam. China blocks access to eleven of the top twenty-five global sites among an estimated 3,000 prohibited foreign websites.[70] This is done in part to restrict access to political speech directed at the Chinese Communist Party. Vietnam's 2018 cybersecurity law requires retention locally of a range of personal and other data of Vietnamese users,[71] in part in order for the state to regulate online content, which could include information opposing or offending the Socialist Republic of Vietnam or "defamatory propaganda," such as any critical or dissenting statements made against the government.

Data localization measures are also being enacted for protectionist reasons. China's blocking or degrading of internet access has supported the development of local champions. For instance, blocking access to Google and Facebook has been to the benefit of search engine Baidu, microblog

Renren, and social networking site Sina Weibo. India's data localization laws also seem in part aimed at supporting the development of local businesses.

There are other trade barriers that affect digital trade. For instance, domestic licensing or other market access services restrictions affect digitally deliverable services trade. A lack of international standards and the development of different local standards could become important digital trade barriers. For instance, for the development of smart manufacturing, China can limit the scope for interconnection of distributed manufacturing facilities and services, hampering export opportunities. Inefficient customs procedures, barriers to express delivery services, and tariffs also raise the costs of exporting goods that are purchased on digital platforms.[72]

Currently Indonesia is seeking to apply tariffs on what it defines as digital goods, such as downloads of software and books.[73] This is at odds with the WTO moratorium on applying customs duties on electronic transmissions, a moratorium that was renewed at the WTO ministerial meeting in Buenos Aires in 2017.[74]

Developing International Trade Law for Digital Trade

While the negotiations that ushered in the establishment of the WTO were conducted in the 1980s and early 1990s before much of the commercial internet existed, there are several WTO agreements relevant for digital trade. These include the General Agreement on Tariffs and Trade (GATT), the General Agreement on Trade in Services (GATS), the Annex on Telecommunications, Information Technology Agreement (ITA) I & II, and the Agreement on Technical Barriers to Trade (TBT Agreement).[75]

Digital Trade Rules in the WTO

Trade rules are important as enablers of digital trade and as breaks on government regulation that can restrict digital trade opportunities. The WTO was negotiated in the late 1980s and early 1990s before the internet existed. Yet WTO rules are relevant for digital trade.

The General Agreement on Trade in Services (GATS) is particularly relevant given the increasing scope for services trade and the growing role of services in GDP and the scope for improving services productivity. Yet whether the GATS applies to digital trade is not straightforward. For example, one effect of going digital is to transform a goods trade—such as in books, software, and other goods with the advent of 3-D manufacturing—into a service trade.

The GATS covers four modes of services delivery: (1) from the territory of one member into the territory of another member (mode 1); (2) in the territory of one member to the service consumer of any other member (mode 2); (3) by a service supplier of one member through commercial presence in the territory of any other member (mode 3); and (4) by a service supplier of one member through presence of natural persons of a member in the territory of any other member.[76] When it comes to which modes are relevant for digital trade, in the case on U.S. gambling the panel and Appellate Body held that the cross-border supply of online gambling was a mode 1 service delivery.[77]

The GATS is a dual-track framework. Some GATS commitments apply to all services, such as the Most-Favored Nation (MFN) commitment. Other GATS commitments, such as on market access and national treatment, only apply to commitments scheduled by WTO members. Moreover, horizontal exceptions to the MFN commitment could also be made and reflected in members' schedules.

GATS modes of delivery are also technologically neutral. This means that a mode 1 commitment, for instance, applies to "all means of delivery, whether by mail, telephone, internet, etc.," unless otherwise specified in a member's schedule.[78] As a result, where members have made a commitment to allow the delivery of a service, they must allow data to flow across borders where this is needed for the delivery of that service.

There are other areas where the WTO includes support for cross-border data flows. For instance, the WTO Understanding on Commitments in Financial Services includes a commitment that members will not "prevent transfers of information or the processing of financial information, including transfers of data by electronic means."[79] The WTO Annex on Telecommunications paragraph 5(c) also includes a commitment to allow services suppliers to use public telecommunications transport networks for the movement of information within and across borders.[80]

One of the challenges in applying the GATS to digital trade is determining whether the challenged data localization requirement affects trade in a sector where a GATS commitment has been scheduled.[81] When services were being scheduled during the Uruguay Round in the early 1990s, most WTO members used the UN Central Product Classification Provisional (CPC Prov.) System or the Services Sectoral Classifications List (or a combination of both).[82] The CPC Prov. was finalized in 1991, when the internet barely existed. While the CPC Prov. has since been updated, the CPC Prov. classification remains the basis for members' GATS commitments. Relevant services sectors for trade in digital services are in telecommunications, audiovisuals, computer and related services, data-based services, and financial services.

The good news from the perspective of applying the GATS to digital trade is that WTO members made relatively liberal commitments in areas such as computer services. This may have been because governments prepared their GATS commitments in the early 1990s, when cross-border digital delivery of search, audiovisual, cloud computing, and other services had not assumed the scale that exists today.[83] At the same time, the extent to which commitments in these areas apply is not clear, particularly to "new" digital services such as search engines, cloud computing, or online gaming, which did not exist when commitments were scheduled.[84]

Another issue is determining how to classify businesses that bundle various services to provide an online service.[85] For example, in the WTO China–Electronic Payment Services dispute, the panel found that the service at issue—electronic payment services for payment card transactions— was an integrated service that consisted of five services working together to provide a single service.[86] Turning to whether electronic payment services had been scheduled by China as a GATS commitment, the panel found that all those services necessary to provide the integrated service are included within the relevant GATS sector or subsector, whether or not each component service is explicitly listed.[87] One possible reading of this panel finding is that WTO members' GATS schedules cover integrated digital services.[88] However, others have argued that integrated services are themselves "new" and therefore not covered, unless explicitly scheduled.[89]

Having established that a digital service is covered by a WTO member's GATS schedule, it would then be necessary to show a violation of a GATS commitment. For instance, a data localization requirement may violate the GATS market access obligation.[90] Data localization measures that increase the burden on foreign suppliers, such as by requiring a local presence, could also be inconsistent with the GATS national treatment commitment.[91]

A WTO member could then seek to justify a data localization measure under one of the GATS Article XIV exception provisions as being necessary to achieve an enumerated list of public policy exceptions. This could include being necessary to protect public morals (GATS Article XIV(a)) or necessary to secure compliance with laws and regulations not inconsistent with the GATS, including those relating to the prevention of deceptive and fraudulent practices (Article XIV(a)(i)) and the protection of the privacy of individuals (Article XIV(c)(ii)). The WTO Appellate Body has found that whether a measure is "necessary" requires "weighing or balancing" factors including the contribution of the measure to the policy goal, the importance of the common interests or values protected by the measure, as well as the impact on imports.[92] Here is where the contribution of the measure to its objective is assessed. Evidence that data localization can undermine goals such as strengthening cybersecurity and privacy could support a finding that some data localization measures are not "necessary."[93]

In the event that the measure passes this weighing and balancing, the complaining WTO member could then seek to show that there is a less-trade-restrictive alternative that could achieve the responding WTO member's goal. The Appellate Body has found that "to qualify as a genuine alternative," the proposed measure must not only be less trade restrictive than the original measure at issue but should also "preserve for the responding member its right to achieve its desired level of protection with respect to the objective pursued."[94] Here, the complaining member could seek to show that the measure's goal could be achieved in ways that are less restrictive on digital trade, including ways that reduce restrictions on cross-border data transfers.[95]

Having established that a data localization requirement is "necessary" under GATS Article XIV, it would still need to be assessed for consistency with the requirement in the chapeau that it is not "applied" in a manner that constitutes a "means of arbitrary or unjustifiable discrimination between countries where like conditions prevail, or a disguised restriction on trade in services."[96] The WTO Appellate Body has stated that the assessment of the consistency of a measure with the GATS Article XIV chapeau is about "locating and marking out a line of equilibrium between the right of a Member to invoke an exception under Article XX and the rights of other Members under varying substantive provisions."[97] The focus on the application of the measure emphasizes how the measure works in practice rather than the measure's justification.[98]

Other WTO Agreements Applicable to Digital Trade

In addition to the GATS, there are other WTO commitments relevant for digital trade. The General Agreement on Tariffs and Trade (GATT) regulates trade in goods, which matters for goods purchased online and delivered in physical form across borders. Lower tariffs in response to WTO Information and Technology Agreement I & II have also supported access to the hardware needed to expand internet access and build out data centers.

The WTO Trade Facilitation Agreement (TFA) should also support trade in goods purchased online by reducing the costs of moving goods through customs, costs that are particularly significant for digital trade in goods in lower value and smaller quantities. The WTO Technical Barriers to Trade (TBT) Agreement is also potentially very important. The TBT Agreement includes MFN and national treatment obligations, as well as a commitment to base domestic technical regulation on international standards where they exist.[99] As outlined above, governments are taking divergent approaches to standards that affect digital trade in areas such as standards for broadband networks, encryption, privacy, and data storage. Failure to find ways to harmonize or support systems of interoperability will negatively impact the development of digital trade. The importance of effective protection and enforcement of intellectual property rights as an enabler of digital trade underscores the ongoing relevance of the WTO Trade-Related Aspects of Intellectual Property Rights (TRIPS) Agreement.

The WTO has also contributed to creating an enabling environment for digital trade by fostering competition in the telecommunications markets, which has contributed to expanding internet access and reducing its cost. The WTO Telecommunications Reference Paper includes pro-competitive principles. Regulatory principles for the telecommunications sector have been aimed at preventing major telecommunications suppliers from engaging in anticompetitive practices.

WTO E-commerce Negotiations

Since 1998 the WTO has had a Work Programme on Electronic Commerce where e-commerce issues are discussed, but it is not a forum for formal negotiations. At the 2019 World Economic Forum meeting in Davos, seventy-six countries, including the United States, China, the EU, and Australia, agreed to launch e-commerce negotiations at the WTO.[100] WTO members have also managed agreement on a permanent moratorium on the levying of customs duties on electronic transmissions that is renewed at each WTO ministerial meeting.

Digital Trade Rules in FTAs

While WTO rules are relevant for digital trade, as noted, these rules were not developed with digital trade in mind, and as a result there are gaps in the rules and the extent of their application remains uncertain. Since 2003 at least seventy FTAs include an e-commerce chapter.[101] While initially e-commerce chapters appeared in developed countries' FTAs, this is changing as more developing countries realize what is at stake. For instance, Colombia and Costa Rica have also included robust e-commerce chapters in their FTAs.[102] The EU has been less ambitious when it comes to digital trade rules in FTAs. For instance, in the Japan–EU Economic Partnership Agreement, instead of a commitment to cross-border data flows there is agreement to revisit this issue within three years of entry into force of the agreement.[103]

Recent FTAs include even more robust rules than previous FTAs. The Korea–United States FTA, for instance, includes the first explicit general commitment to cross-border data flows. However, unlike more recent FTAs such as the Comprehensive and Progressive Agreement on TPP, the commitment is only hortatory, calling on the parties to "endeavor to refrain from imposing or maintaining unnecessary barriers to electronic information flows across borders."[104] The Trans-Pacific Partnership (TPP) Agreement—a twelve-nation trade agreement before the United States withdrew in January 2017—includes a comprehensive e-commerce chapter. The remaining eleven parties revived the TPP as the Comprehensive and Progressive Agreement on TPP (CPTPP), which includes the original TPP e-commerce chapter. More recently, the United States, Mexico, and Canada updated NAFTA—now the United States–Mexico–Canada Agreement (USMCA)—which includes further commitments in what is now called the digital trade chapter.

Key new rules in CPTPP and USMCA are agreement to avoid data localization measures and to allow the free flow of information, subject to a GATS Article XIV–style exceptions provision.[105] The CPTPP and USMCA also include a commitment to abstain from requiring companies to provide source code as a condition of entering the market and to allow use of all devices on the internet.[106] The CPTPP and USMCA also build on previous FTAs with respect to privacy and include a requirement for all parties to protect privacy and a best endeavors commitment to develop compatibility among domestic privacy regimes.[107] USMCA goes further and includes a commitment by the parties to develop privacy frameworks that take into account "principles and guidelines of relevant international bodies" such as the Asia-Pacific Economic Cooperation (APEC) Privacy Framework and the OECD Privacy Guidelines, as well as a commitment to developing interoperability among the parties' different privacy systems.[108] These commitments get at the need for regulatory cooperation in order to build confidence that commitments to cross-border data flows and effective domestic regulation can coexist.[109]

The importance of FTAs for digital trade goes beyond e-commerce chapters. When it comes to intellectual property (IP), for instance, CPTPP and USMCA included WTO-plus commitments relevant for digital trade. One of these is a commitment to develop third-party intermediary liability regimes.[110] The CPTPP also includes a recognition of the need for "an appropriate balance in its copyright and related rights systems, among other things, by means of limitation or exceptions that are consistent with Article 18.65 (Limitations and Exceptions), including those for the digital environment."[111] This is the first time the United States included such a provision in an FTA, and it was not replicated in USMCA. This provision aims to capture the U.S. fair use exceptions to copyright—a principles-based set of exceptions that have been part of the legal underpinning in the United States for development of a digital economy.[112]

While not about IP but certainly relevant in terms of shaping the scope of liability of internet platforms for material they host, the USMCA also includes a commitment to not treat "interactive computer services" as "information content providers."[113] The aim here is to replicate the United States' approach, which distinguishes between publishers of information, who are liable for the content they publish, and platforms, which are not held liable for claims or instance of harm caused by the content they host.[114]

Conclusion

The global internet and cross-border data flows are transforming international trade and providing new opportunities for productivity and growth in jobs. Underpinning much of digital trade is the global internet and cross-border data flows. Yet governments are increasingly restricting cross-border data flows, which can undermine the economic and trade opportunities of digital trade. Restrictions on data flows and requirements for data to be localized are driven by a range of reasons, including protection of privacy, law enforcement, and cybersecurity concerns. Some governments are also restricting internet access and data flows to protect domestic companies—a form of digital protectionism.

International trade commitments at the WTO and in FTAs provide an important discipline on unnecessary restrictions on digital trade. Trade rules in FTAs are also beginning to go further than merely preventing digital trade restrictions and are also including commitments for regulatory cooperation and the development of interoperability among regulatory systems. This is significant, as more international regulatory cooperation is needed in order to give domestic regulators confidence that moving data outside of their jurisdiction won't undermine domestic regulatory goals. At the moment, the absence of common standards or mechanisms for interoperability among regulatory systems is one reason governments are increasingly requiring data to remain local.

NOTES

1. Bernard and others (2007).
2. Wu (2017).
3. Cisco (2017).
4. United States International Trade Commission (2014).
5. World Bank (2016).
6. Organisation for Economic Co-operation and Development (2013).
7. U.S. Department of Commerce (2016).
8. Manyika and others (2016).
9. Manyika and Chui (2015).
10. United States International Trade Commission (2014); Castro (2013).
11. Barefoot and others (2018).
12. United Nations Conference on Trade and Development (UNCTAD) (2017).
13. Castro and McQuinn (2015); United States International Trade Commission (2014, p. 29).
14. Meltzer (2014b).
15. Baily and Montalbano (2016, p. 9).
16. Baily and Montalbano (2016, p. 11).
17. Gordon (2012).
18. Byrne, Fernald, and Reinsdorf (2016); Syverson (2016).
19. Byrne, Fernald, and Reinsdorf (2016); Syverson (2016, p. 5).

20. Dutz, Orszag, and Willig (2009); Rosston, Savage, and Waldman (2010); Syverson (2016, pp. 11–12).

21. Goolsbee and Klenow (2006, p. 108–11).

22. Syverson (2016, p. 14).

23. Syverson (2016).

24. Gordon (2014, p. 29).

25. Manyika and others (2015).

26. Brynjolfsson and others (2017, p. 10).

27. Brynjolfsson and others (2017, p. 10).

28. Brynjolfsson, Hui, and Liu (2018).

29. Andrews, Criscuolo, and Gal (2016).

30. Manyika and others (2015).

31. Haskel and Westlake (2018).

32. Acemoglu and Linn (2004).

33. Andrews, Criscuolo, and Gal (2016).

34. Andrews, Criscuolo, and Gal (2016).

35. Calvino and Criscuolo (2019).

36. Statista (2019). Retrieved on October 7, 2019.

37. Evans (2017).

38. De Leon (2016).

39. Katz (2018).

40. Katz (2018).

41. Lambrecht and Tucker (2015, p. 9); Yun and others (2017).

42. Lambrecht and Tucker (2015).

43. Farrell and Klemperer (2007).

44. Pasquale (2017, p. 3).

45. Rubinfeld and Gal (2017).

46. Soper (2014).

47. Productivity Commission (2016, p. 98).

48. Manyika and others (2016).

49. Greer (2013).

50. World Trade Organization (1998b).

51. United States International Trade Commission (2014, p. 29).

52. Meltzer (2016).

53. Meltzer (2016).

54. Meltzer (2014a).

55. Organisation for Economic Co-operation and Development (2009); Schoonjans and others (2013, p. 41).

56. eBay (2015).

57. United States International Trade Commission (2014, p. 42).

58. United States International Trade Commission (2017, pp. 58–66).

59. PricewaterhouseCoopers (2016).

60. Hoekman and Mattoo (2008); Liu and others (2017).

61. Baldwin (2016).

62. Organisation for Economic Co-operation and Development (2012).

63. Helpman (2011).

64. Miroudot and Cadestin (2017, p. 16).

65. De Backer and Flaig (2017).

66. Ferracane (2017, p. 2).

67. General Data Protection Regulation (2018), Article 45. Personal data can also be transferred under Binding Corporate Rules (BCRs), Standard Contractual Clauses (SCCs), and in a limited number of other circumstances (see article 47).

68. Reserve Bank of India (2018); Kaltra (2018).

69. Cyberspace Administration of China (2017)

70. Office of the United States Trade Representative (2017, pp. 89–90).

71. Government of Vietnam (2018).

72. Meltzer (2014a).

73. Indonesian Ministry of Finance (2018).

74. World Trade Organization (2017).

75. Meltzer (2019).

76. World Trade Organization (1994b, art. 1.2.)

77. World Trade Organization (2004, para. 6.285–87); World Trade Organization (2005, para. 215).

78. World Trade Organization (2004, para. 6.285); World Trade Organization (2009, para. 364).

79. World Trade Organization (1994b).

80. World Trade Organization (1994b).

81. World Trade Organization (1998a); World Trade Organization (2004); World Trade Organization (2009).

82. World Trade Organization (1991).

83. Wunsch-Vincent (2006, pp. 90–91).

84. Tuthill (2017, p. 114).

85. Mitchell and Mishra (2018, p. 1095).

86. World Trade Organization (1998a); World Trade Organization (2012).

87. World Trade Organization (2012).

88. Crosby (2016, p. 4).

89. Zhang (2015, p. 24).

90. World Trade Organization (1998a); World Trade Organization (2005).

91. Hestermeyr and Nielsen (2014, p. 588).

92. World Trade Organization (2007); World Trade Organization (2005).

93. Anupam and Le (2014, p. 5).

94. World Trade Organization (2014, para. 5.261).

95. See Meltzer and Lovelock (2018) for a discussion of how to achieve legitimate policy goals while minimizing restrictions on cross-border data transfers.

96. World Trade Organization (1994b).

97. World Trade Organization (1998a, para. 159).

98. World Trade Organization (1998a, para. 115–16).

99. World Trade Organization (1994a, art. 2.1, 2.4).

100. World Trade Organization (2019).

101. Wu (2017, p .6).

102. Wu (2017, p .7).

103. Agreement Between the European Union and Japan for an Economic Partnership (2018, art. 8.81).

104. Free Trade Agreement Between the United States of America and the Republic of Korea (2018, art. 15.8).

105. Comprehensive and Progressive Trans-Pacific Partnership (2018, art. 14.11); United States–Mexico–Canada Agreement (2018, art. 19.11, 19.12).

106. Comprehensive and Progressive Trans-Pacific Partnership (2018, art. 14.10, 14.13); United States–Mexico-Canada Agreement (2018, art. 19.16, 19.10).

107. Comprehensive and Progressive Trans-Pacific Partnership (2018, art. 14.8); United States–Mexico-Canada Agreement (2018, art. 19.8).

108. United States–Mexico-Canada Agreement (2018, art. 19.8).

109. Mattoo and Meltzer (2018).

110. United States–Mexico-Canada Agreement (2018, art. 20.J.11).

111. Comprehensive and Progressive Trans-Pacific Partnership (2018, art. 18.66).

112. Anupam (2014, p. 639).

113. United States–Mexico–Canada Agreement (2018, art. 19.17).

114. Communications Decency Act of 1996 (1996, sec. 230); see also Anupam (2014, 650–52).

REFERENCES

Acemoglu, D., and J. Linn. 2004. "Market Size in Innovation: Theory and Evidence from the Pharmaceutical Industry." *The Quarterly Journal of Economics* 119, no. 3, pp. 1049–90.

Agreement Between the European Union and Japan for an Economic Partnership. Signed in Brussels in July 2018 (https://trade.ec.europa.eu/doclib /press/index.cfm?id=1684).

Andrews, Dan, Chiara Criscuolo, and Peter Gal. 2016. "The Best versus the Rest: The Global Productivity Slowdown, Divergence across Firms and the Role of Public Policy," OECD Productivity Working Papers 2016-5 (Paris: OECD Publishing), December.

Anupam, Chander. 2014. "How Law Made Silicon Valley." *Emory Law Journal* 63, no. 3, pp. 639–94.

Anupam, Chander, and Uyen P. Le. 2014. "Breaking the Web: Data Localization vs. the Global Internet," Legal Studies Research Paper Series 378 (UC Davis), April.

Baily, Neil Martin, and Nicholas Montalbano. 2016. "Why Is U.S. Productivity Growth So Slow?" Hutchins Center Working Paper 22 (Brookings Institution), September.

Baldwin, R. 2016. *The Great Convergence: Information Technology and the New Globalization* (Harvard University Press).

Barefoot, K., and others. 2018. "Defining and Measuring the Digital Economy," Bureau of Economic Analysis Working Paper (Suitland, Md.: Bureau of Economic Analysis), March.

Bernard, Andrew B., and others. 2007. "Firms in International Trade." *Journal of Economic Perspectives* 21, no. 3 (Summer), pp. 105–30.

Brynjolfsson, Erik, and others. 2017. "Artificial Intelligence and the Modern Productivity Paradox: A Clash of Expectations and Statistics," NBER Working Paper 24001 (Cambridge, Mass.: National Bureau of Economic Research), November.

Brynjolfsson, Erik, Xiang Hui, and Meng Liu. 2018. "Does Machine Translation Affect International Trade? Evidence from a Large Digital Platform," NBER Working Paper 24917 (Cambridge, Mass.: National Bureau of Economic Research), August.

Byrne, David M., John G. Fernald, and Marshall B. Reinsdorf. 2016. "Does the United States Have a Productivity Slowdown or a Measurement Problem?" Papers on Economic Activity (Brookings Institution), March 10–11.

Calvino, Flavio, and Chiara Criscuolo. 2019. "Business Dynamism and Digitilisation," OECD Science, Technology, and Industry Policy Papers 62 (Paris: OECD Publishing), March.

Casalini, Francesca, and Javier Lopez Gonzalez. 2019. "Trade and Cross-Border Data Flows," OECD Trade Policy Papers 220 (Paris: OECD Publishing), January.

Castro, Daniel. 2013. "The False Promise of Data Nationalism" (Washington, D.C.: Information Technology & Innovation Foundation (ITIF)), December (www2.itif.org/2013-false-promise-data-nationalism.pdf).

Castro, D., and Alan McQuinn. 2015. *Cross-Border Data Flows Enable Growth in All Industries*. Report. Washington, D.C.: Information Technology & Innovation Foundation (ITIF), February.

Cisco. 2017. "The Zettabyte Era: Trends and Analysis." White paper. *Cisco.com*, June 2017 (https://webobjects.cdw.com/webobjects/media/pdf/Solutions /Networking/White-Paper-Cisco-The-Zettabyte-Era-Trends-and -Analysis.pdf).

Communications Decency Act of 1996. Pub. L. No. 104-104, sec 230.

Comprehensive and Progressive Trans-Pacific Partnership. Signed in March 2018 (https://www.mfat.govt.nz/assets/CPTPP/Comprehensive-and -Progressive-Agreement-for-Trans-Pacific-Partnership-CPTPP-English .pdf).

Crosby, Daniel. 2016. "Analysis of Data Localization Measures under WTO Services Trade Rules and Commitments," E15 Initiative Policy Brief (Geneva: International Centre for Trade and Sustainable Development (ICTSD) and World Economic Forum), March.

Cyberspace Administration of China. 2017. "Notice of the National Internet Information Office on Public Consultation on the 'Regulations on the Safety Protection of Key Information Infrastructures (Draft for Comment).'" Office of the Central Cyberspace Affairs Commission. Beijing, July 10.

De Backer, Koen, and Dotothee Flaig. 2017. "The Future of Global Value Chains," OECD Science, Technology and Innovation Policy Papers 41 (Paris: OECD Publishing), July.

De Leon, Ignacio. 2016. "Competition Policy in the Internet-Based Industries: Do We Need to Reboot the Debate?" Paper. April 2016 (http://dx.doi.org /10.2139/ssrn.2870576).

Dutz, Mark, Jonathan Orszag, and Robert Willig. 2009. The Substantial Consumer Benefits of Broadband Connectivity for US Households. Report. Washington, D.C.: Compass Lexecon, July.

eBay. 2015. "Empowering People and Creating Opportunity in the Digital Single Market," Executive Summary (Washington, D.C.: eBay Public Policy Lab), October.

eBay. 2016. "Small Online Business Growth Report," eBay Public Policy Lab, January.

European Parliament and Council of the European Union. 2016. "Regulation on the Protection of Natural Persons with Regard to the Processing of Personal Data and on the Free Movement of Such Data, and Repealing Directive 95/46/EC (Data Protection Directive)," Regulation (EU) 2016/679, L119, p. 1–88 (https://eur-lex.europa.eu/legal-content/EN/TXT/PDF/?uri =CELEX:32016R0679).

Evans, David S. 2017. "The Emerging High-Court Jurisprudence of the Antitrust Analysis of Multisided Platforms." *Competition Policy International Antitrust Chronicle* (February), pp. 1–9.

Farrell, J., and P. Klemperer. 2007. "Coordination and Lock-in: Competition with Switching Costs and Network Effects," Chapter 31 in *Handbook of Industrial Organization*, vol. 3, pp. 1967–2012, edited by Mark Armstrong and Robert H. Porter (Amsterdam: Elseiver).

Ferracane, Martina F. 2017. "Restrictions on Cross-Border Data Flows: A Taxonomy." European Centre for International Political Economy (ECIPE) Working Paper 1/2017 (Brussels: ECIPE), November.

Free Trade Agreement Between the United States of America and the Republic of Korea. Signed September 2018 (https://ustr.gov/trade-agreements/free-trade-agreements/korus-fta/final-text).

General Data Protection Regulation. 2018 (https://gdpr-info.eu).

Goolsbee, Austan, and Peter J. Klenow. 2006. "Valuing Consumer Products by the Time Spent Using Them: An Application to the Internet." *American Economic Review Papers and Proceedings* 96, no. 2, pp. 108–11.

Gordon, Robert. 2012. "Is U.S. Economic Growth Over? Faltering Innovation and the Six Headwinds," NBER Working Paper 18315 (Cambridge, Mass.: National Bureau of Economic Research), August.

———. 2014. "The Demise of U.S. Economic Growth: Restatement, Rebuttal, and Reflections," NBER Working Paper 19895 (Cambridge, Mass.: National Bureau of Economic Research), February.

Government of Vietnam. 2018. "Decree No. 27/2018/ND-CP Amending and Supplementing Decree No. 72/2013/ND-CP on Internet Services and Online Information." Hanoi, March (https://vnnic.vn/sites/default/files/vanban/decree_no._27.2018.nd-cpof1march2018.pdf).

Greer, David. 2013. "Big Data Security, Privacy Concerns Remain Unanswered." *CSO*, December 3 (https://www.csoonline.com/article/2134203/big-data-security--privacy-concerns-remain-unanswered.html).

Haskel, Jonathan, and Stian Westlake. 2018. *Capitalism without Capital: The Rise of the Intangible Economy* (Princeton University Press).

Helpman, E. 2011. *Understanding Global Trade* (Harvard University Press).

Hestermeyr, H. P., and L. Nielsen. 2014. "The Legality of Local Content Measures under WTO Law." *Journal of World Trade* 48, no. 3, pp. 553–91.

Hoekman, Bernard, and Aaditya Mattoo. 2008. "Services Trade and Growth," Policy Research Working Paper 4461 (Washington D.C.: World Bank).

Indonesian Ministry of Finance. 2018. "Regulation No. 17/PMK.010/2018." Jakarta, February 2018 (http://www.gbgindonesia.com/en/main/legal_updates/intangible_goods_are_now_subject_to_import_duty.php).

Kaltra, Adiyta. 2018. "India Panel Wants Localization of Cloud Storage Data in Possible Blow to Big Tech Firms." *Reuters*, August 4 (www.reuters.com/article/us-india-data-localisation-exclusive/exclusive).

Katz, Michael L. 2018. *Exclusionary Conduct in Multi-sided Markets.* Report. Paris: Organisation for Economic Co-operation and Development (https://one.oecd.org/document/DAF/COMP/WD(2017)28/FINAL/en/pdf).

Lambrecht, Anja, and Catherine E Tucker (2015). Can Big Data Protect a Firm from Competition? December 18 (http://dx.doi.org/10.2139/ssrn.2705530).

Liu, Xuepeng, and others. 2017. "Services Development and Comparative Advantage in Manufacturing." Policy Research Working Paper 8450 (Washington D.C.: World Bank).

Manyika, James, and Michael Chui. 2015. "By 2025, Internet of Things Applications Could Have $11 Trillion Impact." *mckinsey.com*, McKinsey Global Institute, July 22.

Manyika, James, and others. 2015. *Digital America: A Tale of Haves and Have-Mores*. Report. McKinsey Global Institute, December.

———. 2016. *Digital Globalization: The New Era of Global Flows*. Report. McKinsey Global Institute, February.

Mattoo, Aaditya, and Joshua P. Meltzer. 2018. "Data Flows and Privacy: The Conflict and Its Resolution." *Journal of International Economic Law* 21, no. 4 (December), pp. 769–89.

Meltzer, Joshua P. 2014a. "Supporting the Internet as a Platform for International Trade: Opportunities for Small and Medium-sized Enterprises and Developing Countries," Global Economy and Development Working Paper 69 (Brookings Institution), February.

———. 2014b. "The Importance of the Internet and Transatlantic Data Flows for US and EU Trade and Investment," Global Economy and Development Working Paper 79 (Brookings Institution), October.

———. 2016. "Maximizing the Opportunities of the Internet for International Trade," E15 Initiative Policy Options Paper (Geneva: International Centre for Trade and Sustainable Development (ICTSD) and World Economic Forum.

———. 2019. "Governing Digital Trade." *World Trade Review* 18, no. S1, pp. S23–S48, April.

Meltzer, Joshua P., and Peter Lovelock. 2018. "Regulating for a Digital Economy: Understanding the Importance of Cross-Border Data Flows in Asia," Global Economy and Development Working Paper 113 (Brookings Institution), March.

Miroudot, S., and Charles Cadestin. 2017. "Services in Global Value Chains: From Inputs to Value-Creating Activities," OECD Trade Policy Paper 197 (Paris: OECD Publishing).

Mitchell, Andrew D., and Neha Mishra. 2018. "Data at the Docks: Modernising International Trade Law for the Digital Economy." *Vanderbilt Journal of Entertainment and Technology Law* 20, no. 4, pp. 1073–1134.

Office of the United States Trade Representative. 2017. 2017 National Trade Estimate Report on Foreign Trade Barriers (https://ustr.gov/sites/default/files/files/reports/2017/NTE/2017%20NTE.pdf).

Organisation for Economic Co-operation and Development. 2009. Top Barriers and Drivers to SME Internationalization, OECD Working Party on SME and Entrepreneurship Report (Paris: Organisation for Economic Co-operation and Development).

———. 2012. *Mapping Global Value Chains*. Report TAD/TC/WP/RD(2012)9 (Paris: Organisation for Economic Co-operation and Development).

————. 2013. "Measuring the Internet Economy: A Contribution to the Research Agenda," OECD Digital Economy Papers 226 (Paris: OECD Publishing).

Pasquale, Frank. 2017. "When Antitrust becomes Pro-Trust: The Digital Deformation of US Competition Policy," Francis King Carey School of Law Legal Studies Research Paper 2017-24 (University of Maryland).

PricewaterhouseCoopers. 2016. *Industry 4.0: Building the Digital Enterprise.* 2016 Global Industry 4.0 Survey (https://www.pwc.com/gx/en/industries/industrial -manufacturing/publications/assets/pwc-building-digital-enterprise.pdf).

Productivity Commission of the Australian Government. 2016. Digital Disruption: What Do Governments Need to Do? Commission Research Paper (Canberra: Commonwealth of Australia), June (https://www.pc.gov.au /research/completed/digital-disruption).

Reserve Bank of India. 2018. "Storage of Payment Systems Data," Notification RBI/2017-18/153 (https://www.rbi.org.in/scripts/NotificationUser.aspx?Id =11244).

Rosston, Gregory, Scott J. Savage, and Donald M. Waldman. 2010. "Household Demand for Broadband Internet in 2010." *The B.E. Journal of Economic Analysis & Policy Advances* 10, no. 1 (September), pp. 1–45.

Rubinfeld, Daniel L., and Michal S. Gal. 2017. "Access Barriers to Big Data." *Arizona Law Review* 59, pp. 339–81.

Schoonjans, Bilitis, and others. 2013. "Formal Business Networking and SME Growth." *Small Business Economics* 41, no. 1 (June), pp. 169–81.

Soper, Taylor. 2014. "Google's Erik Schmidt: Our Biggest Search Competitor Is Amazon—Not Microsoft or Yahoo." *GeekWire*, October 13 (www .geekwire.com/2014/google-amazon/).

Statista. "Search Engine Market Share Australia, Sep 2018–Sep 2019." Statcounter (https://gs.statcounter.com/search-engine-market-share/all/worldwide /2019).

Syverson, Chad. 2016. "Challenges to the Mismeasurement Explanations for the U.S. Productivity Slowdown," NBER Working Paper 21974 (Cambridge, Mass.: National Bureau of Economic Research), February.

Tuthill, L. 2017. "Implications of the GATS for Digital Trade and Digital Trade Barriers in Services." *DigiWorld Economic Journal* 107, pp. 95–115.

United Nations Conference on Trade and Development (UNCTAD). 2017. UNCTAD Information Economy Report 2017: Digitalization, Trade and Development. Report. Switzerland: United Nations Publications.

U.S. Department of Commerce. 2016. *Measuring the Value of Cross-Border Data Flows.* Report (www.ntia.doc.gov/files/ntia/publications/measuring_cross _border_data_flows.pdf. 2).

United States International Trade Commission. 2014. Digital Trade in the U.S. and Global Economies, Part 2. Publication 4485. August.

————. 2017. *Global Digital Trade 1: Market Opportunities and Key Foreign Trade Restrictions.* Publication 4716. August.

United States-Mexico-Canada Agreement. Signed November 30, 2018 (https://ustr.gov/trade-agreements/free-trade-agreements/united-states-mexico-canada-agreement/agreement-between).

World Bank Group. 2016. *World Development Report 2016: Digital Dividends.* Report. Washington, D.C.: World Bank.

World Trade Organization. 1991. Services Sectoral Classification List (http://www.wto.org/english/tratop_e/serv_e/mtn_gns_w_120_e.doc).

————. 1994a. *Agreement on Technical Barriers to Trade.* Uruguay Round of Multilateral Trade Negotiations, Annex 1. Marrakesh, April 15 (https://www.wto.org/english/docs_e/legal_e/17-tbt.pdf).

————. 1994b. *General Agreement on Trade in Services.* Uruguay Round of Multilateral Trade Negotiations, Annex 1B. Marrakesh, April 15.

————. 1998a. *U.S.-Import Prohibition of Certain Shrimp and Shrimp Products.* Appellate Body Report WT/DS58/AB/R. United States, October 12.

————. 1998b. "Work Programme on Electronic Commerce." WT/L/274. Adopted by the WTO General Council September 30, Geneva (https://www.wto.org/english/tratop_e/ecom_e/ecom_e.htm).

————. 2004. *Measures Affecting the Cross-Border Supply of Gambling and Betting Services.* Panel Report WT/DS285/R. United States, November 10.

————. 2005. *Measures Affecting the Cross-Border Supply of Gambling and Betting Services.* Appellate Body Report WT/ DS285/AB/R. United States, April 7.

————. 2007. *Measures Affecting Imports of Retreaded Tyres.* Appellate Body Report WT/DS332/AB/R. Brazil, December 3.

————. 2009. *Measures Affecting Trading Rights and Distribution Services for Certain Publications and Audiovisual Entertainment Products (China-audiovisuals).* Appellate Body Report WT/DS363/AB/R. China, December 21.

————. 2012. *Certain Measures Affecting Electronic Payment Services.* Panel Report WT/DS413/R. China, July 16.

————. 2014. *Measures Prohibiting the Importation and Marketing of Seal Products.* Appellate Body Report WT/DS4-00/AB/R. European Communities, May 22.

————. 2017. *Work Programme on Electronic Commerce.* Ministerial Decision of 13 December 2017." WT/MIN(17)/65. Buenos Aires, December 18 (https://www.wto.org/english/tratop_e/ecom_e/ecom_e.htm).

————. 2019. "Joint Statement on Electronic Commerce." WT/L/1056. Davos, January 25 (https://trade.ec.europa.eu/doclib/docs/2019/january/tradoc_157643.pdf).

Wu, Mark. 2017. "Digital Trade-Related Provisions in Regional Trade Agreements: Existing Models and Lessons for the Multilateral Trade System,"

RTA Exchange Overview Paper (Geneva: International Centre for Trade and Sustainable Development (ICTSD) and Inter-American Development Bank (IDB)), November.

Wunsch-Vincent, Sascha. 2006. *The WTO, The Internet and Trade in Digital Products: EC–US Perspective* (Oxford: Hart Publishing).

Yun, John M., and others. 2017. "Comment on the Global Antitrust Institute, Antonin Scalia Law School George Mason University, on the Canadian Competition Bureau's White Paper, 'Big Data and Innovation: Implications for Competition Policy in Canada,'" George Mason University Law & Economics Research Paper Series, no. 17–44, November (https://dx.doi .org/10.2139/ssrn.3079763).

Zhang, Ruosi. 2015. "Covered or Not Covered: That Is the Question," WTO Staff Working Paper ERSD-2015-11 (World Trade Organization), December 7 (https://www.wto.org/english/res_e/reser_e/ersd201511_e.pdf).

PART II

Country Perspectives on a Changing Growth Agenda: Korea

SIX

A Shift in the Economic Policy Paradigm

HYEON-WOOK KIM

One notable change faced by major countries in the wake of the 2008 global financial crisis is the shift in the economic policy paradigm related to expanding the government's role in the market. The 2008 crisis revealed diverse and negative aspects of the market-based economy. In addition, the old policy paradigm turned out to be a bitter failure, and the pressures of continued slow growth and income inequality issues generated more attempts to seek a new paradigm suited to the new reality. Unlike before the crisis when the policy paradigm targeted growth while pursuing efficiency and stability, the new paradigm in the post-crisis world aims to improve the sustainability of economic growth, emphasizing long-term fairness and equality.

The growth agenda under the newly emerging policy paradigm combines policies and strategies to bolster the potential for growth and at the same time solve structural problems. The slowing growth in major countries is in fact a structural phenomenon that existed before the global financial crisis, and its causes are known to be lower input growth—such as population aging—and slower productivity growth, according to the mechanics of classical growth accounting. Some argue that slower productivity growth is a natural consequence of the slowing of technological progress, while others say that productivity growth is simply not keeping up with technological progress—producing the "productivity paradox."[1] The statistics available to us today may not fully account for recent technological progress and the resulting growth effects, but technological developments over the past ten to twenty years are one explanation for the productivity paradox in recent discussions about growth policy.

Other discussions link the productivity paradox to problems in the market structure. For example, one analysis says that the structural difference in technology acceptance between industries and firms gives rise to the paradoxical phenomenon between technical progress and productivity growth. These structural problems have implications that cannot be drawn from aggregate data on performance or reward differentiation between companies or employees, and this analysis helps to explain the route by which the productivity paradox is logically related to discussions of income inequality.[2] Thus, in the face of mounting demands for active government intervention in the market to resolve the problems inherent in the market economy system in the post-crisis world, a discussion of the productivity paradox helps address not only growth policy but also market distortions and problems related to distribution efficiency.

Accordingly, in the process of decomposing the structure of pending problems and figuring out necessary policy targets, even the growth agenda is naturally connected to—not distinguished from—the distribution agenda under the new policy paradigm emphasizing an active government role in the market. To put it another way, policy alternatives that are not supported by an analysis based on distribution perspectives, such as resolving market competition and distortion problems, would not achieve social consensus as a growth agenda.

Meanwhile, others make a direct connection between slow growth and inequality—the two phenomena commonly observed in major countries after the crisis—and are exploring policies to counter them. Although a growing number of empirical analyses show that income inequality is negatively correlated with robust growth and that redistribution makes more positive contributions to growth,[3] economic theory is not yet capable of providing definitive explanations regarding not only the source of the relationship but also the causality between economic growth and societal structural problems like income inequality. Conventional economics assumes that policy responding to social issues will hinder economic growth if it entails government intervention; at the same time, excessive inequality can weaken growth potential by destabilizing political and economic conditions and thereby eroding the investment and social cohesion that is required when the government takes active actions to cope with an economic shock.

A Growth Agenda for the Korean Economy

In the Korean economy, some have connected slowing economic growth to societal structural problems such as income inequality, and before the crisis most analysts argued for one of two different, and incompatible, interpretations. One side argues that regulations and systems designed to address inequality impede corporate innovation and productive investment, and instrumental factors such as rigidity and a dual labor market structure hinder corporate restructuring and delay economic growth. The other side argues that growth-oriented reform could weaken protections for the vulnerable and exacerbate social problems. Thus it can be said that the pre-crisis policy discussions about how to deal with the consequences of slow economic growth were quite different in nature from the productivity paradox perspective and still closely associated with the viewpoint of trade-off between economic growth and distribution.

After the Korean economic crisis in 1997, worries mounted about the existing growth model (which relied heavily on large exporting companies), the slowing growth of productivity, and the weakening potential for job creation in industry. Accordingly, ensuing discussions about growth policy became more inclined to consider social issues such as distribution in their evaluation of policy feasibility and effectiveness.

Since the 2008 global financial crisis, several discussions conducted in Korea credit a more active response to social issues with leading to more sustainable economic growth. In other words, more people accept the view that policy goals for growth and for more equitable income distribution are not necessarily conflicting, but rather can be implemented in a complementary manner. In an academic and political environment where opinions were highly polarized about the necessity and effects of structural reform, a new consensus is building on the desirable path to sustainable growth.

Policies enacted after the 2008 global financial crisis were designed in line with the growing demand for a change in the policy paradigm. The government adopted a policy stance to strengthen economic equality, referred to as "economic democratization," which includes the three-policy package to enhance household income and a corporate accumulated earnings tax; the latter aims to reduce inequality by consolidating fairness in market competition and redistributing corporate earnings into households. Nevertheless, the economic recovery remained tepid, and the political situation deteriorated with the impeachment of the former president, Park Geun-hye, in 2017. Several policy efforts did not meet their intended goals for the establishment of a fair market competition system; instead, extra taxes on chaebol (family-owned conglomerate firms) added more policy uncertainty to the overall economy.

The demand for a shift in the policy paradigm, however, has not weakened, and the effort to redefine growth policy that emerged as an urgent priority in the process of seeking a new policy paradigm reflects the unprecedentedly fast aging of the Korean population and the resulting slowdown in productivity and economic growth. It is in this context that the term "growth" appears in both of the two key policy directions—"income-led growth" and "innovative growth"—of the national policy paradigm that the administration of President Moon Jae-in has pushed forward since taking office in 2017.

Even if the new growth policy conforms well to the demands of the era, and is also committed to responding to the environment signaling persistent "secular stagnation," it is necessary to continuously check the feasibility and effectiveness of the policy and revise it to fit changing circumstances. Changing economic conditions, unmet goals, and unexpected developments call for policies to be adjusted in a timely manner in order to minimize long-term negative impacts.

In this regard, there have been several structural changes to the Korean economy since the global financial crisis. Part II of this book analyzes and evaluates the key phenomena viewed as factors undermining the sustainability of Korea's economic growth. It first reexamines income distribution and the labor share of income, which serves as a significant indicator for checking the exacerbation of income inequality—known as the most pressing social problems in Korea—and also for seeking countermeasures. Next, it examines the current condition and causes of the increase in corporate savings, which has been blamed for the slowing growth of the

Korean economy, and whether or how to revise or complement the current policy perspective. Last, it examines the macroeconomic risks inherent in the increase in household debt, often viewed as Korea's Achilles' heel, and then it suggests policy alternatives based on an analysis of possible impacts on mid- to long-term growth potential.

Changing Distributional Dynamics

Chapter 7 by Youngsun Koh examines the evolution of wage inequality in Korea. Wage inequality fell in the period between 1980 and 1994 (the first subperiod), rose between 1995 and 2007 (the second subperiod), and then fell again between 2008 and 2016 (the third subperiod). By decomposing wage inequality into sex, age, education, and other worker characteristics, Koh finds that the changes in wage inequality were largely the result of the changes in the prices of these characteristics. For example, the college wage premium fell in the first subperiod, rose in the second, and then fell again in the third.

Koh then examines the educational wage premium in greater detail. Because the wage premium, like other prices, is determined through an interaction between supply and demand, changes in the demand for and supply of workers with different levels of education—middle school, high school, and college graduates—can explain the changes in their wage premiums. He argues that the wage premium on higher education fell slightly, contributing to improving wage equality in the third subperiod, for instance, based on the finding that the demand for college graduates stopped increasing while their supply continued to grow, albeit slowly. In the second subperiod, the roles of demand and supply were reversed: the relative demand for college graduates increased faster than the supply, as it did in the United States, which contributed to deteriorating wage inequality.

Koh discusses the possible reasons for his observations and proposes some reasons for the stagnation of the college wage premium in the third subperiod, when wage inequality in Korea fell: the stagnation of skill-biased technical change (SBTC) as would be suggested by stagnant wage growth in the upper part of wage distribution; the deteriorating quality of college education; endogenous technological change; or a combination of these factors. Then he argues that in any case the room for maneuver for policy makers is rather limited: boosting technological change to accelerate wage

growth could lead to a widening wage gap, and increasing the supply of college graduates to reduce the wage gap could further undermine the quality
of college education. Based on these findings, it is argued that breaking the
impasse—for example, by introducing a "flexicurity" system combining a
high degree of market friendliness in economic policy with a high level of
social protection—may require a fundamental change in the way Korea's
economy and society work.

Chapter 8 by Jiyoon Oh analyzes the decline in the labor share of income in Korea. The labor share of income is an indicator of the functional
distribution of national income; thus labor share and household income inequality may be highly correlated, but the relationship is not direct. Nevertheless, the discussion of income inequality in Korea tends to center more
on issues of labor and capital income distribution than on ways to eliminate
unfair competition in the market or to take advantage of the government's
financial functions. This is probably because the rise in income disparity
between businesses and households was a primary criticism of the capital-
ist economic system after the financial crisis.

The Moon administration's national agenda aims to address rising economic inequality and social discontent caused by the spread of market tri-
umphalism by promoting the income-led growth policy. This income-led
growth concept follows the post-Keynesians who consider the unequal income distribution between capital and labor to be the main reason for the
persistence of economic slowdown. Furthermore, they call for a paradigm
shift in distribution policy from pro-capital to pro-labor as a prerequisite
to reducing income inequality and improving economic growth at the same
time. Thus, under the policy framework for income-led growth, the policy
approach to income inequality issues needs to be in a direction that can enhance labor income share, and the agenda's rationale seems to be based on
general observations that the share of labor income has receded over the
last twenty years before and after the global financial crisis of the late 2000s.[4]

As of 2018, 23 percent of Korean workers were self-employed, the fifth-
largest share of self-employed among Organization for Economic Cooperation and Development (OECD) member countries. Separating the
so-called mixed income of the self-employed is therefore important in looking at the trend of labor income shares in the overall economy. Most domestic studies of Korean labor income shares use Gollin's methodology to account for mixed income.[5] They conclude that the decreasing labor share after
the Asian financial crisis had a huge impact on all aspects of the economy and

society. However, these results rely on adjustments that are not sufficient to correct for the mixed income of the self-employed. Counting the labor share in only the corporate sector is one way to avoid the adjustment problem, but this is not possible in Korea since the time-series data for the corporate sector are only available after 2010 in the National Account Statistics.

In order to overcome these difficulties, Oh uses each firm's financial statement information to calculate aggregate corporate labor share. She finds that, for externally audited firms, the labor share has trended up since the 2000s after the Asian financial crisis. These results may seem unusual at a time when labor income shares are declining worldwide. Technological changes and international trade, which are blamed for the decline in the global labor share, are equally applicable in Korea. Oh also looks at whether the increase in monopoly power of superstar firms is the main driver of the change in labor share.[6] However, the superstar firm effect did not appear in Korea, unlike in the United States. Her analysis is expected to serve as an important reference point for understanding what caused social structural problems such as income inequality and how to seek viable solutions.

Rise in Corporate Saving and Household Debt

Chapter 9 by Duksang Cho presents findings from an analysis of the increase in corporate savings. According to general definitions in economics about the roles of economic entities in their respective sectors, the phenomenon of firms piling up more savings cannot be treated as business as usual. The role of the household is to spend a portion of its income on consumption and to save the rest, while the role of firms is to produce by borrowing and investing the resources saved by households in order to enhance their production capacity for the future.

In this context, an increase in corporate savings implies that firms are not upgrading their future production capacity, thus creating an inauspicious possibility that total factor productivity—including technological progress and capital input required for growth—will decelerate and cause the economy to enter a phase of slow growth. Moreover, the increase in corporate savings suggests that the share of corporate income far outpaces that of household income, pointing to an excessively low share of labor income, and hence it can even serve as a linkage that can explain both the global slow growth and income inequality trends.

Based on this perspective, the post-crisis policy stance in Korea has been dedicated to denouncing and downsizing the increase in corporate savings. One example, as mentioned, is the corporate accumulated earnings tax in the three-policy package to enhance household income formulated as a part of the 2014 tax reform proposals.[7] The current government's income-led growth policy is also based on the implicit recognition that corporate savings are too large and that downsizing could lead to an increase in the share of household income (or labor share of income) and a reduction in income inequality.[8]

It is also conceivable that the firms hoarding cash and hesitating to invest may be putting downward pressure on the growth rate of the Korean economy. On the other hand, some argue that the increase in cash holdings is an optimal choice for firms coping with mounting uncertainties; most cash holdings are used to finance fixed assets, and hence there is no need to condemn the practice. Cho begins by investigating the validity of this argument. Korea's corporate savings have risen mainly on the consumption of fixed capital and the increase in the balance between savings and investment. In particular, the greater corporate savings after the 2000s can be seen as the firm's choice optimized to tackle a situation in which technological changes are devouring more capital than before. One result may be that the productivity gap widens further between firms actively pursuing technological changes and those not doing so. In other words, his analysis confirms that corporate savings have a meaningfully positive correlation with productivity growth. This result implies that restraints on corporate savings could prevent optimal corporate decision making and discourage the incentive for the firm to pursue technological change, eventually undermining the efficiency of the market.

Chapter 10 by Young-il Kim analyzes the macroeconomic risks inherent in the problem of growing household debt and finds implications for growth policy. The increase in household debt has been continuously regarded as a risk to the Korean economy over the past several years, and even the most significant one since the deleveraging of household debt occurred in advanced countries after the housing bubble burst in the wake of the global financial crisis.

Just as the U.S. subprime mortgage crisis was a trigger for the global financial crisis, the excessive increase in household debt poses a huge risk to the financial market, but the situation can be viewed as an outcome of the aforementioned structural changes being reflected in the Korean economy. In other words, a huge increase in household debt, just like the increase in corporate savings, is a structural problem that needs to be corrected in the light of the shared role of households and firms in saving and borrowing that are assumed in traditional economics.

On the other hand, unlike most advanced economies that have successfully prevented a sudden collapse of economic growth by expanding fiscal debt in the wake of the global crisis, Korea has always made fiscal soundness a policy priority, perhaps even sacrificing the financial soundness of households for the sake of economic growth. In other words, what such a policy stance would bring to economic growth must be taken into account if some future situation calls for reducing household debt to improve the financial soundness of the household sector without burdening the country's fiscal soundness.

Securing financial stability by resolving household debt problems can play a valuable role in enhancing productivity. For instance, the commercialization of advanced technologies developed by innovative firms requires initial investment and employment while also serving to reduce investment and employment by existing competitors and in conventional sectors. Rapid technological progress can increase productivity in the pertinent sector, but it could entail a decrease in investment and employment in the entire economy, thereby hindering economic activity.[9] However, in the situation where household debt issues are resolved and sound financial stability is ensured, if monetary and fiscal policies can be fully managed in an expansionary manner, long-term balanced growth can be pursued by encouraging investment in rising industries and strengthening the capacity to absorb the labor force displaced by technological advances.

In response to rising economic and social concerns over household debt, the Moon administration includes household debt risk as one of the top 100 national tasks. In its "Comprehensive Measures to Curb Household Debt," a plan announced in 2017, the government seeks a soft landing for household debt through aggregate risk management, noting that household debt is a burden on the Korean economy, including consumption and growth. With regard to mitigating risks, the income-led growth policy goes one step further, emphasizing the need to stabilize household disposable income by providing financial support to highly indebted low-income households, including by writing off long-term microcredit liabilities. Still, it is not entirely clear what path or direction household debt should take to improve the growth of the real economy; more detailed analyses will provide a more concrete basis for policy choices and interpretations.

In this regard, Kim's analysis is significant for future discussions on growth policy since it explores the role of household debt in relation to the post-crisis slump in private consumption, and it draws inferences about slow growth. His study empirically demonstrates that growing instability in Korea's household debt leads to less consumption and slower economic growth. Adverse effects of debt on consumer spending, especially during a macroeconomic downturn, could take a huge toll on economic activity and delay a recovery. This is why household debt is regarded as a financial accelerator that could weaken domestic demand when economic conditions falter, since macroeconomic resilience would suffer while household balance sheets become less sound.

Thus one negative effect of household debt is to impair the sustainability of growth. Hysteresis might occur because the economic slowdown is increasingly likely to deepen further and persist longer, and this could pose a risk to the supply-side growth potential.[10] Experiences such as long-term recession leave a scar, constraining the accumulation of physical and human capital and even undermining productivity. If the increase in household debt served to help ease the shocks from economic crashes and the hysteresis phenomenon after the global financial crisis, now is the time to be concerned about what would happen if household debt were to move in the opposite direction, since there is a nonlinear relationship between household debt and growth.

Kim's study calls for a more active approach to curbing excessive household debt in order to prevent huge harms to social welfare resulting from an economic downturn. It recommends that, in normal times, the government should strengthen its macroeconomic policy stance to create a soft landing for household debt—for instance, by limiting the portion of overly indebted borrowers. In contrast, in a downturn, with stagnating domestic demand, expansionary monetary and fiscal policies should be carried out in tandem with measures to stabilize the financial market—as the stabilization alone would not be enough to prevent prolonged downward pressure on aggregate demand among heavily indebted households. In addition, considering that a full-fledged recovery in consumption is not likely unless the financial soundness of households improves, Kim emphasizes the need to pursue efforts to ameliorate the financial vulnerability of the household sector on an ongoing basis.

Conclusion

These chapters in this part of the book trace the post-crisis developments in Korea's socioeconomic climate represented by slow growth and income inequality. The authors attempt to determine whether social structural conditions can be blamed for causing those problems and can thus be the target of new policies. In particular, they analyze the structural changes in major economic sectors, where those changes have great significance in the design and implementation of policies for sustainable growth. They also look at what relationship the changes have to key growth factors, including productivity.

The changes in financial structure are analyzed in aggregate terms and from micro-perspectives, since they can affect discussions of economic growth issues such as income share, distribution, debt, savings, and investment after the crisis. In addition, the chapters empirically analyze the background of these structural changes through recent domestic and foreign literatures and scrutinize the ripple effect on productivity and growth in the Korean economy.

The analyses in these chapters have significant implications for a more sophisticated growth agenda in the future by strengthening the logical link between the mid- to long-term strategy for sustainable growth and the shift in policy paradigms and policies for social equality enhancement, a topic that has gained increasing attention since the global crisis. These analyses may be small in number, but their evaluations of structural problems and their underlying causes in Korea's household and corporate sectors will be important in establishing future policy directions. These studies of the impact of slow growth and socioeconomic structural changes on growth, including productivity, contribute to developing a policy stance and instruments that will enable sustainable growth.

NOTES

1. Research findings and statistics imply that productivity growth has slowed in major countries since the digital revolution of the early 2000s, and slide even further after the global financial crisis (Adler and others, 2017).

2. Several studies have already taken an interest in the link between slowing productivity growth and deteriorating income inequality. See, for example, OECD (2018) and Brookings Institution and Chumir Foundation (2019).

3. Ostry, Berg, and Tsangarides (2014).

4. Increasing the minimum wage, one of the most representative policies intended to realize income-led growth (when the employment situation is

assumed to experience no changes), is known to raise the income share of low-income households, thereby helping to improve income distribution and increase the labor share of income; hence it is distinguished from existing income redistribution policies such as the earned income tax credit (EITC).

5. Gollin (2002).

6. Autor and others (2017).

7. Park (2016) commented that the three-policy package to enhance household income, including the corporate accumulated earnings tax, is one of the most innovative policies ever adopted in the history of the Korean economy and would have been inconceivable under preceding policy frameworks.

8. At a press conference held in Cheong Wa Dae in August 2018, chief policy maker Jang Ha-sung said that of all gains achieved from economic growth, the share for households declined significantly owing to increasing economic inequality. The continued decline in the share of household income caused a decrease in consumer spending, but despite the increases in the share of corporate profit and savings, corporate investment has not risen. His diagnosis was that, because benefits from economic growth are not properly transferred to household income, domestic demand is stagnating and corporate investment is outpaced by corporate savings, implying that the economy's growth potential is declining (Yonhap News 2018).

9. Basu, Fernald, and Kimball (2006).

10. A similar logic applies in discussions about the relationship between monetary policy and economic growth. For instance, it argues that an expansionary monetary policy acts to increase spending and lower the unemployment rate among economic entities, thereby providing an environment conducive to productivity growth. Especially in the economic downturn, as in the hysteresis phenomenon stressed by Blanchard and Summers (1986), if the short-term monetary policy fails, the unemployment rate will climb, and given that the longer people remain unemployed the less chance they will have of returning to the labor market, the economy is most likely to experience a long-term supply shortage. On the contrary, if monetary policy takes more active approaches to counter the economic downturn, unemployed people will have a greater incentive to return to the labor market and companies may be induced to provide better retraining programs and work facilities, thereby making a long-term contribution to the supply side of the economy.

REFERENCES

Adler, Gustavo, and others. 2017. "Gone with the Headwinds: Global Productivity," IMF Staff Discussion Note 17/04 (Washington, D.C.: International Monetary Fund).

Autor, David, and others. 2017. "The Fall of the Labor Share and the Rise of Superstar Firms," NBER Working Paper 23396 (Cambridge, Mass.: National Bureau of Economic Research).

Basu, Susanto, John G. Fernald, and Miles S. Kimball. 2006. "Are Technology Improvements Contractionary?" *American Economic Review* 96, no. 5 (December), pp. 1418–48.

Blanchard, Olivier, and Lawrence Summers. 1986. "Hysteresis and the European Unemployment Problem," *NBER Macro Annual* (Cambridge, Mass.: National Bureau of Economic Research).

Blanchard, Olivier, Eugenio Cerutti, and Lawrence Summers. 2015. "Inflation and Activity—Two Explorations and Their Monetary Policy Implications," IMF Working Paper 21726 (Washington, D.C.: International Monetary Fund).

Brookings Institution and Chumir Foundation. 2019. *Productive Equity: The Twin Challenges of Reviving Productivity and Reducing Inequality.* Report, Washington, D.C.

Gollin, Douglas. 2002. "Getting Income Shares Right." *Journal of Political Economy* 110, no. 2, pp. 458–74.

OECD. 2018. *The Productivity-Inclusiveness Nexus.* OECD, Paris.

Ostry, Jonathan D., Andrew Berg, and Charalambos G. Tsangarides. 2014. "Redistribution, Inequality, and Growth," IMF Staff Discussion Note 14/02 (Washington, D.C.: International Monetary Fund).

Park, Jong-Gyu. 2016. "Macroeconomy and Income Distribution," in *Income Distribution in Korea,* edited by Yoon-Je Cho (Seoul: Han-Ul Academy Press). [In Korean]

Yonhap News. 2018. "Jang Ha-sung Committed to Accelerate the Income-Driven Growth Policy Using All Available Means," August 26.

SEVEN

Growth and Distribution

No Longer Compatible with Each Other?

YOUNGSUN KOH

Over the past sixty to seventy years Korea has achieved remarkable economic growth combined with equitable income distribution.[1] Many developing countries, in contrast, have experienced slow or intermittent growth and deteriorating income distribution.[2] However, this happy combination came to a close in Korea in the 1990s. Figure 7-1 shows the changes in Gini coefficients in the period from 1990 to 2016. Income inequality stopped falling in the early 1990s and began to rise, with a brief acceleration during the financial crisis in the late 1990s. But it underwent another reversal in the late 2000s, falling again until the mid-2010s.

A similar trend can be found in wage inequality. In figure 7-2, wage inequality is measured with the Q5–Q1 gap and the P90–P10 gap.[3] A large (small) value of Q5–Q1 or P90–P10 indicates a large (small) wage gap among workers. Dividing the whole period into three subperiods, 1980–94, 1995–2007, and 2008–16, one can see that the wage gap decreased in the

FIGURE 7-1. **Gini Coefficients (Market Income)**

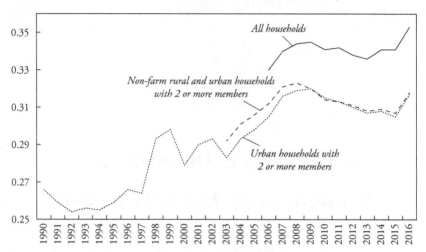

Source: Statistics Korea (http://kosis.kr/statisticsList/statisticsListIndex.do?menuId=M_01
_01&vwcd=MT_ZTITLE&parmTabId=M_01_01#SelectStatsBoxDiv).

FIGURE 7-2. **Inequality of Hourly Wage[a]**

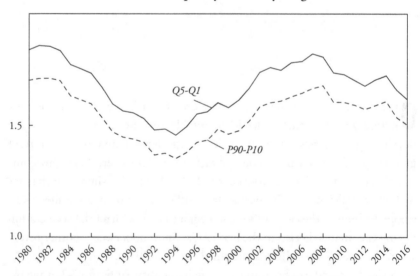

Source: Koh (2018).

a. The Q5–Q1 gap is the difference between the average log hourly wages of the top quintile and
the bottom quintile. The P90–P10 gap is the difference between the 90th percentile and the
10th percentile of the log hourly wage.

Table 7-1. *The Annual Growth of Real Hourly Wages*[a]

Percentile	1980–94	1994–2007	2007–16
90th	6.6	5.6	1.1
50th	9.2	4.0	1.1
10th	9.2	3.1	3.0

Source: Ministry of Employment and Labor, *Wage Structure Survey*, various years.
a. Values given as percent. Only establishments with ten or more workers were included in the sample. Real values were obtained with the consumer price index.

first subperiod, increased in the second, and decreased in the third, following the pattern observed for income inequality in figure 7-1. This result is not surprising given that wages are the most important source of income for most households.

While the wage gap was growing or shrinking, wage growth slowed throughout all subperiods. Table 7-1 shows the real value of the 50th percentile (median) hourly wage grew by 9.2 percent and 4.0 percent per year in the first and second subperiods, respectively, and then by 1.1 percent in the third. Such an abrupt drop in wage growth in the third subperiod was also observed for the 90th percentile. On the other hand, the 10th percentile grew by 3.0 percent per year in the third subperiod, narrowing the gap with the 90th and 50th percentiles.

In short, the first subperiod combined improving wage distribution with healthy wage growth. In the second subperiod wage growth continued, albeit at a lower level, but the wage distribution deteriorated. In the third subperiod, the opposite was true: wage growth collapsed but the wage distribution improved. Growth and distribution appear to have become incompatible with each other after the mid-1990s.

Since the 1980s, many advanced countries have witnessed rising wage inequality.[4] This has often been attributed to skill-biased technical change (SBTC), which is said to increase the demand for high-skilled labor.[5] In particular, the demand for college graduates has increased rapidly since the 1980s with the widespread use of information and communications technology (ICT) and raised the wage premium on higher education. According to this view, which has gained currency among economists in the United States, college enrollment needs to be expanded further to win the race between education and technology.

This chapter studies wage inequality in Korea to understand the factors that have affected its evolution. I propose a novel approach that decomposes wage inequality into sex, age, education, and other worker character-istics. The analysis finds that the changes in wage inequality were largely the result of the changes in the prices of these characteristics.[6] For instance, the college wage premium fell in the first subperiod, rose in the second, and then fell again in the third, much like the Q5–Q1 or P90–P10 gap shown in figure 7-2.

Next I examine the educational wage premium in greater detail. The wage premium, like other prices, is determined through an interaction be-tween supply and demand. In the first subperiod, the supply of high school graduates increased relative to that of college graduates, but the relative de-mand for the former increased faster, and consequently the wage premium for the latter declined. In the second subperiod, the roles of demand and supply were reversed: the relative demand for college graduates increased faster than the supply, as it did in the United States. In the third subpe-riod, the relative demand stayed largely unchanged but the relative supply kept growing, pulling down the wage premium.

Possible reasons for these observations are discussed. For instance, rea-sons for the stagnation of the college wage premium in the third subperiod could include the stagnation of SBTC, as would be suggested by stagnant wage growth in the upper part of the wage distribution; the deteriorating quality of college education; endogenous technical change;[7] or a combination of these factors. In any case, the room for maneuver for policymakers is rather limited: boosting technical change to accelerate wage growth could lead to a widening wage gap, and increasing the supply of college graduates to reduce the wage gap could further undermine the quality of college education. Breaking the impasse—for example, by introducing a flexicurity system—might require a fundamental change in the way Korea's economy and soci-ety work.

Decomposition of Wage Inequality

In this section we attempt to discern what part of the changes in wage in-equality is due to the changing returns to skill—for example, the changing wage premium on college education.

Data

The main source of data used in this chapter is the Wage Structure Survey (WSS) for 1980–2016. The WSS is carried out by the Korean Ministry of Employment and Labor on a sample of establishments. It contains information on the workers' wages, hours worked, sex, age, highest level of education completed, work experience, tenure with their current employer, occupation, industry, and the size of the establishment in which they work. Since it relies on company documents for data collection, it is considered more reliable than household surveys, which often rely on workers' memories.

Note, however, that workers with no fixed workplace and workers in the agricultural and government sectors are excluded from the WSS. In addition, the size of establishments surveyed has changed from those with ten or more permanent employees (1980–98) to those with five or more (1999–2005) and finally to those with one or more (2006–16). For the sake of consistency, establishments with fewer than ten employees are dropped from the sample for 1999–16 in the following analysis.[8] As there exist no other sources that cover the 1980s, the somewhat limited coverage of the WSS is deemed a price worth paying.

I use the hourly wage to measure wage inequality.[9] The hourly wage is closer to the textbook concept of price of labor than monthly or yearly earnings and better represents the quality of the job. For example, a part-time job with a higher hourly wage and lower yearly earnings is likely of better quality than a full-time job with a lower hourly wage and higher yearly earnings.

Table 7-2 reports the dramatic change in worker characteristics between 1980 and 2016. The average age of workers rose from 28.6 years to 41.2 years. The share of middle school graduates plummeted from 59.8 percent to 3.8 percent, while that of (four-year) college graduates jumped up from 8.6 percent to 40.6 percent. The share of workers with ten or more years of experience increased from 8.2 percent to 33.9 percent of the total, and the average firm tenure grew from 2.8 years to 7.1 years. At the same time, workers in establishments with 300 or more employees declined from 45.2 percent to 21.7 percent of the total. The occupational mix also witnessed significant changes, with the share of professional, technical, and managerial jobs rising from 10.9 percent to 28.0 percent and that of craft workers and operators falling from 65.7 percent to 27.9 percent.[10] The

Table 7-2. *Worker Characteristics*[a]

		1980	1990	2000	2010	2016
Sex	Male (%)	60.1	67.2	71.1	69.2	66.2
Age	Average no. of years	28.6	32.7	36.6	39.0	41.2
Highest education completed	Middle school (%)	59.8	33.1	17.6	6.1	3.8
	High school (%)	29.4	48.0	48.0	39.8	38.9
	Junior college (two-year) (%)	2.3	5.9	12.3	17.4	16.7
	College (four-year) (%)	8.6	13.0	22.2	36.6	40.6
Work experience	Less than 3 years (%)	57.7	39.2	28.7	31.4	32.3
	3–10 years (%)	34.1	40.6	38.7	36.5	33.9
	10 or more years (%)	8.2	20.2	32.6	32.1	33.9
Firm tenure	Average no. of years	2.8	3.8	5.4	6.8	7.1
Establishment size	10–299 employees (%)	54.8	63.1	75.8	76.0	78.3
	300 or more employees (%)	45.2	36.9	24.2	24.0	21.7
Occupation	Professional, technical, and managerial (%)	10.9	21.9	26.7	28.0	28.0
	Clerks (%)	16.2	16.3	22.1	25.1	25.6
	Services and sales (%)	6.0	7.2	4.4	7.9	9.6
	Craft workers and operators (%)	65.7	52.2	39.0	31.2	27.9
	Elementary occupations (%)	1.2	2.3	7.7	7.9	8.9
Industry	Light manufacturing (%)	35.4	27.5	14.8	8.6	7.8
	Heavy and chemical manufacturing (%)	35.1	36.4	32.3	29.5	28.3
	Industry exc. manufacturing (%)[b]	5.9	4.6	5.8	5.9	5.6
	Services (%)	23.7	31.5	47.0	56.0	58.4

Source: Ministry of Employment and Labor, *Wage Structure Survey*, various years.
a. Hours worked were used as weights in the calculation.
b. Industry excluding manufacturing is composed of mining, utilities, and construction.

industrial structure also changed substantially, with the service industry increasing its share from 23.7 percent to 58.4 percent at the expense of light manufacturing, whose share fell from 35.4 percent to 7.8 percent.

Estimating Wage Equations

As a first step in the investigation, I estimate a Mincerian wage equation separately for each year, starting with equation 7-1:

$$y_{it} = X_{it}\beta_t + \varepsilon_{it}. \tag{7-1}$$

In equation 7-1, y_{it} stands for the log hourly wage of individual i in year t and X_{it} includes sex, age, age squared, education, experience, firm tenure, firm tenure squared, establishment size, occupation, and industry. In the literature, β_t is often called the "price," or the returns to skill. The regression result is denoted by equation 7-2.

$$y_{it} = X_{it}\hat{\beta}_t + \hat{\varepsilon}_{it}. \tag{7-2}$$

The results for 1980, 1990, 2000, 2010, and 2016 are reported in table 7-3. All coefficient estimates have expected signs with high statistical significance.

Approximating Percentiles with Quintile Averages

I now suppress time subscripts in our notation for the moment and approximate the 10th and 90th percentiles of log wage, y_i, by the averages over the bottom (first) and top (fifth) quintiles, respectively. For example, the 10th percentile of y_i, y_{P10}, is approximated by $y_{\overline{Q1}} = \frac{1}{n_1}\Sigma_{i \in Q1}\, y_i$ so that $y_{P10} \approx y_{\overline{Q1}}$, where $Q1$ is the group of workers belonging to the bottom quintile and n_1 is their number. Adopting similar notations, we have $y_{P90} \approx y_{\overline{Q5}}$. The percentile gap, a common measure for inequality, is then approximated by the quintile average gap: $y_{P90} - y_{P10} \approx y_{\overline{Q5}} - y_{\overline{Q1}}$. The right-hand side of this semi-equality will be called the Q5–Q1 gap. Figure 7-2 shows that this produces fairly good approximations.

Now setting $X_{\overline{Q1}} = \frac{1}{n_1}\Sigma_{i \in Q1} X_i$ and $\hat{\varepsilon}_{\overline{Q1}} = \frac{1}{n_1}\Sigma_{i \in Q1}\hat{\varepsilon}_i$, and similarly for the top quintile, we can derive from equation 7-2 equation 7-3 and equation 7-4:

$$y_{\overline{Q1}} = X_{\overline{Q1}}\hat{\beta} + \hat{\varepsilon}_{\overline{Q1}} \text{ and } y_{\overline{Q5}} = X_{\overline{Q5}}\hat{\beta} + \hat{\varepsilon}_{\overline{Q5}}. \tag{7-3}$$

$$y_{P90} - y_{P10} \approx y_{\overline{Q5}} - y_{\overline{Q1}} = (X_{\overline{Q5}} - X_{\overline{Q1}})\hat{\beta} + (\hat{\varepsilon}_{\overline{Q5}} - \hat{\varepsilon}_{\overline{Q1}}). \tag{7-4}$$

The right-hand side of equation 7-4 has two components, the first measuring the contribution of observable worker characteristics (X) to wage inequality and the second being residual inequality. In the literature, the first component is often called "between-group" inequality and the second "within-group" inequality.[11]

Table 7-3. *Regression of Log Hourly Wage*[a]

		1980	1990	2000	2010	2016
Sex	Male	0.350***	0.275***	0.202***	0.236***	0.193***
		(0.002)	(0.002)	(0.003)	(0.002)	(0.002)
Age		0.045***	0.025***	0.037***	0.041***	0.037***
		(0.001)	(0.001)	(0.001)	(0.001)	(0.000)
Age squared × 10		−0.005***	−0.003***	−0.004***	−0.004***	−0.004***
		(0.000)	(0.000)	(0.000)	(0.000)	(0.000)
Highest education completed	Middle school	−0.142***	−0.104***	−0.124***	−0.049***	−0.041***
		(0.002)	(0.002)	(0.003)	(0.004)	(0.003)
	Junior college	0.167***	0.064***	0.039***	0.092***	0.093***
		(0.006)	(0.003)	(0.003)	(0.003)	(0.002)
	College	0.435***	0.334***	0.235***	0.300***	0.263***
		(0.004)	(0.003)	(0.003)	(0.003)	(0.002)
Work experience	Less than 1 year	−0.184***	−0.225***	−0.223***	−0.171***	−0.104***
		(0.003)	(0.003)	(0.004)	(0.004)	(0.003)
	1–3 years	−0.061***	−0.063***	−0.082***	−0.062***	−0.042***
		(0.002)	(0.002)	(0.004)	(0.003)	(0.002)
	5–10 years	0.077***	0.047***	0.025***	0.050***	0.040***
		(0.003)	(0.002)	(0.003)	(0.003)	(0.002)
	More than 10 years	0.163***	0.129***	0.071***	0.135***	0.120***
		(0.004)	(0.003)	(0.004)	(0.004)	(0.003)
Firm tenure		0.035***	0.032***	0.036***	0.027***	0.027***
		(0.001)	(0.001)	(0.001)	(0.001)	(0.000)
Firm tenure squared × 10		−0.008***	−0.005***	−0.005***	−0.001***	−0.001***
		(0.000)	(0.000)	(0.000)	(0.000)	(0.000)
Establishment size (no. of employees)	10–29	−0.109***	−0.099***	−0.114***	−0.121***	−0.110***
		(0.004)	(0.003)	(0.003)	(0.003)	(0.002)
	30–99	−0.074***	−0.069***	−0.082***	−0.059***	−0.065***
		(0.002)	(0.002)	(0.002)	(0.002)	(0.002)
	300–499	0.017***	0.068***	0.111***	0.107***	0.084***
		(0.002)	(0.001)	(0.001)	(0.003)	(0.002)
	500 or more	0.047***	0.147***	0.116***	0.231***	0.264***
		(0.002)	(0.001)	(0.002)	(0.002)	(0.002)
Occupation		O	O	O	O	O
Industry		O	O	O	O	O
Observations		404,120	473,785	475,472	628,027	674,100
R-squared		0.740	0.715	0.665	0.604	0.610

Source: Koh (2018).

a. The coefficient estimates for the constant term and the occupation and industry dummies are not shown. Robust standard errors in parentheses. ***$p < 0.01$, **$p < 0.05$, *$p < 0.1$. Observations on workers were weighted by the number of hours worked.

Decomposing the Level of Wage Inequality

The between-group inequality can be further decomposed into individual characteristics in X. For example, consider the first three variables in the regression—sex, age, and age squared—and denote them by x_1, x_2, and x_3, respectively. Also denote the coefficient estimates of these variables by $\hat{\beta}_1$, $\hat{\beta}_2$, and $\hat{\beta}_3$. Then the contribution of sex to the Q5–Q1 gap is given by $(x_{1,\overline{Q5}} - x_{1,\overline{Q1}})\hat{\beta}_1$, and that of age is given by $(x_{2,\overline{Q5}} - x_{2,\overline{Q1}})\hat{\beta}_2 + (x_{3,\overline{Q5}} - x_{3,\overline{Q1}})\hat{\beta}_3$. Similarly, let x_4, x_5, and x_6 denote the three education dummies (middle school, junior college, and college) and $\hat{\beta}_4$, $\hat{\beta}_5$, and $\hat{\beta}_6$ their coefficient estimates. Then the contribution of education is given by $(x_{4,\overline{Q5}} - x_{4,\overline{Q1}})\hat{\beta}_4 + (x_{5,\overline{Q5}} - x_{5,\overline{Q1}})\hat{\beta}_5 + (x_{6,\overline{Q5}} - x_{6,\overline{Q1}})\hat{\beta}_6$. Interestingly, the choice of baseline dummies (for example, female rather than male) does not affect the result of the computations. Figure 7-3 illustrates the results of decomposition using equation 7-4.

Decomposing the Changes in Wage Inequality

Having discussed the decomposition of the *level* of wage inequality, we now turn to the decomposition of the *change* in wage inequality. Let $g_t = y_{\overline{Q5},t} - y_{\overline{Q1},t}$ denote the Q5–Q1 gap in year t, and similarly define $z_t = X_{\overline{Q5},t} - X_{\overline{Q1},t}$ and $\mu_t = \hat{\varepsilon}_{\overline{Q5},t} - \hat{\varepsilon}_{\overline{Q1},t}$. Here, z_t represents the difference in worker characteristics between the top and bottom quintiles. In the following discussions, we refer to z_t simply as the "distribution." Then we have $g_t = z_t \hat{\beta}_t + \mu_t$ and equation 7-5, where the upper bars denote averages over the sample period:

$$g_t - \overline{g} = \overline{z}\left(\hat{\beta}_t - \overline{\hat{\beta}}\right) + (z_t - \overline{z})\overline{\hat{\beta}} + (z_t - \overline{z})\left(\hat{\beta}_t - \overline{\hat{\beta}}\right) + \left(\overline{z}\overline{\hat{\beta}} - \overline{z}\overline{\hat{\beta}}\right) + (\mu_t - \overline{\mu}). \quad (7\text{-}5)$$

In equation 7-5, $g_t - \overline{g}$ is the deviation of the Q5–Q1 gap from its mean, $\hat{\beta}_t - \overline{\hat{\beta}}$ is the deviation of $\hat{\beta}_t$ from its mean, and $z_t - \overline{z}$ is the deviation of the distribution from its mean. The first term on the right-hand side, $\overline{z}\left(\hat{\beta}_t - \overline{\hat{\beta}}\right)$, is the contribution of the price to $g_t - \overline{g}$, and the second term, $(z_t - \overline{z})\overline{\hat{\beta}}$, is the contribution of the distribution. The third term is an "interaction term," and the fourth term is a constant adjustment. The last term, $(\mu_t - \overline{\mu})$, is the contribution of the within-group inequality. Note that the sum of the first three terms is equal to $z_t\hat{\beta}_t - \overline{z}\overline{\hat{\beta}}$ (equation 7-6),

FIGURE 7-3. Contributions to the Q5–Q1 Gap

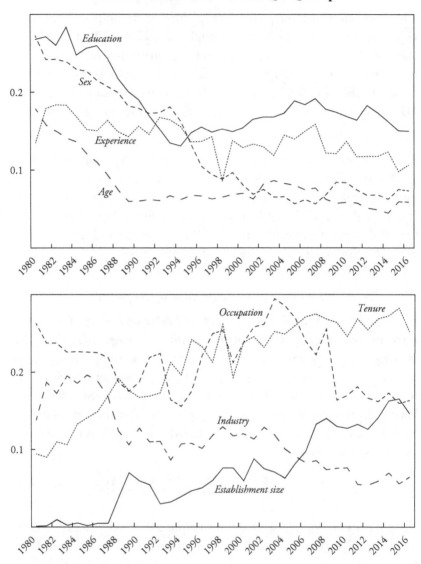

Source: Koh (2018).

and represents the deviation of between-group inequality from its mean (with a constant adjustment, $\overline{z}\hat{\overline{\beta}} - \overline{z}\hat{\overline{\beta}}$).

$$z_t\hat{\beta}_t - \overline{z}\hat{\overline{\beta}} = \overline{z}\left(\hat{\beta}_t - \hat{\overline{\beta}}\right) + (z_t - \overline{z})\hat{\overline{\beta}} + (z_t - \overline{z})\left(\hat{\beta}_t - \hat{\overline{\beta}}\right). \tag{7-6}$$

Figure 7-4 plots for each worker characteristic "total deviation," "price," and "distribution," which are defined, respectively, as $z_t\hat{\beta}_t - \overline{z}\hat{\overline{\beta}}$, $\overline{z}\left(\hat{\beta}_t - \hat{\overline{\beta}}\right)$, and $(z_t - \overline{z})\hat{\overline{\beta}}$.

Looking at panel A, we see that both the "price" and "distribution" of sex played similar roles in explaining the "total deviation." The same is true for age (panel B). As for education (panel C), the "total deviation" and the "price" are almost indistinguishable from each other, indicating that price was the dominant factor in determining education's impact on wage inequality. Much the same can be said about work experience (panel D). On the other hand, in the case of firm tenure (panel E) and establishment size (panel F), a better part of the "total deviation" can be attributed to the "distribution." In the case of occupation (panel G) and industry (panel H), both "price" and "distribution" played important roles, as in the cases of sex and age.

From figure 7-4 we can compute the changes within each subperiod (1980–94, 1995–2007, 2008–16) by taking the difference between the values in the final year and the starting year. In each subperiod, with F and S denoting the final and starting year, respectively, differencing equation 7-6 across F and S yields equation 7-7:

$$z_F\hat{\beta}_F - z_S\hat{\beta}_S = \overline{z}(\hat{\beta}_F - \hat{\beta}_S) + (z_F - z_S)\hat{\overline{\beta}} + \text{other terms.} \tag{7-7}$$

Table 7-4 reports the results. For each subperiod, the first column (T) shows the total change in between-group inequality $(z_F\hat{\beta}_F - z_S\hat{\beta}_S)$, the second column (P) shows the change due to price changes $(\overline{z}(\hat{\beta}_F - \hat{\beta}_S))$, and the last column (D) shows the change due to distributional changes $\left((z_F - z_S)\hat{\overline{\beta}}\right)$.

The next-to-last-row of table 7-4 reports the sums of the columns. The sums of the T columns are −0.022 in 1980–92, 0.012 in 1995–2007, and −0.008 in 2008–16. Various worker characteristics as a whole thus decreased the Q5–Q1 gap in the first subperiod, increased it in the second,

FIGURE 7-4. **Decomposition into the Price Effect and the Distribution Effect**

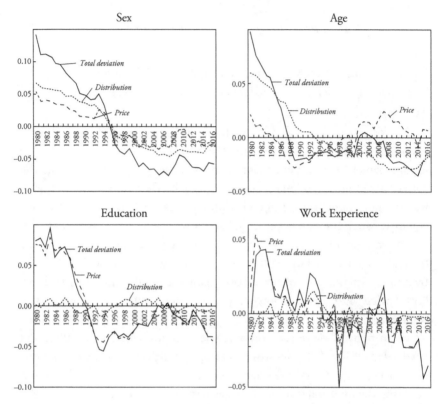

Source: Koh (2018).

Note: "Total deviation" corresponds to $z_t \hat{\beta}_t - \bar{z}\bar{\hat{\beta}}$, "Price" to $\bar{z}(\hat{\beta}_t - \bar{\hat{\beta}})$, and "Distribution" to $(z_t - \bar{z})\bar{\hat{\beta}}$.

and decreased it in the third. This coincides with the movement of the Q5–Q1 gap as shown in figure 7-2 and reported in the last row of table 7-4.

The sums of the T columns are also close in value to the sums of the P columns, which are –0.021 in 1980–92, 0.013 in 1995–2007, and –0.015 in 2009–16. In other words, the changes in wage inequality were largely the result of the changes in the prices of worker characteristics.[12] Looking at individual worker characteristics, one can see that in each subperiod the values in the P column for age, education, and experience have the same signs as the sum in the P column. These characteristics therefore appear to have been important in leading the overall price movement.

FIGURE 7-4. (continued)

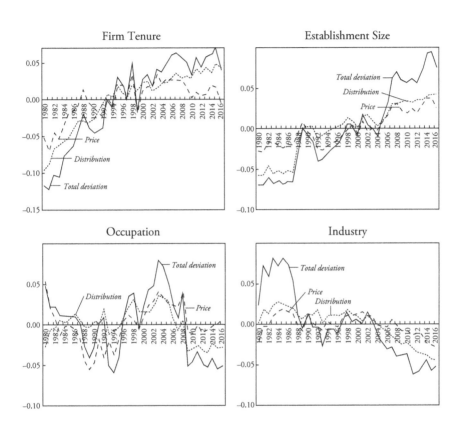

Changing Prices of Education

The previous section demonstrated that wage inequality has been strongly influenced by the prices of worker characteristics. The returns to skill have fluctuated over the decades and shaped the development of wage inequality and, by extension, income inequality. In particular, the final education completed by workers, together with age and experience, has led the change in total prices. Price is determined through the interaction between demand and supply. This section studies the changes in demand for and supply of education in 1980–2016. We follow the standard approach in the literature but allow for different movements of demand shifters across subperiods. Then a more complicated picture than that suggested by the argument of "the race between education and technology"[13] emerges.

Table 7-4. *Changes within Each Subperiod*

	1980–92[a]			1995–2007			2009–16		
	T	P	D	T	P	D	T	P	D
Sex	-0.008	-0.003	-0.003	-0.006	-0.003	-0.004	-0.002	-0.003	0.001
Age	-0.010	-0.004	-0.005	0.001	0.003	-0.002	0.000	-0.001	0.002
Education	-0.010	-0.009	0.000	0.004	0.003	0.000	-0.004	-0.005	0.001
Experience	0.003	-0.001	0.003	0.002	0.002	0.000	-0.002	-0.003	0.001
Tenure	0.007	0.002	0.008	0.003	0.001	0.001	-0.002	-0.003	0.002
Establishment size	0.002	0.000	0.004	0.007	0.004	0.003	0.002	0.001	0.001
Occupation	-0.003	-0.008	0.004	0.004	0.003	0.000	0.000	0.002	0.001
Industry	-0.002	0.002	0.001	-0.002	0.001	-0.002	-0.002	-0.003	-0.003
Sum	-0.022	-0.021	0.012	0.012	0.013	-0.005	-0.008	-0.015	0.004
Q5–Q1	-0.030			0.027			-0.017		

Source: Koh (2018).

a. Sample periods (1980–92, 1995–2007, 2009–16) were adjusted to match the changes in occupational and industrial classifications.

b. **T** refers to the total change of the contribution of each worker characteristic to the Q5–Q1 gap, **P** the part due to changes in price, and **D** that due to changes in distribution. The changes were annualized by dividing them by the number of years in each period.

FIGURE 7-5. **Relative Labor Supply and Demand**

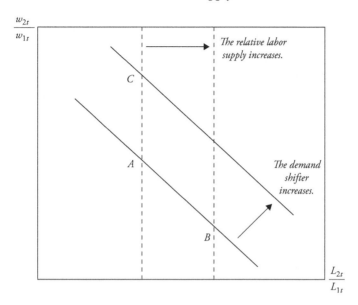

Source: Acemoglu (2002, p. 20).

Theoretical Framework

To better understand the movement of prices, the following regressions are run:

$$\log\left(\frac{w_{2t}}{w_{1t}}\right) = \gamma D_t - \gamma \log\left(\frac{L_{2t}}{L_{1t}}\right) + \epsilon_t, \ t = 1980, \ldots 2016. \qquad (7\text{-}8)$$

In equation 7-8, w_{1t} and w_{2t} are the wages of group 1 and group 2, respectively, L_{1t} and L_{2t} are their labor supplies, and D_t is the demand shifter. For example, if group 1 is high school graduates and group 2 is college graduates, then $\log\left(\frac{w_{2t}}{w_{1t}}\right)$ is the relative price of college education to high school education, and $\log\left(\frac{L_{2t}}{L_{1t}}\right)$ is the relative supply.

The relation between $\frac{w_{2t}}{w_{1t}}$, D_t, and $\frac{L_{2t}}{L_{1t}}$ can be explained with the help of figure 7-5. Assume for the moment $\gamma > 0$. Starting from point A, when $\frac{L_{2t}}{L_{1t}}$ increases, $\frac{w_{2t}}{w_{1t}}$ falls along the demand curve to point B. When D_t increases, on the other hand, $\frac{w_{2t}}{w_{1t}}$ rises from point A to C.

In the literature, D_t is often interpreted as reflecting the different speeds of technological progress for different factors. Following Daron Acemoglu,[14] suppose the production function for the aggregate economy takes the constant elasticity of substitution (CES) form $Q_t = [(A_{1t} L_{1t})^\rho + (A_{2t} L_{2t})^\rho]^{\frac{1}{\rho}}$ where A_{1t} and A_{2t} are factor-augmenting technology terms. In a competitive labor market, the wage for group 1 is equal to its marginal product:

$$w_{1t} = \frac{\partial Q_t}{\partial L_{1t}} = A_{1t}^\rho L_{1t}^{\rho-1}[(A_{1t} L_{1t})^\rho + (A_{2t} L_{2t})^\rho]^{\frac{1}{\rho}-1},$$

and similarly for group 2:

$$w_{2t} = \frac{\partial Q_t}{\partial L_{2t}} = A_{2t}^\rho L_{2t}^{\rho-1}[(A_{1t} L_{1t})^\rho + (A_{2t} L_{2t})^\rho]^{\frac{1}{\rho}-1}.$$

Then the relative price is given by equation 7-9:

$$\frac{w_{2t}}{w_{1t}} = \left(\frac{A_{2t}}{A_{1t}}\right)^\rho \left(\frac{L_{2t}}{L_{1t}}\right)^{\rho-1}. \tag{7-9}$$

Taking logs on both sides of equation 7-9 gives equation 7-10:

$$\log\left(\frac{w_{2t}}{w_{1t}}\right) = \frac{1}{\sigma}\log\left(\frac{A_{2t}}{A_{1t}}\right)^{\sigma-1} - \frac{1}{\sigma}\log\left(\frac{L_{2t}}{L_{1t}}\right), \tag{7-10}$$

where $\sigma = \dfrac{1}{1-\rho}$ is the elasticity of substitution.

The relation in equation 7-10 holds even when there are more than two factors of production L_{it} ($i = 1,2,3, \ldots$) and the production function is of the form $Q_t = [\Sigma_i (A_{it} L_{it})^\rho]^{\frac{1}{\rho}}$, in which case equation 7-11 holds:

$$\log\left(\frac{w_{it}}{w_{1t}}\right) = \frac{1}{\sigma}\log\left(\frac{A_{it}}{A_{1t}}\right)^{\sigma-1} - \frac{1}{\sigma}\log\left(\frac{L_{it}}{L_{1t}}\right), \quad i=2,3, \ldots . \tag{7-11}$$

From equations 7-8 and 7-10, we have $D_t = \log\left(\dfrac{A_2}{A_1}\right)^{\sigma-1}$ and $\gamma = \dfrac{1}{\sigma}$. So if group 1 and group 2 are substitutes ($\sigma > 0$), and if the elasticity of substitution is sufficiently large (that is, if $\sigma > 1$), then a technological progress that favors group 2 over group 1 will shift the demand curve out, while if the elasticity is small (that is, if $0 < \sigma < 1$), such a progress will

FIGURE 7-6. **Enrollment Rate**

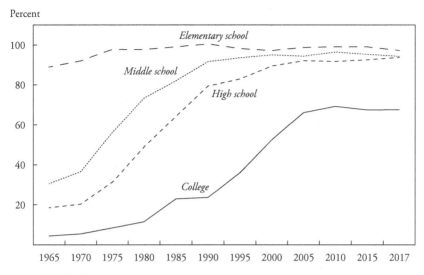

Source: Koh (2018).

shift the demand curve in.[15] On the other hand, if group 1 and group 2 are complements ($\sigma < 0$), then such a progress will always shift the demand curve out.

Estimation

In the literature, γD_t is often assumed to be a linear function in time.[16] In this chapter, a spline function for three periods (1980–94, 1995–2007, 2008–16) is assumed for γD_t as in equation 7-12, where $1(\cdot)$ is an indicator function:

$$
\begin{aligned}
\gamma D_t = \alpha_0 + \alpha_1 t \cdot 1(1980 \le t \le 1994) \\
+ \, [1994(\alpha_1 - \alpha_2) + \alpha_2 t] \cdot 1(1995 \le t \le 2007) \\
+ \, [1994(\alpha_1 - \alpha_2) + 2007(\alpha_2 - \alpha_3) + \alpha_3 t] \cdot 1(2008 \le t \le 2016).
\end{aligned}
\tag{7-12}
$$

A positive (negative) estimate for α_1, for example, will indicate that the relative demand tended to increase (decrease) during the first period.

In estimating equation 7-8, care should be taken to prevent those variables not included in the regression from affecting the results. For example, suppose group 1 is high school graduates and group 2 is college graduates. Given the rapidly rising college enrollment rate over the past decades (figure 7-6),

L_{2t} will contain more and more and L_{1t} less and less young workers as time passes. In addition, given the rising share of women among college students, L_{2t} will also contain more and more and L_{1t} fewer and fewer women. Without an appropriate correction, the estimate of γ would reflect not only the effect of college education but also that of age and sex.

This paper follows Lawrence Katz and Kevin Murphy to address this problem.[17] First, workers are sorted into 600 sex–age–education–tenure–experience groups.[18] Next, the average share of each group is calculated over the whole sample period (1980–2016). These averages are then assigned as fixed weights to the groups. The average wage of, say, college graduates is then calculated with these fixed weights for each year.

Regression Results

Two regressions were run for education, and the results are reported in table 7-5. In the first regression, high school graduates were chosen as group 1, and the regression was run for middle school, junior college, and

Table 7-5. *Regression of Relative Wage on Relative Supply*[a]

| | | Seemingly Unrelated Regression | | | |
		Middle school / high school (1)	Junior college / high school (2)	College / high school (3)	College equivalents / high school equivalents (4)
	α_1	−0.005 (0.005)	−0.008*** (0.002)	−0.014*** (0.001)	0.008 (0.006)
Slope	α_2	−0.013*** (0.003)	0.003 (0.003)	0.028*** (0.004)	0.041*** (0.008)
	α_3	−0.013*** (0.004)	−0.005*** (0.001)	−0.000 (0.003)	0.004 (0.004)
$-\gamma$		−0.185*** (0.047)	−0.043 (0.041)	−0.346*** (0.050)	−0.446*** (0.100)
Observations		37	37	37	37
R-squared		0.922	0.940	0.916	0.899

Source: Koh (2018).
a. Constant estimates not shown. Standard errors in parentheses. ***$p < 0.01$, **$p < 0.05$, *$p < 0.1$.

Table 7-6. *Share and Relative Supply of Graduates*

Subperiod		First		Second		Third	
Year		1980	1994	1995	2007	2008	2016
Share (%)	Middle school (A)	59.8	26.1	24.3	8.3	7.4	3.8
	High school (B)	29.4	50.1	50.0	43.0	42.8	38.9
	Junior college (C)	2.3	7.7	8.3	17.5	18.0	16.7
	College (D)	8.6	16.1	17.4	31.1	31.9	40.6
Relative supply	Middle school (A/B)	2.03	0.52	0.49	0.19	0.17	0.10
	High school (B/B)	1.00	1.00	1.00	1.00	1.00	1.00
	Junior college (C/B)	0.08	0.15	0.17	0.41	0.42	0.43
	College (D/B)	0.29	0.32	0.35	0.72	0.75	1.04

Source: Koh (2018).

college graduates over this group using the SUR (seemingly unrelated regression) method. In the second, the regression was run for college equivalents (a combined group of junior college and college graduates) over high school equivalents (a combined group of middle school and high school graduates). These two equivalence groups were constructed by utilizing "efficient units," that is, wage ratios.

In the first subperiod, the estimate of α_1 is negative in columns 1, 2, and 3, indicating that the demand for high school graduates increased relative to all other education groups. This relative increase was statistically significant for junior college and college graduates.

It is notable that the supply of high school graduates also increased rapidly in this subperiod, as can be inferred from figure 7-6. Table 7-6 reports the share and the relative supply of each education group. It shows that the share of high school graduates nearly doubled from 29.4 percent to 50.1 percent during the first subperiod while the share of middle school graduates more than halved from 59.8 percent to 26.1 percent. Accordingly the supply of middle school graduates collapsed from being twice as large as that of high school graduates to being half as large.

Now from equations 7-8 and 7-12, the change in log relative wage in the first subperiod can be written as equation 7-13, omitting the error term:

$$\Delta\log\left(\frac{w_{2t}}{w_{1t}}\right) = \gamma\left(\frac{\alpha_1}{\gamma}\Delta t\right) - \gamma\Delta\log\left(\frac{L_{2t}}{L_{1t}}\right). \qquad (7\text{-}13)$$

Table 7-7. *Predicting the Change in Relative Wages*[a]

Subperiod		First	Second	Third
	Middle school	−9.3	−7.4	−4.6
Change in log relative supply	Junior college	4.9	7.8	0.2
	College	0.7	6.3	4.3
	Middle school	−2.7	−6.8	−6.8
Change in relative demand	Junior college	−17.0	7.2	−11.0
	College	−4.0	8.4	0.0
Predicted change in log relative wage	Middle school	1.3	0.1	−0.4
	Junior college	−1.0	0.0	−0.5
	College	−1.6	0.7	−1.4

Source: Koh (2018).
a. Expressed as percent per annum.

Here $\Delta \log \left(\dfrac{w_{2t}}{w_{1t}} \right)$ is the change in log relative wage, $\dfrac{\alpha_1}{\gamma} \Delta t$ is the change in relative demand, and $\Delta \log \left(\dfrac{L_{2t}}{L_{1t}} \right)$ is the change in log relative supply.

We can derive similar expressions for other subperiods. Table 7-7 reports the values for these variables. In this table, all log changes were converted into percent changes per annum.

Table 7-7 shows that in the first subperiod a substantial decline in the relative supply of middle school graduates (−9.3 percent per annum) was only marginally offset by a decline in the relative demand (−2.7 percent per annum) and led to an increase in the relative wage of middle school graduates (1.3 percent per annum). On the other hand, the small increase in the relative supply of college graduates (0.7 percent per annum) combined with a large fall in the relative demand for them (4.0 percent per annum) to produce a large fall in their relative wage (−1.6 percent per annum). Earlier studies often attributed the falling wage premium for college graduates to their increased supply,[19] but this result indicates that an increased demand for high school graduates rather than an increased supply of college graduates was the decisive factor. In any case, a rising relative wage of middle school graduates and a falling relative wage of college and junior college graduates led to narrowing wage gaps between education groups in the first subperiod, as shown in figure 7-7. This eventually led to the falling contribution of education to wage inequality as illustrated in figure 7-3.

FIGURE 7-7. **Relative Wages of Education Groups**[a]

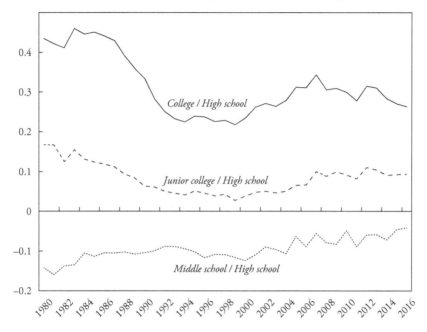

Source: Koh (2018).

a. Coefficient estimates from wage equation 7-1.

The picture changes completely in the second subperiod. The estimate of α_2 in column 3 of table 7-5 is 0.028 and that of γ is 0.346, and both are significant at the 1 percent level. Thus, the relative demand for college graduates increased by 8.4 percent annually.[20] At the same time, the relative supply of college graduates more than doubled from 0.35 to 0.71 in this subperiod (table 7-6), and their relative supply increased by 6.3 percent (table 7-7). But such an increase in supply was not enough to meet the increasing demand, and their predicted relative wage rose by 0.7 percent. The rising college wage premium led to a rising contribution of education to wage inequality (figure 7-3).

The demand for college graduates stopped increasing in the third subperiod. The estimate of α_3 in column 3 of table 7-5 is −0.000 and is not statistically significant. While the relative demand stood still, the relative supply of college graduates increased by 4.3 percent, and the relative wage fell by 1.4 percent (table 7-7). The relative wage of junior college graduates also fell, and the overall contribution of education to wage inequality declined (figure 7-3).

Lastly, comparing columns 3 and 4 of table 7-5, we can see that the coefficient estimates are similar to each other except for α_1. The estimate of α_1 in column 3 is negative and significant, while that in column 4 is positive and insignificant. Studies that employ college and high school equivalents, following Lawrence Katz and Kevin Murphy,[21] would thus miss an important role played by the increasing demand for and supply of high school graduates in Korea in the early years.

Explaining the Changing Demands

What were the driving forces behind the changing relative demands for education? This section attempts an explanation for these changes.

The First Subperiod

The most notable development in the first subperiod was the increasing demand for high school graduates. During this subperiod, Korea was moving away from light manufacturing toward heavy and chemical industries (HCIs). The Korean government had announced the HCI drive in the early 1970s in response to the intensifying competition from other low-wage countries and the increasing need to climb up the value chain. Since then, the share of HCIs rose continuously in manufacturing. For instance, the share of manufacturing workers in HCIs increased from almost half in 1980 to about 80 percent in 2016 (table 7-2). The changing industrial structure could have reduced the demand for low-skilled middle school graduates and increased that for mid-skilled high school graduates.

Another possibility is that all industries—not only manufacturing but also services and other industries—were affected more or less by technical changes that increased the demand for high school graduates. For instance, Daron Acemoglu claims that technological progress is initiated by profit motives and sustained by market demands and that an increased supply of a specific group of workers can increase the demand for them by prompting technical changes that make better use of them.[22] He presents several cases in history as circumstantial evidence for his endogenous technical change hypothesis. One example is the early nineteenth century when the supply of unskilled labor increased in English cities as a result of enclosures, population growth, and other changes. As would be predicted by the endogenous technical change hypothesis, important unskilled labor–biased technologies were introduced in this period, the most notable of which was the factory system replacing tasks previously performed by skilled artisans.

Applying the endogenous technical change hypothesis to the Korean labor market in the 1980s, the increasing demand for high school graduates could have come from their increasing supply following the rapidly rising enrollment rate in high schools since the 1970s (figure 7-6). The increasing supply prompted technical changes in workplaces (again, not only in manufacturing but also in other industries) that made more use of high school graduates. Acemoglu originally proposed this hypothesis and constructed a theoretical model to explain the increasing demand for college graduates in the United States,[23] but his argument can be applied equally to other cases as well. Here causality runs from an increasing supply to technical changes and then to an increasing demand.

It is beyond the scope of this chapter to examine whether the increasing demand for high school graduates in the first subperiod was caused by the changing industrial structure or by technical changes that raised the productivity of high school graduates. But the issue certainly deserves close investigation in the future.

The Second Subperiod

Many studies have pointed a finger at SBTC as the reason for the increasing demand for high-skilled workers in the 1990s and 2000s.[24] In particular, it is claimed that the widespread use of ICT has increased the demand for high-skilled labor in Korea as in the United States. Even without the advancement of ICT, it is quite possible that the demand for high-skilled workers increased in the second subperiod as Korea moved closer to the technological frontier in many areas on the back of prolonged investment in research and development.

Meanwhile, the endogenous technical change hypothesis would argue that the increasing supply of college graduates in the 1990s and 2000s accelerated SBTC and increased the demand for college graduates. As such, this hypothesis offers an explanation for the cause of SBTC and does not refute the SBTC-based explanations for the increasing demand for college graduates.

All things considered, the second subperiod appears to have been a period of accelerated technological progress, which raised the premium on college education and widened the wage gap among workers.

The Third Subperiod

The subdued increase in the demand for college graduates observed in the third subperiod could have many causes. First, SBTC may have decelerated significantly in recent years. Korea's annual GDP growth recorded 9.4 percent and 5.1 percent in the first and second subperiods, respectively, but only 3.1 percent in the third. The real hourly wage growth experienced a similar slowdown, as reported in table 7-1, with the annual growth rate of median wage falling from 9.2 percent and 4.0 percent to 1.1 percent. Many countries witnessed a slowdown in capital accumulation and total factor productivity growth after the global financial crisis, and Korea was not an exception.[25] The declining growth potential of the Korean economy could have put a brake on the demand for high-skilled workers.

Second, the deterioration in the quality of higher education could have reduced the demand for college graduates. The college enrollment rate has risen significantly as a result of policy changes in the early 1980s and the mid-1990s (figure 7-6).[26] College education has since become almost universal, but the concern about the poor quality of education has increased. At the same time, according to Ju-Ho Lee, Hyeok Jeong, and Song-Chang Hong,[27] the bottom 20 percent of college graduates and bottom 40 percent of junior college graduates receive wages that are lower than the average wage of high school graduates. If the educational quality has indeed been compromised as a result of the explosive growth of quantity, *ceteris paribus*, the demand for college graduates must have decreased.

Third, according to the endogenous technical change hypothesis, the stagnant demand for college graduates in the third subperiod could have been caused by the slower growth of their supply following the flattening of college enrollment rates (figure 7-6).

Policy Implications

The three possibilities offered above for the third subperiod suggest that policymakers' room for maneuver is rather limited. If they believe that technical change has indeed slowed down and led to slower economic growth and wage increase, and if they want to reverse the trend by accelerating technical change, then they would need to accept the worsening of wage and income inequality, as it happened in the second subperiod. If they attempt to counter the worsening wage inequality by expanding the supply of college education and thereby reducing the college wage premium, then they may exacerbate the deterioration of college education, as has been observed since the 1990s. They may also see the demand for college graduates increase further according to the endogenous technical change hypothesis.

The two goals of robust economic growth and equitable income distribution may no longer be compatible with each other. In the 1970s and 1980s, when Korea was starting from a low technological level, the demand for mid-skilled workers increased rapidly, and the government could combine growth and equity by expanding the supply of high school graduates fast enough to narrow the wage gap with middle school graduates but slow enough to avoid widening the gap with college graduates. With industrial upgrading, however, the demand has shifted from mid-skilled toward high-skilled workers. A sustained economic growth will require continued technological progress, which will further increase the demand for skills and widen the wage gap, given the bottleneck in the supply of high-quality college education.

Breaking the impasse may require a radical departure from the way Korea's economy and society are currently organized. In addition to facilitating innovation and boosting productivity, the government needs to raise the quality of education and strengthen the social safety net. However, the country appears to lack public consensus on the need for changes in policies and institutions to meet the current challenges. The following subsections discuss these points in turn.

Boosting Productivity with Deregulation

To facilitate innovation and boost productivity, wide-ranging deregulation is needed. According to the Organisation of Economic Co-operation and Development (OECD) indicator of Product Market Regulation (PMR),

FIGURE 7-8. **OECD Product Market Regulation Indicator, 2013**[a]

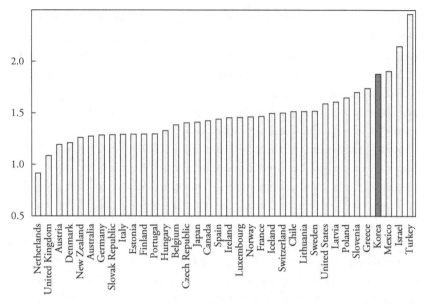

Source: *OECD.Stat* (http://www.oecd.org/economy/reform/indicators-of-product-market
-regulation/), accessed April 3, 2019.

a. The scale is from zero (least) to six (most restrictive).

Korea has the fourth most regulated economy, next to Turkey, Israel, and
Mexico (figure 7-8). In almost all categories of PMR, Korea ranks very low
(table 7-8). The only exceptions are scope of state-owned enterprises
(ranked fifth), communication and simplification of rules and procedures
(ranked first), differential treatment of foreign suppliers (ranked ninth), and
a few others. But in other categories Korea has a very restrictive system,
such as in governance of state-owned enterprises (ranked thirtieth),
price controls (ranked thirty-fifth), antitrust exemptions for incumbents
(ranked twenty-seventh), barriers in network sectors (ranked thirty-third),
barriers to FDI (ranked thirty-first), trade barriers (ranked thirty-sixth),
and barriers to trade facilitation (ranked thirtieth). The widespread in-
volvement of government in economic activities should be reexamined and
reduced.

Labor market regulation is also believed to be restrictive in Korea. The
OECD indicator of Employment Protection Legislation (EPL) ranks Korea
in the twenty-third place among thirty-four countries in the category of

Table 7-8. *OECD Product Market Regulation Indicator, 2013*

Category	Korea's ranking out of 36 countries
Product market regulation	33
State control	29
Public ownership	16
Scope of state-owned enterprises (SOEs)	5
Government involvement in network sectors	12
Direct control over enterprises	10
Governance of state-owned enterprises	30
Involvement in business operations	32
Price controls	35
Command and control regulation	13
Barriers to entrepreneurship	27
Administrative burdens on startups	17
Administrative burdens for corporation	23
Administrative burdens for sole proprietor firms	17
Barriers in services sectors	11
Complexity of regulatory procedures	21
Licenses and permits system	22
Communication and simplification of rules and procedures	1
Regulatory protection of incumbents	31
Legal barriers	25
Antitrust exemptions	27
Barriers in network sectors	33
Barriers to trade and investment	35
Explicit barriers to trade and investment	36
Barriers to foreign direct investment	31
Tariff barriers	36
Other barriers to trade and investment	25
Differential treatment of foreign suppliers	9
Barriers to trade facilitation	30

Source: *OECD.Stat* (http://www.oecd.org/economy/reform/indicators-of-product-market-regulation), accessed April 3, 2019.

individual dismissals of regular workers, in twenty-sixth place in the category of temporary contracts, and in fourth place in the category of collective dismissals (table 7-9).

In the case of individual dismissals of regular workers, perhaps the most stringent is the requirement to reinstate dismissed workers once the dismissal is found unfair (figure 7-9). In most OECD countries, employers can resort

Table 7-9. *OECD Employment Protection Legislation Indicator, 2013*

	Korea's ranking out of 34 countries
Individual dismissals (regular contracts)	23
Temporary contracts	26
Collective dismissals	4

Source: *OECD.Stat* (https://www.oecd.org/els/emp/oecdindicatorsofemployment
protection.htm), accessed April 3, 2019.

FIGURE 7-9. **Protection of Permanent Workers against Individual Dismissals: Difficulty of Dismissal, 2013**[a]

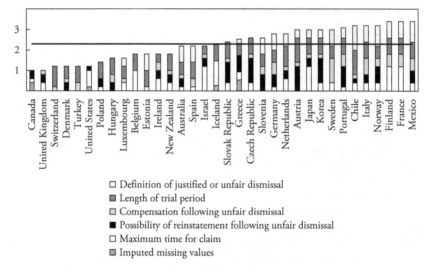

□ Definition of justified or unfair dismissal
■ Length of trial period
□ Compensation following unfair dismissal
■ Possibility of reinstatement following unfair dismissal
□ Maximum time for claim
▨ Imputed missing values

Source: Organisation for Economic Co-operation and Development (2013b).

a. The scale is from zero (least) to six (most restrictive).

to monetary compensation in lieu of reinstatement to end disputes with dismissed workers.[28] But monetary compensation is rarely used in Korea, and reinstatement is the rule. This increases uncertainty significantly on the part of employers when hiring workers.

In the case of temporary contracts, the use of temporary work agency (TWA) workers and fixed-term contract (FTC) workers is tightly controlled in Korea. Only thirty-two tasks are open for TWA workers. In contrast, the United States and the United Kingdom have no regulations, and Germany and Japan allow TWA workers for all tasks with some exceptions (for example, construction). FTC is also limited up to two years in Korea, much shorter than in Japan (five years), Spain (three years), or Germany (two years, but the extension and repeated renewal of contracts is allowed through collective bargaining).

In the case of collective dismissals, fewer restrictions are in place, but labor relations in Korea are known for their adversarial tendency. Firms face many difficulties when confronting organized labor. For instance, the temporary replacement of workers on strike by TWA or FTC workers or utilizing outside suppliers is strictly prohibited, while they are allowed in most countries.

Deregulation of product and labor markets has been found extremely difficult, except in times of crisis (for example, the Asian financial crisis of 1997). Many attempts were made but met with strong opposition from various quarters, not least of which was from labor unions.

Strengthening the Social Safety Net

Korea has traditionally focused more on education and other public services (transportation, housing, water supply, sanitation, and so forth) than on redistribution through welfare programs. Spending on education, for instance, occupied one-fifth of total public spending and 4 percent of GDP in the 1970s. Most of the spending was directed toward primary education for the general public. The strategy has been very effective in equalizing opportunities and supporting job creation.

Welfare spending began to rise rapidly in the 1990s, but it is still far below the level often witnessed in many advanced economies. In 2015 total social expenditure corresponded to 10 percent of GDP in Korea, far below 19 percent observed across OECD countries (figure 7-10). A large part of the discrepancy originates from the relatively short history of Korea's pension system, but almost all other programs also spend less in Korea than in other OECD countries. Spending on unemployment benefits, for instance, is 0.3 percent of GDP in Korea, while it is 0.7 percent in OECD countries on average. The net replacement rate in unemployment for a single person with an unemployment duration of twelve months amounts to 21 percent of his or her previous earnings, far lower than in many other OECD countries (figure 7-11).

The weak social safety net owes to the relatively small tax revenue. Total tax revenue, including social security contributions, was 27 percent of GDP in Korea in 2017, while it was 34 percent in OECD countries on average

FIGURE 7-10. Social Expenditure, 2015

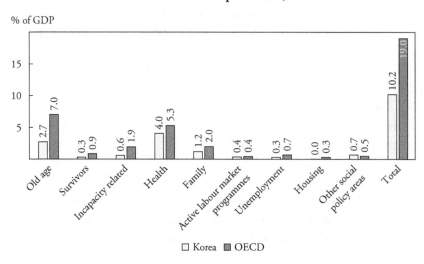

% of GDP

Korea   OECD

Source: *OECD.Stat* (https://stats.oecd.org/Index.aspx?DataSetCode=SOCX_AGG), accessed April 3, 2019.

FIGURE 7-11. Net Replacement Rate in Unemployment, 2017[a]

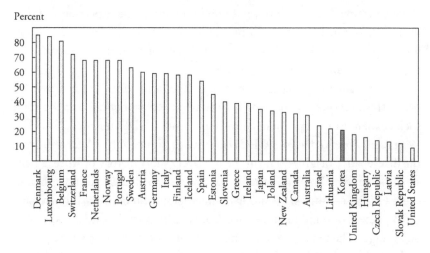

Percent

Source: *OECD.Stat* (https://stats.oecd.org/Index.aspx?DataSetCode=NRR), accessed April 3, 2019.

a. For a single person without children, with an employment duration of twelve months and previous in-work earnings equal to 67 percent of the average wage, and not including housing benefits.

Table 7-10. *Tax Revenue*[a]

Country	Korea	OECD						
Year	2017	1965	1975	1985	1995	2005	2015	2016
Total tax revenue	26.9	24.9	28.7	31.6	33.1	33.4	33.7	34.0
Taxes on income, profits, and capital gains of individuals	4.8	6.8	9.1	9.9	8.6	8.0	8.3	8.2
Taxes on income, profits, and capital gains of corporations	3.8	2.1	2.1	2.5	2.6	3.3	2.8	2.9
Social security contributions	6.9	4.5	6.3	7.3	8.7	8.5	9.0	9.2
Taxes on property	3.1	1.9	1.7	1.6	1.6	1.8	1.9	1.9
General taxes on goods and services	4.3	3.2	4.1	5.0	6.5	6.8	6.9	7.0
Taxes on specific goods and services	2.7	5.7	4.6	4.6	3.9	3.4	3.2	3.3
Other taxes	1.2	0.8	0.8	0.6	1.1	1.6	1.6	1.6

Source: *OECD.Stat* (https://stats.oecd.org/Index.aspx?DataSetCode=REV), accessed April 3, 2019.
a. Expressed as percent of GDP.

(table 7-10). Revenues from personal income taxes are particularly small, as are the revenues from social security contributions and value added taxes.

In order to strengthen the social safety net, it is absolutely necessary to increase the tax revenue. But it is not easy, given the public hostility against tax increases. Public surveys reveal a generally favorable view on welfare spending increases, but once asked how the government should finance the spending increases, only a very small part (less than 10 percent) of the population agrees to a tax increase (figure 7-12). The majority (80 percent) of them believe that the government can squeeze money out of other inefficient spending programs. This presumably reflects a lack of public trust in government.

The Way Forward

These discussions indicate both the necessity of radical changes and the difficulty of achieving them. Continuous efforts to communicate the necessity

FIGURE 7-12. **Public Survey on National Fiscal Management**

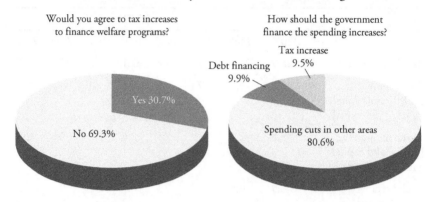

Source: Gallup Korea (2016).

to the public are needed. It will also help to have political leadership that can see through the current challenges and is willing to mobilize its political capital to carry out reforms. Korea's future will depend critically on the choices made by the public and its politicians in the coming years.

Conclusions

In Korea, income inequality declined in the early 1990s, then rose until the late 2010s, and then began to decline again. Wage inequality experienced similar changes in 1980–2016, declining in the first subperiod (1980–94), rising in the second (1995–2007), and declining again in the third (2008–16). The decomposition of wage inequality indicates that most of the changes in inequality came from the changes in the price of skill.

Price is determined through an interaction between demand and supply. In the case of education, the changes in the demand for and supply of different education groups—middle school, high school, and college graduates—can explain the changes in their wage premiums. In the first subperiod, a rapidly increasing demand for high school graduates narrowed the wage gap between high school and college graduates, while an increasing supply of high school graduates and a decreasing supply of middle school graduates narrowed the wage gap between these two groups. This contributed to a falling wage inequality in this subperiod.

In the second subperiod, the college wage premium rose significantly, leading to a rising wage inequality. Skill-biased technical change could be one possible driver of the rising college premium. In the third subperiod, the premium on higher education fell, reversing the upward trend in wage inequality observed in the previous subperiod. At the same time, however, wage growth dropped to 1 percent per year in the upper and middle part of the wage distribution. This may reflect a deceleration of SBTC and a setback in Korea's growth potential.

A key question concerns the relation between growth and distribution. The first subperiod witnessed a happy combination of robust economic growth and improving wage distribution. When the Korean economy was starting from a low level of technology, an increasing demand for and supply of mid-skilled workers helped expand the mid-level wage earners. In the second subperiod, however, wage distribution deteriorated substantially while wage growth was maintained (albeit at a slower pace than before). As the Korean economy came closer to the technological frontier, the demand for high-skilled workers increased. Despite the rapid expansion of higher education, the college wage premium rose rapidly and inequality increased.

In the third subperiod the opposite happened; inequality decreased but growth stalled. If this reflects a deterioration in Korea's growth prospect, then more efforts are needed to facilitate technological progress and boost productivity. At the same time, the social safety net needs to be strengthened to counter the increasing inequality. Overcoming the oppositions that are blocking the efforts for deregulation and building public consensus on tax increases to finance safety nets would be the first step toward harmonizing growth and distribution.

NOTES

1. World Bank (1993, figure 1.3).

2. Goldberg and Pavcnik (2007).

3. The note in figure 7-2 defines the Q5–Q1 gap.

4. Katz and Autor (1999, table 9).

5. Juhn, Murphy, and Pierce (1993); Katz and Autor (1999); Goldin and Katz (2007).

6. This finding is in line with the findings of Juhn, Murphy, and Pierce (1993).

7. As proposed by Acemoglu (2002).

8. In addition, minors younger than 15 years of age, whose employment is prohibited by law, are dropped from the sample, as are workers in such industries as agriculture, water supply, and communications, for which there are many years of missing data. These omissions reduced the number of workers in the sample by less than 2 percent before 1999, by 3 percent to 6 percent in 1999–2005, and by 5 percent to 9 percent in 2006–16.

9. Following DiNardo, Fortin, and Lemieux (1996).

10. The classifications of occupations and industries have each undergone several changes. For the purposes of this study, new and time-invariant classifications were constructed. In reclassifying the occupations, extensive reference was made to International Labour Organization (2012). Despite my best efforts, of course, the consistency of new classifications over time cannot be fully guaranteed.

11. Lemieux (2006).

12. This finding is in line with the findings of Juhn, Murphy, and Pierce (1993), who employed a very different approach from the one I use here.

13. Goldin and Katz (2007).

14. Acemoglu (2002).

15. Acemoglu (2002, p. 21).

16. Katz and Murphy (1992, p. 89); Katz and Autor (1999, p. 1519); Acemoglu (2002, p. 27).

17. Katz and Murphy (1992).

18. Cross-tabulating two sex groups (male and female), three age groups (15–29 years, 30–54 years, and 55+ years), four education groups (middle school, high school, junior college, and college), five experience groups (less than 1 year, 1–3 years, 3–5 years, 5–10 years, and 10+ years), and five tenure groups (less than 1 year, 1–3 years, 3–5 years, 5–10 years, and 10+ years) yields a total of 600 $(= 2 \times 3 \times 4 \times 5 \times 5)$ groups.

19. For example, Kim and Topel (1995).

20. $8.4 = (\exp (0.028 / 0.346) - 1) \times 100$.

21. Katz and Murphy (1992).

22. Acemoglu (2002).

23. Acemoglu (2002).

24. Kwon and Kim (2001); Shin (2007).

25. Kim, Han, and Lee (2017).

26. In the early 1980s the government began to place graduation quotas on colleges while increasing entry quotas above graduation quotas by 30 percent. According to the plan, 30 percent of entrants would not be able to graduate from college. The government's intention was to reduce competition among high school students to enter colleges while encouraging hard work among college students. But the strong opposition from students and their parents to graduation quotas led to the abolition of the latter in later

years, while leaving the increased entry quotas intact. In addition, in the mid-1990s, the government adopted a rule-based license system to allow anybody to open colleges whenever certain conditions set by the government are met. Both changes helped to rapidly expand the number of colleges and college students.

27. Lee, Jeong, and Hong (2014).

28. Organisation for Economic Co-operation and Development (2013a).

REFERENCES

Acemoglu, Daron. 2002. "Technical Change, Inequality, and the Labor Market." *Journal of Economic Literature* 40, no. 1, pp. 7–72.

DiNardo, John, Nicole M. Fortin, and Thomas Lemieux. 1996. "Labor Market Institutions and the Distribution of Wages, 1973–1992: A Semiparametric Approach." *Econometrica* 64, no. 5, pp. 1001–04.

Gallup Korea. 2016. "Public Survey on National Fiscal Management." March 29 (http://news1.kr/articles/?2617409).

Goldberg, Pinelopi K., and Nina Pavcnik. 2007. "Distributional Effects of Globalization in Developing Countries." *Journal of Economic Literature* 45, pp. 39–82.

Goldin, Claudia, and Lawrence F. Katz. 2007. *The Race between Education and Technology* (Harvard University Press).

International Labour Organization. 2012. *International Standard Classification of Occupations: Structure, Group Definitions and Correspondence Tables*, vol. 1. Report ISCO-08. Geneva.

Juhn, Chinhui, Kevin M. Murphy, and Brooks Pierce. 1993. "Wage Inequality and the Rise in Returns to Skill." *Journal of Political Economy* 101, no. 3, pp. 410–42.

Katz, Lawrence F., and David H. Autor. 1999. "Changes in the Wage Structure and Earnings Inequality," in *Handbook of Labor Economics*, vol. 3, edited by Orley Ashenfelter and David Card (Amsterdam: North Holland), pp. 1463–1555.

Katz, Lawrence F., and Kevin M. Murphy. 1992. "Changes in Relative Wages, 1963–1987: Supply and Demand Factors." *Quarterly Journal of Economics* 107, no. 1, pp. 35–78.

Kim, Dae-Il, and Robert H. Topel. 1995. "Labor Markets and Economic Growth: Lessons from Korea's Industrialization, 1970–1990," in *Differences and Changes in Wage Structures*, edited by Richard B. Freeman and Lawrence F. Katz (University of Chicago Press).

Kim, Dowan, Jinhyung Han, and Eunkyung Lee. 2017. "Estimating Korea's Potential Growth Rates." *Bank of Korea Monthly Bulletin* 71 (September), pp. 16–32.

Koh, Youngsun. 2018. "The Evolution of Wage Inequality in Korea," Policy Studies 2018-01 (Sejong: Korea Development Institute).

Kwon, Namhoon, and Jong-Il Kim. 2001. "Changes in Employment Structure in Korea and the Role of Information Technology." *Journal of Korean Economics Studies* 8, pp. 61–89.

Lee, Ju-Ho, Hyeok Jeong, and Song-Chang Hong. 2014. "Is Korea Number One in Human Capital Accumulation? Education Bubble Formation and Its Labor Market Evidence," KDI School Working Paper 2014-03 (Sejong: KDI School of Public Policy).

Lemieux, Thomas. 2006. "Increasing Residual Wage Inequality: Composition Effects, Noisy Data, or Rising Demand for Skill?" *American Economic Review* 96, no. 3, pp. 461–98.

Organisation for Economic Co-operation and Development. 2013a. "Detailed Description of Employment Protection Legislation, 2012–2013," EPL Database (Paris).

———. 2013b. "Protecting Jobs, Enhancing Flexibility: A New Look at Employment Protection Legislation." *OECD Employment Outlook 2013*, pp. 65–126.

Shin, Sukha. 2007. "Technology and the Demand for Unskilled Labor after the Economic Crisis." *KDI Journal of Economic Policy* 29, no. 1, pp. 1–39.

World Bank. 1993. *The East Asian Miracle: Economic Growth and Public Policy* (Oxford University Press).

EIGHT

Change in Labor Income Share in Korea

Findings from Firm-Level Data

JIYOON OH

In macroeconomics the share of labor and capital is almost constant regardless of the flow of time, a well-known empirical rule discovered by Nicholas Kaldor.[1] However, many studies have documented a decline of the share of GDP going to labor over recent decades in many nations.[2] It is generally accepted that the trend of labor income share has been declining since the 1980s. With the emergence of empirical studies showing that the share of labor income in developed countries such as the United States has fallen over the past thirty years, studies on the causes of these changes in labor share have begun to draw quite a bit of attention. In particular, the worsening income inequality in some countries, including the United States, since the 1980s, when labor income share began to fall, has sparked a great deal of interest in labor income share, a functional index of production factors.

As socioeconomic maturity has progressed in Korea, the interest in income and asset inequality has greatly increased. In this context, the interest in the trend of labor income share has greatly increased. In Korea, several studies have reported that labor share has declined since the Asian financial crisis of 1997–98. Baegeun Kim, Byung-hee Lee, Daehee Jeong, Sangyoung Joo and Cheon, and Jangpyo Hong report that the labor share began to decline around 1997–98, during the Asian financial crisis.[3] These studies generally conclude that Korea's trends in labor income distribution fell until the 2000s after the financial crisis.

However, it is very difficult to get the labor share right in Korea, where not only are there many self-employed laborers but also the composition of self-employed laborers changes with time. The studies mentioned above are based on the adjustment of Douglas Gollin,[4] which is not satisfactory in this case. Gollin's method is weak for comparing levels of labor income share between countries at a single point in time because countries have different characteristics of self-employed laborers. In Korea, it is not appropriate to use Gollin's adjustment when examining the trend of labor shares over time, since characteristics such as the industrial or capital equipment rate of the self-employed vary with time.

Recently, many studies only calculate labor shares of the corporate sector due to the difficulty of adjusting for self-employment. However, there is no official way to calculate the labor share of the corporate sector in Korea using the Bank of Korea's National Accounts system before 2010. Income accounts by institutional sectors were first released in 2010. This study is the first attempt at directly measuring the labor share of incorporated firms using companies' financial statement data.

The Trend of Labor Share in Korea's Total Economy

This chapter looks at the key features of the Korean labor market and explains why the indicators of labor share using macrovariables are biased. An alternative is to use financial statement data to calculate and present the labor income share of the corporate sector.

Characteristics of the Korean Labor Market

The proportion of nonsalaried workers in the domestic labor market is not at all negligible. In fact, it is a large part of the labor market.

FIGURE 8-1. **Composition of Labor Force by Status**

Source: Current Population Survey.

Figure 8-1 shows how quickly the Korean labor market went through structural changes. The number of self-employed (nonsalaried) workers is equal to the sum of independent businessmen and unpaid family workers. In the 1970s the weight of industries such as agriculture, forestry, and fishing stood out, effectively reducing the number of self-employed laborers. Of the total employed, the proportion of nonwage workers stood at 25.4 percent in 2017, which is very high compared to other countries. The change in the proportion of nonsalaried workers also shows that the rate of nonsalaried workers has changed so fast that it has declined by an average of about 2 percent per year from 1980 to the present. Figure 8-2 shows the percentage of nonsalaried workers in OECD countries as of 2017. As shown in the figure, Korea is one of the countries with a very high proportion of nonsalaried workers, following Turkey and Mexico. Figure 8-3 shows the scatterplot of nonsalaried workers as related to per capita GDP. The white diamond is Korea. Korea is located much higher than the trend line, meaning the proportion of nonsalaried workers is higher than per capita GDP.

The labor share includes labor costs in the numerator, and the denominator includes labor costs, operating surplus, and fixed capital consumption. The self-employed sector accounts for a nontrivial share of each component. Table 8-1 shows what a large part self-employed laborers play in the total economy. The proportion of wage workers employed as self-employed, not corporate, was about 25 percent in 2016. According to the National

FIGURE 8-2. **Percent of Nonsalaried Workers in OECD Countries, 2017**

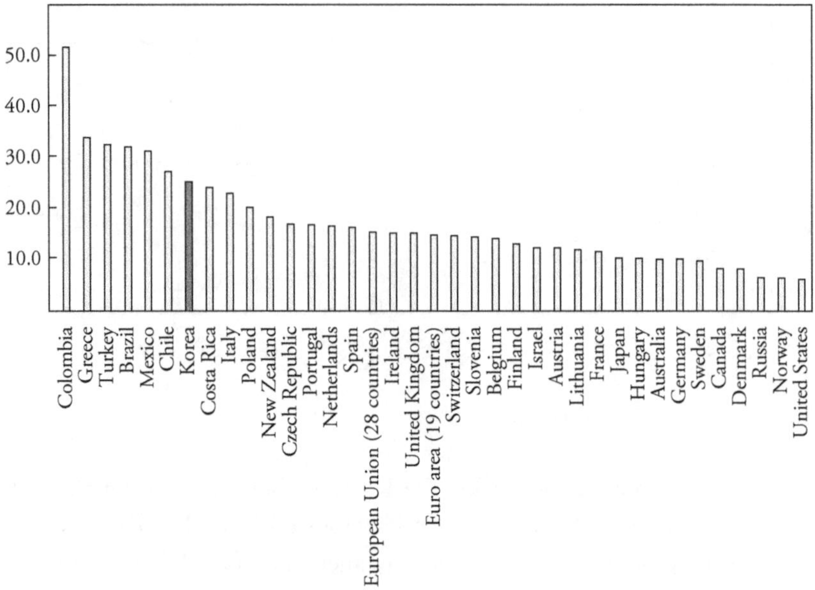

Source: OECD Employment and Labour Market Statistics.

Accounts by institutional sectors, the proportion of employee compensation paid by the self-employed during the period 2010–17 is 18 percent, which is not negligible.

Figure 8-4 shows the average nominal household income of self-employed households and wage earners' households. This data comes from the Korean household trend survey. Until the early 1990s, income for households with a self-employed main breadwinner was higher than that for wage-earning households, but thereafter it was the reverse. This implies that there is no consistent way of dividing the self-employed's mixed income into returns to labor and capital, since the nature of self-employed labor has changed greatly.

Such features in the Korean labor market suggest how difficult it is to separate the mixed income of the self-employed. Therefore, attention is needed to interpret the level and trend of the labor income distribution rate of the Korean economy due to the problem of self-employment correction.

FIGURE 8-3. Proportion of Nonsalaried Workers Relative to GDP in OECD Countries

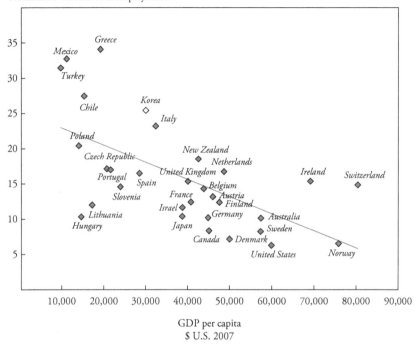

Nonsalaried workers % of employment

GDP per capita
$ U.S. 2007

Source: OECD National Accounts Statistics.

Table 8-1. *Scale of the Self-Employed to the Total Economy*

	Percent		
	2000	*2010*	*2016*
The proportion of wage workers employed by the self-employed in the total employed	31	24	24
The proportion of compensation paid by the self-employed in the total compensation	n.a.	19	18

Source: Current Population Survey, National Accounts.
n.a.: Not available.

FIGURE 8-4. **Average Household Income by Worker Type**

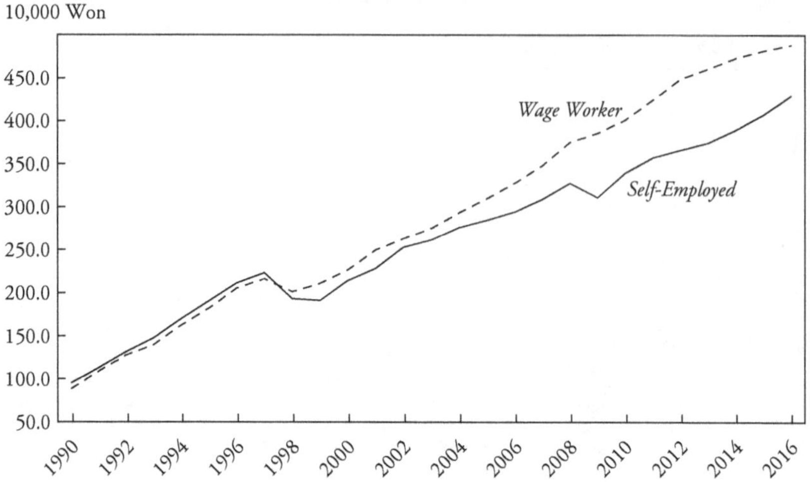

10,000 Won

Source: Data from the Survey of Household Income and Expenditure of Statistics Korea.

Typical Labor Share in Korea

Domestic research relies on the three adjustments of Douglas Gollin's approach to break down the mixed income of the self-employed.[5] However, in Korea all three of Gollin's correction methods seem to have a large measurement error. The central bank, the Bank of Korea, publishes the labor income share, consisting of compensation and operating surpluses, without adjusting for mixed income. Therefore, the labor income share published by the Bank of Korea may have a large measurement error when the share of self-employed laborers changes greatly.

In the National Account system, there are operating surpluses in the corporate, government, and household sectors, respectively, and their sum is defined as the operating surplus in the overall economy. Gollin (2002) regards the operating surplus of the household sector to be the surplus of the self-employed and discusses how to divide the self-employed surplus into a share of labor and capital. Here are three ways to do it.

Gollin's first adjustment in equation 8-1 assumes that the operating surplus of the self-employed is all derived from labor.[6] This assumes that the contribution of capital to self-employed income is negligible. However, such a correction may have a large measurement error in Korea. From 1990 to 2017, fixed assets of households accounted for about 15.1 percent of the fixed assets of the economy as a whole, making it difficult to consider capital input by the self-employed as zero.

$$LS1 = \frac{compensation + OSPUE}{GVA} \tag{8-1}$$

Gollin's second adjustment in equation 8-2 assumes that the average labor income of nonsalaried workers is equal to the average labor income of wage workers. However, if Korea's labor income share is calculated in this way, the labor share exceeds 90 percent. Considering that there is no country in which the labor share is as high as 90 percent, the error in the second adjustment is shown to be serious.

The second adjustment's measurement error stems from failure to reflect that the quality level of the Korean self-employed workforce is significantly lower than that of wage earners. Since the salaried worker's average wage income is higher than the average mixed income of the self-employed, the assumption that a certain portion of nonsalaried workers' operating surplus is equal to the average wage of salaried earners leads to an overestimation of the labor share.

$$LS2 = \frac{compensation \times \dfrac{Total\ employed}{salaried\ worker}}{GVA} \tag{8-2}$$

Gollin's third adjustment in equation 8-3 is based on the assumption that the labor income share in the self-employed sector is the same as that of the corporate sector. In order to make such an adjustment, the numerator of the labor share should exclude the compensation of the employees from the self-employed sector, and the value added of the self-employed sector should be excluded from the denominator of the labor share as well. However, in many countries, Korea included, the statistics of the National Accounts by institutional sectors are not complete. Thus, Gollin assumes that compensation of those hired by the self-employed and the consumption of fixed capital in the self-employed sector are negligible. As seen above, the compensation and the consumption of fixed capital in the self-employed sector in Korea is considerable. Therefore, the measurement error is also considered significant in the correction method.

OSPUE: operating surplus of private unincorporated enterprises

$$LS3 = \frac{compensation}{GVA - OSPUE} \qquad (8\text{-}3)$$

Finally, the labor share of the Bank of Korea is the net labor share, which is the sum of the total employee compensation for the national account and the total operating surplus. The net labor share is the value excluding depreciation or fixed capital consumption. This measure does not consider the decomposition of mixed income of the self-employed. Thus, the measurement error may increase at a time when the share of the self-employed changes sharply.

OS: operating surplus in the total

$$bok = \frac{compensation}{compensation + OS} \qquad (8\text{-}4)$$

Figure 8-5 graphs the labor shares of the three adjustments by Gollin and the Bank of Korea. Adjustment 1 and adjustment 2 began at a high level in 1975 and declined until 2010, but after that, adjustment 1 slightly increases and adjustment 2 remains stagnant. Adjustment 3 trends downward from the early 1990s to the end of 2010, but it has been rising since 2010. The labor share of the Bank of Korea is steadily rising from past to present.

As shown in figure 8-5, Gollin's adjustment makes it difficult to accurately judge the representative trend of the labor income share of the

FIGURE 8-5. Representative Labor Share Calculations for Korea

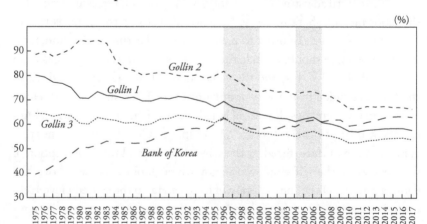

Source: Data from the National Accounts of the Bank of Korea.

Table 8-2. *Maximum and Minimum Labor Share Calculations*[a]

	Gollin's 1	Gollin's 2	Gollin's 3	Bank of Korea
Maximum	80.2 [1975]	94.4 [1980]	64.5 [1975]	63.3 [2016]
Minimum	57.1 [2011]	66.3 [2017]	52.5 [2010]	39.7 [1975]
2017	57.7	66.3	53.9	63.0
Average	66.7	78.3	58.8	56.5

Source: National Accounts.
a. The value in [ ] is the year in which the maximum and minimum values of the labor share are recorded.

Korean economy. For three consecutive years, which are shaded in figure 8-5, the four indicators move in the same direction. There are only short periods in which the orientation of the four metrics match for three consecutive years. From 1996 to 2000 all indicators fell. We can conclude that the fall in labor share before and after the Asian financial crisis is obvious, although there are differences in degree. Meanwhile, the trends indicated by the four indicators were consistent between 2004 and 2007; but the trend was not monotonic, as it fell again in 2007 after rising in 2005 and 2006.

It is difficult to make consistent conclusions about the direction of labor share from 1975 to the mid-1990s and the direction and change of labor share after the Asian financial crisis. Korea's labor share has not continued to fall, unlike that of major countries. In a country such as Korea that has rapidly developed from agriculture to manufacturing and service industries, it is not easy to figure out the right trend of labor income share by way of Gollin's simple adjustments.

Table 8-2 shows the years of maximum and minimum levels of labor income share. According to adjustment 1 and adjustment 2, the maximum value of Korea's labor share is achieved in 1975. The maximum of adjustment 2 is reached in 1980, and the maximum of the Bank of Korea index is reached in 2016. All minimum values appear after 2010 for Gollin's adjustment indicators, but for the Bank of Korea indicator the year is 1975. As the four indicators differ greatly, it seems difficult to compare the level of Korea's labor share using Gollin's adjustment method or the Bank of Korea index.

Gross vs. Net Labor Shares

Benjamin Bridgman emphasizes that the rapid decline in gross income share in the United States and other major countries is mainly attributable to the increase in the proportion of fixed capital consumption.[7] Even Japan's labor share shifts to a trend that has increased significantly over the past two decades, if fixed capital consumption is excluded from value added. In this section Korea's gross labor share and net labor share are compared.

The gross value of the National Accounts, as shown in equation 8-5, consists of employee remuneration, surplus in operations, fixed capital consumption, and taxes.

$$
\begin{aligned}
\text{Gross value added} = {} & \text{compensation} + \text{operating surplus} \\
& + \text{consumption of fixed capital} \\
& + \text{net taxes on production and imports.} \quad (8\text{-}5)
\end{aligned}
$$

Gross labor share is the proportion of compensation divided by gross value added, and net labor income share is the sum of the compensation and operating surplus. The indicators of labor share in Table 8-2 are all gross labor shares. The gross value added reflects the structure of production of labor and capital more directly, while the allocation of net value between labor and net capital share means the income ultimately attributable to labor versus capital. The consumption of fixed capital is not an income that can be obtained and consumed by an individual, so the net labor income share can be more closely related to the discussion of distribution and inequality issues than the gross labor share.

Figure 8-6 is a time trend of the proportion of consumption of fixed capital to gross value added. It was 6.9 percent in 1970 but increased by 2.8 percent annually until 1994 and increased significantly from 1995 to 1998 to reach 20 percent, where it stayed fairly consistent in the 2000s. The difference between the gross and net labor share widened when the proportion of fixed capital consumption increased. Figure 8-7 is the result of calculating the gross and net labor shares using Gollin's adjustment 3.[8] Overall, the net labor share rose faster than the gross labor share until the 1980s and the mid-1990s. This is because the proportion of fixed capital consumption has steadily increased. Since the proportion of fixed capital consumption remained at a similar level after the Asian financial crisis, the gap between the gross and net labor shares in the 2000s remained constant.

In summary, consumption of fixed capital effectively lowered the trend of gross labor share from the 1980s to the mid-1990s, when its proportion increased. In other words, with the exception of consumption of fixed capital, the labor share clearly increased from 1981 to 1996. Since then,

FIGURE 8-6. Ratio of Fixed Capital Consumption to Total Value Added

Percent

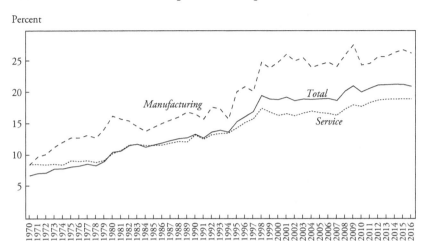

Source: National Accounts.

FIGURE 8-7. Gross vs. Net Labor Shares

Percent   Percent

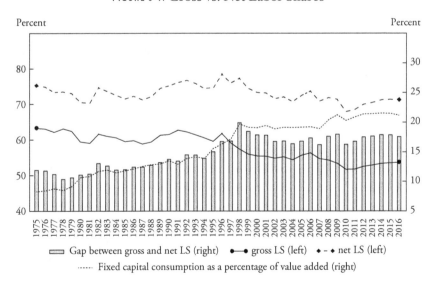

Source: National Accounts.

the increase in the proportion of fixed capital consumption in Korea in the 2000s did not significantly affect the trend in the gross labor share, which is different from the results obtained by Bridgman for other major countries.[9]

The Trend of Labor Share in the Korean Corporate Sector

In this section, the labor share of the nonfinancial corporate sector is calculated using macro- and microdata. All firms mentioned in this section are nonfinancial corporations. National Accounts are typical sources of macrodata. For the microdata, financial statement data (KISdata) and the Korean Annual Manufacturing Survey are used.

Recent studies have used the corporate labor share as a primary measure. The main reason for limiting the calculation of the labor share to the corporate sector is that it is difficult to correct the mixed income of the self-employed. Because the self-employed themselves cannot clearly identify the contributions made by labor and capital out of their operating profit, simple adjustment of mixed income without taking into account the qualitative characteristics of the self-employed can make a big difference in terms of trends and levels. According to the current National Accounts system, the operating surplus of households and nonprofit entities includes imputed rents from owner-occupied dwellings that do not exactly match the operating surplus of the self-employed. We can avoid this measurement issue if the subject of the labor share is limited to the corporate sector.

Whether the corporate labor share is the correct indicator or not depends on the questions addressed. When we study the causes of change in labor shares, most of the major candidates are closely related to changes in the market economy, such as changes in technology, international trade, and monopoly profits of firms that are not directly related to the government sector and housing prices. The overall labor share includes imputed rents from owner-occupied dwellings and the government sector, so it is desirable to exclude areas that are far from market changes.

Corporate Labor Shares Using Macrodata

The biggest problem in measuring Korea's corporate labor share is that data is only available for a short period of time. The Bank of Korea's National

FIGURE 8-8. **Labor Share of Nonfinancial Corporations**

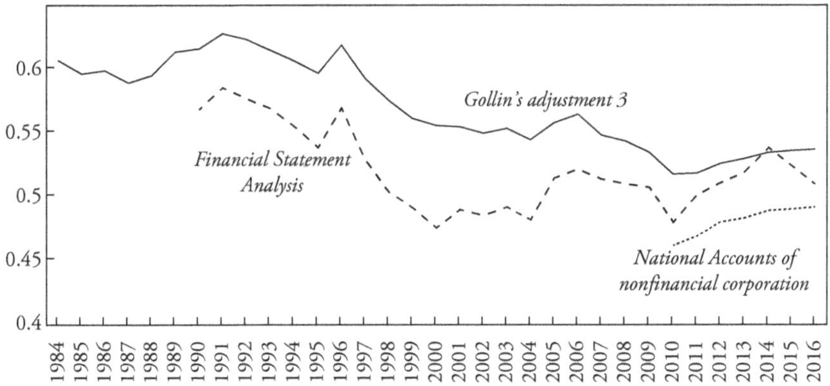

Source: National Accounts, Financial Statement Analysis, and KISdata.

Accounts is a time series covering all nonfinancial firms with excellent representation and easy international comparison. However, data on employee compensation by institutional sectors has existed only since 2010 and therefore can represent corporate labor share for only eight years, from 2010 to 2017. The Bank of Korea's Financial Statement Analysis has been available since 1990, although the survey method and sample selection have been revised several times. We can use this data as a supplement to the National Accounts to look at the corporate labor share.

Figure 8-8 shows three graphs of the labor share of nonfinancial corporations. The first long one is Gollin's adjustment 3, which is the same as in figure 8-5. The second is the labor share calculated directly from the National Accounts of nonfinancial corporations since 2010. The third is the proportion of labor costs to value added in the Financial Statement Analysis. The value added of the Financial Statement Analysis consists of operating surplus, labor cost, interest and tax and deductions, and depreciation. Since operating surplus is the value of eliminating interest expense after adding loan-loss allowance from operating profit, net interest expense is not counted from value added in this data. This graph is based on a simple correction of the level gap in the year in which the time series break occurred in proportion to labor cost in the Financial Statement Analysis.[10] Considering that the value added of National Accounts consists of surplus operations, employee compensation, consumption of fixed capital, and taxes, it is believed that the labor share of the National Accounts and the proportion of labor costs in the Financial Statement Analysis are similar measures. Both types of labor shares are gross income share, which includes depreciations and taxes on value added.

Comparing all the gross labor shares in aggregate data, we found a significant difference since 2000. In the 1990s, Gollin's adjustment and labor cost in the Financial Statement Analysis showed similar trends, although they differed in terms of level. However, the trend since 2000 is different. The gross labor share in the Financial Statement Analysis rose by about 4 percentage points between 2000 and 2007, but Gollin's adjustment in the National Accounts decreased by 1 percentage point. The labor share in the National Accounts began to fall in 1991, and the trend continued until 2010 and has since increased slightly. Comparing the time between 2000 and 2016, the labor share for 2016 is 1.8 percentage point lower for Gollin's adjustment compared to what it was in 2000. On the other hand, the labor share in the Financial Statement Analysis fell significantly in the 1990s, recovered greatly from the decline until the mid-2000s, fell again during the financial crisis, and rose sharply until 2014. Comparing the time between 2000 and 2016, the labor share for 2016 was 3.4 percentage points higher than it was in 2000, which trends in the opposite direction of the labor share given in the National Accounts.

Corporate Labor Shares Using Microdata

Many researchers, such as David Autor and coauthors,[11] are turning to firm-level microdata to study the causes of change in labor shares, but it seems that no research has been conducted using corporate microdata in Korea. As mentioned above, Korea has difficulty correcting the mixed income of the self-employed, making it hard to grasp the trend of labor share through a macrodata time series.

The main firm-level data used in this study is KISdata, consisting of firms' financial statements. In this study we exclude financial and insurance industries, state-owned companies, and nonprofit corporations from KISdata. The analysis is based on KISdata's externally audited firms for two reasons. First, the financial statements of externally audited firms are more credible than those of firms that do not have any disclosure obligation. Second, the attention paid to externally audited firms is relatively higher.

As samples are limited to entities of external audits including listed firms, it is necessary to look at whether the sample of KISdata used in this study can represent the entire body of nonfinancial corporations. Comparing the operating surplus of the nonfinancial corporations of the National Accounts and the surplus of the sample of KISdata, KISdata's operating profit amounted to about 57 percent of the operating profit of the National Accounts. In the same way, the compensation is equal to about 48 percent. A comparison between the Financial Statement Analysis and the sample of KISdata shows that KISdata's operating profit amounted to about 73.3 percent of that in the Financial Statement Analysis. In the same way, compensation in the sample of KISdata is about 50 percent of total compensation in the Financial Statement Analysis.

Many studies control for outliers and data entry errors by winsorizing (i.e., eliminating) observations from the top 1 percent and bottom 1 percent of the reference variable when dealing with firm-level microdata. In this study, the upper and lower 0.01 percent of the calculated labor shares are excluded from the analysis. Excluding some of the top and bottom portions of the ratio variables, such as the labor share, does not have a meaningful effect on the aggregate trend.

It is not trivial to generate variables such as labor costs and value added from financial statement data. Value added is defined by the additive method, which is a method of adding income attributable to those who contributed to production, as is the case with the Financial Statement Analysis by the Bank of Korea. Labor costs are generated by combining labor costs in the income statement (in sales and management expenses) and labor costs in the manufacturing cost statement (in expense). In 2004 the obligation to disclose manufacturing cost statements was abolished. For periods in which no manufacturing cost statement information exists, we use value added components in the notes of the financial statements.

The specific variable definitions are as follows:

Compensation = Employee salaries and benefits (SG&A in income statements) + labor costs (COGS in manufacturing costs statements) + employee benefit (COGS in manufacturing costs statements).

Gross value added = Operating income before tax + compensation + depreciation and amortization.

Net value added = Operating income before tax + compensation.

FIGURE 8-9. Gross Labor Share over Time (α_t)

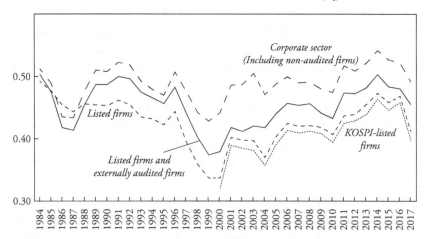

Source: KISdata.

Following Loukas Karabarbounis and Brent Neiman,[12] we run a regression as in equation 8-6 and equation 8-7, where $S_{i,t}$ is firm i's labor share at time t. Regression is weighted by the firm's value added, which is the denominator of $S_{i,t}$. Variable α_t is normalized so that the first observation in 1984 is consistent with the actual labor share level.

$$S_{i,t} = \alpha_t + \epsilon_{i,t}. \tag{8-6}$$

$$S_{i,t} = \varphi_i + \alpha_t^f + \epsilon_{i,t}. \tag{8-7}$$

In equation 8-6, α_t corresponds to the weighted average labor share of the sample population. In equation 8-7, α_t^f is the labor share within firm-level data after controlling for firm entry and exit effect on average.

Figure 8-9 shows the time effect (α_t) of equation 8-6, which is the aggregate gross labor share of the corporate sector. The time series of aggregate labor shares of different sample coverage show very similar patterns. All the samples in KISdata, externally audited firms, listed companies, and KOSPI-listed companies have moved together, with only the level being slightly different. As firms grow, the labor share declines. The labor share of externally audited firms was 50 percent in 1991, dropped to 37 percent in 1999, and rose in the 2000s up to 50 percent in 2014, then fell again from 2015 to 2017. This movement is similar to the labor share shown by the Financial Statement Analysis.

FIGURE 8-10. Gross Labor Share with Firm Fixed Effects (α_t^f)

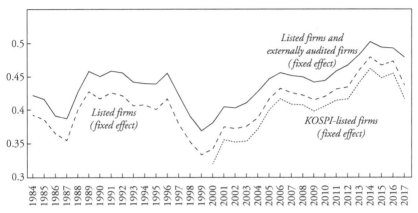

Source: KISdata.

Figure 8-10 shows the result of extracting the time effect (α_t^f) of equation 8-7. In contrast to figure 8-9, because of the firms' fixed effect, it can be interpreted as the result after controlling for the entry and exit of firms. If we look at the trend of the aggregate labor share after controlling for the fixed effects of firms, the average labor share has greatly increased beginning a few years after the Asian financial crisis. Particularly, the labor income share in the corporate sector has greatly increased since 2000. This pattern is common to all, regardless of sample selection.

Figure 8-11 and figure 8-12 show the results of the net labor income share by the above methods of equation 8-6 and equation 8-7. Figure 8-11 indicates (α_t) and figure 8-12 implies (α_t^f) with firms' fixed effect. The net labor income share is the labor cost divided by the sum of labor cost and operating profit. It can be seen that the trends of net labor share and gross labor share move in almost similar directions. Therefore, the proportion of depreciation and amortization does not alter the aggregate trend of labor share significantly.

In sum, the corporate labor share has fallen since the early 1990s and dropped sharply before and after the Asian financial crisis. The corporate labor share fell in the 1990s. In particular, the decline is marked at the Asian financial crisis. It rose again from 2000 to recover its early 1990s level in 2014. This pattern appears in both gross and net labor share. The upward trend in the 2000s is greater when the firms' fixed effect is controlled. The trends of labor share in all categories (full sample, externally audited, listed,

FIGURE 8-11. Net Labor Share over Time (α_t)

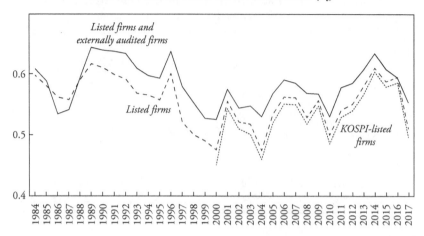

Source: KISdata.

KOSPI) are very similar. Figure 8-13 shows that the trend of the 2000s is mainly driven by manufacturing companies. These results are somewhat different from the labor share adjusted by Gollin in the National Accounts. The key difference is the trend between 2000 and 2014, after the Asian financial crisis and up to now.

Within- and Between-Firm Effect in Labor Shares

David Autor and coauthors argue that the emergence of superstar firms was an important factor in the declining trend of the U.S. labor share in the last thirty years.[13] This study uses U.S. census data to decompose the changes in the labor income share of firms using the methodology of J. Marc Melitz and Sašo Polanec called DOPD (Dynamic Olley-Pakes Productivity Decomposition).[14] It shows that the decline in the labor share was small within firms, but large between firms. This implies that the growth of firms with low labor share is the major reason behind the decline of the labor share.

In this section the changes in the labor share in KISdata are decomposed using Autor and others' method. In equation 8-9, S, X, and E stand for survivors, exits, and entrants, respectively. Net entry effect is

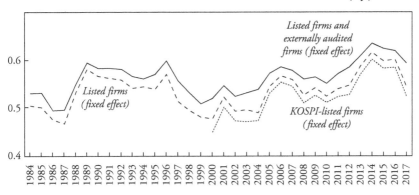

FIGURE 8-12. **Net Labor Share with Firm Fixed Effects (α_t^f)**

Source: KISdata.

FIGURE 8-13. **Gross Labor Share over Time (α_t) by Sector**

Source: KISdata.

$\omega_{X,1}(S_{S,1} - S_{X,1}) + \omega_{E,2}(S_{E,2} - S_{S,2})$. The labor share of firm i is S_i and ω_i is the value added share of firm i. Variables with a bar denote averages. Within-firm effect is $\Delta \overline{S}_S$. Between-firm effect that represents the reallocation effect is $\Delta[\Sigma(\omega_i - \overline{\omega})(S_i - \overline{S})]_S$. Net entry effect is $\omega_{X,1}(S_{S,1} - S_{X,1}) + \omega_{E,2}(S_{E,2} - S_{S,2})$.

$$\begin{aligned} \Delta S = \Delta \overline{S}_S &+ \Delta[\Sigma(\omega_i - \overline{\omega})(S_i - \overline{S})]_S \\ &+ \omega_{X,1}(S_{S,1} - S_{X,1}) + \omega_{E,2}(S_{E,2} - S_{S,2}). \end{aligned} \tag{8-9}$$

Figure 8-14 shows that the between-firm effect is not dominant enough to pull down labor share. Over the analysis period, the average company's labor share increased, but the reallocation of resources to those with low labor share also increased. The decomposition of Korea's labor share in the corporate sector indicates that the resource allocation to companies with low labor share is not large enough to reduce the overall corporate labor share. Unlike the U.S. results, the between-firm effect is not enough to bring down labor share in the whole period. In the 1990s the within-firm effect and the between-firm effect show the same negative direction. In the 2000s, the within-firm effect is dominant over the between-firm effect.

Figure 8-15 is the result of DOPD carried out in the manufacturing and service industries, respectively. The between-firm effect for firms with low labor share is underway in the manufacturing sector but is not serious in the service sector. On average, the labor share within firms has been increasing over time in both sectors.

Conclusions

This study examined Korea's corporate labor share. During 1984–2017 the corporate labor share in KISdata did not show a consistent tendency, unlike the declining trend of labor share in developed countries such as the United States. This can be understood in view of the economic development of Korea, where the industrial structure has shifted from agriculture to manufacturing to service and the proportion of wage workers has increased significantly.

The issue of Korea's labor share was more focused on what it looked like after the Asian financial crisis than on the long-term trend of decades. Korea's labor share has drawn much attention since the Asian financial cri-

FIGURE 8-14. **Decomposition of Labor Share Change**

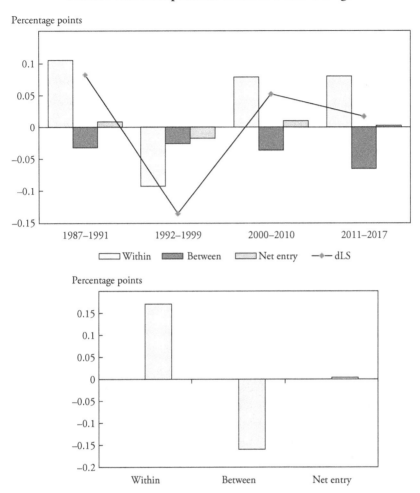

Source: KISdata.

sis and is deeply related to Korea's economic and social changes. Korean society faced a labor market segmentation problem as dualism became serious after the Asian financial crisis. As growth slowed, sensibility to inequality increased greatly. Moreover, the labor share has recently received great social attention as the main driving force of the new government's income-led growth target.

Domestic studies in Korea so far have mainly corrected the mixed income of the self-employed through Gollin's adjustments. In this way, since

FIGURE 8-15. **Decomposition of Labor Share Change by Sector**

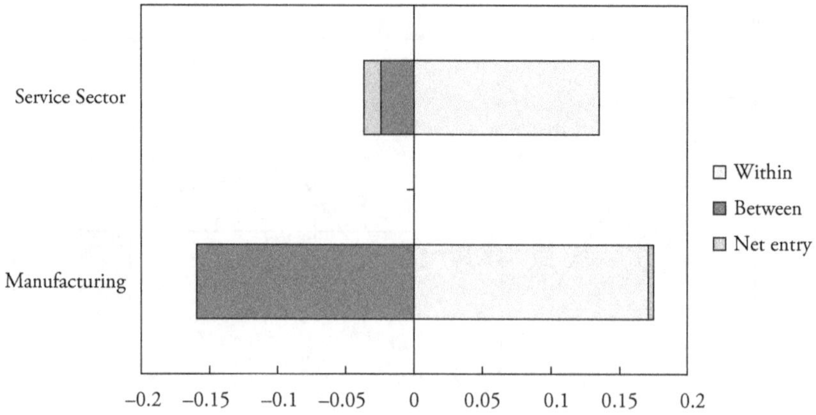

Source: KISdata.

the labor share is falling from the Asian financial crisis to the global financial crisis, many studies have concluded that the labor share in Korea deteriorated after 1997–98.

In this study the labor share of relatively large firms in KISdata is shown to trend up in the 2000s, although there are fluctuations during that period. This upward trend in the 2000s is the same for both the gross and net labor share. It does not depend on whether the firm fixed effect is controlled. Immediately after the crisis (1997–99), the labor share declined sharply, but it steadily rose from 2000 to 2014, reaching the highest level during the analysis period. This pattern is also observed in the Financial Statement Analysis of the Bank of Korea. This implies that large firms thought to be stingy in labor income distribution are actually becoming generous since the Asian financial crisis. These results are primarily for large companies, so care needs to be taken with their interpretation.

Market power can be an important driver of changes in the labor share, empirically as well as theoretically. David Autor and his coauthors argue that "superstar firms" such as Google and Amazon can account for the decline of the labor share in the United States.[15] However, the superstar firm effect is not yet dominant in Korea. Superstar firm effects were not expected to show up simply because the labor share of relatively large firms in Korea has risen, nor did it in reality.

Public concern about the decline in labor share mostly comes from its potential negative welfare effect. However, whether decline in labor share leads to deterioration of welfare or not is theoretically ambiguous. Labor share's effect on welfare is dependent on the reasons behind its changes. According to Loukas Karabarbounis and Brent Neiman, capital-biased technological change reduces the labor share of income. Eventually, however, technological development—even if capital biased—raises labor income and leads to higher aggregate output and welfare. On the other hand, if the labor share declines because of market frictions such as increasing markups, then it is negative for welfare.[16]

This study emphasizes the necessity of studying two directions. First, attention to the labor share has been greatly increased, but the correction of mixed income is still highly dependent on Gollin's methodology.[17] The measurement error has to be sufficiently considered. In order to discuss the trend of labor share in Korea, empirical finding should be demonstrated. This study is meaningful in that it uses microdata to show corporate labor share from various perspectives. Further, the fluctuation of labor share itself does not give a qualitative direction on the welfare effect. It is important to explore causes behind fluctuation of labor share in Korea. Policy responses should differ depending on the type of shock driving the labor share change.

NOTES

1. Kaldor (1957).
2. Elsby, Hobjin, and Sahin (2013); Karabarbounis and Neiman (2014).
3. Kim (2013); Lee (2015); Jeong (2015); Joo and Cheon (2014); Hong (2013).
4. Gollin (2002).
5. Gollin (2002).
6. Gollin (2002).
7. Bridgman (2018).
8. Gollin (2002).
9. Bridgman (2018).
10. In the Financial Statement Analysis, the time series has been cut off due to multiple changes in the survey's methods and sample populations.
11. Autor and others (2017).
12. Karabarbounis and Neiman (2014).
13. Autor and others (2017).
14. Melitz and Polanec (2015).
15. Autor and others (2017).
16. Karabarbounis and Neiman (2014).
17. Gollin (2002).

REFERENCES

Autor, David, and others. 2017. "The Fall of the Labor Share and the Rise of Superstar Firms," NBER Working Paper 23396 (Cambridge, Mass.: National Bureau of Economic Research).

Bridgman, Benjamin. 2018. "Is Labor's Loss Capital's Gain? Gross Versus Net Labor Shares." *Macroeconomic Dynamics* 22, no. 8, pp. 2070–87.

Elsby, Michael, Bart Hobijn, and Aysegul Sahin. 2013. "The Decline of the U.S. Labor Share," Brookings Papers on Economic Activity, pp. 1–63. Fall.

Gollin, Douglas. 2002. "Getting Income Shares Right." *Journal of Political Economy* 110, no. 2, pp. 458–74.

Hong, Jangpyo. 2013. "Analysis on the Variation of Labor Income Share in Korean Manufacturing Industry." *Journal of Industrial Labor Studies* 19, no. 1, pp. 1–34.

Jeong, Daehee. 2015. "Estimation of Elasticity Between Capital and Labor: Focused on the Implication of Labor Income Share," KDI-Policy Research Series, 2015–22 (Seoul: Korea Development Institute).

Joo, Sangyoung, and Soomin Cheon. 2014. "Measurement of Labor Income Share: Searching for an Alternative for Korea." *Social and Economic Review* 43, pp. 31–65.

Kaldor, Nicholas. 1957. "A Model of Economic Growth." *The Economic Journal* 67, no. 268, pp. 591–624.

Karabarbounis, Loukas, and Brent Neiman. 2014. "The Global Decline of the Labor Share." *Quarterly Journal of Economics* 129, no. 1, pp. 61–103, February 2014.

Kim, Baegeun. 2013. "Study on the Measurement and Determinants of Labor Income Share." *Economic Analysis* 19, no. 3, pp. 1–48.

Lee, Byung-hee. 2015. "The Issues and Trends in Measuring Labor Income Distribution Rate." *Nodong Review*, January, pp. 25–42.

Melitz, J. Marc, and Sašo Polanec. 2015. "Dynamic Olley-Pakes Productivity Decomposition with Entry and Exit." *RAND Journal of Economics* 46, no. 2, pp. 362–75.

NINE

Technological Change and the Rise of Corporate Saving

A Korean Case Study

DUKSANG CHO

C orporate saving, which can be defined as the value added produced by and retained in corporations, has been increased globally. Peter Chen, Loukas Karabarbounis, and Brent Neiman fuse the national accounts of the United Nations to show that the ratio of global corporate saving to GDP has been trending up since the 1980s.[1] Figure 9-1 shows that global sectoral savings relative to global GDP have changed. Two lines for each sector, one until 2010 and another since 2000, respectively, represent the ratio of global aggregate sectoral saving to global aggregate GDP evaluated by using the 1993 and 2008 System of National Accounts (SNA). Despite cyclical fluctuations in the short run and level shifts between the 1993 SNA and 2008 SNA, it is clear that corporate saving shows an increasing trend up to 2015.

FIGURE 9-1. **Global Saving by Sectors**[a]

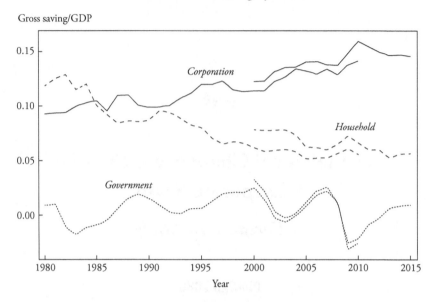

Source: United Nations, National Accounts Statistics.

a. The units of the vertical axis are ratios. All values of gross saving and GDP are the global aggregates of countries in the UN data. Time series of each sector from 1980 to 2010 are based on 1993 SNA data and those from 2000 to 2015 are based on 2008 SNA data.

Why has corporate saving increased? Chen, Karabarbounis, and Neiman suggest that the savings of the corporate sector increased due to the combination of a decreasing relative price of investment goods and sticky dividends. They argue that the declining relative price of investment goods due to technological changes can decrease labor share and make households save less, given that the share of dividends is unchanged in spite of rising corporate profits due to institutional reasons. Thus, they argue that the increase in corporate savings is a mirror of the declining labor share. Figure 9-2 shows that the global labor share in the corporate sector has decreased since the 1980s simultaneously with an increase in corporate savings rates, which is the ratio of gross saving to gross value added (GVA) in the corporate sector.

If rising corporate savings is a consequence of the declining labor share, which is derived from undistributed profits, changes in sectoral savings

FIGURE 9-2. **Global Labor Share in Corporate Sector**[a]

Share of corporate GVA

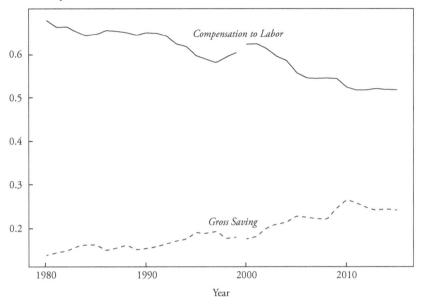

Source: United Nations, National Accounts Statistics.

a. The units of the vertical axis are ratios. All values of gross value added (GVA), compensations to labor, and gross saving in the corporate sector are the global aggregates of countries in the UN data. Time series from 1980 to 1999 are based on 1993 SNA data and those from 2000 to 2015 are based on 2008 SNA data.

could result in households' subdued consumption and dampened aggregate growth. This is because the corporate saving gluts derived from frictions such as sticky dividends can be a source of inefficiency. It might, then, be effective to use policy measures to prompt corporations to distribute more profits to households to help increase aggregate demand.[2]

Many questions, however, still need to be answered. What makes a firm more profitable than before? What are the incentives for a firm to retain more profits than before? What prevents a firm from transferring its profits to households, the ultimate owners of the firm? Why does a corporate dividend policy look sticky—not for years but for decades?

This study examines the possibility that firms save their profits in order to prepare for and cope with technological changes. Technological changes, including not only advances in scientific or engineering knowledge but also changes in market structures such as more integrated global markets, make the more technologically advanced firms more profitable. It is a high-tech, frontier firm that can experience soaring profits in the midst of technological changes. The frontier firm, thus, can have an incentive to save more profits and use them to cope with technological changes in order to stay in the frontier.

Given the expected, persistent changes in technologies, saving more and tapping into internal capital markets can be a better strategy than distributing out profits and raising external capital. If a frontier firm distributes out its profits, it could send to external capital markets a negative signal that the firm has no more power to follow the frontiers and continue to earn profits. This negative signal can deteriorate the firm's ability to raise external capital, which is essential to pursue technological changes. In addition, investments in risky projects are inevitable for the frontier firm to keep the lead. These risky investments can further weaken the firm's ability to raise external capital and make it save more. Thus, technological changes as an incentive for firms to save more can be in line with the arguments of financial constraints and the precautionary motive for firms' cash holdings.[3]

For instance, let's look at the investments of Samsung Electronics Company, which is the world's largest memory chips manufacturer. The semiconductor market is a high-tech, capital-intensive industry experiencing persistent technological changes. To survive in this industry, Samsung Electronics must stay in the quickly evolving technological frontiers, or the firm will become obsolete in the market, like past competitors Samsung pushed out. The firm acknowledges this threat and needs to prepare for the persistent increase in investments.

Figure 9-3 shows the net profits and investments of Samsung Electronics since 2004. It can be observed in the top panel that the size of investments in equipment and construction (solid line) is comparable to or in some years even larger than that of net profits (dashed line). Moreover, the size of the accumulated profits in the bottom panel is almost identical to that of accumulated investments since 2004. This implies that most of the retained earnings of Samsung Electronics are used to make investments.

Semiconductor makers have been competing to integrate the greater number of transistors required in a tiny-sized memory chip in order to in-

FIGURE 9-3. **Net Profits and Investments of Samsung Electronics**[a]

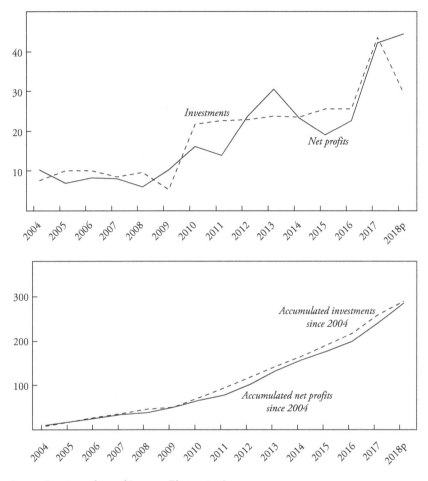

Source: Earnings release of Samsung Electronics Company.

a. The units of the vertical axis are trillions of KRW (Korean Republic Won). Investments consist of investments in equipment and construction to form fixed capital. The top panel shows annual flows of net profits and investments. The bottom panel shows accumulated flows of net profits and investments since 2004.

crease the amount of data stored. Thus, they must keep innovating their manufacturing process. We call it tech migration. Figure 9-4 shows the history of tech migration in which Samsung Electronics proceeded. The problem is that the technological barriers of tech migration are getting higher as the size of transistors is getting smaller. This means that more

FIGURE 9-4. **Timing of Tech Migration, Samsung Electronics**[a]

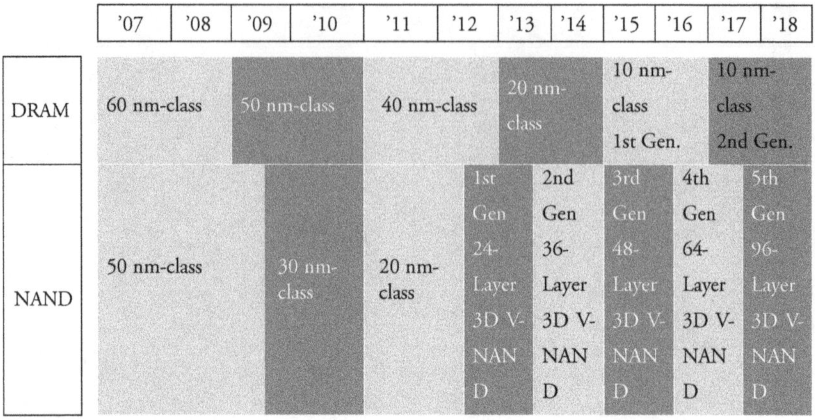

	'07	'08	'09	'10	'11	'12	'13	'14	'15	'16	'17	'18
DRAM	60 nm-class		50 nm-class		40 nm-class		20 nm-class		10 nm-class 1st Gen.		10 nm-class 2nd Gen.	
NAND	50 nm-class		30 nm-class		20 nm-class	1st Gen 24-Layer 3D V-NAND	2nd Gen 36-Layer 3D V-NAND	3rd Gen 48-Layer 3D V-NAND	4th Gen 64-Layer 3D V-NAND	5th Gen 96-Layer 3D V-NAND		

Source: Samsung Electronics Company.

a. First year of a new technology being used to produce memory chips. For example, Samsung Electronics began to produce 50nm-class DRAM and 20nm-class NAND in 2009 and 2011, respectively.

capital is required and the success of tech migration is more uncertain as tech migration becomes more complicated.

Note that investment hikes can be observed in 2010 and 2017 in figure 9-3. The increments of investments in 2010 and 2017 were sizable, 16 trillion and 18 trillion Korean Republic Won (KRW), respectively. These numbers are larger than 10 percent of annual equipment investments in all of South Korea, which are not only too large but also too abrupt for a firm to raise them from external capital markets. It is, therefore, very likely that Samsung Electronics expected tech migration and prepared for the expected increase in investments by retaining its net profits. In general, tech firms such as Amazon, Apple, Google, Microsoft, Alibaba, or Tencent become the biggest investors in the world.[4]

The case of Samsung Electronics is consistent with the following hypothesis. Given expected, persistent technological changes, we can think of a cycle as one in which a firm makes profits, saves them, invests them, and makes larger profits and saves them again. A high-tech frontier firm may have more incentive to follow this cycle and to retain its profits rather than distribute them out with dividends, because what lies beyond the technological frontier is unknown by definition. Thus, corporations can save more due to this impending uncertainty in a time of expected, persistent technological changes.

This study examines the possibility that firms increase their saving in order to cope with technological changes. Specifically, national accounts and firm-level microdata of South Korea are used to test the hypothesis that an increase in corporate saving is related to technological changes and that productivity dispersion occurs due to the cycle described above: a virtuous cycle for the frontier firms and a vicious cycle for the laggards.

The rest of this paper proceeds as follows. In the second section, changes in the corporate saving of South Korea are examined and show that the rise of corporate saving stems from an increase in the consumption of fixed capital and an increase in the corporate saving rate. In the third section, I introduce and inspect the hypothesis that firms save more in order to prepare for the expected, persistent changes in technologies. In the fourth section, an increase in productivity dispersion among firms is suggested as a possible outcome of rising corporate saving. Lastly, the fifth section discusses policy implications and the limitations of this study.

Changes in Corporate Saving

What is corporate saving? Following previous studies such as Chen, Karabarbounis, and Neiman, let's define corporate saving as undistributed corporate profits or value added that firms produce and retain by themselves rather than distribute out. Note that corporate saving is a flow measure, which is distinct from corporate cash holding, a stock measure. Corporate saving can be accumulated as financial assets, including cash, or used as investments in equipment and construction to form fixed capital.

This definition of corporate saving is consistent with the sectoral gross saving of the system of national accounts (SNA), which is defined as the retained value added in a sector. Specifically, a sectoral gross saving of national accounts consists of consumption of fixed capital (CFC), net investment (= gross fixed capital formation – CFC), net lending, acquisitions less disposals of nonfinancial nonproduced assets, changes in inventories, and net capital transfers.

Gross saving = changes in inventories + gross fixed capital formation
                    + acquisitions less disposals of nonfinancial nonproduced
                    assets + net lending – net capital transfers.

For instance, gross saving by nonfinancial corporations in South Korea in 2016 was 307.4 trillion KRW in nominal terms, which is the sum of gross fixed capital formation (291.7 trillion KRW), acquisitions less disposals of nonfinancial nonproduced assets (36.4 trillion KRW), net lending (–7.4 trillion KRW), and changes in inventories (–8.4 trillion KRW) minus net capital transfers (4.8 trillion KRW).

A Trend in Corporate Saving in South Korea

The rise of corporate saving is a global phenomenon. Chen, Karabarbounis, and Neiman use UN data of national accounts to show that the share of saving by corporations relative to global GDP has increased.[5] Figure 9-1 shows changes in sectoral savings relative to global GDP over time. Savings by corporations relative to global GDP have been increasing gradually while savings by households have been decreasing and government savings have been fluctuating without a significant trend.

Changes in sectoral savings over time are also observed in South Korea. Let's look at the sectoral savings to GDP ratios in the national accounts of South Korea. In figure 9-5 the ratio of nonfinancial corporations' gross savings to GDP shows an increasing trend since 1975 (about 0.25 percent annual increase) and an increase to 18.3 percent by 2017. The sizable increments of corporate saving were observed mainly before 1990, the early 2000s, and the late 2000s. Since 2010 the ratio of corporate savings to GDP has slightly declined, but it still remained at historically high levels.

As the share of corporate savings has increased in the long run, the shares of other sectors have decreased. The household sector's savings to GDP ratio had abruptly dropped in the period of economic turmoil, the 1997–98 financial crisis of South Korea. Since then households' savings to GDP ratio has remained in the range of 5 percent to 10 percent of GDP. Compared to global government savings in figure 9-1, the government savings of South Korea have been relatively stable and stayed positive without the prominent fluctuations of business cycles. The ratio of government savings to GDP decreased by about 2.5 percent from 10 percent of GDP in

FIGURE 9-5. Sectoral Saving in South Korea

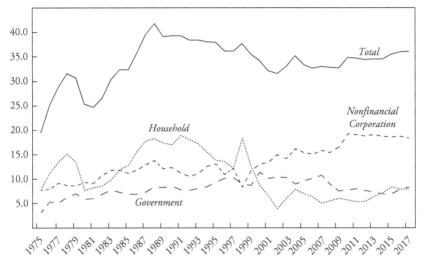

Source: Bank of Korea.

the 2008 global financial crisis. Since then, the government's savings to GDP ratio has remained quite stable.

Decomposition of Corporate Savings

Changes in the corporate savings to GDP ratio can be decomposed in two ways. First, an increase in corporate saving can be decomposed into an increase in the share of the corporate sector's value added and an increase in the savings rate of corporations. If the share of value added produced by corporations relative to GDP increases, the ratio of corporate savings to GDP can increase even though firms do not change their saving behavior. The corporate savings to GDP ratio is also able to increase if firms increase their savings rates, although the sectoral share of GDP by corporations does not change.

In figure 9-6, we can see that since 2000 the rising corporate savings relative to GDP was attributed to both the increase in the share of the corporate sector's value added and the increase in corporations' savings rate. The increase in the corporate savings rate of South Korea, however, played a major role in the rise of corporate saving since 2000. Note that the scales of vertical axes are different between the two panels. The bottom panel of the corporate savings rate has larger scales than the top panel. The savings rate of nonfinancial corporations increased by 8.1 percentage points from

FIGURE 9-6. Sectoral Share of Value Added and Sectoral Saving Rate[a]

Sectoral Share of Value Added

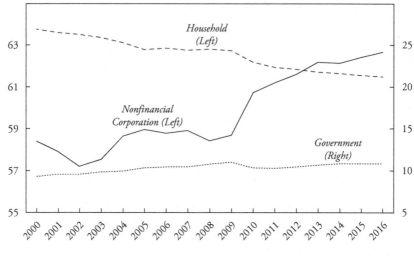

Sectoral Saving Rate (=Gross Saving / GVA)

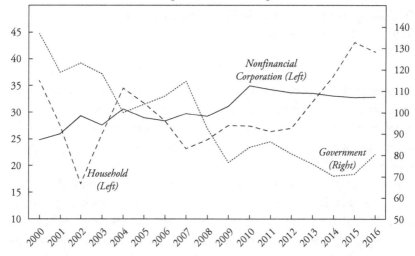

Source: Bank of Korea.

a. The units of the vertical axis in the top panel are the percent of the sum of sectoral gross value added (GVA). The units of the vertical axis in the bottom panel are the percent of GVA.

2000 to 2016, while the share of value added by nonfinancial corporations increased by 4.3 percentage points from 2000 to 2016.

Observe the changes in figure 9-6 by periods. In the early 2000s the
increase in corporate savings was mainly due to an increase in the corporate savings rate. The corporate savings rate increased from 25 percent to
30 percent. In the late 2000s, corporate saving increased as both the corporate savings rate and the share of corporate value added increased. Since
2010, the ratio of corporate savings to GDP has decreased slightly but still
remained at a historically high level of above 30 percent. The share of the
corporate sector's value added has been increasing since 2010, while
households' share of value added has declined.

It is worth noting that the corporate share of value added and the corporate savings rate show an abrupt increase in 2010 when Samsung Electronics ramped up its investments in semiconductor and display facilities
from 5.2 trillion KRW to 21.6 trillion KRW. The company's increase in
investments was so sizable that it affected the nominal machinery equipment investments of South Korea, which was 87.6 trillion KRW in 2010.

Second, corporate savings also can be decomposed into capital account
components. With this decomposition, we can examine what components
mainly contributed to the increase in corporate saving over time. Figure 9-7

FIGURE 9-7. Decomposition of Corporate Saving

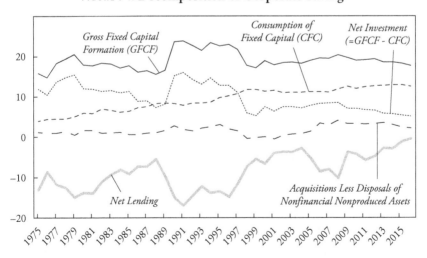

Source: Bank of Korea.

Note: The units of the vertical axis are the percent of GDP.

Table 9-1. *Changes in Gross Fixed Capital Formation of Nonfinancial Corporations*[a]

	Gross fixed capital formation (GFCF)	Consumption of fixed capital (CFC)	Net investment (GFCF − CFC)	Acquisitions less disposals of nonproduced nonfinancial assets	Net lending
Annual changes (trend)	0.03	0.22	−0.19	0.05	0.25
1975	15.90	3.90	11.90	1.20	−13.10
2016	17.80	12.60	5.20	2.20	−0.40

Source: Bank of Korea.
a. Values expressed as percent of GDP.

shows the components of the nonfinancial corporations' capital account as a percentage of GDP. We can observe that both consumption of fixed capital (CFC) and net lending show an increasing trend and that net investment (gross fixed capital formation – CFC) shows a decreasing trend.

The ratio of corporate CFC to GDP mainly increased in the pre-1990s, the mid-1990s, and the late 2000s. The pre-1990s and the late 2000s roughly coincide with the periods when the ratio of corporate savings to GDP increased, as shown in figure 9-5.

It is also worth noting that the ratio of corporate gross fixed capital formation (GFCF) to GDP has barely deviated from a constant level of slightly less than 20 percent of GDP since 1975, while its composition has considerably changed. Since 2010 the ratio of corporate net lending has increased in particular, while the other components have declined or stayed at a constant level.

Table 9-1 shows that the GFCF of nonfinancial corporations barely changed, 15.9 percent to 17.8 percent of GDP from 1975 to 2016. The CFC of nonfinancial corporations, in contrast, increased from 3.9 percent to 12.6 percent of GDP in the same period, while the net capital investment (GFCF – CFC) of nonfinancial corporations decreased from 11.9 percent to 5.2 percent. Meanwhile, the net lending of nonfinancial corporations increased from −13.1 percent to −0.4 percent of GDP from 1975 to 2016.

The increasing share of CFC and the decreasing share of net investment in the components of the nonfinancial corporations' capital account can be understood with a standard growth theory. As Korea's economy approaches its balanced growth path, the speed of capital accumulation decreases with the decreasing share of net investments and the increasing share of depreciation. However, it is not easily explained by the standard growth theory that the ratio of GFCF to GDP has remained at a similar level to that of the late 1970s when Korea's economy experienced rapid capital accumulation. Standard growth theories expect that as an economy matures and approaches its balanced growth path, the incentive for capital accumulation weakens and the share of gross fixed capital formation relative to GDP decreases.

The fact that the share of GFCF remains high suggests that the demand for gross fixed capital formation is still high in South Korea due to some structural factors such as technological changes. For example, when technology changes from a typewriter to a computer, the obsolescence of capital using existing technologies can be accelerated, consumption of fixed capital can increase, and the demand for gross fixed capital formation can increase. When the structure of industries changes from light industry to heavy industry or from heavy industry to information technology (IT) industry, consumption of fixed capital can also increase and the demand for gross fixed capital formation can rise. When Samsung Electronics undergoes tech migration, its production facilities using old technologies become obsolete and its consumption of fixed capital can increase.

In the next section we examine the possibility that a firm has increased its savings rate to cope with the rise of CFC, which could be driven by technological changes.

Hypotheses on the Rise of Corporate Saving

In this section we set the hypotheses on the rationale behind rising corporate saving and examine their validity. The following two hypotheses together suggest that technological changes have resulted in an increase in consumption of fixed capital (CFC) and that firms are increasing their saving in response to an expected, persistent rise of CFC.

Hypothesis A: Firms increase savings in order to prepare for the expected, persistent rise of consumption of fixed capital.

Hypothesis B: Technological changes increase the consumption of fixed capital.

Verification of Hypothesis A

Does a firm increase its saving in order to prepare for expected, persistent technological changes, which can be captured by the rise of CFC? In order to verify this hypothesis, let's define the voluntary saving of corporations as gross saving less inelastic costs for which firms must pay. If firms' voluntary saving does not increase with the rise of CFC, we can reject hypothesis A.

Suppose that among the components of gross saving in national accounts, firms' inelastic costs are changes in inventories and acquisitions less disposals of nonfinancial nonproduced assets, which are mostly net purchases of land. The reason for categorizing changes in inventory as firms' inelastic expenses is that they are likely to fluctuate with business cycles. It is, however, unclear whether net purchases of land are inelastic costs from the perspective of firms. Firms' net purchases of land are sizable and able to have a significant impact on the results in the case of South Korea, in which corporations' net purchases of land have been larger than 1 percent of GDP for decades. Voluntary saving, thus, is defined in two ways: one is a voluntary saving with net purchases of land, and another is a voluntary saving without net purchases of land.

Voluntary Saving 1 = net saving (= gross saving – CFC)
            – changes in inventories = net investment
            + net lending – net capital transfers
            + acquisitions less disposals of nonproduced
              nonfinancial assets.

Voluntary Saving 2 = net saving (= gross saving – CFC)
            – changes in inventories – acquisitions less
              disposals of nonproduced nonfinancial
              assets = net investment + net lending
            – net capital transfers.

If an increase in CFC is temporary, then firms can increase borrowing and mitigate the cost pressures stemming from this temporary increase in CFC. Thus, firms have no incentive to increase their saving in order to cope with unexpected, temporary increases in CFC. They are likely to reduce their saving and increase borrowing. As a result, we can expect a negative or no correlation between the previous period's CFC and the present period's voluntary saving.

Corr (CFC$_{t-1}$, Voluntary Saving$_t$) ≤ 0 given a temporary CFC shock.

If an increase in CFC, however, is expected to be persistent, firms can choose to increase their saving rather than increase their borrowing. For instance, if an increase in CFC is the result of the obsolescence of tangible assets due to technological changes, the increase in CFC can lead to the decrease in the collateral value of tangible assets and tightening of the borrowing constraints of firms. In addition, intangible assets are difficult to objectively evaluate, and their amortization costs are high. Therefore, if the share of intangible assets increases due to technological changes, it can lead to a decline in the collateral value of corporate assets, which can weaken further the ability of firms to borrow. Lastly, in the period of technological changes, firms' investments in exploring technological frontiers are inherently riskier. External capital markets could play less of a role in these investments, and hence firms are more likely to depend on their internal capital, savings. As a result, we can expect a positive correlation between the previous period's CFC and the present period's voluntary saving.

Corr (CFC$_{t-1}$, Voluntary Saving$_t$) > 0 given an expected,
persistent CFC shock.

In order to examine hypothesis A, correlation coefficients between nonfinancial corporations' CFC of the previous year (t-1) and their voluntary saving of the present year (t) are examined with a ten-year rolling window. Specifically, the ten-year rolling window correlation coefficient for year t measures the correlation between CFC from t-11 to t-1 and voluntary saving from t-10 to t. To evaluate correlations, we use the first differences in the ratio of CFC to GDP and the ratio of voluntary saving to GDP because their levels show a nonstationary trend.

Figure 9-8 shows that the correlation coefficients between nonfinancial corporations' CFC (t-1) and their voluntary saving (t) declined in the 1990s, increased in the 2000s, and exceeded 0.5 after 2010. This result suggests that hypothesis A, which argues that corporations can increase their saving

FIGURE 9-8. Correlation Between CFC and Voluntary Saving
(Normalized by GDP)[a]

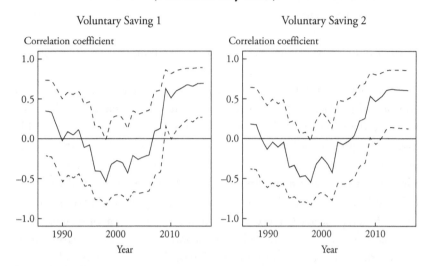

Source: Bank of Korea.

a. The first differences of the level variables are used to evaluate ten-year rolling window correlations. The level variables of corporate CFC and voluntary savings are normalized with GDP. Dashed lines show a 90 percent confidence interval.

in order to cope with the expected, persistent shocks to CFC, starts to work from the early 2000s. Dashed lines in the figure show a 90 percent confidence interval.

Figure 9-9 shows the correlation coefficients between nonfinancial corporations' CFC (t-1) and their voluntary saving (t) using nonfinancial corporations' gross value added (GVA) as a numeraire instead of GDP. Note that the ratio of corporate saving to GVA is a more suitable measure to capture corporate savings rates because it measures how much firms save out of the value added they produce. Although we cannot confirm the long-term trend due to the short time span of sectoral GVA, data of which are available since 2000, the figure shows that the correlation coefficients have exceeded zero significantly since 2012, which is consistent with the result using the ratios relative to GDP.

An increase in CFC can lower the collateral value of firms' fixed capital and weaken the external financing ability of firms. Therefore, the simultaneous increases in CFC and the corporate savings rate in the 2000s suggest the possibility that firms increase their saving in order to prepare for

FIGURE 9-9. Correlation Between CFC and Voluntary Saving
(Normalized by GVA)ᵃ

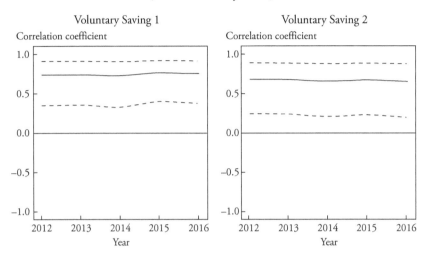

Source: Bank of Korea.

a. First differences of the level variables are used to evaluate ten-year rolling window correlations. The level variables of corporate CFC and voluntary savings are normalized with GVA. The dashed line shows a 90 percent confidence interval.

shocks to investments due to technological changes given borrowing constraints.

Figure 9-10 shows changes in CFC rates by type of capital goods over time. A CFC rate is calculated by this year's CFC (=investments less increases in net capital stock) divided by last year's net capital stock. As can be seen in the figure, the CFC rate of facilities or equipment, which is corresponding to tangible assets, increased until the early 2000s and has stayed at a historically high level since then. The CFC rate of intellectual property products (IPP), which is corresponding to intangible assets, increased until the late 2000s and has also stayed at a historically high level since then. These high CFC rates since the 2000s are consistent with the previous observation that firms' voluntary saving started to show a positive correlation with firms' CFC since the 2010s. Note that the correlation is backward in the sense that it is evaluated by using the observations in the past ten-year window. It is also worth noting that the CFC rate of construction has not increased. This may represent the fact that construction is not the sector of technological changes nowadays.

FIGURE 9-10. **CFC Rates**[a]

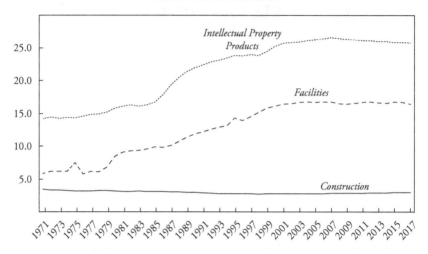

Source: Bank of Korea.

a. The units of the vertical axis are the percent of the real net capital stock. A CFC rate by type of capital goods is calculated by this year's CFC (=investments less increases in net capital stock) divided by the last year's net capital stock. All variables are in real terms valued at chained 2010 year prices. The CFC rate by type of capital goods represents the whole economy, not sectors. Although a sectoral CFC rate is more suitable to the context, an aggregate CFC rate is used because a sectoral investment by type of capital goods is not available in the national accounts.

Hypothesis A seems to fit well with the tech migration story of Samsung Electronics. Few researchers in the literature have focused on the tech migration story to explain the rise in corporate saving. Among them, Antonio Falato, Dalida Kadyrzhanova, and Jae Sim argue that the rise of corporate cash holdings, which is the result of the increase in corporate saving, stems from the rise of intangible capital.[6] Their argument might suggest technological changes from tangible to intangible assets. The tech migration hypothesis, however, encompasses not only the rising intangible assets but also the increases in depreciation derived from changes in tangible assets. John Graham and Mark Leary show that the U.S. corporate cash holdings were large in the mid-1900s when structural changes took place and that the recent rise of U.S. cash holdings is relatively moderate and mainly observed in newly public firms.[7] They suggest that the recent rise of U.S. corporate cash holdings might be linked to changes in aggregate investment and profitability.

Verification of Hypothesis B

Do technological changes increase the consumption of fixed capital? In order to examine hypothesis B, I use Statistics Korea's Survey of Business Activity (SBA), which is a firm-level microdata set including all firms in South Korea with fifty or more regular employees and 300 million KRW or more in capital stock from all industries. The dataset covers the period from 2006 to 2016. Firms with missing values of tangible assets, intangible assets, and depreciation are dropped. In addition, I exclude industries that have distinct characteristics, including finance and insurance, public administration, and real estate and leasing.

It is necessary to set up variables that can capture technological changes to test the hypothesis. I use the ratio of intangible assets to tangible assets as a variable to measure a firm's technological change. A positive correlation between a change in the intangible to tangible assets ratio and the degree of technological changes is assumed. This is because firms' research and development expenditure accounts for most of the firms' intangible assets, which corresponds to intellectual property products (IPP) in national accounts. It is quite plausible that the more research and development expenditure a firm spends, the more technological changes the firm experiences. In addition, intangible assets have been the main driver of economic growth in recent years.[8] The ratio of intangible assets to tangible assets, however, can vary widely across industries. Some industries can have a high intangible to tangible capital ratio due to their intrinsic characteristics. Every firm-level variable, thus, is standardized by subtracting the annual average value of its corresponding two-digit industry.

I use depreciation of tangible assets in the firm-level data as the variable that corresponds to CFC in national accounts. The two concepts are similar but slightly different, especially in their timing. CFC is an economic concept that captures a change in the value of capital that can produce future streams of value added. Depreciation, in contrast, is an accounting concept that allocates the cost of a tangible asset over its useful life. In spite of their differences, they should have similar values in the long run, which is of interest to this study. Figure 9-11 shows the CFC to GVA ratio of a corporate sector in national accounts and the depreciation to value added ratio of all firms in the SBA. We can observe that both time series have similar levels and business cycles over time. Note that the CFC to GVA ratio has

FIGURE 9-11. **Depreciation of Tangible Assets**[a]

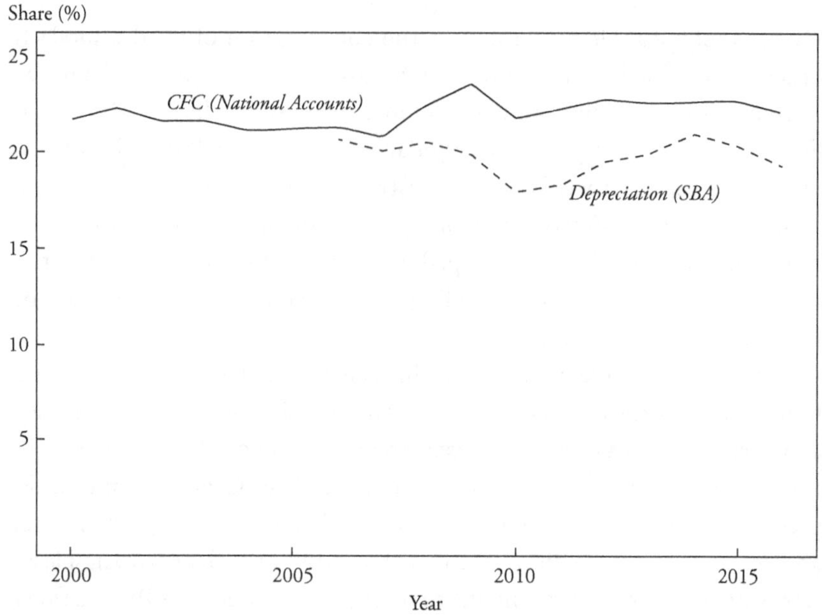

Source: Statistics Korea and Bank of Korea.

a. The shares for depreciation and CFC represent the ratio of depreciation to value added of all firms in the SBA and the ratio of CFC to GVA of corporations in national accounts, respectively.

larger levels than the depreciation to value added ratio. This is because CFC includes amortization of intangible assets but depreciation does not.

To verify hypothesis B arguing a positive correlation between technological changes and CFC, let's first look at the correlation between changes in the ratio of intangible to tangible assets and changes in the ratio of depreciation to tangible assets across two-digit industries from 2006 to 2016.

As can be seen in figure 9-12, industries with a larger increase in the intangible assets ratio show a larger increase in the depreciation ratio. The solid line in the figure is the weighted least squares (WLS) regression estimate using an industry's average real value added for the period from 2006 to 2016 as a weight. Table 9-2 shows the result of this regression. The estimate shows a clear positive, upward trend. This implies that an industry accumulating intangible assets faster than tangible assets experienced an increase in the depreciation rate of tangible assets. Note that depreciation

FIGURE 9-12. **Intangible Assets and Depreciation of Tangible Assets, Between Industries**[a]

Δ (Depreciation / Tangible asset)

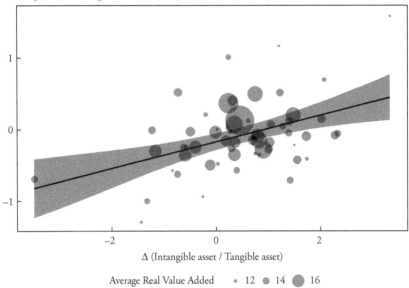

Δ (Intangible asset / Tangible asset)

Average Real Value Added   • 12   ● 14   ⬤ 16

Source: Survey of Business Activities, Statistics Korea.

a. The horizontal axis shows changes in the ratio of intangible assets to tangible assets from 2006 to 2016. The vertical axis represents changes in the ratio of depreciation to tangible assets from 2006 to 2016. The size of the circle represents the average real value added for 2006 and 2016. A solid line shows the weighted least squares regression estimate with the average value added as a weight. Shaded areas represent 95 percent confidence intervals.

Table 9-2. *Intangible Assets and Depreciation of Tangible Assets, Between Industries*[a]

Dependent variable	Independent variable
Changes in the ratio of depreciation to tangible assets	Changes in the ratio of intangible assets to tangible assets
From 2006 to 2016, 59 observations	0.187** (3.743)

Source: Survey of Business Activities, Statistics Korea.
a. The number in the parentheses shows t-statistics. Asterisks indicate statistical significance; ** $p < 0.01$. The average real value added of each industry for 2006 and 2016 is used as a weight.

FIGURE 9-13. **Probability Densities of Depreciation of Tangible Assets**[a]

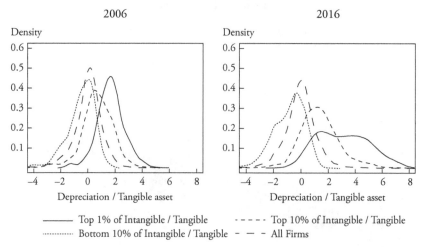

Source: Survey of Business Activities, Statistics Korea.

a. All firm-level variables are standardized by subtracting the two-digit industry annual average.

does not include amortization of intangible assets, and so the result does not stem from the composition effects. It is more likely that industries spending more on research and development expenditure experienced faster depreciation of tangible assets.

A positive correlation between the intangible assets ratio and the depreciation ratio is observed not only across industries but also across firms. Figure 9-13 shows that firms with a larger intangible assets ratio are likely to have a larger depreciation ratio and that this positive correlation is further strengthened in 2016 than in 2006. Firms having the top 10 percent intangible assets ratio show a statistically significant (first order stochastic dominance) increase in the depreciation ratio compared to firms having the bottom 10 percent intangible ratio. This pattern also can be observed between firms having the top 1 percent intangible assets ratio and firms having the top 10 percent intangible assets ratio. Note that all firm-level variables are standardized by subtracting the two-digit industry's annual average. Thus, it is less likely that the increases in the gap of depreciation ratios among groups from 2006 to 2016 derive from the compositional effects of industries.

The more intuitive observation can be found in figure 9-14. The figure shows that in 2016 the correlation between the intangible assets ratio and

FIGURE 9-14. **Intangible Assets and Depreciation of Tangible Assets, Scatter Plots**[a]

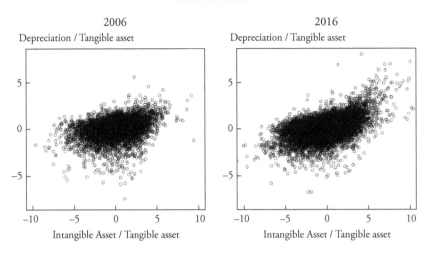

Source: Survey of Business Activities, Statistics Korea.

a. All firm-level variables are standardized by subtracting the two-digit industry annual average.

the depreciation ratio is mainly reinforced by the firms for which both ratios are large. This observation is in accord with the reinforcement cycle story in the periods of technological changes described in the introduction: a virtuous cycle for the frontiers and a vicious cycle for the laggards. Given that technologies are expected to change, the frontier firms can earn profits, prepare for the changes by saving and investing in them, and earn larger profits. In contrast, the laggard firms cannot earn enough, they save less, and they invest less.

Figure 9-15 shows that the standard deviations of both the intangible assets ratio and the depreciation ratio have been trending up since 2006. This figure reflects the possibility that the gaps between the frontier firms and the laggards are increasing.

Lastly, Figure 9-16 presents changes in estimated association between the intangible to tangible assets ratio and the depreciation to tangible assets ratio by using a fixed-effect model. It shows that the association becomes strengthened over time. Note that the association between the two variables showed a rapid increase in the late 2000s when the ratio of corporate savings to GDP increased.

FIGURE 9-15. **Standard Deviation of Intangible Assets and Depreciation of Tangible Assets**[a]

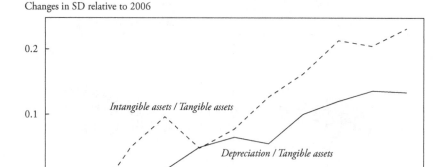

Changes in SD relative to 2006

Source: Survey of Business Activities, Statistics Korea.

a. All firm-level variables are standardized by subtracting the two-digit industry annual average.

To sum it up, the ratio of intangible assets to tangible assets and the ratio of depreciation to tangible assets are positively correlated, and this relationship has been strengthening since the 2000s. This trend is likely to be caused by the widening gap across firms. Thus, if the ratio of intangible assets to tangible assets is an appropriate variable to capture a firm's technological change, this increasing positive correlation can be viewed as supporting evidence of hypothesis B.

Expected Effects of Rising Corporate Saving

An increase in depreciation stemming from persistent technological changes can be a headwind for all firms. Firms are likely to pay high depreciation costs when they actively embrace technological changes. Firms that are not actively embracing technological changes, on the other hand, need to endure declining profits due to relative productivity declines.

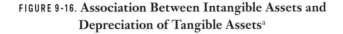

FIGURE 9-16. Association Between Intangible Assets and
Depreciation of Tangible Assets[a]

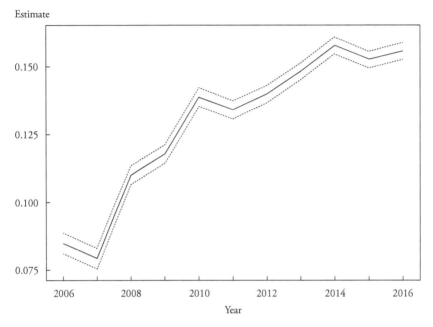

Source: Survey of Business Activities, Statistics Korea.

a. A fixed-effect model is used to estimate the effects of the intangible asset ratio on the depreciation ratio. Controlling variables include sales, the ratio of capital to labor, and two-digit industry dummies. Dashed lines show ±1se. The units of the vertical axis are the regression coefficients of Log (Depreciation / Tangible asset) on Log (Intangible assets / Tangible assets).

Firms' heterogeneity arises from the difference in their ability to stand against the headwind. The laggard firms can fall behind due to the headwind, while the frontier firms are able to proceed in spite of the headwind by actively adopting technological changes. A rising trend of CFC due to technological changes, thus, can be observed simultaneously with the expansion of the productivity gap among firms with the ability to increase their saving for accommodating technological changes and those without the ability.

The expansion of the productivity gap among firms due to technological changes may not be a recent phenomenon. It could be a general phenomenon in the period of technological changes. For instance, Hyunbae Chun and coauthors show that the heterogeneities in firm characteristics increase more in industries that adopt IT more intensively.[9]

Depreciation and Productivity

I use the SBA to examine the relationship between depreciation and productivity. The dataset covers a time span from 2006 to 2016. Firms with missing values of tangible assets, intangible assets, and depreciation are dropped. I exclude industries that have distinct characteristics, including finance and insurance, public administration, and real estate and leasing.

A firm's productivity is measured by its total factor productivity (TFP). I use a growth accounting method with the following Cobb-Douglas production function to estimate a firm's TFP denoted by A:

$$Y_{i,j,t} = A_{i,j,t} K_{i,j,t}^{1-\alpha_j} L_{i,j,t}^{\alpha_j} \text{ for firm } i, \text{ industry } j, \text{ time } t.$$

Output, Y, is measured as the deflated value added of a firm with producer prices of Bank of Korea. Capital input, K, is measured as the deflated tangible assets with GDP investment deflator Bank of Korea. Labor input, L, is total hours worked constructed as the product of the number of regular employees and the industrial average of hours worked taken from Statistics Korea. Labor elasticity of the production function, α, is measured as the two-digit industrial average of labor shares for the whole sample period from 2006 to 2016.

A cross-industry analysis suggests a positive association between depreciation and productivity: the more an industry experiences depreciation, the more productivity gain it has. Figure 9-17 shows that industries with a larger increase in the ratio of depreciation to tangible assets are likely to have a larger increase in TFP. A solid line in the figure represents the WLS regression estimate using the industrial average of real value added for the sample period from 2006 to 2016 as a weight. Table 9-3 shows the regression results, which are statistically significant and positive.

The above result suggests that technological changes can result in a productivity gap among industries. Given the characteristics of recent technological changes featuring advances in general purpose technologies such as artificial intelligence or data science, it is also possible that a similar pattern can be observed across firms within an industry.

By looking at firm-level productivity distributions, indeed, we can observe a positive correlation between depreciation and productivity.

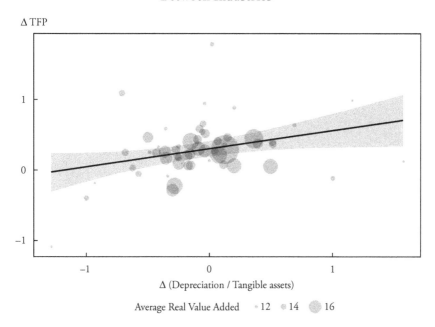

Source: Survey of Business Activities, Statistics Korea.

a. The horizontal axis shows changes in the ratio of depreciation to tangible assets from 2006 to
2016. The vertical axis represents changes in total factor productivity (TFP) from 2006 to 2016.
The size of the circle represents the average real value added for 2006 and 2016. A solid line
shows the weighted least squares regression estimate with the average value added as a weight.
Shaded areas represent 95 percent confidence intervals.

Table 9-3. *Depreciation of Tangible Assets and TFP, Between Industries*[a]

Dependent variable	Independent variable
Changes in TFP	Changes in the ratio of depreciation to tangible assets
From 2006 to 2016, 59 observations	0.257*
	(2.46)

Source: Survey of Business Activities, Statistics Korea.
a. The number in the parentheses shows t-statistics. An asterisk indicates statistical
significance; * $p < 0.05$. The average real value added of each industry for 2006 and 2016
is used as a weight.

FIGURE 9-18. **Probability Densities of TFP**[a]

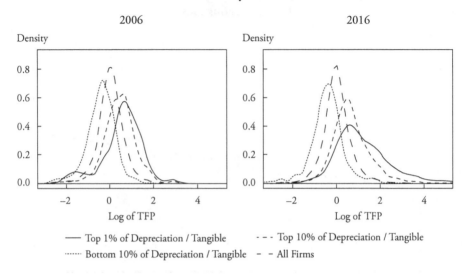

2006

2016

— Top 1% of Depreciation / Tangible   - - - Top 10% of Depreciation / Tangible
······ Bottom 10% of Depreciation / Tangible   – – All Firms

Source: Survey of Business Activities, Statistics Korea.

a. All firm-level variables are standardized by subtracting the two-digit industry annual average.

Figure 9-18 shows that firms with a larger ratio of depreciation to tangible assets are likely to have the larger TFP in the sense of first order stochastic dominance. The TFP distribution of firms with the top 10 percent (top 1 percent) depreciation ratio lies to the right of that of firms with the bottom 10 percent (top 10 percent) depreciation ratio. In addition, this positive correlation is further reinforced in 2016 as compared to 2006.

This positive correlation between the depreciation ratio and TFP of firms suggests that technological changes are associated with the productivity gaps among firms within an industry. Note that the gaps increased from 2006 to 2016.[10]

Figure 9-19 shows scatterplots of the depreciation ratio and productivity in 2006 and 2016. As can be seen in the figure, a positive correlation between the depreciation ratio and TFP is strengthened over time. In particular, the correlation appears to be reinforced primarily by firms for which both ratios are large. This implies that the frontier firms proceed relatively further and that the gaps between the frontiers and the laggards expand.

Let's look at the association between the depreciation ratio and TFP of firms through the following fixed-effect model, $\text{TFP}_{i,j,t} = \beta_1 dep.sale_{i,j,t} + \beta_2 dep.cap_{i,j,t} + \beta_3 X_{i,j,t} + \Sigma_j \delta_j + \Sigma_t \delta_t$, where i, j, and t represent firm, two-digit indus-

FIGURE 9-19. **Depreciation of Tangible Assets and TFP, Scatterplots**[a]

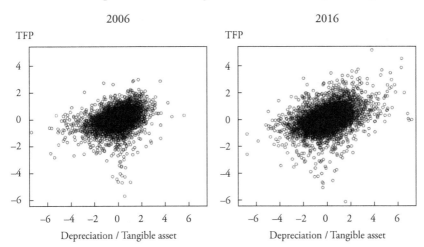

Source: Survey of Business Activities, Statistics Korea.

a. All firm-level variables are standardized by subtracting the two-digit industry annual average.

try, and year, respectively. A dependent variable is total factor productivity (TFP). Independent variables are the depreciation to sales ratio (*dep. sale*) that captures a firm's short-term cost pressure and the depreciation to tangible assets ratio (*dep.cap*) that captures changes in a firm's production structure due to technological changes. Control variable (*X*) includes a firm's size measured by the log of the number of a firm's regular employees (*log.size*) and a one-year lagged TFP of a firm (*lag*(TFP)). A two-digit industry dummy (δ_j) and a year dummy (δ_t) are also included.

Table 9-4 shows the estimation results. In the first three columns (1)–(3),[11] *dep.sale* shows statistically significant negative correlations with TFP. These negative correlations are consistent with the interpretation that the depreciation to sales ratio captures a firm's short-term cost pressure. As the tangible assets of a firm depreciate out, the firm needs to invest more to keep its capital input status quo and to maintain its current output. This necessary amount of investment derived from depreciation is a firm's cost, and it decreases its profits.

In the last three columns (4)–(6) in Table 4,[12] *dep.cap* shows statistically significant positive correlations with TFP. These positive correlations are compatible with our expectation that the depreciation to tangible assets

Table 9-4. *Depreciation of Tangible Assets and TFP, Between Firms*[a]

| | Dependent variable | | | | | |
| | *tfp* | | | | | |
	(1)	(2)	(3)	(4)	(5)	(6)
dep.sale	−0.115***	−0.095***	−0.164***			
	(0.003)	(0.004)	(0.015)			
dep.cap				0.235***	0.226***	0.256***
				(0.003)	(0.003)	(0.012)
log.size	−0.220***	−0.208***	−0.230***	−0.214***	−0.202***	−0.213***
	(0.004)	(0.005)	(0.007)	(0.004)	(0.005)	(0.007)
lag (tfp)		0.283***			0.281***	
		(0.004)			(0.003)	
Observations	79,092	63,346	63,346	79,092	63,346	63,346
R²	0.062	0.112	0.084	0.126	0.164	0.131

Source: *p<0.1; **p<0.05; ***p<0.01
Note: Survey of Business Activities, Statistics Korea.
a. All firm-level variables are standardized by subtracting the two-digit industry annual average. In models (3) and (6), lagged independent variables are used as instrumental variables for dep.sale and dep.cap.

ratio, *dep.cap*, can measure the degree of technological changes: how quickly a firm changes its composition of tangible assets when it adopts new technologies. For instance, if a semiconductor manufacturing company upgrades its production lines from a 20nm technology to a 10nm technology, many parts of the existing production equipment used in the 20nm production process must be replaced. As a result, the depreciation will increase rapidly, and the ratio of depreciation to tangible assets can be greatly increased.

Besides, the lagged productivity (*lag*(TFP)) shows positive correlations with the current period productivity (TFP), which is in line with our expectation. The size of a firm (*log.size*), however, shows negative correlations with TFP although positive correlations are expected theoretically. This might be a symptom of resource misallocation among firms in South Korea or the result of firms adopting labor-saving technologies.[13]

To sum, the regression results in table 9-4 suggest that the increase in depreciation is closely related to the increase in productivity and that the productivity gap can expand among firms: those with the ability to in-

FIGURE 9-20. Widening Gap Between Frontier and Laggard Firms[a]

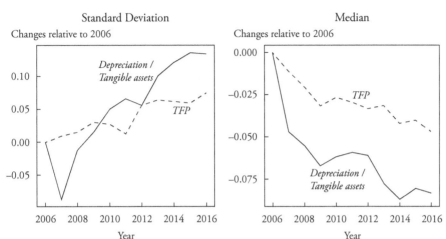

Source: Survey of Business Activities, Statistics Korea.

a. All firm-level variables are standardized by subtracting the two-digit industry annual average.

crease their saving against the headwind for accommodating technological changes and those without the ability. Figure 9-20 shows this widening gap. Note that both the depreciation rate and TFP, which are standardized by subtracting their two-digit industry annual average, have an increasing trend for their standard deviations and a decreasing trend for their medians.

This rising trend of standard deviations together with the decline in median values shows that a firm distribution in South Korea becomes more right-skewed, which implies that some frontier firms grow faster while many laggard firms grow slower. This widening productivity gap between the frontier firms and the laggard firms is not only observed in South Korea. Dan Andrews, Chiara Criscuolo, and Peter N. Gal report that the productivity gap among large global firms in OECD countries has been expanding and that the productivity improvement of the frontier firms does not spread fast enough to the laggard firms.[14] In a time of technological changes, as argued in this paper, it might be the frontier firms that make changes in technologies and enlarge the frontiers by earning, saving, investing, and again earning more profits.

Conclusion

In this study, I show that South Korea's corporate saving measured by the ratio of nonfinancial corporations' gross savings to GDP has been increasing in the long term and that the increase is mainly due to the increase in consumption of fixed capital (CFC) and net lending. It is also argued that the increase in the corporate saving rate since 2000 can be a firm's optimal choice to cope with the expected, persistent increase in CFC due to technological changes and that the productivity gap can expand between firms that actively adopt technological changes and those that do not.

If technological changes are behind the increase in corporate saving as shown in this study, the high level of South Korea's corporate savings rate could suggest that its economy struggles to follow or to lead technological changes. Then, a policy measure that directly suppresses corporate saving could distort firms' optimization behaviors and hinder them from adopting technological changes.

This study, however, is a partial equilibrium analysis examining corporate saving with firms' perspective. A general equilibrium analysis studying a relationship among corporate saving, household income, and aggregate demand is required to set more concrete policy suggestions.

NOTES

1. Chen, Karabarbounis, and Neiman (2017).
2. For example, Park (2013).
3. For example, Almeida and Campello (2007); Bates, Kahle, and Stulz (2009); Choi and Lim (2007).
4. For example, "Tech Firms" (2018).
5. Chen, Karabarbounis, and Neiman (2017).
6. Falato, Kadyrzhanova, and Sim (2013).
7. Graham and Leary (2018).
8. For example, Corrado, Hulten, and Sichel (2009).
9. Chun and others (2008).
10. Both the depreciation ratio and TFP for each firm are standardized by subtracting the two-digit industrial annual average. Distributions are constructed by pooling these standardized values of all firms across all industries. Thus, compositional changes in industries are expected to be controlled for and hence have at most minor effects on the increase in TFP gaps among firms.
11. In the model (3), a one-year lagged variable of dep.sale is used as an instrument variable for dep.sale to control for the simultaneity between TFP and dep.sale.

12. In the model (6), a one-year lagged variable of dep.cap is used as an instrument variable for dep.cap to control for the simultaneity between TFP and dep.cap.

13. These unexpected positive correlations are beyond the scope of this paper. Further studies are required for detailed explanations.

14. Andrews, Criscuolo, and Gal (2016).

REFERENCES

Almeida, Heitor, and Murillo Campello. 2007. "Financial Constraints, Asset Tangibility, and Corporate Investment." *The Review of Financial Studies* 20, no. 5, pp. 1429–60.

Andrews, Dan, Chiara Criscuolo, and Peter N. Gal. 2016. "The Best versus the Rest: The Global Productivity Slowdown, Divergence across Firms and the Role of Public Policy," OECD Productivity Working Papers 2016-5 (Paris: Organisation of Economic Co-operation and Development).

Bates, Thomas W., Kathleen M. Kahle, and René M. Stulz. 2009. "Why Do US Firms Hold so Much More Cash Than They Used To?" *The Journal of Finance* 64, no. 5, pp. 1985–2021.

Chen, Peter, Loukas Karabarbounis, and Brent Neiman. 2017. "The Global Rise of Corporate Saving." *Journal of Monetary Economics* 89, pp. 1–19.

Choi, Yong-Seok, and Kyung-Mook Lim. 2007. "A Study on the Pattern Changes and Determinants of Corporate Cash Holding." *KDI Journal of Economic Policy* 29, no. 2, pp. 75–116. [In Korean]

Chun, Hyunbae, and others. 2008. "Creative Destruction and Firm-Specific Performance Heterogeneity." *Journal of Financial Economics* 89, no. 1, pp. 109–35.

Corrado, Carol, Charles Hulten, and Daniel Sichel. 2009. "Intangible Capital and US Economic Growth." *Review of Income and Wealth* 55, no. 3, pp. 661–85.

Falato, Antonio, Dalida Kadyrzhanova, and Jae Sim. 2013. "Rising Intangible Capital, Shrinking Debt Capacity, and the US Corporate Savings Glut," FEDS Working Paper 2013-67 (Washington, D.C.: Federal Reserve Board), September (http://dx.doi.org/10.2139/ssrn.2350863).

Graham, John R., and Mark T. Leary. 2018. "The Evolution of Corporate Cash." *The Review of Financial Studies* 31, no. 11, pp. 4288–344.

Park, Jongkyu. 2013. *Structural Problems in Korean Economy: Wageless Growth and Paradox of Corporate Thrift*. KIF Research Paper (Seoul: Korea Institute of Finance). [In Korean]

"Tech Firms Are Suddenly the Corporate World's Biggest Investors." 2018. *The Economist* (July 28).

TEN

Rise of Household Debt and Spending in Korea

Evidence and Policy Implications

YOUNG-IL KIM

Household debt is a source of great concern in Korea due to the size, growth rate, and quality of that debt. Compared to other Organization for Economic Co-operation and Development (OECD) countries (figure 10-1), the share of household debt to GDP is high, and there is growing unease over the possible repercussions of such a large amount of debt on the real economy.[1] The debt-related risks are even amplified by Korea's inadequate social safety nets and pension system. Korea's household debt-to-GDP ratio has continued to increase since the early 2000s, while those in many OECD countries have shown significant adjustments following the global financial crisis (figure 10-2). Excessive credit growth can be a significant threat, as it can exacerbate a recession.[2]

In addition to the size and growth rate of household debt, the quality of debt also deserves attention. As shown in figure 10-3, the loans from

FIGURE 10-1. Household Debt/GDP Ratio

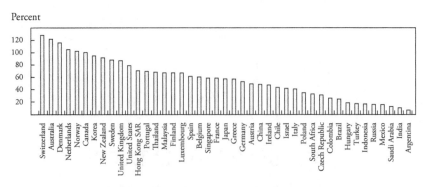

Source: BIS Statistics Explorer, 2017.

nonbank financial institutions, which tend to charge higher interest rates, have grown rapidly, and their share of the aggregate household loans has increased. This and the above factors can weaken the sustainability of debt as more households become vulnerable to shocks to the economy. Household debt is a risk not only to financial and social stability but also to the real economy.

Risks to Financial Stability

A large share of the total debt is reported to be held by credit-worthy households with high incomes and sufficient wealth. As such, the possibility of massive defaults is low in the short run. The majority of household loans from banks are borrowed by credit-worthy households in the form of mortgage loans, which record fairly low loan-to-value (LTV) ratios in comparison to those of countries such as the United States. In addition, Korean banks have been assessed to have adequate loss-absorbing capacities such as loan loss provisions and capital buffers. Hence, banks, which are systemically important financial institutions, will not face difficulties in the short term. Accordingly, it is often argued that household debt may not give rise to imminent systemic risks for the financial system.[3]

Although the risk of insolvency is low, there still seems to be a liquidity mismatch in the household credit market.[4] A large number of households in Korea tend to borrow short-term loans while their assets are held mostly in nonliquid forms such as real estate. Hence, there is a liquidity mismatch

FIGURE 10-2. **Trends in the Household Debt/GDP Ratio**

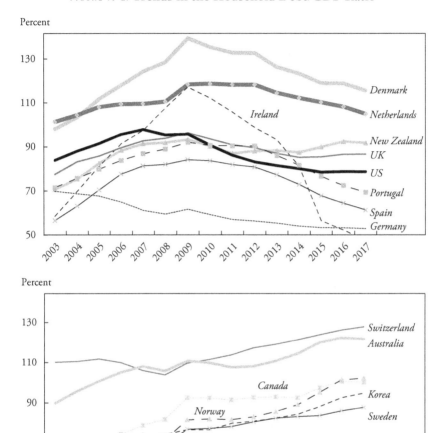

Source: BIS Statistics Explorer, 2017.

between the asset side and the liability side in households' balance sheets. The liquidity mismatch may enhance the interaction between asset markets such as the housing market and the credit market. For example, depression in the housing market could put indebted households into a difficult position in the credit market. Additionally, a depression in the credit market could also result in a depression in the housing market.

FIGURE 10-3. **Household Debt from Banks and Nonbank**
Financial Institutions

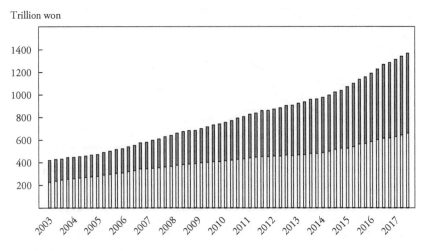

Trillion won

Source: Bank of Korea.

In short, the current level of household debt may be considered to be a potential risk to financial stability although it is not likely to result in systemic risks in the immediate future.

Risks to Financial and Social Inclusion

Still, there are a large number of vulnerable indebted households whose debt payment capacities are weak due to low income or insufficient wealth. They are often borrowers from nonbank financial institutions, which charge relatively high interest rates due to the household's lack of creditworthiness. The amount of debt they hold is relatively small and is a relatively small part of the aggregate amount of debt in the economy. Meanwhile, a large share of their debt is often borrowed from nonbank financial institutions whose systemic importance is low—hence, systemic risks to the financial system are unlikely. However, the majority of vulnerable borrowers may be a source of concern in terms of financial and social inclusion.

Risks to the Real Economy

As household debt grows, the leverage ratio (households' level of debt relative to their debt-payment capacity) has continued increasing. The debt-to-income ratios of Korean households are high in comparison with other

OECD countries, suggesting that their debt repayment burdens are also relatively high. It is often argued that the growing amount of debt relative to economic activity poses risks to the real economy, as it can suppress households' consumption expenditures and, hence, aggregate demand. Furthermore, it can also threaten the sustainability of economic growth itself. This study investigates how the leverage of the household sector of the economy affects households' spending to weigh down the real economy. The relationship between household debt and spending in Korea is the main focus of this study.

To understand how household debt is related to sluggish domestic demand, the empirical analysis of this study investigates how the leverage of the household sector can hinder the growth of expenditure. For the empirical and quantitative analysis, household-level data is used to find out how the leverage of households affects their expenditure growth. In this study, how household leverage ratios have affected expenditure growth in the period after the global financial crisis is analyzed and how changes in the household leverage ratio would affect household spending and domestic demand is predicted.

Furthermore, this study attempts to draw implications for economic growth from a mid- to long-term perspective, as well as from a short-term, business-cycle aspect. With this in mind, related literature on the relationship between household debt, sluggish aggregate demand, and potential GDP is reviewed.

This study analyzes the role of household debt in relation to the real economy. If the leverage of the household sector destabilizes the real economy or weakens the sustainability of economic growth, a set of public policy tools should be sought to prevent increasingly negative outcomes and to improve economic performance. The discussion then turns to what policies are necessary in order to deal with household debt in the periods both before and after it affects the real economy.

The remainder of this study is organized as follows. The second section discusses the performance of private consumption in the period after the global financial crisis, while the third section discusses the economy-wide conditions that may have affected private consumption. The fourth section discusses why debt may matter to the performance of the real economy. The fifth section shows the results of empirical analyses on the relation between debt and household spending. The sixth section further discusses the possible effects of debt on the real economy from a medium- to long-term perspective. And the last section concludes with discussions of policy implications.

Weak Growth of Household Spending since the Global Financial Crisis

Korea's private consumption growth rates have been very low since the global financial crisis—with especially low figures during the crisis as well as during the Eurozone fiscal crisis (figure 10-4). Accordingly, the contribution of private consumption to the GDP growth rate has also been very weak, as shown in figure 10-5.

GDP can be a dominant predictor of private consumption, as it is closely related to household income. The change in GDP can explain movements in private consumption to a large extent, as shown in figure 10-4. However, there may be other variables that can affect private consumption.

The Role of GDP as a Determinant of Private Consumption

In order to assess the role of GDP as a determinant of private consumption, how well the GDP growth rate predicts private consumption in the period after the global financial crisis is analyzed. Based on the following simple regression model, with the GDP growth rate as the main predictor of private consumption growth (equation 10-1), private consumption for the period after the global financial crisis can be predicted. First, year-to-year logarithmic growth rates of quarterly real private consumption are regressed on year-to-year logarithmic growth rates of quarterly real GDP, as seen in equation 10-1 by using data from the first quarter of 1961 to the fourth quarter of 2007. The forecast for the private consumption growth rate based on the estimated equation (10-1) for the period from the fourth quarter of 2010 to the fourth quarter of 2017 are shown in comparison with the actual consumption growth rate in figure 10-6.

$$\Delta_4 \ln(\textit{real private consumption}_t) = \beta_0 + \beta_1 \Delta_4 \ln(\textit{real GDP}_t) + \epsilon_t. \quad (10\text{-}1)$$

It appears that, to a certain degree, the GDP growth rate alone can explain the changes in the private consumption growth rate. But this may not be enough to explain the actual growth rate of private consumption. Based on the historical relationship captured by the simple regression

FIGURE 10-4. **Growth Rates of Private Consumption and GDP**

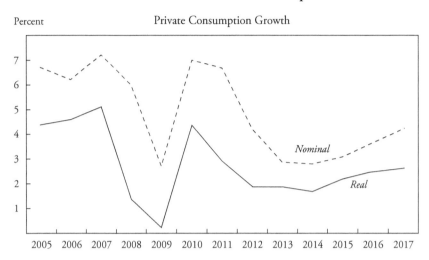

Percent   Private Consumption Growth

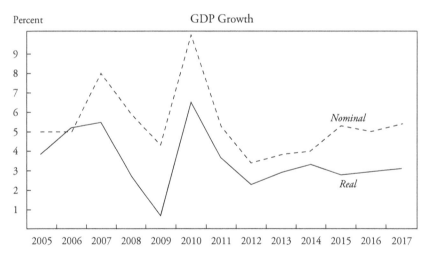

Percent   GDP Growth

Source: National Income Account, Bank of Korea.

model, the GDP-based forecasts tend to overpredict private consumption following the global financial crisis, as shown in figure 10-6. In other words, the actual private consumption growth rate seems to be smaller than what the GDP predicted in the past. As a robustness check, the regression model (equation 10-1) can be estimated with only nominal variables included for the period after 1990, during which the nominal variables were relatively

FIGURE 10-5. GDP Growth and Contribution of Private Consumption to GDP Growth

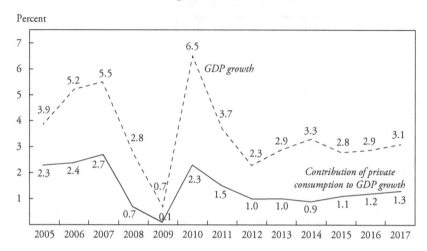

Source: National Income Account, Bank of Korea.

FIGURE 10-6. Year-on-Year Private Consumption Growth: Actual vs. Forecast

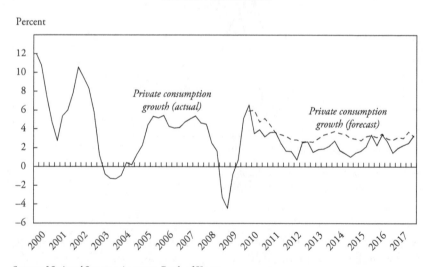

Source: National Income Account, Bank of Korea.

stable. The forecasts for nominal private consumption based on the estimated regression model also overpredicted private consumption, although the degree was smaller. Hence, it is suspected that there may be other variables that affected private consumption during the period of interest.

Other Variables as Possible Determinants of Private Consumption

This study seeks to explain the weak growth in private consumption since the global financial crisis, focusing on the role of debt in the real economy. In addition to households' income, net worth, credit constraints, precautionary motives, and so forth can be considered important factors that can affect household spending, according to previous studies in the economic literature. For example, the weakness of household balance sheets during the period when economic conditions were worsening may be related to their access to credit markets as well as to their precautionary motives. Hence, the spending patterns of highly leveraged households may be different from those of other households.

With regard to explaining the weak growth phenomena of aggregate consumption, it is worth mentioning the possibility of other approaches and arguments, although such alternative views are not pursued in this study. For example, the increase in life expectancy, which is an important aspect of Korea's demographic structural change, may be linked to the slowdown in aggregate consumption propensity.[5] In addition, distributional changes in wealth would be related to the change in aggregate consumption if less wealth were associated with a higher marginal propensity to consume.[6] In other words, an increase in wealth inequality could result in bigger adjustments in the aggregate consumption during a recession if more households were credit constrained and their consumption was made difficult. The credit constraint in the latter approach may also be an important mechanism in this study, as higher leverage tends to be associated with more credit constraints.[7]

Economic Background behind the Slowdown in Household Spending

In this section the economy-wide conditions that may have affected household spending in the period after the global financial crisis are examined. Under consideration are asset market conditions, levels of uncertainty, and credit market conditions, as they can affect household spending through changes in net worth, credit constraints, precautionary motives, and so forth.

GDP, which is the main predictor of private consumption, has weakened in terms of the growth rate since the global financial crisis. However, the weak growth rate of GDP or of household income may be insufficient in fully explaining the weak growth of household expenditure, as discussed in the previous section. The changes in the macroeconomic conditions that may have affected private consumption can be explored. In particular, asset market conditions, levels of uncertainty, and credit market conditions in relation to private consumption are examined in this section.

Asset Market (Housing Market) Conditions

Housing prices recorded low growth rates during the global financial crisis and eurozone crisis (figure 10-7). As housing prices can affect households' net worth in their balance sheets, they can change spending behaviors through the channel of wealth effects. Housing prices are closely related to households' wealth because a large share of households' assets is held in

FIGURE 10-7. Annual Growth Rate of Housing Prices

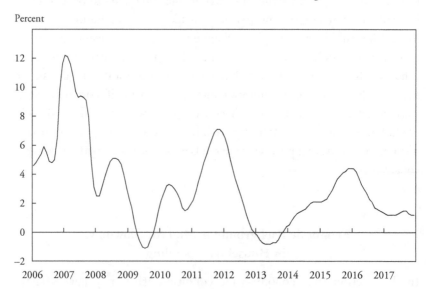

Source: Housing Purchase Price Index, KB Kookmin Bank.

the form of real estate in Korea. Hence, changes in housing prices directly affect the amount of net worth in household balance sheets.

Level of Economic Uncertainty

The level of uncertainty rises during crisis periods. Indicators related to uncertainty such as stock market volatility as well as unemployment rates show that the level of uncertainty may have risen during past crisis periods (figure 10-8). The rise in uncertainty may induce risk-averse households to cut back their current expenditures and to prepare themselves against possible economic downturns. The higher the level of uncertainty, the larger the impact on expenditure, as risk-averse households attempt to adjust their spending downward more aggressively due to precautionary motives.

Credit Market Conditions

Credit market conditions worsened during the crisis periods. For example, surveys on lending practices, especially for credit to households, show that households' access to the credit market may have worsened during the crisis periods (figure 10-9). Worsening credit market conditions can keep indebted or highly leveraged households from accessing credit resources. Hence, they may prevent households from smoothing out their consumption expenditure. The worse credit market conditions become, the more likely credit-constrained households are to adjust down their expenditures because they may not have sufficient credit buffers to smooth out their consumption.

Why Does Debt Matter in Household Spending?

Household leverage has increased rapidly in Korea since the global financial crisis of 2007–09, while it has decreased in many other countries in the OECD. Korea's household debt-to-GDP ratio is higher than other OECD economies and it is often argued that the household debt in Korea may be related to the sluggish growth of private consumption. The change in household income may explain the changes in household spending to a large extent, but it could be insufficient to explain the slowdown, as discussed above. With this in mind, how the composition of household balance sheets affects their decisions regarding consumption expenditure and how these

FIGURE 10-8. **Stock Market Volatility and Unemployment**[a]

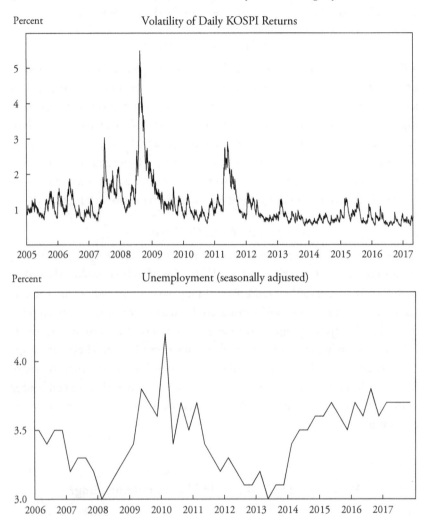

Percent   Volatility of Daily KOSPI Returns

Percent   Unemployment (seasonally adjusted)

Sources: Korea Stock Exchange and Statistics Korea.

a. Stock market volatility is the conditional standard deviation of daily returns of KOSPI index calculated based on the GARCH(1,1) model.

FIGURE 10-9. **Senior Loan Officers' Opinion on Banks' Lending Practices**[a]

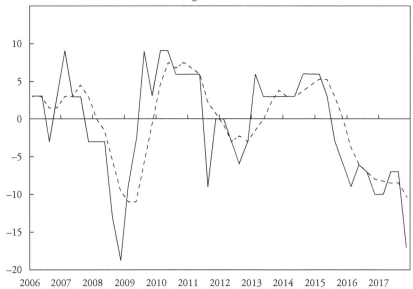

Banks' Lending Attitude Toward Households[b]

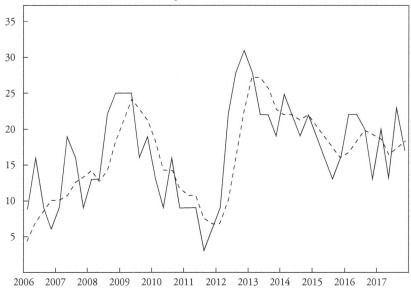

Banks' Judgment of Households' Credit Risk[c]

Source: Survey on Lending Practices, Bank of Korea.

a. Dotted lines are the four-quarter moving averages of black lines.

b. An index reading above 0 indicates that the number of financial institutions responding "easing" is greater than that of those responding "tightening." A reading below 0 indicates the opposite.

c. The index shows how large the number of financial institutions responding "increase in credit risk" is compared to that of those responding "decrease in credit risk."

FIGURE 10-10. **Household Balance Sheet Composition**

Asset (A)	Debt (D)
	Net Worth (NW)

changing balance sheets may be related to the sluggish performance of private consumption after the global financial crisis is considered.

Debt, Balance Sheet Composition, and Resilience to Shocks

The share of debt from households' balance sheets can reflect their financial vulnerability. The debt-to-asset ratio is inversely related to the net worth–to-asset ratio because the former is equal to a 1- net worth–to-asset ratio (figure 10-10). The net worth–to-asset ratio can work as a buffer against shocks, hence contributing to households' resilience. The higher the leverage ratio, or debt-to-asset ratio, the smaller the net worth–to-asset buffer. As such, households with higher leverage may be more vulnerable to worsening economic conditions such as economic downturns.

Credit Constraint Channel

High-leverage households face difficulties in accessing credit markets if economic conditions worsen. Lenders would be more likely to decline their demand for credit if credit market conditions deteriorated. Such credit constraints may prevent borrowers or highly leveraged households from smoothing out their spending. Accordingly, credit-constrained households tend to show a larger marginal propensity to consume.[8] In short, households with higher leverage would be forced to further adjust down their spending in periods of economic downturn.

Precautionary Motive Channel

High-leverage households may also show more precautionary behaviors in times of rising uncertainty in comparison with other households because their financial position is vulnerable to shocks. Households with high leverage may fear becoming overindebted or going bankrupt, as they expect bad events to occur more frequently.[9] Hence, risk-averse households with high leverage would attempt to adjust down their spending growth in order to avoid worse outcomes during an economic downturn.

Empirical Analysis of the Relationship between Household Debt and Spending

In this section, household-level data is analyzed to understand the effects of leverage ratios (debt to asset, debt to income) on households' spending. Of particular interest is whether the differences in households' leverage ratios can explain the changes in their consumption expenditure after the global financial crisis. The sample period can be divided into economic downturns (the 2007–09 global financial crisis and the 2011–13 eurozone fiscal crisis) and normal periods to figure out how economic conditions influence the effects of households' debt on spending.

Empirical Specifications and Data Description

The role of household leverage in relation to household expenditure is analyzed in this study based on an empirical model. How the model is specified and what data is used for the estimation are discussed in the following.

MAIN EMPIRICAL SPECIFICATIONS. A household's current income can affect spending if they are myopic or face credit constraints. Their net worth may also affect spending through the wealth effect. Characteristics such as the number of household members, their ages, their education levels, and so forth are expected to reflect the preferences of households and, hence, may explain the heterogeneity in household spending. In addition to the conventional explanatory variables, debt-related variables are examined for their effects on households' spending in this study. Based on the above discussion, households' expenditure growth rates are regressed on such debt-related variables as leverage ratios in addition to the traditional explanatory variables, including income, net worth, household characteristics, and so forth, as in the following regression model.

$$\Delta C_{i,t\sim(t+s)} = \beta_0 + (\beta_1 + \beta_2 \; Leverage_{i,t}) \; Debt\_dum_{i,t} + \beta_3 \; \Delta Y_{i,t\sim(t+s)}$$
$$+ \beta_4 \Delta NW_{i,t\sim(t+s)} + \beta_5 \Delta HHsize_{i,t\sim(t+s)} + \beta_6 X_{i,t} + \epsilon_{i,(t+s)}. \qquad (10\text{-}2)$$

The regression model includes households' expenditure growth (ΔC) as a dependent variable and income growth (ΔY), net worth growth (ΔNW), and the change in the number of household members ($\Delta HHSize$) as control variables and X as other control variables that may reflect household preferences. A dummy variable for debt holding (*Debt_dum*: 1 if indebted, 0 otherwise) is used to distinguish borrowers from nonborrowers because their spending behaviors can differ, especially in the face of a credit crunch or market uncertainties. The leverage ratio of households (*Leverage*) is the main variable of interest, as discussed above.

($\beta_1 + \beta_2$ *Leverage*) · *Debt_dum* in the regression model shows the effects of households' liability on their expenditure growth; β_1 captures the difference in expenditure growth between debtors and nondebtors, while β_2 captures the marginal effect of the leverage on expenditure growth. The regression model shows whether the differences in balance sheet composition—measured by the leverage ratio (debt to asset)—at the beginning of the period across households affect the changes in their spending behavior in the period that follows (figure 10-11).

The variables of households' expenditure, income, and net worth are inverse hyperbolic sine transformed to deal with certain statistical issues associated with extreme values often raised in microdata analyses.[10] The transformation also allows for the use of such a variable as the net worth, which records "0" or negative (–) while allowing for an interpretation similar to logarithmic transformation. Hence, the difference (Δ) of the transformed variables may be interpreted as the growth rate.

The empirical model is then estimated for the whole sample period, periods of economic downturns, and normal periods, respectively, to examine whether the effects of debt on households' expenditure are dependent on macroeconomic conditions.

DATA FOR THE EMPIRICAL STUDY. Household-level data is analyzed to estimate the effects of debt on spending. This study uses the National Survey of Tax and Benefits (NaSTaB), which has been surveying households through face-to-face interviews, with an original sample of 5,634 households, annually since 2008. The NaSTaB is widely used and is a nationally repre-

FIGURE 10-11. **Time Dimension of Main Variables**

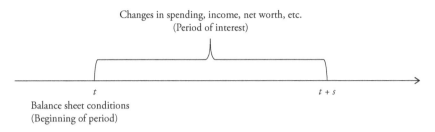

sentative sample of households, showing how individuals and households perform in their economic activities, such as income, expenditure, wealth, liabilities, taxes, benefits, and so forth, every year. The dataset represents the experiences of households in the periods of interest for this study.

The main variables for the empirical analysis are computed based on data from the NaSTaB. Disposable income is the gross income minus non-consumption expenditure (current taxes, public pension, social insurance, and transfers). Household expenditure is the total amount of purchases of various services and goods during the year, excluding nonconsumption expenditure. Net worth is total assets, including financial assets and nonfinancial assets (real estate, security deposits, and so forth) minus the gross debt. The total debt includes housing-related loans, nonhousing loans, unsecured loans, lease deposits to be returned to tenants, and so forth.

HETEROGENEITY IN EXPENDITURE GROWTH AND THE DEBT-TO-ASSET RATIO. The expenditure growth rate is different across households, as shown in figure 10-12. The difference in spending behaviors can be explained by many explanatory variables included in the regression model, equation 10-2. Households also differ in their leverage ratios, again as shown in figure 10-12. This study analyzes how the differences in households' leverage ratios are related to the differences in their expenditure growth rate.

Empirical Findings

As discussed above, sluggish income growth alone cannot explain the weak growth rate in private consumption observed after the global financial crisis. The suspicion for this study was that the vulnerability in households' balance sheets in terms of leverage ratios may be affecting their spending

FIGURE 10-12. **Distribution of Household Expenditure Growth and Debt/Asset Ratio**[a]

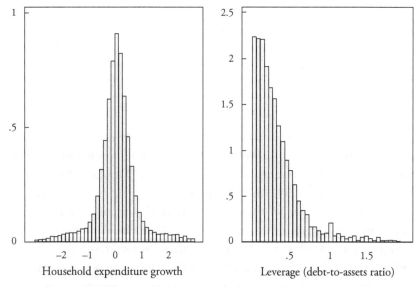

Distribution of Consumption Growth and Leverage

Household expenditure growth

Leverage (debt-to-assets ratio)

Source: The histograms are drawn using National Survey of Tax and Benefits (NaSTaB) data.

a. Distributions are shown by histograms that are scaled to density units so that the sum of the areas equals 1.

behavior. Estimates made through the regression model, equation 10-2, are used to figure out whether debt affects household spending after the global financial crisis.

ESTIMATION RESULTS AND INTERPRETATION. The estimation results in equation 10-2 for the full sample period, periods of economic downturns, and normal periods are shown in table 10.1. As can be seen, the liability-side information such as debt holding (Debt_dummy) and leverage ratio (debt to asset, debt to income) matters, and it can explain households' spending behaviors in the period since the global financial crisis. The expenditure growth rate of indebted households is lower than that of nonborrowing households. Households with higher leverage ratios (debt to asset, debt to income) tend to show a lower expenditure growth rate in comparison to households with lower leverage ratios. The effects of debt on households' spending are significant and sizable, especially during macroeconomic

Table 10-1. *Estimating the Relation between Household Debt and Expenditure Growth*[a]

Sample period (economic conditions)	Full sample period (recession + normal)		Recessionary period (2007-09, 2011-13)		Normal period (2009-11, 2013-15)	
Debt_dummy	−0.050*** (0.014)	−0.045*** (0.014)	−0.072*** (0.020)	−0.062*** (0.020)	−0.031 (0.020)	−0.030 (0.020)
(Debt/Asset) * Debt_dummy	−0.066*** (0.019)		−0.092*** (0.026)		−0.041 (0.028)	
(Debt/Income) * Debt_dummy		−0.011*** (0.003)		−0.017*** (0.003)		−0.006 (0.004)
Income growth	0.191*** (0.008)	0.196*** (0.008)	0.178*** (0.011)	0.186*** (0.011)	0.206*** (0.012)	0.209*** (0.012)
Net worth growth	0.009*** (0.002)	0.007*** (0.002)	0.011*** (0.002)	0.007*** (0.002)	0.008*** (0.003)	0.006*** (0.003)
Other control variables			—omitted—			
R-squared	0.064	0.065	0.069	0.070	0.063	0.063
Number of Observations	16,446		8,019		8,427	

Source: Coefficients of the regression model are estimated using National Survey of Tax and Benefits (NaSTaB) data.
a. Numbers in ( ) are standard errors. Statistical significance within 1 percent, 5 percent, and 10 percent indicated by ***, **, and *, respectively.

downturns (recessionary periods). However, the effects of debt on households' expenditure are neither significant nor sizable during normal periods. Hence, it is clear that the leverage ratios of the household sector contributed to amplifying the severity of the recessions by further depressing households' spending growth.

QUANTITATIVE INTERPRETATION OF THE ESTIMATION RESULTS. The effects of households' leverage ratios on their expenditure growth rate are statistically significant as well as economically sizable. The effects of debt on spending in quantitative terms can be assessed through the following.

A 10 percentage point (%p) difference in the debt-to-asset ratio (debt/asset) can explain the 0.33%p/year (=0.066 * 10%p / 2 years) difference in households' expenditure growth rate in 2007–15 (the full sample period). In other words, a 10%p increase in households' debt-to-asset ratio can explain the −0.33%p decline in annualized expenditure growth rate on average from 2007 to 2015.

The negative effects of debt on households' spending were significant and even bigger, especially during a recessionary period. A 10%p difference in the debt-to-asset ratio (debt/asset) can explain the 0.46%p/year (=0.092 * 10%p / 2 years) difference in households' expenditure growth rate during the recessionary period of the global financial crisis (2007–09) and the eurozone crisis (2011–13).

The estimation results show that a 10%p difference in the debt-to-asset ratio can explain the 0.21%p/year (=0.041 * 10%p / 2 years) difference in households' expenditure growth rate in the normal period (2009–11, 2013–15). However, the estimates are not statistically significant, even at the 10 percent significance level.

IMPLICATIONS FOR THE RELATIONSHIP BETWEEN HOUSEHOLD DEBT AND SPEND-ING. In short, debt may have contributed to the weak growth rate of households' spending in the period from 2007 to 2015 since the global financial crisis. The negative effects of debt on households' expenditure growth have been sizable and statistically significant but appear to be driven mostly by the relatively strong impacts during the recessionary periods of both the global financial crisis and the eurozone crisis.

Further Discussions on the Relation between Debt and Economic Growth

The analysis above provides empirical evidence for the effect of debt on households' spending based on household-level microdata analysis. It may be worthwhile to discuss the role of debt in relation to economic growth with macroeconomic and global perspective. This section reviews arguments and implications of previous studies about the relationship between debt and economic growth.

Household Leverage and Slumps in Demand during Economic Downturns

The empirical findings of this study suggest that excessive debt can affect the severity of economic downturns because households with higher leverage may attempt to adjust down their spending in response to worsening economic conditions. This implies that the aggregate demand of the economy would further decrease during economic downturns if the economy were populated by more indebted households with higher leverage. Hence, the high leverage of Korea's household sector must have made the economy more vulnerable to the downside risks.

The negative effects of household leverage on the demand side during and after the global financial crisis have also been reported in advanced economies. Several studies have reported that the contraction in household expenditure in the United States after the global financial crisis was associated with household leverage.[11] Similarly, some other studies reported the relevance of debt to the depression of household expenditure after the global financial crisis in the United Kingdom and Denmark, respectively.[12] The findings of these studies suggest that the higher leverage of the household sector can amplify and lengthen economic downturns—although the countries studied were different.

Household Leverage and Rising Unemployment during Economic Downturns

Household debt can amplify economic downturns through direct impact on private consumption, according to empirical studies on the relation between household debt and spending. There are also arguments that household debt can exacerbate economic downturns through direct negative effects on employment.[13] This argument suggests that debtors may ask for a relatively high reservation wage due to their limited liability, resulting in a significant increase in unemployment. However, the latter argument may not be very relevant to Korea, at least up until recently, because bankruptcy and indemnification of debts are permitted in a somewhat limited way in Korea, unlike in the United States.

Private Debt and Severe Recessions in World History

The experiences of advanced economies may support the fact that excessive private debt leads to deeper and longer recessions. For example, it was reported that, based on the empirical analysis of fourteen major advanced economies, recessions following excessive credit activities were more severe than normal recessions.[14]

Some argue that many of the severe recessions in the twentieth century, which are globally noteworthy, are related to debt. Irving Fisher pointed to the important role of debt in the U.S. Great Depression,[15] while Richard Koo pointed to excessive debt problems in Japan's long-term recession in the "Lost Decade" of the 1990s.[16] Mervyn King pointed to the relevance of excessive private debt in the severe recessions experienced by Europe in the early 1990s.[17]

With respect to the Great Depression, Fisher asserted that debt deflation was at the core of the long period of severe recessions.[18] According to his argument on debt deflation, excessive debt may have caused the recession to intensify and prolong. The liquidation of assets can begin when it becomes difficult to maintain the excessive debt within the economy. The resulting downward pressure on price and deflation can cause real debt to rise. This may, in turn, accelerate the liquidation of assets to reduce the debt, thereby depressing economic activity even further.

As for the so-called Lost Decade of Japan, Koo proposed that a balance sheet recession was the cause of the long-term depression.[19] This suggests that the recession may have been prolonged as firms with high leverage made decisions to invest, hire, and produce with the aim of reducing debt, not maximizing profits. The long-term severe economic downturn may be an outcome to which agents with high leverage contributed in the process of rebuilding their balance sheets through debt reduction. The same argument can be applied not only to firms with high debt ratios but also to households with high debt ratios, suggesting that sluggish domestic demand may be prolonged if households with high leverage prefer to reduce their debt within a long time span.

Household Credit Activities and GDP Growth

Household debt can contribute to economic growth as long as credit resources are efficiently allocated. Hence, household debt up to a certain level relative to economic activity may help the economy to grow. However, household debt beyond a certain level may exert negative effects on economic growth because such cases as inefficient allocation of credit resources can occur. For example, the International Monetary Fund (IMF) reported that, based on cross-country studies, household debt showed positive effects on GDP growth to a certain degree but gradually declined and turned negative beyond that.[20] Lombardi, Nohanty, and Shim reported that the effect of household debt on GDP growth was positive in the short run but turned negative in the long run, while the negative impact of debt on consumption was stronger with higher leverage.[21] These studies appear to imply that excessive credit activities may be harmful to the real economy as excessive risk taking and the consequent inefficient allocation of resources tend to increase.

According to time series studies on macroeconomic variables, the GDP of many countries has been reported to follow a difference-stationary process, suggesting that the trend in GDP can shift permanently down after major recessions.[22] As such, debt-driven recessions, if severe, may have been related to the permanent decline in the potential output level, resulting in larger losses in social welfare.

A prolonged slump in aggregate demand could also affect factors of production (labor, physical capital, and so forth) through hysteresis, as it can hinder the accumulation of physical and human capital with negative effects on productivity.[23] For example, it was reported that the potential GDP in the United States fell by 7 percent compared with the pre-crisis growth path due to the global financial crisis, suggesting the possibility of a permanent decline in the GDP level.[24] In addition, it was argued that the supply side of the economy would have been seriously damaged by the sluggish aggregate demand, suggesting the need to respond to the hysteresis, which has a negative impact on long-term growth.

Conclusion

The high leverage in the household sector may result in further downward adjustments in household spending during economic downturns, magnifying the downside risks. In other words, household debt works as a financial accelerator that exacerbates economic recessions if accumulated beyond a certain level relative to economic activity. Hence, an economy with too much household debt would go into a deeper recession during an economic downturn even without much disruption to the financial system. If the debt problem resulted in significant disruption in the process of financial intermediation, the effect of debt on recessions would be more severe.[25] Hence, more preemptive policy measures may be necessary to deal with the excessive debt problem in that case.

In addition, the spending cuts of highly leveraged debtors may not be easily compensated by other households' expenditure in a world with friction, contributing to deflationary pressures.[26] The negative effects of high leverage on aggregate demand could become even bigger if resources are not easily reallocated due to frictions in the economy.

The negative effects of household debt on the aggregate demand side, which are discussed in this study, are likely to threaten the sustainability of economic growth. As recessions become more severe and become prolonged, hysteresis can occur, which may weaken even the supply side production capacity. Accordingly, active policy responses may be necessary to resolve the excessive debt problem.

The effects of debt on the real economy are severe during economic downturns as compared with normal periods. Hence, prudential policy measures may be considered in normal periods while attempting to ease the deflationary pressure of debt during recessions.

In a normal period, the weaknesses of households' balance sheets may need to be repaired while preventing too much debt accumulation by implementing macroprudential policy measures to keep households' balance sheets sound. As prudential policy measures, the following may be considered: regulations on borrowers' borrowing limit such as loan-to-value and debt-to-income regulations; regulations on the asset and liability side activity of financial institutions such as restrictions on asset growth rates; regulations on the loss-absorbing capacity of financial institutions such as provisioning requirements and capital regulation; and taxation of specific assets (real estate properties).[27]

Macroprudential policy has received much attention since the global financial crisis because it was recognized that monetary policy alone can no longer guarantee macrofinancial stability. Fluctuations in credit activity may differ from business cycles. For example, credit activity tends to fluctuate within a longer cycle and can even stand at different stages from real economic activity. Hence, a separate macroprudential policy framework to deal with excessive credit activities may be needed. On the other hand, macroprudential policy can have an indirect effect on the real activity, which affects the effectiveness of monetary policy. Monetary policy can also affect the effectiveness of macroprudential policy. In order to achieve financial as well as real economic stability, macroprudential policy and monetary policy can be implemented to work in cooperation with each other by taking into account the interaction between the two policy tools. For example, a regular cooperation body can be established to share information and assessments on the economy with relevant policy authorities for effective collaboration.

In a recessionary period with household debt exerting further downward pressure on the demand side, aggregate demand can be stimulated with an expansive stance through monetary and fiscal policies while making efforts to repair households' balance sheets. Such a policy stance can relieve households' debt burdens and make up for weakness on the demand side. Still, there are pros and cons in terms of the effectiveness of monetary versus fiscal policies depending on assessments of the economic conditions and the capacities of each policy tool.

Monetary policy aimed at raising inflationary expectations can be implemented in order to ease deflationary pressure. However, it may be difficult to gain credibility for the central bank's willingness to raise expectations, considering its concerns over inflation in the past.[28] On the other hand, fiscal policy can play an active role if the policy interest rate is already low and cannot be further lowered. However, it would be worthwhile to note that fiscal soundness can be damaged if the troubled balance sheets of households cannot be resolved in a short period of time in spite of the expansive stance of fiscal policy. In addition, it would be difficult to expect a full recovery in households' spending unless their balance sheets have been repaired. Therefore, efforts to improve the financial soundness of households need to be pursued at all times. For example, debt-restructuring programs can be run for households with troubled balance sheets. The government can also assist the restructuring of troubled debt if an agreement between the creditor and debtor is not feasible.

In a much longer time horizon, the overall incentives system, which is related to household debt, can be examined and fixed. Such an incentives system may be associated with state-run credit or housing programs, taxes, costs of defaults, and so forth. For example, the government is involved in credit programs and running housing finance / guarantee corporations to support the access of households to credit resources and housing, particularly low- and middle-income families. Easy access to credit or housing ownership can help financial and social inclusion. However, it is worth considering borrowers' lifetime debt-payment capacities and preventing them from becoming overindebted. In addition, the government provides depositors of a number of nonbank financial institutions with tax reduction benefits on interest income, hence contributing to their capacities of loan generation. Taking into account that too much credit can be harmful, whether such tax incentives are still necessary at the current development stage of the credit market can be considered. Recently, the cost burden of delinquent or defaulted loans has shifted in favor of debtors in Korea. For example, personal bankruptcy and the rehabilitation system and debt-adjustment programs have changed to become more debtor friendly. The decline in insolvent debtors' burdens can contribute to social welfare by enabling minimal consumption spending and a fresh start. However, the shift in the cost-sharing between debtor and creditor can also change borrowers' decisions to borrow, the labor supply, and consumption spending, also affecting credit market, labor market, and product market outcomes. Therefore, policymakers need to deal with the incentives embedded in credit market contracts from an integrated and longer-term perspective.

NOTES

This article is based on Kim, Young-il. 2018. "Household Debt and Private Consumption," in *Decade after Global Crisis and New Growth Agenda for Korean Economy*, edited by Hyeon-Wook Kim. Research Monograph (Sejong: Korea Development Institute). [In Korean]

1. International Monetary Fund (2017); Lombardi, Nohanty, and Shim (2017).

2. Jorda, Schularick, and Taylor (2013).

3. Kim and Yoo (2013).

4. Kim (2013).

5. Kwon (2016).

6. Amromin, De Nardi, and Schulze (2018); Carroll, Slacalek, and Tokuoka (2014).

7. Kaplan, Violante, and Weidner (2014).

8. Carroll, Slacalek, and Tokuoka (2014); Kaplan, Violante, and Weidner (2014).

9. Eggertsson and Krugman (2012); King (1994); Mishkin (1977).

10. Dynan (2012); Browning, Gørtz, and Leth-Petersen (2013).

11. Dynan (2012); Mian and Sufi (2010); and Mian, Rao, and Sufi (2013).

12. Bunn and Rostom (2015); Andersen, Duus, and Jensen (2016).

13. Donaldson, Piacentino, and Thakor (2019).

14. Jorda, Schularick, and Taylor (2013).

15. Fisher (1933).

16. Koo (2011).

17. King (1994).

18. Fisher (1933).

19. Koo (2011).

20. International Monetary Fund (2017).

21. Lombardi, Nohanty, and Shim (2018).

22. Barro (2009); Obstfeld (1994); Cogley (1990).

23. Reifschneider, Wascher, and Wilcox (2015); Summers (2014a); Summers (2014b).

24. Reifschneider, Wascher, and Wilcox (2015).

25. Jorda, Schularick, and Taylor (2013).

26. Eggertsson and Krugman (2012).
27. Claessens (2015).
28. Eggertsson and Krugman (2012).

REFERENCES

Amromin, Gene, Mariacristina De Nardi, and Karl Schulze. 2018. "Inequality and Recessions." *Chicago Fed Letter*, Federal Reserve Bank of Chicago, no. 392.

Andersen, Asger L., Charlotte Duus, and Thais L. Jensen. 2016. "Household Debt and Spending during the Financial Crisis: Evidence from Danish Micro Data." *European Economic Review* 89, pp. 96–115.

Barro, Robert J. 2009. "Rare Disasters, Asset Prices, and Welfare Costs." *American Economic Review* 99, no. 1, pp. 243–64.

Browning, Martin, Mette Gørtz, and Søren Leth-Petersen. 2013. "Housing Wealth and Consumption: A Micro Panel Study." *The Economic Journal* 123, no. 568, pp. 401–28.

Bunn, Philip, and May Rostom. 2015. "Household Debt and Spending in the United Kingdom," Staff Working Paper 554 (London: Bank of England).

Carroll, Christopher D., Jiri Slacalek, and Kiichi Tokuoka. 2014. "The Distribution of Wealth and the MPC: Implications of New European Data." *American Economic Review* 104, no. 5, pp. 107–11.

Claessens, Stijn. 2015. "An Overview of Macroprudential Policy Tools." *Annual Review of Financial Economics* 7, pp. 397–422.

Cogley, Timothy. 1990. "International Evidence on the Size of the Random Walk in Output." *Journal of Political Economy* 98, no. 3, pp. 501–18.

Donaldson, Jason Roderick, Giorgia Piacentino, and Anjan V. Thakor. 2019. "Household Debt Overhang and Unemployment." *The Journal of Finance* 74, no. 3, pp. 1473–502.

Dynan, Karen. 2012. "Is a Household Debt Overhang Holding Back Consumption?" *Brookings Papers on Economic Activity* 43, no. 1 (Spring), pp. 299–362.

Eggertsson, Gauti B., and Paul Krugman. 2012. "Debt, Deleveraging, and the Liquidity Trap: A Fisher–Minsky–Koo Approach." *The Quarterly Journal of Economics* 127, no. 3, pp. 1469–513.

Fisher, Irving. 1933. "The Debt-Deflation Theory of Great Depressions." *Econometrica* 1, no. 4, pp. 337–57.

International Monetary Fund. 2017. "Household Debt and Financial Stability," in *Global Financial Stability Report*. Report. Washington, D.C. (October).

Jorda, Oscar, Moritz Schularick, and Alan M. Taylor. 2013. "When Credit Bites Back." *Journal of Money, Credit and Banking* 45, no. 2, pp. 3–28.

Kaplan, Greg, Giovanni L. Violante, and Justin Weidner. 2014. "The Wealthy Hand-to-Mouth." *Brookings Papers on Economic Activity* 45, no. 1 (Spring), pp. 77–138.

Kim, Young-il. 2013. "Household Debt Vulnerability and Directions for Risk Management: Analysis and Implications of the Household Asset-Liability Structure," in *Structural Changes and New Policy Directions in the Korean Housing Sector*, edited by Man Cho. Research Monograph (Sejong: Korea Development Institute). [In Korean]

Kim, Young-il, and Joohee Yoo. 2013. "Assessing Korean Households' Credit Risk: Stress Tests with Household Level Data." *Economic Analysis* 19, no. 2, pp. 59–95. [In Korean]

King, Mervyn. 1994. "Debt Deflation: Theory and Evidence." *European Economic Review* 38, no. 3, pp. 419–45.

Koo, Richard. 2011. "The World in Balance Sheet Recession: Causes, Cure, and Politics." *Real-World Economics Review* 58, no. 12, pp. 19–37.

Kwon, Kyooho. 2016. "Increase in Life Expectancy: Macroeconomic Impact and Policy Implications," Feature Article 2016(2) (Sejong: Korea Development Institute).

Lombardi, Marco Jacopo, Madhusudan Nohanty, and Ilhyock Shim. 2017. "The Real Effects of Household Debt in the Short and Long Run," Working Paper 607 (Basel: Bank for International Settlements).

Mian, Atif, Kamalesh Rao, and Amir Sufi. 2013. "Household Balance Sheets, Consumption, and the Economic Slump." *The Quarterly Journal of Economics* 128, no. 4, pp. 1687–726.

Mian, Atif, and Amir Sufi. 2010. "Household Leverage and the Recession of 2007–09." *IMF Economic Review* 58, no. 1, pp. 74–117.

Mishkin, Frederic S. 1977. "What Depressed the Consumer? The Household Balance Sheet and the 1973–75 Recession." *Brookings Papers on Economic Activity* 8, no. 1, pp. 123–74.

Obstfeld, Maurice. 1994. "Evaluating Risky Consumption Paths: The Role of Intertemporal Substitutability." *European Economic Review* 38, no. 7, pp. 1471–86.

Reifschneider, Dave, William Wascher, and David Wilcox. 2015. "Aggregate Supply in the United States: Recent Developments and Implications for the Conduct of Monetary Policy." *IMF Economic Review* 63, no. 1, pp. 71–109.

Summers, Lawrence H. 2014a. "Reflections on the 'New Secular Stagnation Hypothesis,'" in *Secular Stagnation: Facts, Causes, and Cures*, edited by Coen Teulings and Richard Baldwin (London: Centre for Economic Policy Research).

———. 2014b. "U.S. Economic Prospects: Secular Stagnation, Hysteresis, and the Zero Lower Bound." *Business Economics* 49, no. 2, pp. 65–73.

Contributors

SINEM KILIC CELIK   is an economist in the Prospects Group of the World Bank. Her research interests lie in macroeconomics, international macroeconomics, and public finance. She previously worked in the International Monetary Fund's Research Department, where she contributed to several analytical chapters of the *World Economic Outlook*. Her recent papers include work on potential growth, productivity, and structural reforms. She holds a Ph.D. in economics from George Washington University.

DUKSANG CHO   is an associate fellow in the Department of Knowledge Economy at the Korea Development Institute. His research interests cover various areas in macroeconomics, with an emphasis on firm dynamics. Recent research topics include the effects of business groups on resource allocation, technological change, and the rise of corporate saving. He holds a Ph.D. in economics from Washington University in St. Louis.

BRAHIMA COULIBALY   is a senior fellow and director of the Africa Growth Initiative at Brookings. Previously, he was chief economist and head of the emerging market and developing economies group at the Board of

Governors of the Federal Reserve System. He has taught at George-
town University, the Darden Graduate School of Business at the
University of Virginia, and the University of Michigan. He holds a
Ph.D. in economics from the University of Michigan.

KARIM FODA   is an economist in the European Department of the International Monetary Fund. Formerly an associate fellow at Brookings,
his research has focused on technological change, productivity,
growth linkages between advanced and emerging economies, and
income inequality. He is cocreator of the Brookings–Financial Times
TIGER index. He has also worked at KPMG, Accenture, and the
Central Bank of Egypt. He holds an M.A. in economics from Duke
University.

HYEON-WOOK KIM   is a senior fellow and director of Macroeconomic
Analysis and Forecasting at the Korea Development Institute (KDI).
He is also a professor at the KDI School of Public Policy and Management. Previously, he served at the Bank of Korea, including as an
advisor to the Monetary Policy Committee and secretary to the
governor. He has also worked as senior director and vice president at
the SK Group. He holds a Ph.D. in economics from Columbia
University.

YOUNG-IL KIM   is a fellow in the Department of Markets and Institutions
at the Korea Development Institute (KDI). He has served as a director
of the Department of Financial Policy Research at KDI. He has been
a visiting scholar at George Washington University. He has conducted
research on consumption, housing cycles, economic forecasting, stock
market volatility, macrofinancial linkages, household indebtedness,
and systemic risk regulation. He holds a Ph.D. in economics from the
Ohio State University.

YOUNGSUN KOH   is a senior research fellow and director of the Center
for International Development at the Korea Development Institute.
Previously, he served as director of the Department of Macroeconomic and Financial Policy and the Department of Public Finance
and Social Policy and as chief economist. He has served as second vice
minister for policy coordination and as vice minister for the Ministry
of Employment and Labor in the government of Korea. He holds a
Ph.D. in economics from Stanford University.

M. AYHAN KOSE   is director of the World Bank's Prospects Group. He manages the Bank's publications on global trends, including *Global Economic Prospects*. Also a nonresident senior fellow at Brookings and a research fellow at the Center for Economic Policy Research, he previously worked in the Research Department of the International Monetary Fund. He has taught at the Booth School of Business, INSEAD, and Brandeis International Business School. He holds a Ph.D. in economics from the University of Iowa.

WARWICK J. McKIBBIN   is a professor of public policy and the director of the Center for Applied Macroeconomic Analysis at the Australian National University. He is also a fellow of the Australian Academy of Social Sciences and nonresident senior fellow at Brookings. He was awarded the Order of Australia "For Distinguished Service to Education as an Economist." He has worked at the Reserve Bank of Australia, including serving on its board. He holds a Ph.D. in economics from Harvard University.

JOSHUA P. MELTZER   is a senior fellow at Brookings. His research covers international trade law and policy, with a recent focus on digital trade. He has testified on trade issues before the U.S. Congress and other forums. He has taught at Melbourne University Law School, Georgetown University Law School, and Johns Hopkins School for Advanced International Studies. He holds an S.J.D. and L.L.M. from the University of Michigan, Ann Arbor, and law and commerce degrees from Monash University.

JIYOON OH   is a fellow in the Department of Economic Policy and Strategy at the Korea Development Institute (KDI). Her research interests span a range of issues in macroeconomics, with an emphasis on firm dynamics. Since joining KDI, she has worked on studying allocation efficiency, implications of size-dependent policies, macroeconomic effects of state-led housing supply, and market structure and income distribution. She holds a Ph.D. in economics from the University of Rochester.

FRANZISKA OHNSORGE   is manager of the Prospects Group at the World Bank. She is a lead author of the Bank's *Global Economic Prospects* report. Previously, she worked at the International Monetary Fund, covering a range of Asian, European, and Central Asian economies.

Earlier, she worked in the Office of the Chief Economist at the EBRD on regional surveillance, forecasting, and financial sector policies. She holds a Ph.D. in economics from the University of Toronto.

ZIA QURESHI is currently a visiting fellow at Brookings. His research covers a broad range of global economic issues, including a recent focus on how technology is reshaping the economic agenda. He previously worked at the World Bank and the International Monetary Fund (IMF), including serving as director of Development Economics at the Bank and executive secretary of the IMF–World Bank Joint Ministerial Development Committee. He holds a D.Phil. in economics from Oxford University, where he was a Rhodes Scholar.

ADAM TRIGGS is director of research at the Asian Bureau of Economic Research in the Crawford School of Public Policy at the Australian National University. A nonresident fellow at Brookings, he has worked in research and advisory roles at Australia's Department of the Prime Minister and Cabinet, office of the Shadow Assistant Treasurer, and the Australian Competition and Consumer Commission. He holds a Ph.D. in economics from the Australian National University.

Index

CPSIA information can be obtained
at www.ICGtesting.com
Printed in the USA
LVHW111822070220
646195LV00001B/17